THE ULTIMATE HOME OFFICE SURVIVAL GUIDE

SUNNY BAKER AND KIM BAKER

PETERSON'S
Princeton, New Jersey

About Peterson's

Peterson's is the country's largest educational information/communications company, providing the academic, consumer, and professional communities with books, software, and online services in support of lifelong education access and career choice. Well-known references include Peterson's annual guides to private schools, summer programs, colleges and universities, graduate and professional programs, financial aid, international study, adult learning, and career guidance. Peterson's Web site at petersons.com is the only comprehensive—and most heavily traveled—education resource on the Internet. The site carries all of Peterson's fully searchable major databases and includes financial aid sources, test-prep help, job postings, direct inquiry and application features, and specially created Virtual Campuses for every accredited academic institution and summer program in the U.S. and Canada that offers in-depth narratives, announcements, and multimedia features.

Visit Peterson's Education Center on the Internet (World Wide Web) at www.petersons.com

Library of Congress Cataloging-in-Publication Data

Baker, Sunny.
    The ultimate home office survival guide / Sunny Baker and Kim Baker.
        p.   cm.
    Includes index.
    ISBN 0-7689-0007-7
    1. Home-based businesses—Management. 2. New business enterprises.
I. Baker, Kim, 1955– . II. Title.
HD62.38.B353   1998
658'.041—dc21   98-13278
                                                                            CIP

Composition and design by Peterson's

Printed in the United States of America

10   9   8   7   6   5   4   3   2   1

CONTENTS

CONTENTS

Acknowledgments

Our appreciation goes to the person who helped us the most in assembling the data for this book, Michelle Sbraga, our Research Director at Baker & Baker. Her unwavering organization, attention to detail, and practical viewpoint have assured that this first edition of *The Ultimate Home Office Survival Guide* contains all the information that real-world home-based entrepreneurs and home-based workers can turn to with confidence.

Michelle, with the assistance of her husband Michael, also helped with the chapter on office design. Michael holds a degree in architecture from Temple University and specializes in office environment planning as a facilities project manager for major corporations.

Special thanks also go to all the people from the directories, trade and professional associations, and online companies who responded to our calls or sent information for inclusion in the book. Without their help, this book and CD-ROM set would not be as complete or as helpful to you, the user.

Kudos to the staffs of Mesa Community Library, Phoenix Library, and Tempe Library. The librarians were invaluable resources, though we are sure some are relieved not to see us camped in the reference sections everyday.

And finally, to Bill Gates, Chairman of Microsoft Corporation, Sunny's former boss, and a former client of Baker & Baker in Microsoft's early days after they moved out of the garage. Bill doesn't know it, but he was instrumental in motivating us to work at home for ourselves. After all, Bill really doesn't need our help any more, does he?

An Invitation from the Authors

Are you one of the weary workers in America who lament the unproductive hours spent commuting in rush-hour traffic? Do you dream of freedom from the shackles of the corporate time clock? Are you looking for new challenges and more independence in your career? If so, you are like millions of people who are looking for the independence and security that working at home can bring.

Most people dream romantically about the fun and freedom of working at home. No commutes. No boss looking over your shoulder. More time with the kids. But are you ready to really do it? Do you really know what it takes to succeed? This book can help you decide if you have what it takes to prosper at home.

Today, because of new communications technologies and changing corporate policies about "attendance" in the office, millions of people have moved from corporate headquarters to home office. Millions of others have left the corporation altogether and started businesses of their own. In fact, most home-based workers are more productive in a home office than in a traditional setting, if they know how. You can do it too! Gain the freedom and prosperity that no office-based existence provides. Think about moving your work to your home. Even if you only work part of the week in your home office, or if you go full tilt and decide to start your a business from your home, this book can help you make home-based prosper-

ity a possibility. This first edition of *The Ultimate Home Office Survival Guide* is a book and CD-ROM compendium that provides a combination of instructions, inspirations, guidelines, tools, forms, spreadsheets, resource listings, and company offers for starting and running almost any home-based office.

Take a moment to review the Table of Contents before you start flipping through the pages. You'll see that *The Ultimate Home Office Survival Guide* has been organized into distinct parts to meet the needs of various types of home-based workers. Each part of the book details a major topic for home-based workers—whether they run their own businesses or work at home for another company.

The bound-in CD-ROM that accompanies this book could be called "The Ultimate Yellow Pages for Home-Based Workers." It provides contact information for agencies, data, publications, products, and other frequently required business sources. Included are listings for the information that home-based businesspeople have most often needed. If we missed something that you need, please tell us about it. We will track down the information for you and include it in the next edition.

We invite you to send us your ideas, success stories, and tips to help us maintain *The Ultimate Home Office Survival Guide* and CD-ROM as an indispensable resource for all home-based workers. Those ideas and suggestions that are used will be acknowledged in the next edition of the book.

Please e-mail your comments, suggestions, articles, and interests to sunnybaker@aol.com or kimbaker@aol.com. We look forward to hearing from you and hope that you will enjoy reading and using *The Ultimate Home Office Survival Guide.* We hope it makes your home-based work more productive, comfortable, and rewarding.

Sunny Baker, Ph.D., and Kim Baker
Baker & Baker
Marketing Consultants and Home-Business
   Advisors
Johnson City, Tennessee

INTRODUCTION

Home-Based Workers—The Force of the Future

You embody significant hope for the economic future and are thinking about becoming a home-based worker. You are among the more than 40 million people in America who now work from their homes (either full- or part-time) or one of even more millions who is considering a home-based business as an alternative to a traditional job or as a second source of income. As a home-based entrepreneur, you are a part of the "invisible workforce" that is changing the face of American enterprise.

Currently, the home-based workforce already generates income of more than $100 billion a year (and growing). If you work out of your home, it's no longer an embarrassment, it's a testament to your role in keeping the world a prosperous place.

IT'S EASIER THAN EVER TO PROSPER FROM HOME

Because of advances in computer technologies and electronic communications, home-based careers are more feasible, less costly, and potentially more rewarding than ever before. With the growing variety of tools and electronics to support work-at-home endeavors and the increasing number of professionals choosing to work at home, the home office is quickly becoming a standard feature of the domiciles of families worldwide.

Of course, prospering in a home-based career or business venture requires more than just moving a used desk and a telephone into the back bedroom. Home-based success requires planning, organization, marketing, budgeting, and scheduling, just like any business venture or office job. The right tools and technology must also be selected to make working at home efficient. If you choose to start a business at home (instead of working at home for someone else) your business must be promoted and financed, just like a storefront business. Most of all, success as an employee or entrepreneur demands vision and drive to reap the full benefits of working at home.

A NEW BREED OF EMPLOYEE AND A NEW CLASS OF ENTREPRENEUR

There are two types of home-based workers, and *The Ultimate Home Office Survival Guide* can help with both categories. The first category is the new breed of home-based employees, people who work for other businesses from their homes or negotiate new work arrangements with existing employers. These telecommuters may work three or four days at home and occasionally drop by corporate headquarters to keep in touch. Some corporate employees work full-time in their home-based offices using teleconferencing facilities and e-mail instead of attending traditional meetings. In fact, there's no reason why most office workers need to go into the office at all if the office and communications facilities are in place to support them.

The second breed of home-based worker is the home entrepreneur. These people are setting up offices at home to start full-time ventures or to supplement income with after-hours projects.

A WIN-WIN SITUATION FOR EVERYONE

Working at home is the ultimate win-win situation. Home-based workers save money for employers in office space and utilities. Home-based workers save time by eliminating long commutes to the office. In some cases, home-based workers prove to be more productive than their office counterparts.

Still, for many home-based workers and home-based entrepreneurs, the hopes of independence and freedom ultimately fall short. Dreams turn into disenchantment, and people reluctantly find themselves looking for another dull 9-to-5 job in impersonal cubicles, lacking flexibility but offering structure to stay on track. These failures are completely avoidable, however, if people know the right methods and are able to sidestep the common pitfalls of working at home.

In picking up this book, you are looking for good advice and inspiration. You want to succeed. You already know that there are shelves full of small and home-based business books in your favorite bookstore. Why spend your money and time on this one? What makes this book different and worthwhile?

A TRUE SUPPORT SYSTEM

You may have read the detailed profiles of some of these homemade successes in our book *Million Dollar Home-Based Businesses*. The businesspeople profiled in that book inspired this one. After the publication of *Million Dollar Home-Based Businesses*, people began asking us how they could prosper from working at home. We wanted to give them good advice and looked for books that detailed the processes, techniques, and methods that actual entrepreneurs used to achieve their success in working at home. We assumed that a book that fit the bill had already been written, and so we searched for it. As we reviewed books on home-based offices to recommend to our friends and readers, we found some good books. (You'll find them listed in the resources section in this book.) We also discovered some surprises.

Significant success factors, necessary management techniques, and mandatory financial procedures were simply missing from other volumes about home-based enterprise. When good advice was included, the tools necessary to put the information to work were notably absent. It would take three, four, or more of these incomplete volumes to get all the information needed to successfully run an office from scratch.

It became apparent that our friends needed a book that synthesized in one volume the success secrets, tools, and advice collected from the multitudes of prosperous home-based professionals around the country. The book we were looking for hadn't been written yet.

While researching home-based entrepreneurship further, we began to visualize the book we wanted—a comprehensive resource for home-based workers, a system that would take people from idea to independence, from worry to wealth, from struggle to success. Our goal for the book, and the bound-in CD-ROM, became simply to create the ultimate resource

for people who work at home. *The Ultimate Home Office Survival Guide* is our attempt to meet that goal.

The book concept evolved and the outline expanded as we talked to more people. We learned that the complexities and requirements for a successful home-based office are no less encompassing than any other format for an office, although being home-based presents unique opportunities and challenges. From choosing a location for the office in your home to setting up operations, from managing time to integrating life and work, from keeping records of operations for the IRS to dealing with growth—the more we learned about home-based offices, the more we realized we had to do more than write a book—we had to create an entire system of resources and ongoing information.

In creating this support system for home-based workers, we sought the advice and insights of hundreds of entrepreneurs and we reviewed more than 100 books, countless newsletters, and even more government publications on entrepreneurship, small business, and home-based business. We have borrowed what we consider to be the best expert advice to develop a comprehensive reference system for home-based entrepreneurs, telecommuters, and home-based employees.

EVERYTHING YOU NEED TO GET STARTED—FROM IDEA TO INDEPENDENCE

From developing the office layout to using new technologies for keeping in touch with the outside world, *The Ultimate Home Office Survival Guide* covers the most important requirements for home-based success. Our goal has been to guide businesspeople through the home office process without wasting time on poor strategies, detours, or the quicksand in which unwary home-based workers may find themselves mired. Because we are home-based entrepreneurs ourselves, our experience guided us in choosing one technique over another.

Included in this book are more techniques, forms, references, and sources than any other home office guide. As the book evolved, it became clear that the same techniques do not work for everyone. As you read the book you'll find something unique—multiple techniques for similar functions. For example, there are multiple ways to handle your recordkeeping and various techniques for managing your time. We let you choose the forms, techniques, and concepts that best fit your profession, personality, and lifestyle.

All the forms, checklists, and spreadsheets are included on a CD-ROM bound with the book, so you can duplicate and adapt them to your own home-based career or business. The forms are formatted in Microsoft Word and the spreadsheets are formatted in Microsoft Excel. In addition, we have provided instructions for converting the documents for use with other products on PCs and Macintosh computers.

Because we couldn't fit everything into one volume, any omissions are justified by the inclusion of hundreds of listings for information sources, government agencies, private associations, helpful books, and useful products for people who work from their homes.

WHO SHOULD USE THIS BOOK?

As authors we obviously would like to have a large audience reading this book, but there are some specific people we had in mind as we compiled the information, techniques, resources, and worksheets of *The Ultimate Home Office Survival Guide*. These people include:

Work-at-Home Corporate Employees (Telecommuters). Companies and corporations are finally getting the message that for highly creative and productive employees, working at home is not heresy. With quality employees becoming expensive and irreplaceable, many companies would rather allow someone to work at home than lose their skills. Working at home also accommodates workaholics who don't respond well to an office environment and also benefits the growing number of businesspeople who want to spend more time with their families. Research shows that home-based employees consistently produce superior work in considerably less time than office-based employees. A home office with technological links to the parent company is required to succeed, and *The Ultimate Home Office Survival Guide* explains the mechanics of setting up a high-tech office at home and making it productive. This book also covers the lifestyle issues that may intrude upon work-at-home professionals and provides ways around each one.

Workers Who Want to Establish Independence. Armies of managers, professionals, and tradespeople inside companies and corporations are readying themselves to move toward independence by starting their own home-based businesses and leaving the corporate ranks behind. Unfortunately, many of these home-based businesses never reach their full potential of creating true independence. For these people *The Ultimate Home Office Survival Guide* provides a complete game plan for establishing a transition time line, methods for choosing a career direction, fine-tuning techniques for adapting to a home office environment, and guidelines for making it work.

Early Retirees. Many talented and productive employees are being forced to take early retirement from companies in the process of downsizing. Unfortunately, a large percentage of these retirees won't find a comparable job. Most of these retirees (some only in their 40s) want to keep active in the business world and many have an early-retirement settlement that could be used wisely in a home-based business venture. *The Ultimate Home Office Survival Guide* offers the practical advice to make postretirement pay off. Since many newly retired workers have never worked outside the traditional office environment, *The Ultimate Home Office Survival Guide* explains how to choose and assemble a prosperous and satisfying business at home.

People "Just Waiting for the Axe to Fall." Jobs in major corporations and medium-size companies were once considered secure. Today, cutbacks, buyouts, and mergers are an ugly reality facing even the most qualified tradespeople and professionals in business. *The Ultimate Home Office Survival Guide* provides options for people in potentially shaky positions by helping them put together an alternative plan and preparing them for new opportunities. By following the book's advice, workers will have a proactive alternative ready and the finances needed to make a home-based business work.

Practicing Home-Based Entrepreneurs. Many of the target readers for this book are already home-based businesspeople or home-based corporate workers in various stages of transition from an office job to an at-home career. *The Ultimate Home Office Survival Guide* is a resource for completing the transition, improving performance, and fixing past mistakes. It shows how planning can be used to identify and solve problems. Techniques for improving promotion and distribution are also provided. In addition, case studies and real-life profiles encourage struggling home entrepreneurs to persevere by demonstrating that "Yes, it can be done!"

HOW TO USE *THE ULTIMATE HOME OFFICE SURVIVAL GUIDE*

Because no home-based career or business is the same as any other, no one will use this guide and its resources in exactly the same way. With this in mind, we have tried to make the system flexible to accommodate a wide range of working styles and home-based information needs.

The book contains chapters that cover every aspect of starting, managing, and maintaining a home-based office and workstyle. Each chapter contains a narrative that describes key processes, strategies, and methods. These narratives are accompanied by specific checklists, worksheets, forms, and other resources found on the CD-ROM that implement the advice of each chapter. There is a chapter at the end of this book that offers guidelines for using the forms, checklists, and other resources you'll find on the CD-ROM.

The most relevant sections and chapters for you will depend on your personal skill levels, experience, and office needs. Not all chapters will be necessary for all business-people, but every home-based worker, whether new or experienced, should find much of use in these pages.

We hope we have succeeded in creating "the ultimate book for home-based workers," since this was our goal. Where the book falls short, we take full responsibility, but where it excels and motivates successful home enterprises, we give credit to the people who gave us their time, advice, and insights.

GO FOR YOUR DREAMS

We all have dreams of a better world. In our dreams, we see a world where people can depend on themselves and their own ingenuity, perseverance, and drive to succeed. In our minds, home-based entrepreneurs are a key component of turning the dream of economic stability into reality. Home-based businesses can transform the downtrodden commuters into energetic producers. It isn't magic, but it can be done. Millions of businesspeople have done it already.

We have written this book to help you get established and for use as an ongoing reference after you succeed. Enjoy the book. Use the CD-ROM. Help make the dream come true. Start a home-based career or a home-based business and prosper. Stop commuting! Use the time to do what matters and what matters to you!

PART

1

HOME SWEET OFFICE:
GETTING STARTED AT HOME

1

THERE'S NO PLACE LIKE HOME

This chapter is for people who are thinking about starting a business of their own from home. If you already operate a home-based business, this chapter will help you to reinforce why you started your business in the first place, identify personal strengths, and reach your home-based work goals. If you're considering working for someone else in a telecommuting position, most of the advantages of working at home spelled out in this chapter apply to you as well.

As the twenty-first century approaches, people are looking for security, something large corporations no longer provide. Those who start their own home-based businesses want freedom from the shackles of working for someone else. Telecommuting workers in corporate jobs gain flexible schedules and increased productivity by working part or all of the week from their home offices. Many home-based entrepreneurs desire new challenges in their lives. In their quests, all these home-based workers are discovering the independence and security that working at home can bring.

By choice and coercion, businesspeople are leaving their traditional 9-to-5 jobs in droves to work at home. Some have dreamed about a home-based enterprise for several years and are finally making the break. Others have been the victims of job cutbacks and layoffs, now common in the formerly stable white-collar world and standard in the blue-collar ranks. Many are looking for more time with their families. Most are tired of the unproductive hours spent commuting in rush-hour traffic.

DON'T JUST PUT UP—HEAD HOME INSTEAD

Few things in life are less rewarding than working for a boss you don't respect within a company that treats its employees like disposable commodities. Living under the threat of layoffs and cutbacks is stressful and often humiliating for a seasoned professional. There is an alternative. You can depend on yourself instead!

You can use your own time-honed skills to prosper. You can do work you love. You don't have to depend on others for income or security. You can set up almost any kind of business venture from a family room, garage, or spare bedroom. Manufacturing businesses, direct marketing businesses, service businesses—there are surprisingly few restrictions on home-based enterprises. Of course, there are city ordinances and zoning laws to contend with if you want to start some types of manufacturing businesses, but other than that, you can start almost any company from your home.

We encourage you to become part of the work-at-home revolution, whether you start your own business or become a telecommuter for another company. But before you quit your job, invest the family savings, or give an ultimatum to your boss, take some time to decide if you're really ready to make the commitment required for home-based success.

DISPELLING THE MYTHS ABOUT HOME-BASED ENTREPRENEURS

When you ask people about working from your home, you will certainly encounter some standard prejudices about home-based businesspeople. In fact, you may hold some of these biases yourself without realizing it. It is important to dispel these myths before you get started. We have listed some of the most common myths about home-based business ventures and the facts that negate them.

The Myth: Home-based businesses are hobbies.

The Reality: *It is true that many home-based businesses are started from hobbies, but most are not. Home-based entrepreneurs strive to make significant profits from their business activities, just like entrepreneurs who choose to work from traditional offices or retail facilities.*

The Myth: Home-based workers are not as sophisticated as office-based businesspeople.

The Reality: *The range of business sophistication among home-based businesspeople runs the gamut from novice to tycoon. There are no stereotypes that fit home-based workers other than to say that they share common traits of perseverance and goals of self-sufficiency and independence.*

The Myth: Office-based workers and store-front businesses are more prosperous than their home-based counterparts.

The Reality: *This is simply not true. Hundreds of major corporations have been started from homes. Read our book Million Dollar Home-Based Businesses if you need proof of the prosperity of home-based entrepreneurs. Prosperity has more to do with the person behind the business than the location of the business activities.*

The Myth: Home-based businesses are not real businesses in the view of the law.

The Reality: *Home-based businesses are just as real as any other business, they just operate out of peoples' homes instead of from offices or storefronts. The test of a home-based business is its ability to make profit—and millions of people support themselves from their home-based* *endeavors. Business laws, regulations, and tax requirements apply to businesses run from homes just as they do to businesses run in other facilities.*

The Myth: Home-based businesses and careers take less time to manage than traditional businesses and careers.

The Reality: *A full-time home-based business or home-based job takes just as much time to manage as any job or business. Home-based businesses are, after all, real businesses with all the marketing, finance, administration, and legal requirements of any business. Home-based workers may have more flexibility in scheduling their time, but the amount of invested time is the same as any successful business. The people who don't put in enough time simply don't succeed.*

FACTS ABOUT HOME-BASED BUSINESSPEOPLE

We mentioned earlier that we interviewed hundreds of successful home-based entrepreneurs in assembling this book and our prior book of entrepreneurial profiles, *Million Dollar Home-Based Businesses*. If you are still just thinking about starting your own business or career from home, here are some facts about those hundreds of entrepreneurs that might motivate you to take the plunge:

- Many of the people were unemployed or laid off when they started their businesses.
- Most of the successful entrepreneurs we interviewed started with less than $5,000 in the bank. Some started with no savings at all.
- The ideas for successful businesses ranged from ordinary to weird, mundane to extraordinary. In the final analysis, the

business idea seemed less important than the entrepreneur's motivation to succeed.

- Most of the people had never run a business before and had little formal business training.
- Age, gender, and ethnic background were not relevant in predicting the success of home-based entrepreneurs. We found people from all walks of life, socioeconomic strata, and physical well-being who had become homemade millionaires. Successful entrepreneurs rise above the objections, disregard the stereotypes, and turn handicaps into advantages.
- Education was not a predictable factor in the success of the home-based entrepreneurs we interviewed. Some people had special training to support their businesses, while others never finished high school. Some are college dropouts. Still others have advanced graduate degrees from prestigious universities. Most of the people educated themselves when they found they needed specific business skills.

While many of the people we spoke with run businesses directly related to their formal education, sometimes education propels entrepreneurs in another direction. For example, one entrepreneur with a master's degree in clinical psychology found that he disliked being a psychologist. Using the skills gained from his childhood fascination with electronics, he began a business designing computerized control systems—a long way from the psychologist's couch. All this supports our observation that there are no hard-and-fast rules about the education needed to support a home-based business.

Do what is best for you. Don't let training, or lack thereof, get in the way.

- Home-based entrepreneurs and telecommuters generally feel more satisfied with their lives. They enjoy working for themselves more than working for other people. They are also generally positive about the future—something few cubicle-based corporate employees can say today.

THE BUSINESS ADVANTAGES OF BEING HOME-BASED

If you put aside the myths about home-based businesses and telecommuters, you'll find that almost anyone can succeed from almost anywhere. There are some other advantages associated with working at home that should be considered as well.

The business advantages of starting a home-based business or becoming a telecommuter can be significant. The following are advantages most frequently cited by established home-based businesspeople.

- **Low overhead.** One of the most significant factors in starting a business at home is lower costs. Reduced operational costs mean lower risk of failure. Lower costs also mean you can begin your business sooner, since you won't have to save or raise the money to lease an office or buy additional furniture, phones, or other equipment.
- **High productivity.** Research indicates that home-based workers are consistently 15 to 25 percent more productive than their office-based counterparts. These productivity gains are the result of a decrease in distractions, a reduced number of meetings, and an elimination of wasteful activities to support a bureaucracy. Productivity gains are also partially psychological. People are more comfortable at home and can work at their own pace.

- **Flexible scheduling.** Working from home provides the freedom to structure your life and your career by your own terms. Eliminated from the day are wasteful hours spent commuting, time spent on unproductive meetings, and the general feeling of malaise that accompanies working in a less-than-satisfying career in a company or corporate environment. By working at home, time can be structured any way that works.
- **Ecological and health benefits.** Home-based businesses offer inherent ecological advantages over traditional businesses. They generally reduce the pollution produced when people commute between home and work. Because fewer people are involved in the business operations, the tons of wasted paper from memos, reports, and other documents in large bureaucracies are replaced with efficient, personal communications, thereby significantly reducing the waste of precious natural resources. Home-based businesses are also unbiased. They give people of almost any background or economic condition the opportunity to start a business with only minimal resources. In addition, most home-based entrepreneurs have pointed out that stress is reduced and personal well-being is greatly enhanced when they can control their own destinies through their own efforts.

- **Tax benefits.** Although you'll need to separate your business expenses from your home expenses, if you use a large percentage of your home space exclusively for business activities, you can deduct that percentage of your mortgage payment, depreciation, property taxes, insurance, and utilities from the profit of your business. This means the business directly pays for a portion of your home while you work in it. You can also deduct the work-related expenses of your automobile—something you can't usually do working in an office-based job.

- **Family togetherness.** In many instances home-based businesses have strengthened family relationships because everyone can get involved. Family members can pool their energies and skills to reach a common goal. At the very least you'll be able to schedule your time to go to important family events.

- **Competitive advantages.** Some people don't think that they can compete with the big companies when they work from home. However, there are clear advantages in working at home that can give you a competitive edge. First, you can be more competitive in your charges or prices because you have lower overhead. Second, you can provide better service. An advantage of providing services from home is that you can be reached when clients need you. You can provide a comfortable, welcome atmosphere if customers visit your home. No giant parking lots. No waiting in line. And, because you are more comfortable at home, you can make your customers feel more comfortable at the same time.

If you want to consider owning your own home-based business as opposed to a telecommuting arrangement, there are some additional advantages:

- You have the chance to make more money than you could make working for someone else.

- You'll be your own boss and make the decisions that are crucial to your business' success or failure.

- You'll be the boss of hired associates.

- You'll have job security—no one can fire you.

- You'll put your ideas into practice.

- You'll learn more about every aspect of a business and gain experience in a variety of disciplines.

- You'll work directly with your customers.

- You'll have the personal satisfaction of creating and running a successful business.

- You can work in a field or location that you really enjoy.

- You'll establish roots in a community and provide stability for your family.

- You can participate in every aspect of running the business.

Given all the potential advantages of working at home and working for yourself, you can see why the trend toward home-based businesses and home careers is popular. The dream of owning a business or working at home is no longer a fantasy. The opportunity is simply waiting at your doorstep (or spare bedroom or garage).

UNIVERSAL SUCCESS FACTORS

Home-based entrepreneurs have established a variety of businesses and are involved in diverse jobs. Home-based workers have a wide range of business experiences and skills. For example, formal education is not a predictable component in the success profiles of the home-based workers. Therefore, other factors must be more important in gaining home-based business success.

Based on interviews with home-based entrepreneurs and some informal research, it is apparent that there are four significant factors common to all home office success stories. Since these qualities represent a universal thread in home-based business prosperity, they are highlighted here in an effort to represent the prerequisites of prosperity. These qualities were specified by entrepreneurs from all parts of the country, regardless of their gender, age, personal profiles, or businesses.

Perseverance

Home-based entrepreneurs consistently cite perseverance, their ability to hang onto their dreams through thick and thin, as being the single most important trait responsible for their success. To be successful in a home-based business or home-based career you must be capable of prolonged effort, even in the face of adversity. Many successful entrepreneurs have started businesses that ended in bankruptcy courts. However, they managed to pick up the pieces and try over and over until they made a business work. Others have taken years to establish themselves, but they eventually succeeded. For many of these hard workers, the tenacity to

cling to their businesses in the face of mounting losses and problems saw them through the crises.

Dedication is a related success factor in documented homemade business stories. While the owners of competing companies, especially large, established ones, enjoy a weekend at the beach, the dedicated home-based entrepreneur may work all weekend to satisfy a customer. It is their willingness to put in the extra 3 hours a day or an extra day a week that ultimately helps these home-based entrepreneurs succeed where others would have failed. Successful entrepreneurs simply don't give up or give in.

Need for Independence

After perseverance and drive, homemade millionaires share a fierce determination to remain independent. Many workers had a bad experience with an uncaring boss or unstable company, motivating them to work for themselves. Often, home-based entrepreneurs run enterprises that allow them to make money doing what they would be doing for fun anyway. Many people simply love their work, and this romance fuels the drive required to keep them going.

While there are many variations of this theme, almost all home entrepreneurs dislike or are unsatisfied by working for someone else. They are not corporate players, and some are proud of this fact. Many of these people were regarded by companies and corporations as "problem" employees who liked to make their own decisions and who refused to adapt for the sake of inter-company politics. Instead, these employees voiced their opinions when they felt a decision was unsound, even if it placed them in unpopular positions.

Many office-based workers felt that they had received little or no recognition or financial reward from their previous careers. One homemade millionaire stated, "I made my company a lot of money by recognizing opportunities for growth that they missed. But, on my performance reviews I would get told that I wasn't a good employee in the company's eyes because I made too many political waves."

For some entrepreneurs, running a successful home-based business was a way to "get back" at their old employers by proving that they could succeed on their own. Although some business experts do not recommend competing against previous employers, there are a significant number of homemade millionaires who own flourishing businesses that compete head-to-head with their old companies. These independent entrepreneurs take candid pride in beating their old bosses at their own games.

Willingness to Take Risk

Successful home-based entrepreneurs are willing to take risks when starting a new venture. While the degree of risk varies considerably among individuals and companies, almost no one starts a business without putting something on the line: financial risk, personal failure, or job security. Many entrepreneurs start their businesses against the advice of friends, family, and their employers. They are left to achieve success entirely on their own. Some entrepreneurs even risk their marriages, going ahead with ventures without the approval of their mates.

Like other home-based entrepreneurs, if you are going to start your own business or convince your boss that you are more productive at home than in the office, you must be able to accept the risks. There is no way around it. You must have enough faith in yourself to know that you will succeed.

Adaptability

Successful home-based entrepreneurs are able to change course in midstream. They are able to accept disappointment and move on. When they see that an idea isn't working, they quickly review the situation, try to understand what went wrong, and change their approach. Successful entrepreneurs don't get attached to unproductive ideas or stuck in inefficient ways of thinking about things. They learn to get expert advice and put their egos aside. They learn that it's better to ask questions than to lose the business entirely.

VARYING BUSINESS PRACTICES

While characteristics of persistence, independence, adaptability, and a willingness to take risks are almost universal traits among the homemade millionaires and successful telecommuting employees, the similarities among the success factors stop there. The ways home-based workers conduct their lives and build businesses and careers are as diverse as the products they sell and the work they do.

If you have already read *Million Dollar Home-Based Businesses*, you discovered many differences in the way people select their businesses, get them started, and build the enterprises to success. Where one homemade millionaire turned a hobby into a major business over a period of years with almost no start-up capital, another mortgaged the house and took every possible risk to build a business overnight. Some millionaires used their own good ideas, while others became involved in established multilevel marketing programs (such as Amway or Shaklee).

The types of businesses and jobs that people can pursue from a home are almost limitless. There is no specific formula for success—you need to be flexible and adaptive. Remember—perseverance pays off. Many options and alternatives are suggested in this book.

The variety of start-up capital sources was especially surprising. Some funding came from traditional sources like small business loans or loans from friends or family. Other entrepreneurs put savings away methodically and had specific financial security goals to meet before they allowed themselves to start their own businesses. Most of the capital, however, came from odd or impulsive sources, including insurance settlements for car accidents, money sequestered away for a boat or a vacation, or a reimbursement check for a business trip overseas. Some of the ventures began with no start-up capital whatsoever.

Another unexpected anomaly was the different attitudes about planning. Some entrepreneurs claim that planning is a waste of time—others swear by it. Some cite the development of a solid business plan as the single most important aspect of their success. Others work on a fly-by-night basis, running more on instinct than anything else—and they prefer it that way. Business experts favor planning; however, there will always be adept entrepreneurs who need no design. In addition, home-based entrepreneurs have different working hours, controversial attitudes about personnel, novel approaches about reinvesting profits from the company, and completely diverse methods of marketing their products.

THE PITFALLS OF HOME-BASED OFFICES

Given all the diversity in success, the good news is that there is something out there, somewhere, that can work for you. All you need is perseverance, drive, and flexibility to find it or build it. The bad news is that there is no magic formula for success. As good as home-based enterprise sounds, nothing is perfect. Just because a business or a job is home-based doesn't mean it will succeed. In fact, the success ratio for new home-based businesses is very similar to that for any other new business.

Most experts agree that only 50 percent of people who start any new business (home-based or not) are still in business after one year. According to the U.S. Department of Commerce, over 80 percent of all new businesses fail within the first five years. Of course, it is possible to raise the percentage of success if new businesspeople understand the pitfalls before they start.

Failures anticipated are failures avoided. Thus, it is important to understand why certain home-based endeavors fail. Unsurprisingly, the most common reasons for home-based business failure are the same as those for all businesses.

- **Choosing the wrong business.** Often new entrepreneurs choose a business that sounds fun but lacks financial credibility. Others choose businesses that sound lucrative, but which lack a personal interest to the people involved. Others choose ideas with no market. Be sure to thoroughly investigate any business idea before you invest a large sum of money into the idea. Chapters 2–5 will help you avoid selecting the wrong business for you and your personality.

- **Lack of management skills.** This is a catch-all excuse that covers almost any business problem. Management is the most important skill you can have as an entrepreneur, but it is not a skill that anyone can define for you. Management entails almost every aspect of business. In fact, "Most venture capital firms concentrate primarily on the firm's management. They feel that even mediocre products can be successfully manufactured, promoted, and distributed by an experienced, energetic management group." (quoted from the Small Business Administration)

   This is true of home-based businesses as well. With energetic, focused management, most other problems in a business can be easily solved. It is important, therefore, to make sure that you have the management skills and tools to ensure your success and that poor management is not the excuse for your failure.

- **Inadequate time spent with the business.** This is a frequently cited excuse for home-based business failure. It is an excuse because it is a problem easily solved by simply changing your priorities. You must put in the time necessary to make the business succeed. The choice is yours.

- **Lack of preparation.** Many businesses fail because owners don't understand the requirements of a successful business. Chapter 6 provides guidelines for planning a successful business within your financial, time, and skill limitations. Don't choose a business that overwhelms you. Your chances for success will grow if you choose a business that matches your skills and finances.

- **Inadequate funding.** Some home-based businesses can be started with little or no capital, but most cannot. Be sure to choose a business that fits your budget. There are worksheets and guidelines in Chapter 6 that show you how to determine, plan for, and obtain adequate financing for your business.

In addition to these common reasons for business failure, there are some inherent problems with working at home that must be planned for from the beginning.

- Conflicts with family members who share the same living space with the business.
- Separating the work space from the home space.
- Inability to stay focused on work priorities because day-to-day life gets in the way.
- Archaic laws and city ordinances that restrict home-based activities.

If you're considering owning a home-based business, there are always additional negatives to consider.

- You may have to take a personal financial risk.
- If you operate a full-time venture, you will probably have to work long hours and may have fewer opportunities to play with friends and family.
- You may end up spending a lot of your time attending to the details of running a

business and less time on those aspects of the business that you really enjoy.

- You may find that your income is not steady. Sometimes you won't have much income at all, so you'll need to plan for these fluctuations.
- You may have to undertake tasks you find unpleasant, such as filling out bookkeeping records or dealing with the IRS.
- You may have to learn many new skills, such as general management, filing and bookkeeping, production planning, promotion, market research, and sales.
- You may have trouble attracting qualified employees when (and if) you need them. If you don't find who you need, you or your family may be your only source of labor.
- You may be less accessible to major suppliers and therefore less likely to get the large discounts of vast companies.
- You may have a problem establishing your image as a company.
- You may run out of space at home as your business grows.

Again, a good philosophy is that a problem identified is a problem solved; therefore, some portion of this book looks at the multi-tude of things that can go wrong. This isn't being negative. It's being prepared.

THE BOTTOM LINE

In our minds, there's really no place like home for a business or a career. The ever-lengthening commuting times in office-based jobs, rising transportation costs, changing lifestyles, the desire to combine a career and a family, and the need to escape the daily 9-to-5 grind are all part of the decision to move home. Other factors include the continuing expansion of the services and information sectors and the widespread availability of microcomputers and other affordable technologies—developments that have opened the door on a broad array of new home-based business possibilities. Given all the advantages—including tax benefits, personal freedom, and financial rewards—it's easy to see that it pays to work at home.

And remember, if you've tried working at home in the past and have failed to achieve your goals, don't give up now. The only true failures in life are those who fail to try again. You *can* make it if you keep focused on the business.

C H A P T E R

2

ARE YOU READY TO WORK AT HOME?

This chapter identifies many options for businesses and careers that can be successfully started from a home. If you're considering buying an established business or a franchise, you should start here, but also be sure to master the information contained in Chapters 4 and 5. If you already have a business, just skim through this chapter and Chapter 4 to make sure you've started the best business for you, and then go to Section II to master the steps in planning and reorganizing your business or office-based career. If you're not ready to start your own business but want to try working for someone else from your own home, read Chapter 3 to get started in a telecommuting career. Be aware, however, that most of the chapters in this book apply to telecommuting workers as well as home-based business owners.

DO YOU HAVE WHAT IT TAKES?

Starting a home office takes a lot of courage, but courage doesn't pay the bills. To be successful, you'll need more than just courage. You'll need that special combination of hard work, skill, and perseverance discussed in the last chapter. On occasion, you'll also need some good, old-fashioned luck.

Owning a home-based business or working as a telecommuter is not just another job. It's a totally different lifestyle. You must decide whether you're ready for a complete commitment to the success of your business and home-based operations. Just as importantly, you must ask your family members or housemates whether they are also committed to having you work at home. You need the support of those who share your living space or you might have a hard time finding the time and space to get your work done.

"Believe that you will succeed. Believe firmly and you will then do what is necessary to bring success about."
Dale Carnegie

As a home-based businessperson, you might have more flexible use of your time; however, if you own a business you'll probably also find that you may have less time overall for things like vacations (at least until you get well established). If you're starting a new business, you might be using much of what you own as collateral to raise money for start-up operations. You also must understand and practice the myriad roles you'll need to play to be successful in your home-based business.

THE ROLES NEEDED TO REAP SUCCESS

We've all heard of the beleaguered executive who moans that he's overworked because he has to wear more than one hat at his company. Most home-based businesspeople would give anything if they had to wear only two or three hats. To give you an idea of the number of hats you'll wear, here are some of the roles you can expect to play if you work at home:

- **Business planner.** You'll need to create an initial plan for your business. As your business develops, you'll inevitably want to make changes, perhaps to expand the business or to add a new product line. If you make a change, it is your responsibility to plan it and execute it, and you'll need to consider all of the ramifications of your decisions.

- **Sales and marketing executive.** In addition to planing your marketing or advertising campaign, you'll have to carry it out. You may write advertising copy, do some preliminary market research, visit potential customers, or make sure existing customers stay happy, depending upon the type of business you own, or you may have to join business groups; attend various breakfasts, lunches, and dinners; and network with other businesspeople who could help your business prosper.

- **Chief operations manager.** You'll probably be the one filling out all the bills and insurance forms, answering customer questions and complaints, and making the decisions about the benefits package you offer to yourself (and any employees). You must decide how to invest your income, structure operations, and handle the day-to-day concerns. If there's a decision to be made, you'll be making it.

- **Tax collector.** If you sell goods at the retail level, you're responsible for collecting a sales tax for various government entities. In addition, if you have employees, you're responsible for collecting payroll and federal taxes from them.

- **Accountant.** Even if you have an accountant, you'll need to know a lot about accounting. You must know which records to keep and how to keep them, how to prepare your tax forms, and how to prepare and interpret all of your financial statements.

- **Lawyer.** Even if you have a lawyer, you'll need to know a lot about business law to stay out of trouble. If you don't have a lawyer, you'll have to prepare all of your contracts and understand all of the employment laws if you plan to hire employees.

- **Bill collector.** When customers don't pay, it'll be up to you to collect from them. You'll have to know what you can and can't do when collecting, and you'll have to decide how to collect from slow-paying clients and when to give up and do something more rewarding with your time.

- **Market researcher.** Before you start your business, you'll have to find out who your customers are and where they're located. You may also have to conduct marketing research at various times during the life of your business, such as when you should consider introducing a new product or selling products in a new location.

- **Technology expert.** As a home-based business owner, you will probably depend on your computer for record keeping, correspondence, research, and much more. You'll need to learn to use a fax machine, printer, copier, etc. When things break, you must fix them or find someone who can. Eventually, you'll also need to install upgrades and load software to keep up with the latest changes in technology.

- **Secretary and receptionist.** Even if you have a clerical assistant, you'll inevitably do some basic administrative work, including filing, typing, mailing, and telephone answering.

If you feel comfortable playing all or most of these roles, read on. Home-based business opportunities abound for those who like to wear different hats.

YOUR EXPECTATIONS

Before you decide on a business, you need to thoroughly understand what you expect of the business: Why do you want to start a home-based business or telecommuting career? Money? Recognition? Personal freedom? Were you laid off? If someone were to ask you why you're considering a home-based business or career, what would you say?

Your first step before deciding on a home-based business or career is to focus on what you ultimately want from your business and to begin setting some goals. Your goals for the business will affect the type of operation you choose and how you'll determine if you have the right skills to succeed. If you want to succeed, how will you know when you've arrived? Knowing what you want from your business or career is paramount to success.

To determine your goals, here are a few common reasons why people start home-based businesses and home-based careers:

- **Money.** Some entrepreneurs feel that a corporate setting limits the amount of money they can make, and they want the chance to make the income they feel they deserve. Other businesspeople have been downsized or otherwise laid off, and they want to replace their lost income.

- **Independence.** Some people just don't like working for others, and they want the freedom to make their own decisions.

- **Ideas.** Some employees believe that their ideas are being used improperly and ignored in corporate jobs. These workers want to do things better, faster, and with more personality.

- **Recognition.** Some employees feel unappreciated in jobs where they are required to make lots of money for other people. These workers want to play a more significant, creative, or individual role in their own businesses.

- **Satisfaction.** Some employees feel trapped in office jobs. They want to work in exciting fields that provide not only a good income but personal satisfaction as well.

Of course, your personal goals will determine whether you start a home-based enterprise and play an important role in just about every decision you make along the way—from your business structure and employees to how you sell and market your products or services. Once you have some idea of what your general goals are, the next step is to make those goals concrete by quantifying them. It's not enough to say, for example, that you want to change careers or that you want to be your own boss. You'll need to develop specific targets for your business, including monetary ones.

Quantifying your goals can be a long process. You'll have to gather a lot more information before you're ready to set specific targets. Eventually, you'll probably want to put those goals together in the form of a business plan (which we talk about in detail in Chapter 6). Before you gather all the specific information about your business idea, consider these guidelines for quantifying your goals:

- **Be specific.** Establish targets that can be easily measured, and use numbers as targets whenever possible. For example, you may set a goal of selling your goods or services across a specific county, reaching a defined level of sales, or selling a total number of products. Tie your target numbers to specific time frames (within one year, five years, or even ten years and beyond).

- **Be aggressive, but not too aggressive.** You can aim high and still be realistic. Don't set goals that are too easy. Also, set both short-term and long-term goals. If, after six months in business, you accomplish all of your goals, then what? Don't sell yourself short. Go for something that's a bit beyond the ordinary.

- **Be realistic.** High expectations are great, but make sure that you establish achievable targets.

- **Be consistent.** Beware of setting goals that compete with each other. For example, a goal of selling 1,000 products a month might be inconsistent with a goal of earning $10,000 a month. There is nothing wrong with having both goals, yet be aware when a potential conflict exists and then establish priorities among your goals.

Some people have difficulty setting goals because they just don't know where to start. If this applies to you, start with an attainable goal. For example, set a goal of the amount of money you'll need to support your living expenses since, no matter what, you'll need to make enough to make ends meet. After achieving the basic financial requirements to support your lifestyle, you should look at other goals, such as increasing your profits, broadening your number of customers, or adding more products.

WHY GOALS ARE IMPORTANT

Goals are not just the destination you're driving toward, they're also the painted lines that help keep you on the road. The information and worksheets on the CD-ROM will help you determine if your goals for starting a business at home are similar to those revealed in interviews with hundreds of home-based entrepreneurs.

If you spend time to understand your priorities, your reason for starting a home-based business is probably a good one. Of course, some of your business ideas may not be on the CD-ROM. Don't worry. There are as many reasons for starting home-based businesses as there are different kinds of home-based entrepreneurs. The CD-ROM only covers the most common ones.

NOTE: All the worksheets, forms, and checklists mentioned in this book are provided on the CD-ROM packaged with this book. The worksheets and forms on the CD-ROM can be duplicated for friends and family and used repeatedly. The CD-ROM is organized in the same manner as the book, by chapters, for easy access to the relevant CD-ROM worksheets.

PERSONALITY TRAITS AND WORKING HABITS

"As a general rule, those who thrive on working at home are self-starters who like the line of work they are in and enjoy working independently. They're goal-directed achievers and are comfortable with minimum structure, capable of setting up and following their own schedules and deadlines." (quoted from Paul and Sarah Edwards' *Working at Home,* 1992)

Do the people the Edwards describe sound like you? The personality traits worksheet on the CD-ROM provides questions about your personality and work preferences to help determine if you match the typical home-based success profile. Answer the questions as honestly as possible. Your scores on this worksheet will identify preferences, traits, and working styles that are important to consider before you decide to go into a business from your home.

Of course, not every successful entrepreneur matches the typical profile. If you don't, this doesn't mean that you won't succeed, it just means that you have some areas to work on. If you really don't like being on your own, determining your own schedules, or setting your own priorities, you should use tactics to make sure you get things done and are happy in a home-based enterprise.

Using the worksheet is only an informal approach to determining your working preferences and personality traits, but the worksheet will help you identify those aspects of your life that may interfere with your home-based success.

ARE YOU READY?

If you have a good reason for starting a home-based business and if you also have a personality and working habits that are well-adapted to home entrepreneurship, your next step is to determine if you are psychologically prepared to start your own business. If you are still just thinking about home-based entrepreneurship, the worksheets on the CD-ROM can help you decide if you are ready to start your own business at home. If you already have a home-based business, a review of these worksheets will help reveal potential weak spots in your current business practices and attitudes.

The best way to determine your readiness to succeed as a home-based entrepreneur is to honestly evaluate your strengths, weaknesses, and attitudes toward the work that will be involved. You are the only one who can do that. The worksheets help guide the process. Remember, you are the most important factor in the success or failure of your business.

Answer the questions as if your business depends on the responses. It does. Take your time and be honest with yourself. These forms are not a test. No one else needs to see your responses. There are no right or wrong answers. The worksheets on the CD-ROM will only reveal basic strengths and weaknesses or obstacles to overcome in getting ready for home-based success.

If you've completed the worksheets for this chapter thus far, you now know a lot more about yourself and your thinking regarding a home-based business or telecommuting career. If you are still determined to be a home-based tycoon, it's time to decide on a business that's right for you. Included in the next few pages and on the CD-ROM are a wide range of options and suggestions that should help you find a business idea that's feasible.

CHOOSING AN ENTERPRISE THAT'S RIGHT FOR YOU

Before you choose a home-based business or career, the diverse motivations for starting your home-based enterprise are worth in-depth analysis. Some home-based entrepreneurs suggest that you select a business strictly by the market and income potential. Others suggest a business in a field with which you are already intimately familiar. Many, however, take a different approach and insist that you should choose a business you would enjoy even if you weren't getting paid for it. Home-based literary agent Mike Snell, of Cape Cod, Massachusetts, put it this way: "Look into your heart and make sure that the kind of business you choose is something you would like to do—even if nobody paid you to do it. Do what you love and the money will follow." In contrast, Kyle Roth, a Los Angeles-based entrepreneur who runs a computer consulting firm from his Westwood bungalow, offers less romantic advice: "Pick a field that pays the biggest hourly rate."

So how should you choose? Should you start a business for love or money? The answer depends on your personal capabilities and your work ethic. Obviously, you can make a quick killing if you have special skills that are in demand. You can have the Brink's truck pick up your takings for a daily trip to the bank and settle into quiet retirement. However, if you lack such skills or dislike the work you have done before, then the possibilities are endless, and it might be worthwhile to investigate your hobbies or personal interests as the basis for a money-making enterprise.

As you examine business opportunities in depth in the next chapter, remember that if you try to copy someone else's success, step-by-step, you may not have the same results. That's not to say that you won't succeed if you try to write books, open a consulting agency, start a unique skin care line, or initiate other enterprises that have been successful for other people, but you still need to adapt the idea and the execution to your personal situation and skills. You need to formulate your own idea and your own management style for your business to succeed. Even if you operate a franchise or buy an existing business, you'll need to adapt the business to your own specific strengths and weaknesses if you want to make money.

How do you know if your own ideas are good ones? Is it better to start your own business or get involved with something that already exists (like a franchise or multilevel marketing program)? When you have an exciting idea, you'll want to research the competition and the market potential before you get started. There are numerous places that provide information on the potential and requirements for a business, as well as facts on the competition. The information and checklists discussed in this book should help you decide on a business that you can manage into profitability.

Included in the Business Ideas section of the CD-ROM are a wide range of business opportunities for home-based entrepreneurs. Some are fun and exciting—others are ordinary and obvious. The key is to choose a business that matches your priorities and needs. Remember, it is not necessarily the idea for

the business that secures success. More importantly, success depends on the entrepreneur's dedication to the pursuit of independence and prosperity.

Stop, Look, and Listen: The Basic Rules for Finding a Business Idea

In grade school we learn simple rules for understanding what's happening around us: stop, look, and listen. These fundamental rules are necessary components of finding viable business opportunities. The possibilities for profitable home-based businesses are really endless, from ordinary home-based consulting and bookkeeping firms to businesses based on wacky, wild ideas like Eric Schechter's Rubber Duck Races. (Don't laugh—those rubber ducks made Eric $10 million in one year.) Business opportunities are all around you if you just take time to stop, look, and listen.

Here's how it works. First, *stop* and take some time to understand your own skills and interests. Suggestions for pinpointing your abilities and interests are found in the next section of this chapter.

Next, *look* at other home-based businesses that have succeeded. This book is a good place to start, but there are many other places to look. More suggestions for finding business ideas are located in the resources section on the CD-ROM. We also suggest that you keep clippings of ideas you find. We have hundreds of file folders full of ideas—some will turn into books, some will support our marketing efforts, and some are just inspirations. Every six months or so, we sort our files, and we almost always find something that spawns a useful and prosperous idea.

Finally, learn to *listen* to the people around you. Clients usually tell you the kind of services and products they want. If you listen to consumers talk about their needs and desires, you can often think of a business opportunity that meets their requirements. Being a good listener is the key to being a good businessperson. Listening to people involves getting together with them. Listen to people in stores, in social situations, or through eaves-dropping on conversations. Learn to listen through practicing. When people don't tell you what you want to know, ask them. Most of us really do like to talk about ourselves and our opinions. If you give people the chance to do so, you can gain a great deal of information.

Using the stop, look, and listen approach, you'll find opportunities that meet almost any range of interests, skill levels, and financial goals.

Your Business Choices

What kind of business should you start? If you use the stop, look, and listen technique, you'll discover that there are at least four types of businesses you can start from home:

- A business idea that's yours alone and begins with your own efforts from scratch.
- A home-business that you buy from some-one else, whether a prepackaged home-business opportunity (a *business op* in trade lingo) or a business you're acquiring from an independent seller.
- A franchise that's appropriate for home-based success (listings for over 100 such opportunities are located on the CD-ROM)
- A multilevel marketing (MLM) program that allows you to sell catalog goods

through your own effort and the effort of others (usually other home-based workers). By engaging yourself in the marketing process, you collect a portion of their commission as well as your own. (Again, listings for many such opportunities are on the CD-ROM.)

- Many people who want to start a home-based business have a pretty good idea of what type of business they want to own. Yet there are some who only have a general business idea, while others don't have any ideas at all. Why might you buy an existing business rather than build from the ground up? A premade business or an established franchise can save time and money.

Issues about buying a business opportunity or a franchise and getting involved in MLM programs are explored in detail in Chapter 5, but for now, just choosing an idea for a business (whether your own idea or a purchased venture) involves the same amount of effort as finding a business opportunity that matches your skills and desires.

Healthy and Ecologically Sound Opportunities

In introducing possibilities for home-based endeavors, it's important to acknowledge the growing interests in ecology and health. It's not news that ecology, equality, and health are major concerns, and many successful home-based entrepreneurs want to make a difference in these areas. By starting businesses that have made people healthier, animals safer, and the world stronger, some entrepreneurs have contributed something important to their communities and to the world. Their businesses range from manufacturing natural toothpaste to designing fake fur coats, from selling weight loss formulas and organic vitamins to completing health-care research for critically ill patients.

It's apparent from the diverse ideas and the personal convictions of the entrepreneurs who promote healthy and ecologically sound ideas or products are naturals for home-based prosperity. These businesses prosper simply because the entrepreneurs who started them truly care about people and the world they live in.

There are still many opportunities in these areas to be tapped by new entrepreneurs. Expect to see more of these world-conscious, home-base businesses flourish over the next decade. If you have a passion for protecting animals, making the world cleaner, or using resources in more ecologically sound ways, there is probably a business in your heart that will not only make money but will also make a difference.

Special Business Opportunities for Women and Minorities

Governmental organizations, along with most large businesses, have implemented programs that provide special opportunities for businesses owned by minorities. The definition of a minority and how that definition applies to the various business forms is inconsistent between agencies, so investigate your eligibility as a minority business enterprise. Registering your business on a procurement list opens doors that you would otherwise have had to discover on your own. These types of organizations are also known as Disadvantaged Business Enterprises (DBE) or Woman Business Enterprises (WBE).

These procurement programs are designed to ensure that a certain percentage of government-issued contracts go to special businesses. You are more likely to get a government request for a proposal if you are listed as a DBE or WBE than if you are not. This doesn't guarantee that you will get the business, but at least you get a shot at it. Contact the government procurement office, General Services Commission, or Corporate Purchasing Office to get the necessary packet of information that lists the requirements for becoming a DBE or WBE.

Consider Less Popular Opportunities

Here's another option that many home-based entrepreneurs have turned into a profit: find something that no one else wants to do. There's a rule of thumb to determine the overall feasibility of a business or service: *The more interesting or prestigious the job, the fewer openings available and the lower the pay will be for new entrants in the field.* For that reason, if you should decide one morning to write novels for a living or grow your hobby as a landscape painter into a multimillion-dollar, home-based career, chances of success are less favorable than other less-sought-after careers. That doesn't mean that writing isn't a good career (we obviously like the approach), but it does mean that making it will take some serious effort. Keeping this in mind, business opportunities are abundant if you are willing to consider a mundane or contemptible job that no one else wants and if you do a good job at it while charging a reasonable price.

As an example of how this strategy can pay off, one couple that we interviewed oper-

A STOREFRONT IN THE HOME

Many communities, especially small towns, allow storefronts to be located within or on the grounds of private residences. Such a home-based business may compete with regular store-based retail by selling everything from carpets to cosmetics to computers. Home-based stores work much like conventional stores with outside signs, parking, and sometimes a display window. In addition, the store may also run mail order and make on-site sales calls.

The advantage of a storefront is that it's a retail outlet with lower leasing, equipping, protecting, and stocking expenses than a regular storefront. In-house stores range in complexity from products stacked on fold-up tables to a complete sales floor requiring extensive modification of the house or a new building on the property. Another plus is that, while a conventional storefront requires continuous manning during store hours, home-based store managers can choose to see customers by appointment or have very limited operating hours.

The disadvantage of running any store is the number of hours required if you plan to have regular operating hours. Of course, these hours can be used profitably to run all aspects of the home-based enterprise, including sales outside the home. Set up the home office in the store and, assuming that traffic is light, you can mind the store and operate the business.

Beware that traffic will be light. Unlike the highly visible stores on the main thoroughfare, you must build your business through advertising and promotion. Your store doesn't have the drive-by presence of conventional stores unless it's located on a major street rather than in a quiet neighborhood. While word-of-mouth advertising helps, without additional promotion only the local population becomes aware of your operation.

Another problem is community acceptance. Before planning a home-based store, your first stop should be city hall. You must study regulations and attain the required paperwork to be approved. You may find that such an operation is out of the question or that your neighbors must approve the store first, with it's additional traffic and noise. If you live in a planned community or one with a homeowners' association, their rules might prevent what city hall allows. Finally, it's important that your neighbors are comfortable with your business. You don't want to invest $25,000 in remodeling and inventory only to have a torchlight procession protesting your grand opening.

ates a septic tank clean-out service high in the mountainous area of central Colorado. It was easy to tell that they were embarrassed just talking about what they did for a living, but when the subject of income came up, we found out that after only a couple of years in the business they were making over $150,000 annually—not bad when compared to the unemployment checks they had been receiving. They have a home-based office, enjoy steady income, work their own hours, and get to spend time with their kids.

The formula for their success was simple. They looked at the market area near their home and found some service opportunities that were not being adequately addressed by other companies. After looking into an appliance repair business, a home-based quick print shop, and several other opportunities, they chose the septic tank clean-out service, acquiring the requisite truck for $6,500 from an elderly widow whose husband previously performed the service. After learning about septic tanks and chemicals at a local library and helping a septic tank service in Denver, the couple learned more about doing the dirty work and started their business.

They charged a reasonable fee for each clean out and quickly built a loyal customer base because customers had previously paid much more to a service 75 miles away. While few people would suggest that this is a glamorous business, it's paid off handsomely for this couple, and it will put their three sons through college as well as comfortably support the family.

THE MORE YOU LEARN, THE BETTER OFF YOU'LL BE

A frequent comment from successful businesspeople is that you can never know too much about your profession, the competition, or the market before you get started. Many entrepreneurs recommend that before you start your company, you should track down all of the magazines and newspapers relevant to your new profession and read them religiously.

While you may think that there aren't any magazines that cater to your specific enterprise, with the enormous number of trade and specialty magazines, most likely there are several publications that directly relate to your business. Reading them will help you succeed. For example, if you are thinking of opening a llama ranch on your home's unused acreage, you shouldn't be surprised to find *Llamas Magazine—The International Camelid Journal*!

There are several ways to track down publications that cater to your trade. You might visit a competitor to see what magazines are laid out on the table in the reception area and note the phone numbers for each one. (Look on the masthead located within the first couple of pages for subscription and circulation particulars.) A trip to a library or bookstore is another route, but to really get a handle on all the available magazines and periodicals, look in the SRDS guides from Standard Rate and Data Service in the reference section of most libraries. These volumes list just about every periodical for every industry.

In addition to industry-specific publications, more general interest magazines may be of use to you in your competitive and market analysis. Typically, several publications are available that cater to a broader audience such as small manufacturing companies, craft makers, and office technology. It is smart to keep tabs on general business magazines as well. You may spot a trend that could be an opportunity for expansion; therefore, reading about other struggling businesses can be a source of reassurance in times of rough seas. In addition to *Wall Street Journal*, *Business Week*, and *For-*

tune, look up *Success, Entrepreneur, The Economist, Women Entrepreneur,* and *Home Office Computing.*

While a growing number of computer magazines run columns aimed at home-based businesses, one very useful publication for those with companies at home is *Home Office Computing.* This magazine is full of tips and how-to information written by home-based entrepreneurs for home-based entrepreneurs. In home-oriented business magazines you'll meet people like yourself, hear how they got started, and receive credible advice for making your business more successful.

The home-business magazines also feature regular reviews of home-office technology, including fax machines, copiers, telephones, computers, software, and more. Since only products of use to home-based businesses are profiled, magazines often limit their reviews to the kinds of products a home-based business is likely to buy. Best of all, the reviews of technical products like computers are written for busy business people who need to get work done, not for computer whizzes.

Read the magazines at the library if you can't afford to subscribe, and keep in mind that many business or industry publications are available free to qualified readers by filling out a form that comes with the magazine. Most of the magazines also have Web sites that enable you to review information without buying or storing the magazines. To qualify for subscriptions to some publications you only need to be someone who buys products from advertisers that appear in the magazine. For example, in industry publications on comput-

ers like *PC Week*, you qualify if your company purchases computers or computer-related supplies.

Books and Motivational Tapes

One entrepreneur we met has a great approach for dealing with down days both in life and in her company. On a rainy day she heads to the library and curls up with a book on marketing, sales, promotion, or some other business topic. On really rainy days, she picks up a book on motivation or how to build and maintain a positive attitude. The payoff? The down days have become fewer and farther apart because her knowledge has given her ideas for a million-dollar business. The motivational books help her to maintain a positive attitude even through trying times.

A related suggestion mentioned by several homemade millionaires is to buy motivational tapes on cassette and listen to them while running business errands or on the way to meet clients. These tapes keep them up-to-date with new ideas and help to revive their spirits if a deal falls through or if they suddenly lack enthusiasm for their company.

Clubs, Communities, and Networking

Most home-based entrepreneurs believe that networking is a primary source of business ideas. These entrepreneurs suggest that you join a special interest society or club related to your business, even if it takes a chunk of change to do so. As Donna Hart (founder of *Parent & Child Magazine*) advises, "Join professional societies so you can take advantage of the knowledge of others in your field. These professionals are a source of ideas as well as business." Donna had to fork over $500 to join a society of publishers who specialize in publications on raising children, but she says that it was worthwhile because members have provided her with advice for her magazine and have been very supportive of her efforts.

In addition to advice, many societies and clubs provide social events that allow you to meet colleagues. These contacts may be useful for locating new business and idea sharing. Having the phone numbers of some business-people that operate similar ventures gives you a support system when faced with a difficult problem or issue. Building a strong support system is an important component for many successful home-based business owners.

Most cities have business clubs and entre-preneurial groups that meet regularly and bring in speakers to discuss a business aspect over lunch or dinner. Joining one or more of these organizations may provide you with advantages similar to joining a professional organization. You may also pick up new clients along the way, since many members of these clubs give their business to other members as a way of supporting entrepreneurs. There is usually an events calendar in your local newspaper that will list the meeting times and locations for business groups. The annual membership fees for belonging to these groups can add up, so consider only groups that allow you to "sample" a meeting or two without charge. Join only those groups where the business-building experience of the members is a step or two ahead of your own.

Another place where you can find ideas, meet others like yourself, and chitchat about home-based business is through online services such as America Online and other chat

lines on the Internet. This requires a computer and a modem, which you should already own since modem prices are now under $100. Logging onto America Online, you can attend forums where work-at-home gurus like Paul and Sarah Edwards (homemade millionaires who support other home-based businesses) provide answers to your questions and give advice to those getting started or running into barriers with their home-based companies. You can also contact us online by sending e-mail to us at kimbaker@aol.com. The cost of using these forums varies, but it is generally not very expensive.

Keep In Touch With the Outside World

Some homemade millionaires stake their entire businesses on their ongoing contacts, their work with community organizations, and other activities that get them in front of new people. If you work at home, it's very important that you advertise your business, and networking seems to be one of the cheapest and most popular ways of doing so. Included on the CD-ROM is information to get you started in your networking endeavors on clubs, societies, newsletters, and conferences.

ALL KINDS OF POSSIBILITIES

If you can't find a business idea in the sources mentioned, to help expand your thinking on possibilities take a look at one of the franchises or multilevel marketing companies listed on the CD-ROM.

If none of the home-based business opportunities sound good to you, why not make up one of your own. Take a look at *Million Dollar Home-Based Businesses* and other books on home-based entrepreneurship listed in the resources and books sections of the CD-ROM to get even more ideas.

Now that you have lots of ideas in mind, Chapter 4 will offer you an easy-to-follow methodology for sorting through your ideas to find the business that will meet your lifestyle and financial goals.

C H A P T E R

3

TELECOMMUTING—BRINGING YOUR JOB HOME

· ·

This chapter looks at telecommuting, the work environment of the new millennium, as an option for getting started in a home-based career. The telecommunications revolution is here to stay because the office can be located anywhere—in the office, your car, or at home. It's an "office-on-the-go" depending on the technology you choose and your employer's willingness to try the arrangement and reap the benefits of happier, more productive employees who work at home.

Finally, businesspeople can leave behind driving to work and polluting the air behind. The work done in a cramped office cubicle after a 55-minute trek through rush-hour traffic can be handled equally as well in a comfortable home office. Your employer should appreciate you more as a telecommuter. In fact, Congress is considering a law that will mandate large corporations to offer employees the opportunity to work at home. As a telecommuter, you take up less room at the office, you can't pollute the environment by commuting, you use your own computer and telephone resources, and you are highly motivated and productive, often surpassing your peer's efforts at the office. It's a win-win situation for you and your employer.

IT'S NOT A JOB FOR EVERYONE

Telecommuting is not appropriate for all tasks or all people. In terms of job responsibilities, many tasks lie outside the domain of the home-based worker. In addition to obvious impossibilities such as assembly line chores, in-person customer service, or the use of expensive machine tools, some jobs require that you be there. Face-to-face meetings, supervision of employees, and the quality assurance of manufactured goods require you to watch, evaluate, or supervise the process. Without your motivation, engagement, and enthusiasm, work may slow to a crawl. But many jobs are viable for telecommuters, including most office-based clerical, accounting, information systems, and direct sales jobs.

THE WORK-AT-HOME EMPLOYEE

Throughout this book we've conveyed the nature and personality of the successful home-based worker. Success as a telecommuter involves traits similar to those of successful home-based business owners. With those traits in mind, the only additional criteria you'll need is to be a good communicator for keeping the office apprised of your efforts. You must also be very comfortable with the technology required for conversations with the home office. While many home-based businesses rely little on computers and telecommunications, working away from home as a telecommuter requires considerable electronic communication such as e-mail and teleconferencing facilities.

A Management Perspective

One of the toughest parts of a home-based job is keeping management informed of your productivity while maintaining a team-player status. This chapter presents the basics, but telecommuting is much easier when your managers:

- Accept you as a worker who requires little supervision
- Have other telecommuters successfully working from home
- Regularly use computers for communications and are not uncomfortable working with you via phone, fax, and e-mail
- Appreciate the benefits and contributions of a telecommuter even if they are not always accessible

Obviously not all management teams or companies will be receptive to telecommuters. Some companies may treat you as a disloyal team member no matter how much high-quality work you produce. You need to evaluate the situation before suggesting a telecommuting assignment. For those applying for jobs, telecommuting is best suggested after you've served a term as an in-house employee. Otherwise, choose a job as a consultant, or apply only to positions where telecommuting is common.

On the Upside
Telecommuting gives you freedom to produce quality work without the constant interruption of peers or the discomforts of the impersonal cubicle. You set your own hours and rearrange projects to meet expectations. You work when you want to, whether it's 8:00 p.m. or 4:00 a.m. A properly managed home office is free of noise, people dropping by, and ringing telephones. This freedom from unwelcome interruptions vastly improves productivity, which is why most managers familiar with telecommuting have no doubts that it makes happier employees and gets more accomplished.

WHY TELECOMMUTE INSTEAD OF STARTING YOUR OWN BUSINESS?

Most people choose telecommuting as a bridge between conventional and unconventional work styles. Telecommuting provides a dependable salary and health benefits lacking in a home-based business. In addition, in some enlightened companies telecommuters can work wherever they live, whether it's 10 miles or 1,000 miles away from the office.

Many telecommuters use traditional jobs as stepping stones to running a home-based business. After a year or two, a telecommuter can use their knowledge and new contacts to establish a home-based enterprise. A steady income can purchase the equipment needed for the business while you learn to use it. With or without the traditional employer's knowledge, it's possible to start a new enterprise while working at a conventional job. As the business grows, it's important to decide whether to keep it on the side or to quit the day job and become completely home-based. Learning and experiencing the job before taking the risk of running a full-time, home-based enterprise is commonly how home-based consulting firms get established. First you must learn the ropes and get some clients, then you can set up a business without a traditional employer.

THE STEPS TO TELECOMMUTING

Effective telecommuting requires that you follow a series of steps. First, you'll want your employer to see you as a potential telecommuter, and then you'll need to get ready to work at home. The steps may take some time depending on the job and the employer involved. Remember, if things don't work out for you or your employer, you can always return to the office.

Step 1. Consider the job. Can it be accomplished from home without any problems? Can you effectively interact with management, coworkers, your staff, and clients while working from home? If time must be spent at the conventional work site, how far away is it? How often do you have to go there? If needed, can you get there quickly?

Step 2. Consider the employer. Is this a company that is flexible in its working relationship with employees, or would the suggestion of telecommuting put the boss off? (Surprisingly, some managers won't consider letting you work at home even though it makes logical and economic sense. Even if your boss is willing, his boss may feel that telecommuting contradicts an organized workplace.)

Step 3. Suggest the idea to your boss casually. If he seems receptive follow up with a conversation outlining the relationship and offer him a written plan. A plan should describe how you propose to succeed by working at home and how it will directly benefit the company. If you need equipment for home use, this should also be included.

Step 4. Suggest a trial period. Your managers will be more comfortable if your plan includes a trial period before a permanent commitment. The trial period can take weeks or months depending on the agreement. If new equipment must be purchased for your home office, make sure it can be returned and used in the office if the new arrangement does not pan out.

Step 5. Set up the home office. Establish agreements on the need for quiet time and an "off-limits" office area with members of the household.

Step 6. Commence the trial period. Assume that you'll need to make adjustments since assignments will be delivered differently now and your space at the staff meeting will become a conference call.

Step 7. Evaluate the trial period with your manager. Did it work as planned or are there insurmountable problems? If minor problems cloud the arrangement, consider extending the trial period to see if they can be rectified.

Step 8. Telecommute permanently or return to the traditional work environment. To succeed, you may need to work conventionally while taking projects home that require extra time or more concentration.

THE TELECOMMUTING AGREEMENT

It's important that an agreement is established between you and your management stating the nature of your home-based job. Signed by both parties, the telecommuting agreement sets forth your responsibilities, the time required for you to return to the conventional workplace for meetings, how you will be contacted to provide progress reports, and the length of the trial period. The agreements include measurable performance goals but do not manage your time to the nanosecond.

The letter should be drafted by you, approved by the human resources department if your employer has one, and signed by you and your boss. You should also require additional signatures after the trial period has been completed and before the arrangement becomes permanent. If changes to your salary are involved, such as a reduction in pay, this must be included in the agreement as well. Expense reimbursement should also be specified. Working from home doesn't usually incur addition expenses; however, if you must buy supplies or if you incur long distance telephone calls, these charges should be reimbursed.

If the letter is extremely specific in defining your duties—a common requirement in companies that are skeptical about telecommuting—add a clause requesting a new agreement every ninety days. This will work if you submit the new and amended list together, showing all items that were completed and adding tasks that your job required. This helps your manager receive an overall impression of your work versus the tasks included in the agreement, since some may have shifted in priority during three months.

WORKING WITH YOUR EMPLOYER

In any job, communication is the key to continued success, especially for the telecommuter. If you are not toiling visibly at your desk, your employer may assume that you are at home twiddling your thumbs in front of a daytime TV show. Perhaps, however, you prefer to work at night.

Perception is important when working from home, and communication is the key to building a positive perception. Stay visible while working at home by:

- Attending relevant company functions and meetings

- Interacting with customers
- Responding promptly to e-mail
- Responding quickly to mail and faxes
- Calling your boss every day to "check in" and to obtain important information or instructions
- Providing routine, written reports on projects. Document any roadblocks
- Dropping in for lunch occasionally
- Carrying a pager

FOUR WAYS TO STAY CONNECTED TO THE OFFICE

There are several ways to stay connected to the folks back at work:

Stay connected to your company's e-mail

You can communicate with the office by using e-mail. Get a system that notifies you each time a message arrives in your mailbox. When you receive a message, return it immediately.

Long distance charges may make e-mail infeasible, but at least try it during the usual e-mail hours—first thing in the morning. Another option is a gateway set up by your company for field salespeople in remote locations. Unless you're really isolated, chances are there's an easy and inexpensive way to access your office's network with little more than a local phone call. E-mail does tie up the phone line; therefore, you might want to add another line.

Fax

Sending a handwritten note is very effective for maintaining presence with your employer and your clients.

Linking Computers

With an inexpensive, add-on package, you can make an office-based computer turn on by remote control for easy assess to your files from home. Linking products are available that move your mouse to open and close files and windows by remote control. If you set your office computer to work for you at home, your employer will know you're working hard.

Telephone

To keep a high profile, call your office frequently. Make your employer aware of your progress, and offer suggestions on how to make the telecommuting agreement run smoothly. The telephone can ensure that you will be included in decision processes and can also be used to call clients to secure their happiness as well. Use the telephone to maintain your presence as an active participant in the business.

RULES FOR EFFICIENT ELECTRONIC MAIL

E-mail is a powerful tool for keeping in touch. When using e-mail in a business climate:

Keep It Short

Most e-mail messages are read quickly as harried recipients try to clear their mailboxes. A busy e-mail user may receive more than fifty messages a day, while senior management in large corporations may receive as many as 500 messages a day. While 500 messages seems like a lot, keep in mind that as a telecommuter you will probably receive more mail than before, including problems, special causes, and invitations to company events. On the other hand, sending too much unneeded e-mail makes recipients ignore all of your messages, including the important ones.

Frequent e-mail users employ shorthand and a variety of codes to convey emotions and to make communications faster. For example, the well known :) is a representation for a smile indicating that the last remark should be taken in jest or as a thank you. Take your time to fully understand e-mail shorthand before adopting it. If you don't understand an odd phrase, acronym, or symbol, ask someone who does.

Keep It Simple

If you are having trouble writing a message, the subject may be better discussed in person or on the phone. If you find it difficult to put your message into words, it may be because the subject of the message is too delicate for a medium that's depersonalized.

Avoid Double Meanings

When communicating via e-mail, especially with people who don't know your personality, avoid sarcasm and phrases or words that may reverse the meaning of your message. While e-mail appears to be a very straightforward way to communicate, your remarks may become meaningless or insulting if they are misinterpreted.

Use Blanket Messages Sparingly

E-mail systems make copying your message to many recipients easy. Simply request the system to send a copy of a message to all recipients or to a group of people by an alias. An alias is the system's way of mailing a message to a group of people by simply using one name. For example, MARKETING could be an alias for the entire marketing group consisting of forty marketing managers, administrative assistants, and researchers. Addressing a message to MARKETING sends it to everyone in the department. Use alias messaging sparingly. You don't want to overload the home office with e-mail that is not relevant.

DELEGATING WORK AND TRACKING PROGRESS FROM HOME

If you manage or coordinate employees, you need to keep track of what they are doing as well as their progress. For highly motivated workers, little more than a phone call a day is sufficient. E-mail can be used for short correspondence and less important business. Less motivated employees require regular contact and several telephone calls a day providing specific directions and answering questions.

MEETINGS THROUGH TELECONFERENCING

Meetings are an inevitable part of any business. Working at home will relieve you from some; however, it's important for you to appear either physically or electronically at meetings vital to your department. When you can't attend a meeting, you may be able to teleconference using your computer or arrange conference calling through your long-distance carrier without leaving the house.

Conference Calling

Teleconferencing is nothing new. It's been around as long as the party line. It is as simple as talking to coworkers who share the same line. It can also be as complex as having an advanced telephone system or using the phone company to assemble the call. There are also products that use the Internet to handle the transmission. The advantage? No long distance charges!

Teleconferencing requires quality telephone equipment to be effective. Poor communication is often caused by the speaker phone. Using a single handset, trying to sort out the voices of staff members is not easy. Effective communication is difficult unless every staff member has a personal microphone and a telephone system that effectively routes each voice to you.

Electronic Conferencing

An effective approach for many meetings is to establish a chat room on a company e-mail system, through the Internet, or with an online service like America Online. Within this electronic room, each member converses through typed text. For example, a coworker's question appears on everyone's monitor as it is typed. Responses to the question appear as they are entered. The entire session can be saved, printed, and reviewed later as needed.

Advanced systems feature still pictures of each participant as their comments appear under their names. If someone needs to take a break or leave early, an empty chair appears reminding other participants that a member is absent.

Video Teleconferencing

For the telecommuter who needs access to faces as well as voices, Internet teleconferencing—with the addition of software and hardware to a standard PC—is easy, inexpensive, and

convenient. Unlike pricey picture phones or renting time in a video teleconferencing facility, with Internet protocol (IP) teleconferencing, talking is cheap once a small initial investment is made. You can videoconference all day for only Internet or Intranet connection costs. For the corporate user with fast Internet access and good hardware, video quality approaches the more expensive offerings of long-distance carriers. For one-on-one conferencing with your boss, a cheap PC camera, modem, and the software is all you'll need. The picture won't be as clear as an expensive setup, but it gets the job done.

Picture Imperfect

Naturally, not everything about IP teleconferencing is perfect. Two problems follow the technology that you should be aware of before adoption. This is especially true if you're the decision maker for a high-priced system complete with projection TVs and multiple hook-ups.

The first problem is speed. The basis of the Internet is packet switching technology. In simplified terms, your sound and picture can be routed through any number of computers, depending on computer availability. Occasionally packets arrive slowly, seriously disrupting reception on the receiving end. Likewise, a slow modem makes for reception that is like a slow-motion movie, only slower.

The second problem is common to all kinds of computer technology. If you are attempting to conference with a party who employs a different software package, reception may not be possible. Unrelated software packages are capable of working together, yet it's barely ready for prime time and not universally adopted by teleconferencing software makers.

Still, the power of video is awesome. Unlike audio-only telephony or text conferencing, in which the only nuances are the choice of words or the tone of voice, with IP video teleconferencing, facial expressions and body language are also apparent. You can hold up a 400-page report for the other party to see even if it's really just a fancy cover containing blank pages!

EQUIPMENT AND THE TELECOMMUTER

You should buy few materials and use your employer's equipment wherever possible. This not only saves money, but with technology that tends to date and become obsolete quickly, your employer will take the risk, not you. However, any equipment you use should be insured, especially if your employer's insurance will not cover it while it's in your home office.

When taking anything home—from pencils to portable computers—from your employer's abode, do two things. First, inform your boss or ask their permission. You may need to justify taking the item, especially if your employer must purchase a replacement. Second, keep a written log with serial numbers of everything you borrow. Avoid using bootleg copies just to save the company a little money. Sign each item in or out, and have your boss initial the exit and reentry of all goods, especially costly ones.

This log should be copied each time it changes, and your boss should have a dated copy as well as any departments that track company inventory. By keeping this log your managers know exactly what you have. This habit prevents any disagreements if you leave the company or when it's time to trade in your computer and peripherals for fresh ones.

TRACKING EXPENSES

When you log and track employer-owned equipment, you must also track expenses. As a part of the agreement made with your employer, you can divide expenses into two categories: those reimbursable by your employer and those that can be written off on your income taxes. Your telecommuting agreement should be specific as to what can be collected from your employer. That way, if the IRS decides to audit you, you will have written proof stating which expenses are deductible and which expenses are not.

Paperwork and Records

The telecommuter must keep careful track of work-related activities. Reports submitted, expenses, and an equipment log are just the beginning of record keeping. Written communication, including e-mail, should be tracked and saved in a daily journal of activities. Your journal can be brief but will be very useful if you are ever asked to account for your time by a skeptical manager not accustomed to working with telecommuters.

Printed or saved e-mail should become a part of a permanent record. You can refer to old messages if there are questions or if you need to explain your time. With e-mail rapidly replacing memos and the telephone, it is an important and vital way to communicate. All records should be carefully filed by date or category for easy access.

In summary, telecommuting is the vehicle of choice for employees who prefer to work at home and avoid the hassles and wasted time of traditional commuting. You can be king of your own turf while receiving regular paychecks and health benefits from a conventional employer. Although telecommuting is not for everybody, there are workers who want the structure of a company job and the privacy and quiet of home. If you fall into this category, give it a try!

Ten Steps to Choosing a Viable Home-Based Business

If you've followed our "stop, look, and listen" advice, you should have a list of many possible business opportunities. Some may be business ideas of your own, while others may be franchises or multilevel marketing programs. It's time to make a decision about the best business for you. This chapter outlines the process for helping you select the right business opportunity for your interests, skills, and goals.

Your choice of a business starts with you. Not all good business ideas are good for you. It doesn't matter how good a business idea is if it isn't something you will be able to do. If you won't be able to dedicate yourself to the business, it won't succeed.

The ten steps detailed in this chapter are recommended to help you match your abilities to various business requirements. The steps will enable you to rank various business opportunities and choose a business that has high success potential.

STEP 1. UNDERSTAND YOUR PERSONALITY, SKILLS, AND INTERESTS

If asked whether they had the "right stuff" to run a small business, most entrepreneurs would answer with a resounding "yes." The purpose of this first step is not to arrive at a yes or a no answer, but to help you evaluate your strengths and weaknesses.

You can significantly increase your odds of starting a successful business by first taking several personal factors into account: your interests, your experience, and your qualifications. Carefully considering each aspect of your personality and situation will improve the choice you ultimately make. If you completed the worksheets on the CD-ROM discussed in Chapter 2, you already have a good idea of your strengths and weaknesses as a business owner.

Always be honest as you evaluate your skills, otherwise you'll only hurt yourself. Also, don't panic if you discover that you have weaknesses. Every small business owner has faults. The key to success is not having skills, but finding ways to compensate for weaknesses. You can still be successful even if you don't possess every skill needed to run a small business. There are, however, certain qualities that you should possess if you're to be successful:

- **Willingness to sacrifice.** You must be willing to accept the fact that, as a small business owner, you will be the last one paid. Your bank and employees must all be paid before you see any of the money. You must also be willing to sacrifice much of your free time to your business. If you like working 9 to 5, knowing your exact income, and taking three weeks of vacation every year, don't go into business for yourself.

- **Strong interpersonal skills.** If you thought that getting along with your boss was tough, wait until you have to deal with suppliers,

customers, employees, lawyers, accountants, government officials, and everybody in between. Successful owners are able to work with all personality types and discover their customer's likes and dislikes.

- **Strong leadership skills.** Successful owners understand that employees and clients look to them to be led to the promised land. They will be looking to you for answers, and if you're not ready for that responsibility, you probably shouldn't own your own business.

- **Strong organizational skills.** Successful owners are able to keep track of everything that's going on in their business, set priorities, and get things done. They know that if they lose track of what's going on, they'll sink.

- **Intelligence.** We're not talking about the ability to score well on standardized tests. We're suggesting street smarts and common sense. Successful owners are able to anticipate problems before they arise, take preemptive steps to avoid them, and solve crises after they occur.

- **Management ability.** Small business is all about managing relationships with your customers or clients, employees, suppliers, accountant and lawyer, banker, and family. If you don't think you can effectively manage those relationships, you shouldn't start a new business.

- **Business experience.** Without some solid business experience, you're probably not going to be able to borrow any money. Your banker will want to know about your experience, not just in business, but in the business field you're interested in. If you lack experience, acquire some any way you can: volunteer at an existing business or try a part-time or weekend job in the field.

- **Optimism.** How will you react when your business isn't going as planned? An optimist who believes in the business will keep going in spite of the problems. Successful business owners are optimists who are able to continue with their business plans despite setbacks.

Although the qualities listed above are important to home business success, every owner of every single, successful business does not have all of these desired qualities. Therefore, there's hope for those who don't possess the perfect combination of drive, motivation, and good ideas. Maybe one of these categories applies to you:

- **You have a unique idea.** If you've built a better mousetrap, sometimes people will still beat a path to your door, even if you're poorly organized and pessimistic.
- **You're a genius.** If you possess the gift of greatness, clients will not only overlook your weaknesses, they'll revel in them.
- **You're just plain lucky.** Many successful entrepreneurs have earned success just because of their incredibly good timing.

After examining your strengths and weaknesses, you can consider how to compensate for weaknesses. What should you do if you don't have management skills or talent? Here are some options:

- **Consider hiring someone who can handle these tasks that you may not be good at or who has the traits or skills you lack.** As

your business advances, you may determine that the convenience of paying someone else to do unpleasant work is outweighed by the cost. At the start, however, you need to decide whether an employee could do the work for you.

Make a list of the things you like to do and those you don't. If your list includes things that you can't hire someone else to do, such as working with people, the solution is not as easy. Your best bet may be to join forces with someone whose skills complement yours. For example, a person who likes working with people but not with numbers and forms may be a good match for someone who likes working with numbers but not with people. If you really don't think you can handle the responsibilities on your own, you may want to consider another type of business that better matches your skills and personality.

Finding a good partner can be difficult. Most people partner with someone they know well, such as friends and family. Be aware, however that intimate partnerships do not always work. Some marriages and friendships have been destroyed by business partnerships, while others have been enriched by them. Finding a partner through others means, such as through a business association, is even more tenuous. The best advice is to be careful. Make sure that you're a good match before you go into business together.

- **Learn the new skills you need to succeed.** Another way to develop the traits and skills you need is to get training. Try taking classes at a local business school. If classes are too expensive, time consuming, or don't offer you enough real-world experience, you might get involved with a small business adviser, perhaps one from the Small Business Administration. Many small business programs are sponsored by federal or local government agencies, but there are some private ones as well. For more information and the location of an incubator near you, call the numbers provided on the CD-ROM or the National Business Incubator Association at 614-593-4331 or the Small Business Administration (SBA) at 800-827-5722.

STEP 2. DECIDE ON THE TYPE OF BUSINESS YOU PREFER

Most of the books about finding a small business will tell you that the best place to start is by matching your skills and experiences to a business that requires those skills. For example, if you love to cook, you should open a catering business or a restaurant. This step consists of making a list of what you like to do and what you don't like to do. Generally, people like doing things they're good at and don't like doing things they're not good at. It's a simple approach, but it should help you to narrow the possibilities.

There are thousands of possibilities for home-based businesses, many of which have not been discovered yet. If you've examined the Business Ideas and Opportunities sections of the CD-ROM, you've seen the hundreds of possibilities. As you examine the lists, you should notice that there are only three basic categories of businesses among your choices, whether you start the business on your own or

purchase it: a product-oriented business, a service-oriented business, or a business that combines a product and a service.

A product-oriented business sells products that you manufacture or products that are manufactured by others. A service business sells services that you perform from your home or services that you sell from your home and then perform elsewhere. It is also possible to sell services that someone else performs.

As you consider your skills and interests, ask yourself what you would rather do. Do you want to sell a product that you make yourself or sell a service that you provide? Should you sell a product that someone else makes that you can market for a profit?

If you like to make things or coordinate the production of others, then a product-oriented business is probably a good choice. If you have specific skills for providing professional, domestic, or repair services, and if you like to work directly with other people, then a service business might make sense for you. Of course, you can sell both a service and a product. For example, in our business we provide marketing advice for new businesses. This is the service part. We also sell books and software programs. This is the product part of the business. The two aspects of the business support each other and the diversity of the business keeps us interested in our work.

STEP 3. CONSIDER HOW THE SALES WILL BE MADE

After looking at your own skills and interests and matching these to some service or product businesses, it's smart to consider the sales cycle for the various business ideas on your list. Discovering the sales method that must be used to market your product or service is important in matching the business to your skills and personality.

In any business, there are only four sales options:

- **Direct sales to your customers.** Direct sales can be handled through store fronts (or home fronts), mail order, online through the World Wide Web and other information programs (such as America Online or Microsoft Network), and through face-to-face contact with customers. At some level all businesses involve direct sales to someone—whether the wholesaler, middleman, or end user.

- **Direct or indirect retail sales.** In retail sales your initial customer is actually the company or the distribution firm that will distribute your product (called the "wholesale" purchaser). You will, however, still need to promote your product to the end-users who will purchase your product through retail channels.

- **Consignment sales.** In consignment situations you sell others goods without investing your own money in inventory. You can sell prepackaged goods this way, used furniture, or a variety of other "consignment" wares such as crafts or handmade goods. Other people provide the goods, you make the sale, and then send them their portion of the sales price.

- **Multilevel sales.** In these schemes you sell your products through other salespeople who sell direct and involve more salespeople to sell the products to more salespeople. Some people call these "pyramid" schemes,

and if they are done legally, everyone along the way makes money from selling your products. Many multilevel sales programs are also consignment sales programs.

Some products and services can be sold by multiple methods. Other products or services are limited in the ways they can be sold. Thus, it is important to match not only the business idea to your skills and personality, but also the sales method required for the business. For example, if you are not a good salesperson, a product that requires face-to-face contact with your customers is probably not a good choice for you.

STEP 4. RESEARCH THE MARKET, THE LAWS, AND THE COMPETITION

You probably want to do something you love, but your business idea has to be further analyzed by examining the market potential, competition, resources required, consumer/buyer demand, and uniqueness of the idea. Practical research on your business should involve careful analysis of magazines, journals, the Internet, the library, and personal observation. This same research can also help you find, analyze, and keep customers as your business grows and prospers.

If you believe that a market exists for your business, you'll want to know more about the size and shape of the market before getting started. Researching your customers and your competitors is a critical step for small business owners. If Procter & Gamble puts out a product that doesn't sell, they move on to the next idea. If you put out a product that doesn't sell, you're out of business.

The ranking worksheet on the CD-ROM proposes many important questions about the potential of your business idea. It includes questions about the size and characteristics of the market, the distribution of the market, and the competition for your product. The worksheet will help you answer questions like these:

- **Market assessment.** Is there a market for your product or service? If so, how much income can you expect to derive from it?
- **Legal assessment.** What potential legal liabilities are you exposing yourself to by starting a new business? Are there any special laws that may restrict or benefit your business? Is protecting yourself worth the cost?
- **Industry assessment.** Where can you learn more about your business and about available resources to help you succeed?

Before you decide on any business, it is necessary to answer most of the questions posed in the worksheet. In particular, you should know the number of customers in your market area, the average sales amount per customer, and other facts relevant to your business potential.

STEP 5. CALCULATE THE ECONOMICS OF EACH POSSIBLE BUSINESS IDEA

Some businesses are started from love, while others are implemented strictly for money. We recommend that you do some financial planning before you choose a business for either reason. Assemble the basic elements of a business plan (refer to Chapter 6) and determine the financials for your ideas. How much will a new business cost you? Can you afford a lengthy "red ink" period following startup, as well as periodic lulls in cash flow? Can you afford to fail?

Before jumping in with both feet, you need to decide if your ideas will make you enough money. Fortune tellers may be helpful, but we also suggest some basic financial analyses before you decide on a business idea. Don't worry, you don't have to be an accountant to determine how much money you'll need to get started. You'll simply need to do some basic calculations between how much you'll need to make and how much you'll have available to spend before you make a profit on your business.

It All Comes Down To The Numbers

Only by estimating what you can make, and what it will cost to run your business, will you know whether you should continue to pursue your dream. Remember that you don't have to have lots of cash to start or expand a home-based business. Many people start small, often on a part-time basis, spreading their money between living expenses and business start-up costs. Other home-based business owners get loans or borrow money from relatives.

Always remember, however, that if you cannot make money in a reasonable amount of time, drop the idea. While there are several reasons why you want to start your own home-based business, the first reason must be that you expect to make money. It doesn't matter how much fun you'll have, if you don't cover your costs and make some profit, the business isn't worth pursuing.

How Much Money Do You Really Need?

When trying to calculate how much money you'll need to start your business, you must include your living expenses. Don't assume that you can live on beans and tap water while you wait to make a profit. You might start to resent the business if you find yourself without food, entertainment, and an occasional day off. Too much work and too little money can cloud your judgment and significantly dampen your enthusiasm for the business. In addition, don't decrease your living expenses when you estimate your start-up costs, because if your sales are slower than anticipated, you don't want to be out of business just as you start to succeed.

To estimate the total start-up cost of your company, determine how much money you need to start the business and how much money you need to pay yourself in order to cover your basic living expenses. For example, if your business requires $40,000 to start and you need $48,000 to cover your personal living expenses until the company starts making a profit, then the initial investment required is $88,000, not $40,000. Make sure your total investment costs are reasonable. If no additional money is available, your initial $88,000 could be lost just as the company begins to take off.

When you consider investing your own money in your business, make sure that your business is an investment you believe will pay off. Consider the other things you could be doing with your money. How would you use your cash if not investing it in a business? Be sure to consider other business ideas, especially if they make more sense, or more profit.

Business Costs Start With a Family Budget

Before you start planning for the budget of your new business, you must determine how much cash you will need to survive (especially if you intend to support yourself through the business). You have to plan a budget during the start-up and first few months of your business. Hopefully your business will be profitable from the day you open the doors, but usually this is not realistic.

Your estimates of business expenses should include a family budget schedule that tracks your expenses over the last twelve months. It is advisable to use a monthly family budget schedule because expenses may fluctuate greatly from month to month. For example, if you have children in private school or college where the tuition is due twice a year, those months will require additional expenses.

Usually your budget will include things from home mortgage payments to vacations to doctor bills. When preparing the budget, keep in mind any unnecessary expenses that could be reduced or eliminated. Located on the CD-ROM is a monthly budget template (FAMBUDGET.doc). Because it's a template, you can use the worksheet repeatedly and still retain an original copy. The worksheet projects your family monthly budget schedule for twelve months. The worksheet includes most income and expense descriptions. All you have to do is fill in your numbers.

After you have determined the amount of money you'll need to survive, you should consider how long you are willing to go with a loss in your new business. How long are you willing to scrape by with only enough money to pay the business expenses? Finally, how much income do you want to make in your new business? At this point you should have a goal in mind that answers these questions. If your goal is to make $40,000 per year, you will need to determine whether your new business is realistically capable of generating that much income.

Potential business owners should consider a one- to three-year plan for family survival, at a minimum. A lack of staying power, especially in small businesses that may not initially generate enough cash to live on for a year or two, is one of the most common reasons that small businesses fail.

A Break-Even Analysis

After completing a family budget, you'll have a rough idea of what amount of money you'll need to survive. We suggest that you now do a break-even analysis. In a nutshell, a break-even analysis determines how much you should make in order to cover your costs. Obviously, your goal is to do much better than that, but it's smart to ensure that you can at least pay for the production of your products or services.

A break-even analysis considers three pieces of information:

- **The average price of your product.** Estimate how much your typical sale will be. If you sell a number of products and you can't determine the average price, take the prices of all or most of your products and calculate an average.
- **The average cost of your product.** How much it costs to produce a typical sale.
- **Your total fixed costs per year, which equals your total expenses for the year no matter how much you sold.** This figure

includes expenses like rent, operating costs such as the phone and basic utilities, and other overhead expenses like insurance. If you plan to have employees, you'll need to include that cost as well in the fixed costs figure.

To calculate your break-even sales in dollars use the following equation:

Fixed costs ÷ (1 − (average cost of products ÷ average price of products) = break-even sales

For example, if you have an annual fixed living and business cost of $40,000, and you sell party baskets that are priced at an average of $100 each and cost about $20 to make, your break-even figure in dollars is $50,000. Here's how we got that number:

$$(\$40,000) \div (1 - (20 \div 100) =$$
$$(\$40,000 \div .80) = \$50,000$$

This means that you must sell $50,000 worth of baskets a year for the business to break even and to pay your living expenses. To calculate the number of gift baskets you'll need to sell, just divide $50,000 by the price of the product, which is $100:

$$\$50,000 \div 100 = 500 \text{ gift baskets}$$

These numbers may seem confusing at first glance; however, when you include your estimates, you'll see how much you really need to sell to make a profit. Once you determine the break-even figure, decide whether it seems reasonable. Will you really sell this many baskets? Or will you sell more than this? In the example, consider that you must sell almost ten gift baskets every week, or more than forty per month, to break even.

Keep in mind that calculating your break-even point isn't supposed to be exact. However, the calculation will give you a rough idea of your position and what you'll need to sell to pay your expenses and, more importantly, to make some profit.

Calculating the Break-Even Figure for Consultants

If you're not selling a product, there are other ways of estimating your break-even point. If you are thinking of becoming a consultant, for example, you would determine your hourly rate, and divide your fixed costs by your hourly rate. This demonstrates the minimum number of hours you'll need to bill each month to break even. Remember that the average number of hours a successful consultant bills weekly is around 14. If you need about 11 hours a week or less, or 40 hours a month to break even, you probably have a viable consulting possibility, and you have a good chance of making a profit from the venture. If you're having trouble choosing an hourly rate for your services, call some of your competitors and ask about their rates. This establishes what clients are willing to pay.

Does a profit look feasible after determining the break-even analysis? If not, your business idea may have some problems. Are there ways you can reduce your fixed costs by adding some additional services or products? These are decisions you'll need to make in order to create a successful business.

If your break-even analysis appears reasonable, double check your numbers to be sure you haven't forgotten anything. If you

think you can make enough additional profit to support yourself, your idea may be a potentially profitable business endeavor.

Why Early Cashflow Analysis Is Important

If you determine that your business will have a negative cash flow, you may find yourself digging into your personal savings each month to keep the company afloat. Eventually, if you keep eating into your personal cash reserves, the company may go bankrupt. To avoid this, make sure you look carefully at the financial potential of the business before you get started.

Once you have gathered the necessary financial data to establish some cash flow, you should have a business-savvy friend or an accountant review your numbers to determine their validity. If you still have several businesses on your list, eliminate those that don't make economic sense for you. For example, if a business requires more capital than you can borrow or obtain, you should look into businesses that don't have such intensive cash requirements.

STEP 6. NARROW DOWN YOUR IDEAS AND LIST THE PROS AND CONS

Here are some tips and suggestions for choosing a new business from a list of good possibilities:

- Look at your list and eliminate any of the businesses you won't really enjoy owning. As a small business owner, you'll be living, sleeping, and breathing your business and therefore must enjoy it to succeed.

- Remember that a lot of your time will be spent on tasks such as developing promotional programs, haggling with suppliers, and meeting with people. Be sure you'll enjoy these tasks as much as the business.
- If you don't have a lot of capital to invest, look for a business that pays up front and doesn't have exorbitant start-up costs.

Complete the ranking worksheet on the CD-ROM by listing the pros and cons for each of your business possibilities. Follow the instructions on the worksheet to rank the business ideas from least to most appropriate for your own skills and interests. Here are some things to consider while you do this step:

- Look for businesses that have a lot of repeat customers or that sell necessary supplies.
- Avoid seasonal businesses unless you'll make enough to balance out the slow months. Seasonal businesses can provide you with a lot of time off, but usually the cash flow is harder to manage.
- Avoid competing with discounters or with well-established businesses on price, since it is unlikely that you will be able to beat their prices. Instead, compete with better service or quality.
- Many service businesses are easy and cheap to establish. Consider services that don't require expensive equipment or special facilities.

STEP 7. EVALUATE THE POSITIVE CHOICES

At this point, the businesses that remain on your list are probably viable in some way. Try putting your list of business opportunities away for a few days until the ideas settle in your mind. When you are ready to review the list, make sure you have seriously considered all the pros and cons. Finally, use your best instincts to make a choice. Gut instincts are an important aspect of making a business choice and are usually right. Trust them.

Although there are many reasons why small businesses fail, one of the most common is simply making the wrong choice. To help you avoid that error, here are three popular mistakes:

Error #1: Converting a hobby or interest into a small business without first discovering if there is a sufficient demand for the product or service.

Error #2: Starting the business without adequate planning. Your success is not guaranteed just because you've found a market opportunity that also takes advantage of your skills and experience. There are many other considerations. For example, you still must determine if you can afford to get started.

Error #3: Resisting the urge to ask for help. Since you're reading this book, you may have already avoided this pitfall. A lot of people, however, are reluctant to ask others for advice because they're too proud or because they don't know that help is available. Help is available and usually inexpensive. Some sources are:

- **Expert advice.** Talk to entrepreneurs who operate the same or similar businesses. You may be surprised by the number of small business owners who are willing to share their insights with you. As long as you don't ask for trade secrets—and especially if you won't be a direct competitor—you may pick up some valuable information. The Chamber of Commerce or other business associations, such as the Small Business Association, may provide you with access to business experts. If you don't make any progress by attending meetings or by approaching business owners, you may wish to find a business consultant. This may seem expensive, but if you obtain information about the day-to-day operation of your prospective business, this one-time expense will probably be money well spent.

- **Experience.** If you work for a business, you will not only get on-the-job training, but you'll also get a paycheck while you learn. Look for companies that are successful and well run. Even though you may be able to learn a lot from a poorly run, inefficient enterprise, this can be a waste of time and energy. Although there are different ways to do a job successfully, there are usually even more ways to mess things up!

STEP 8. SET BASIC GUIDELINES THAT LIMIT YOUR EXPOSURE

Edward Paulson and Marcia Layton point out in *The Complete Idiot's Guide to Starting Your Own Business* that starting a business is exciting, exhausting, and (potentially) expensive. To avoid a long, drawn out business failure, set some guidelines to evaluate your company's performance. You should know your budget and the time required to keep your business running. If you eventually exceed your basic goals, your business is a success.

If your business falls short of your goals, then you'll need to make some adjustments in managing the business, including changing the products, the marketing scheme, or your expenses. If your business still fails to meet your expectations, you may need to close, sell, or restructure it to meet your personal business goals.

STEP 9. A LAST LOOK AT YOUR OPTIONS

Now that you've done some initial research into the kind of business you want and what it might cost, step back and consider what else you could do with your time, energy, and money over the next few years. If you weren't starting a business, what would you do? Would you stay with your current employer? Would you find a new job? Would you retire and move to a deserted island? These are valid options that you need to reevaluate before committing to a business.

Remember that just because someone else is making a lot of money in a particular business does not mean that you will too. For example, fitness clubs may be springing up in your area of the country. Many entrepreneurs are jumping at the chance to purchase franchise rights or are starting their own health and exercise programs. What if you're not good at exercise? What if you lack the personal skills (and interest) necessary to advise potential customers about exercise?

Financial tools such as budgets and break-even analyses can determine whether your business has potential, but you also need to ask yourself if this is a business you can enjoy daily. It doesn't matter how much money another person makes in the business, but how much money *you* can make.

Remember that the best business for you combines your interests, abilities, and experience with a market need. Your investment in a new business may also be a limiting factor, since you may not be able to buy basic supplies. Most importantly, if there is no market for the products or services you want to sell, you'll have no business regardless of your personal interest. You must have the right combination of personal skill, affordable product, and market potential to be a success.

STEP 10. NEVER GET DISCOURAGED!

What if you discover that your business does not seem feasible? Be thankful! You have just avoided a bad experience. Use what you learn to look for another more profitable opportunity. If you're still questioning whether you're ready to take the plunge, consider some options until you're ready:

- If you work for a big company, ask for a transfer to another division to learn new things about the business
- If you really hate your job but aren't ready to leave, ask about a telecommuting job where you work at home part time
- If you have the necessary skills, try applying for a job at another company
- If you need more training and business acumen, try taking a course or a seminar to acquire the skills you need

Even after you start a business, you can always change the structure of the operations, add products, invest more money, adjust the marketing plans, or look for a part-time job to help augment the business income. Remember that working for yourself is not necessarily a permanent decision. You can always shut the business down and get a traditional job. You could also find a partner who has the skills you lack. You always have options. Make sure that starting a business is your best option, and go for it!

5

Packaged Business Opportunities, Franchises, and Multilevel Marketing Opportunities

If you're not ready to start a business of your own from scratch, you may want to consider a home-based franchise or a packaged business opportunity. This chapter offers advice for finding legitimate opportunities that meet a wide variety of interests and business goals. If you decide later that you want to own a business of your own, the skills you acquire from your franchise or other packaged business opportunity will serve you well.

Usually, the best and most profitable way of becoming self-employed is to start your own business from scratch. However, if you think that starting a business from scratch is too difficult but you still want a home-based enterprise, you have several choices. You can buy a prepackaged business such as a franchise, a prepackaged business system, or an established business that the owners want to sell. Or you can invest your time in one of the many multilevel marketing programs that are emerging around the country.

If you decide that a prepackaged opportunity is of interest to you, the steps to choosing a business are not very different from those discussed in the previous chapter. Again, you must understand your skills and interests as they relate to the business, research the opportunities thoroughly, and identify a viable market for the business products.

If you find a compatible opportunity, a carefully selected, prepackaged business can allow you to take advantage of a successful concept and still exercise your entrepreneurial urge. However, you must be careful to separate the scams from the legitimate enterprises. There is additional information on the CD-ROM to help you do this.

WHY BUY A PREPACKAGED BUSINESS OR FRANCHISE?

In some cases, buying an existing business may be an excellent alternative to starting your own enterprise, but you must understand the advantages and disadvantages before you decide. First, you must understand exactly what you are buying when considering a franchise or another type of packaged or preexisting business.

When you buy the business or franchise, be specific about what you are buying. Are you buying a specific territory, a line of products, training, marketing plans, equipment, or a well-known name brand? It's important that you truly understand the components of the business and the support you'll receive after you get started.

Second, you must identify exactly what you'll be expected to do when you buy the business. What are the legal expectations and contract terms? How much money is involved? Is there an ongoing relationship with the franchisor or seller? When you think you've found a good opportunity, it's time to find a lawyer to review the contracts, terms, and conditions before you sign anything.

IS A HOME-BASED FRANCHISE FOR YOU?

Although a franchise is not technically a business form, it is a way to start a business using the experience and training provided by an existing company. The franchise process works something like this:

1. You research home-based business franchises in areas that interest you.
2. You find a franchisor who has developed a good home-based business concept with a successful track record.
3. You purchase the franchise rights in exchange for a fee. The fees and conditions vary considerably. Typically, you'll have to pay one or a combination of the following: a one-time payment, ongoing royalties, a continuous flat-fee payment, a sliding scale of payments based on sales volume, and advertising and promotional fees. You may also be restricted to buy certain supplies from the franchisor and use specific services provided by the franchisor while you own the business.
4. After a few years, you may start to resent paying the fees to the franchisor and begin looking for ways to do things on your own. This doesn't always happen, but it has happened enough to successful home-based franchisees that you may as well expect to feel resentful at some point during your relationship with the franchisor.

If you choose a quality franchise, the business arrangement allows you to use your own business expertise, operational guidelines, and market recognition, which improves your likelihood of success. Establishing a franchise relationship may actually decrease the amount of cash required to start your business, because many franchisors assist with the initial funding. However, a franchise may also increase the total initial investment required (cash and loans), because you are buying a share of a proven business concept.

THE PLUSES OF A GOOD FRANCHISE

You can benefit from a quality franchise relationship because it removes a lot of the risk associated with starting a new business. A successful franchisor will know precisely how to run your business for success. Good franchise relationships will provide you with training, marketing support, and services that will guide your franchise operations to success. The experience is not free, but it may help you to obtain profitable operations without the risks associated with starting a business from scratch.

Entering into a franchise agreement with a franchisor means that you are establishing a long-term relationship for mutual benefit. When you purchase a franchise, you'll need to set up a company in the same way as if you started it from scratch. You'll often need to evaluate which business type is best for your situation: sole proprietorship, partnership, or corporation. However, the franchisor will always maintain some control over the way you run your business. The franchisor wants to secure the reputation of the franchise and the value of the company's trademarks. This is in your best interest as well as the franchisor's.

THE TWO TYPES OF FRANCHISES

There are two basic types of franchises: product franchises and business format franchises. The product franchise allows the franchisee to sell and manufacture the franchisor's products. This franchise is typically given an exclusive marketing arrangement for a specific geographic territory or market segment. Large companies such as Coca Cola, McDonalds, and Southland Corporation (7-Eleven Stores) offer product franchising opportunities. Most product franchising opportunities require facilities and services not compatible with home-based operations.

Many business format franchises are ideally suited for home-based operations. Business format franchises generally include everything necessary to start and operate a business in one complete package. They provide the product, trade names, operating procedures, quality assurance standards, management consulting support, and other operational standards. The franchisee's (that's you) main role is to sell the company's products and services under the franchisor's trademark rather than become involved in manufacturing functions.

Most of the home-based franchise opportunities listed on the CD-ROM are of the business format type, distributing services (and occasionally packaged products) defined by the franchisor. In this type of arrangement you are buying the format for doing business. Thus, you must only provide the services predefined and controlled by the franchisor.

HOW TO SELECT A FRANCHISE

When you contact the franchisor, you should receive information in the form of a "prospectus," documents required by the FTC (often called the franchise rule) forcing every franchise in the U.S. to provide detailed information about the franchise. This document is also called the Uniform Franchise Offering Circular (UFOC).

At a minimum you should receive information about the franchisor and the people affiliated with the franchisor; a detailed description of the business; financial information; information on other franchisees and their financial success rates; a history of litigation and bankruptcies of the franchisor; the principal officers of the company; the royalties; continuing expenses; a description of all services, goods, and equipment you must buy, rent, or lease from the franchisor; and all terms of financing provided by the franchisor (if applicable).

Before purchasing a franchise, you may be asked to apply for the opportunity to buy the franchise. This is the time when the franchisor evaluates your ability to run the business. Some franchisors will sell to anybody, while others are more selective.

When you review the actual franchise agreement, you'll need to involve a lawyer and perhaps even a certified public accountant (CPA). The agreement should include clauses that cover:

- A definition of the granting of the franchise to you

- The terms for the use of trademarks, patents, and copyrights (this is the heart of the agreement)
- A definition of the relationship between you and the franchisor
- A description of the fees and terms for payment
- A time length for the agreement (negotiate a longer term if you really want to stay in the business)
- A renewal clause that specifies when and how to renew the franchise
- A definition of the territory or market you'll be serving
- An agreed timetable for establishing operations
- Advertising requirements
- Equipment and supplies you're required to buy or lease
- Training and other support services you'll be provided by the franchisor
- Terms for assigning the franchise to others by both the franchisor and yourself
- Conditions for terminating the agreement

Your lawyer should alert you to any conditions affecting your rights to profit from the business or that otherwise limit your ability to compete with other franchisees.

Do not get involved with the franchise if the franchisor or other representatives fail to provide the required disclosures or suggest that you don't need to have the agreements reviewed by a lawyer. If the franchisor seems to spend more time recruiting franchisees than running the business, beware. Also remain wary of franchises that have not been in business very long. You don't want to get locked into a franchise with an inexperienced company.

MULTILEVEL MARKETING OPPORTUNITIES

Multilevel marketing (MLM or network marketing), is another way to work at home with a packaged business system. MLM is a way to compensate people for the direct sales of established products. There are two components to MLM: first, you sell products and receive a commission. The second component is building a sales organization to sell the products (called your "downline organization"). You receive a commission on the sales as well.

In the beginning, MLM companies sold cosmetics, cleaning products, and jewelry, which is why the best-known MLM companies include Amway, Shaklee, and Mary Kay Cosmetics, among others. Today there are thousands of MLM companies, with more appearing daily. These new companies sell everything from toys to telephones.

Some of the companies are legitimate opportunities, while others are less credible. Legitimate MLM marketing is not a pyramid scheme as some people believe. If the focus of the business is to sell products instead of recruiting salespeople, the MLM business is probably legal.

If you really love to talk and don't expect to get rich quick, then consider getting involved in a multilevel marketing program with a proven distributor. Yes, some MLM distributors make lots of money, but most don't. The attraction of MLM is the low investment in the business. If you're good at MLM, you have the sales and speaking skills you can use to prosper in other home-based enterprises. MLM is often a good way to discover if you are an entrepreneur in your soul.

Be aware that more than 90 percent of MLM distributors work part-time. The majority of MLM distributors are women. Many people distribute MLM products because they use them themselves and can make enough money to buy the products they use. The best way to make money in MLM products is to believe in the products that you sell and have an outgoing personality that allows you to sell constantly to almost everyone you meet.

Although there are many prosperous MLM distributors with large downline organizations who sell products for them, be aware that the average monthly income of MLM distributors from reputable MLM companies is less than $100 a month Before you get involved in an MLM situation, make sure you can afford to spend the time required to make an income.

How You Get Paid in an MLM Opportunity

MLM compensation plans are notoriously complex. Before you get involved with an MLM company full-time, evaluate the compensation plan carefully. Understand the discounts you get on the products you distribute, the depth and width of the downline organization that can work for you, the specifics on how commissions and bonuses are paid, and the ways in which you can achieve different levels of commissions based on what you bring to the company.

OTHER PREPACKAGED BUSINESS OPPORTUNITIES

There are other prepackaged businesses that you may want to consider. Packaged business opportunities differ from franchises and MLM opportunities in that you buy a set of products or services without the specific ongoing support and trademarks associated with a franchise or MLM business. A list of home-based business opportunities that you can buy is provided on the CD-ROM. Business opportunities come in all sizes, flavors, and complexities, and the range of services provided by parent companies varies considerably.

Before you accept any business opportunity, make sure you'll get a good value for your purchase. Sometimes you could put together a similar business on your own for less money than the prepackaging company.

The steps involved in purchasing a business opportunity are similar to those of any major purchase. As with franchises, be sure to review all the legal, financial, and historical data on the business before you sign any agreements. And when purchasing any existing business, never buy the receivables, or at least structure the purchase so that you are reimbursed for any uncollectible receivables.

Overall, you should be cautious not only because caution will help you find the business that is right for you but also to avoid being taken advantage of by unscrupulous sellers. Your attorney or your accountant should be actively involved in your search.

FRANCHISE OR EXISTING BUSINESS?

You can sometimes buy preexisting businesses, although this is uncommon for home-based opportunities. If you want to buy the recipes and clients to manufacture Grandma's Salsa from your kitchen, you might want to consider buying an enterprise from someone who wants to retire.

The decision between buying a franchise or buying an existing business usually involves more than deciding to start a business from scratch. The difficulty lies in the fact that both the franchise and the existing business have many similarities, such as successful business concepts, a clearly identified market, name recognition, and management support. Here are a few things that a franchise provides that an existing business does not:

- Ongoing management and marketing support.
- Greater exposure, usually through national advertising campaigns and trademark recognition.
- Less risk. Franchises are usually based on previously successful franchise arrangements. Franchising succeeds only if individual franchisees are successful. Thus, franchises are packaged in a manner that will enable the franchisee to succeed. In comparison, an existing business may not have a history yet.
- Shared costs of promotion and equipment. Expenses that apply to each franchise, such as advertising, may be pooled to take advantage of discounts.
- Complete business methods. A good franchise provides a training program and

ongoing support to help the franchisees master successful business operations.

In choosing between a franchise and an existing business, you must decide whether the extra features of a franchise are worth the cost you'll pay for them.

HOW TO FIND A BUSINESS OPPORTUNITY OR FRANCHISE

If you're in the market to purchase a business or franchise or get involved in an MLM plan, there are many sources available to you that list businesses for sale. If you know what type of business you are looking for, trade associations and trade magazines may be a good place to start your search. The CD-ROM contains a list of trade magazines that specialize in business opportunities. There are also lists of some franchises and business opportunities to get you started, although there's no way we could list every opportunity, since new ones are being created every day.

Other resources for business opportunities include:

- **Newspapers.** Most newspapers have a classified ad section, which lists businesses for sale. Some, such as *The Wall Street Journal*, have a specific classified section of businesses for sale.
- **The Internet.** There are many Internet sites that list businesses for sale, and more are appearing daily. You can search general sites that offer businesses for sale, or you can specifically search for a particular type of business.

- **Business Brokers.** A business broker matches potential business buyers with sellers. One of the benefits of using a broker is that, if he is a good one, he will screen businesses for sale to determine if there are any major problems. The broker also guides you through the process of selling and helps you deal with snags that may develop along the way. However, because of the broker's fee to sell a business, the resulting sales price will be higher, even if the seller is the one who's nominally paying this commission.

SHOULD YOU BUY IT?

Once you've found out everything you can about the business opportunity, you'll have to make a final purchase decision. Here are a few suggestions to consider before you make a deal:

- Be certain that you've gathered all the information you can. Don't be surprised if gathering the information takes you several months. Above all, don't rush into the decision until you've explored every aspect of the finances, the market, and the operations.
- Show the information you've gathered to your lawyer and to your accountant. Ask them to review the agreements and decide whether the purchase is a good idea.
- If you're considering a preexisting business and not a packaged opportunity, make sure that you fully understand the reasons why the current owner wants to sell. If the business hasn't been doing well, you should know precisely what the problem is and

how to fix it. Don't buy a business with vague hopes that you'll magically turn the enterprise around.

- Don't buy a business unless you are reasonably sure that you can make some money. Make sure that your decision about the business is based on facts, not emotions. Don't purchase a business deal just because you want to be your own boss or because you like the idea or product behind the business.

- Learn something about running the business before you sign anything. Some opportunities will provide guidelines for running the business. These guidelines should be specific to your needs and your market. If you're buying a preexisting business, make arrangements for the current owner to show you the ropes.

If you want to own your own business because of the freedom it will bring you, you probably shouldn't buy a franchise. If you buy a franchise, the franchisor will dictate much of your duties. You'll have far more control if you start your own business.

If you have a good business idea that you want to nurture, you probably shouldn't buy a franchise or invest in a prepackaged business. You won't have much control or be given any opportunities to pursue your ideas. You'll probably be better off starting your own business.

If you want to make a lot of money, disregard most of the MLM opportunities. On the other hand, if you want to own your own business because of the financial opportunities it presents, you should definitely consider the advantages of a good franchise or a well-structured packaged business opportunity. Franchises don't necessarily make more money than other types of businesses, but they sometimes have higher success rates. Of course, you'll pay a portion of your profits in exchange for the higher success rate. You should also consider a franchise if you don't have prior experience running a business. A good franchise will help you learn the ropes.

THE DECISION IS YOURS

Most franchisees will tell you that franchises have a failure rate of about 5 percent, compared to the 50 percent failure rate of independent entrepreneurs. You should be aware, however, of studies that question failure rates. For example, a 1995 study by Dr. Timothy Bates at Wayne State University in Detroit, Michigan, found that the franchise failure rate actually exceeded 30 percent and that franchises made lower profits than independent entrepreneurs.

Ultimately, as with any home-based business decision, you'll need to decide if your personality, interests, budget, and market are designed for a business of your own making or a packaged business. The best advice is to do your homework before you decide.

PART

2

DEVELOPING PLANS AND SETTING UP OPERATIONS

6

THE BUSINESS PLAN: A MAP TO SUCCESS

As the leader of your own company, you need to set a course for success. That course will involve both strategic and tactical plans. In the previous chapters, you learned the importance of understanding your motivations for starting a home-based business, the need to evaluate your skills, and the importance of matching your skills and motivations to a business concept. This chapter shows you how to turn that initial thinking into a business plan which clearly projects your strategy. It is important to strategically and tactically plan when starting or expanding a business. Those plans will fuel the development of a formal business plan, which is also explained in this chapter.

The reality is that people plan more extensively for a trip to another country than they do when starting their own businesses. You can't reach a destination if you don't know where you're going. If success is the goal for your business, you'll need a map to get there. Your business plan is your map to success.

While everyone knows that a business plan is a good idea, not many businesses actually have one. Maybe this explains why only 20 percent of all new businesses will persist after five years! If you plan all the steps involved in starting and running your new business, you'll be on your way to success, along with 20 percent of new business owners.

A formal business plan is simply a document about 20 to 40 pages long that outlines the plans and goals for your business. Some sections of the plan should remain confidential (financial information, new technology overviews, client data); you won't share them with outsiders. However, most formal business plans eventually become public by sharing the information with many different audiences, including investors, bankers, and sometimes even clients.

The general information in a formal business plan will probably include background data on key personnel (that's you), descriptions of your products and services, industry analyses and competitive advantages, and other company background information that would also appear in your marketing literature. Thus, your business plan is also useful for creating exposure with the outside world.

If you don't think you will show your business plan to anyone else, you don't have to create a formal document, but you still should perform all the research described in this chapter. You can jot your plan down in a notebook. What is most important is not how the plan looks but what it says.

Uncertainty in starting a new business is difficult to accept, and the greater the risk, the more you need to minimize that uncertainty. By planning your personal and business goals, you will quickly increase your chances for success. Your business plan is a valuable management tool that helps you make decisions for your business. More importantly, going through the process of writing a business plan will help you determine if your business is really worth starting. A business plan is often a requirement in today's business climate, even for home-based businesses. If you complete the process with vigor and enthusiasm, you will learn a lot about your proposed business idea and yourself.

While you may have heard that you only need a business plan if you are trying to get financing to start a company, this is not true. A business plan, whether a formal printed document or detailed notes in a spiral notebook, helps you to organize your business by putting your goals and ideas down on paper. Once you have a plan, you have a guide that you can refer to regularly to keep on track. If you use your business plan, you'll reduce the chance of the business will becoming sidetracked by less important activities. The plan may change, but as long as you update it and understand why you've changed the priorities, you'll have a better chance of reaching your destination.

GET YOUR FAMILY INVOLVED

Get your family members involved in the business planning process from the onset. Not only do family members often come up with good ideas, but they should know what's involved in the business. Starting a new business may mean sacrificing family routines. You may be at home more often, but you'll be working on your business instead of parenting, housekeeping, or relaxing. If the business does well, the entire family will benefit, but if it fails, make sure that your family realizes that you will apply for a regular job to support them, if necessary, until the next business opportunity comes along.

DETERMINING A STRATEGIC DIRECTION

Before you can even begin creating your business plan, you must identify the strategic direction of the business you're about to start. Many business experts recommend defining the overall company direction in a mission statement. This statement describes why your company exists. The mission statement outlines what your company does and who it does it for. It provides the umbrella under which all other goals and actions fall.

The mission statement should be brief and to the point, determining the overall direction of the company. A complete mission statement also sets limits on your market and your products. An example of a typical mission statement for a home-based marketing consultant who specializes in serving high technology clients might be, "To provide public relations, advertising, and product positioning advice to small to mid-sized high technology firms in the Seattle area. My services will be provided at rates that compete favorably with larger advertising agencies and consulting firms and be responsive to the clients' needs for quick, authoritative information."

When you create your company's mission statement and strategic direction, answer the following questions:

- What do you plan to do or sell? Be specific. Do you want to sell holiday gift baskets or provide marketing consulting?
- Who will buy your products or services? Describe your typical customer. Are they specific businesses, nonprofit groups, or women over age 50?

- What are the benefits of your product or service? Do not confuse benefits with features. The benefits are the reasons people buy from you.

If you have a clear strategy and mission for your company, you'll have an overall guideline for determining the company's priorities. It may take you a while to describe the strategy for your business. Once you have a strategy and a mission statement, you're ready to create your business plan.

WHAT DOES A BUSINESS PLAN LOOK LIKE?

Almost anything is easier to do when you have a picture of how it should look when it's done. It is one thing to read about how a business plan is created and something completely different to read an actual plan. For this reason, there are references for completing business plans available on the World Wide Web and sample plans that you can order from the Small Business Administration. A sample plan also appears on the CD-ROM. The formats used in the sample plans are not unique, but they'll provide you with a starting point for organizing your own business plan.

RESEARCH THE BUSINESS

Before you can begin to write your business plan, you must learn more about your business. You need facts about the market you're working in, the competition for your products and services, and the needs of your customers.

Although you may have years of experience in the type of business that you want to start, you'll still need to do some research on the business.

If you'll be asking investors to get involved in your business, they'll want to feel confident that your instincts are correct. To prove that your ideas are on target, you must show them reliable, published articles, reports, and other statistics. Stating that your market is growing exponentially each year is important, but you must back up that statement with a report from the Department of Commerce or other source. Evidence will give you a lot more credibility, which you'll need with investors. All you need to do is some research.

We've talked about researching your business in other chapters. Virtually all the information you'll ever need is in your public library or on the World Wide Web.

Check out the reference books on business found on the CD-ROM. Note the World Wide Web sites on business planning, such as the Small Business Administration site, which includes lots of free software for business plans. There are also forms for business planning on the CD-ROM to help you put your plan together.

Chances are good that you will find the information you want. Once found, you may need help organizing the information into an advantageous format. Public and university libraries contain a wealth of information. General information is available in books, and current statistics are found in magazines, newspapers, and industry newsletters. Using the *Reader's Guide to Periodicals* or an online search, you can find articles that relate to your specific business.

It is unlikely that you'll find all the information you need in a single article. You may need to piece together information from several sources to get a complete picture of the market or industry you're interested in.

ASK FOR HELP

You are not alone in preparing a business plan, even though it may feel that way. There are organizations with a vested interest in helping you succeed, including the local Chamber of Commerce, entrepreneur associations, and the Federal government.

The Small Business Administration sponsors a business support group that assists businesses like yours in creating a business plan and acquiring funding. A group of retired executives who call themselves SCORE (Service Corps Of Retired Executives) are SBA volunteers who have already been successful. They know how to assemble a plan and guide you through the creation and management process, and their services are free!

There are also more than 750 Small Business Development Centers (SBDCs) across the country to assist you. The SBDCs are collaborative efforts between the SBA and local colleges and universities that provide seminars and free counseling to help people starting a business.

Information is provided on the CD-ROM for contacting the SBA and the SBDC and SCORE volunteers in your area. You can also find a local SBA office by calling 202-205-6766.

THE BUSINESS PLAN

A business plan customarily has certain elements or sections. Each plan element below is listed in the order in which it would usually appear in a plan. Don't feel constrained to follow this exact format if another order or different section titles make more sense for your business.

Most business plans contain the same basic information, and the overall structure is fairly well defined. For this reason, you may find that business planning software is helpful while writing your plan. There are a number of "fill-in-the-blanks" business planning software packages on the market. (Some of them are listed on the CD-ROM.) Your responses are then entered into the appropriate plan sections, and the plan contents are automatically created. That is the good news.

The bad news is that no automated business planning software can add your ideas, personality, and style to a plan, and your ideas are crucial to the success of your business. In addition, it is impossible to predict all of the special situations that apply to your business idea. Thus, you may need to add information to the plan created by the software, especially since some investors don't like the "canned plan" format that results from using one of these packages. The creative aspects of the plan are in your hands. Using an automated, business plan software package is worthwhile because it forces you to organize your thoughts about your prospective business.

Whether you use a software program or write the plan on your own, it pays to at least mention the major topics of a plan, even those that are not pertinent to your business. In general, your business plan should contain these basic chapters or sections that follow:

Table of Contents

The Table of Contents is not the most important element of your business plan, but it outlines the information of the coming pages. If no one else will see your plan, don't bother with a Table of Contents, but if you want to make a good impression on a bank or investor, you may want to include a Table of Contents since they are generally found in well-organized documents.

Executive Summary

The Executive Summary is another optional section of the plan if you're the only person using the document. But again, if you're going to show the plan to anyone else, this section will help readers (especially investors) understand the main benefits and features of your business.

The executive summary should include one paragraph that encapsulates each section of the plan. Conclude the Executive Summary by listing your break-even figure, the projected return on the investment, and the major advantages your company will have over the competition. In total, the Executive Summary should be one to two pages long.

Your summary needs to catch and hold the reader's attention, as this section is often the only part of your plan that a potential investor will read. Based on the few paragraphs in the executive summary, an investor will decide whether to read the rest of the plan. If he doesn't want to read your entire plan, you've lost a potential investor. Although this is the first section of the business plan, you should write it after you have completed all the other sections.

Description of Your Product or Service

This part of the plan describes the product or service your business provides and how it meets the needs of your market. Describe exactly what it is you will be selling and why customers or businesses will buy it. How is it different from similar items already on the market? If your product or service is a revolutionary concept, explain why the world needs this new breakthrough.

This section is your opportunity to describe what your product or service is. For instance, is it a new kind of car, a tasty new type of cookie, or a better house-cleaning service? Explain what the product or service does for the user, what the benefits are, and why they would buy it. If there are similar products or services already on the market, briefly compare them to what you are offering and explain how yours is better. If your new product or service is unlike anything currently available, convince the reader that they need it.

Market and Industry Analysis

The Market and Industry Analysis section describes the market need for your product or service. You should detail all the information you gathered during your research regarding the size of your market, the number of potential customers for your product or service, and the growth rate for your market or for the industry as a whole (which could mean the local, state, nationwide, or even worldwide market—depending on your scope for the

plan). Use the facts and figures you found during your research to support the market potential. You will have to make a number of assumptions when completing your market analysis. For example, the percentage of available customers for your product or service is a key estimate in determining your potential sales revenue.

You can find these numbers through information from other companies who estimated their figures, or from "guesstimates" from experts experienced in your field. No one expects you to know exactly how many sales you will make during the first year, but you can provide fairly accurate estimates by making some educated assumptions.

The Competition

Any entrepreneur who believes that they have no competition is in for a rude awakening, even if you have a revolutionary product. You need to know about the established companies already selling products and services similar to yours. How will they react to your company when you begin to compete with them? Depending upon your idea and how long your product or service has been available, your competition may consist of other new and aggressive companies just like yours or established companies from whom you intend to take business.

There is no reason to be afraid of competition. You should take every opportunity to learn from your competitors. Understand what they are doing that's right and what you can do better. It is okay to copy things that work and to learn from other's mistakes.

In this section, it's a good idea to provide a list of the other businesses in the marketplace, proving that you know exactly who your competition is. You should also indicate your impression of their strengths, weaknesses, and overall success in the market. By learning about your competition, the reader of your plan can better understand how you plan to succeed: by going after a market opportunity that no existing competitor is addressing or by doing what everyone else is doing with a different style.

The Owner (or Management Team)

If you're seeking an investor for your business or asking for a loan, one of the most important elements of your business plan is the section that describes why you are the most qualified person to start and run this business. Investors want to feel confident that you have experience in the type of business you're starting and that other members of your management team complement your skills.

The point of detailing your skills and background in this section of the plan is to convince investors that you have the skills to run the business or that you intend to acquire the skills through training or the use of experts. You also need to make sure that you're not trying to do everything yourself. Recognize that you don't know everything and will need to rely on advisers or professionals occasionally.

Operations Plan

This section describes the production procedures, equipment requirements, production requirements, distribution strategies, and any other aspects related to providing the product or service defined in the product section. For those who are starting service businesses, this section may be very short because service providers, such as management consultants, accountants, and attorneys, sell their time and experience. Assumptions should still be outlined explaining how many hours per month you expect to spend on client-related work.

Marketing Strategy

In this section, you need to explain how you intend to win customers. People have to buy your products or services, or else you're out of business. Thus, the thinking that goes into this part of your plan is paramount to your success. As a part of your marketing strategy, you should describe how you intend to let the public know about your products or services, such as through advertising, public relations, and other promotions. You also need to explain your sales approach, such as selling direct to customers, developing a mail-order catalog, or using retail stores to present your products to the world. At this point the details of your marketing plans (i.e., specific places for your ads or the copy in your brochures) aren't necessary, but the strategies and budget for your marketing program should be specific. (You'll find a detailed discussion of many ways to market your products in Chapters 14 through 22.)

Financial Analysis

Every business plan eventually comes down to the bottom line. Everything else up to this point was presented as the foundation for the financial analysis. This section spells out the actual investment required to start the business and how long it will take to earn a profit.

You'll need to forecast your future earnings based on certain sales and operations projections. You must show how much money will be invested and how much you expect to make in a particular time frame.

You should also include a break-even analysis that covers the volume required to push the company from a deficit profit. You should include an income statement, balance sheet, and cash flow analysis report that projects the first twelve months of operations. This is sometimes called a pro-forma income statement. A pro-forma balance sheet is usually a necessary component for the next three years if you're going to a bank for a loan or looking for investors. (You'll learn more about creating the financial statements mentioned here in Chapter 8.)

Pro-forma simply means that the numbers are projections, or estimates, of future sales and expenses. Your income statement summarizes your profit and expenses for a specified period of time, typically one year. It allows you to clearly see the amount of money you can expect to make. You should use a balance sheet to determine the value of what you own (your assets) and what you owe (your liabilities) at a particular point in time, usually the last day of the year. Bankers are interested in this statement because it describes what your business is worth and whether you can pay off your loan by selling all your assets.

A projected balance sheet determines what your assets and liabilities are expected to be at the end of your first year in business. Estimate your actual cash needs for the first twelve months, by month, and then for years two and three on an annual basis. Sometimes you'll have a lag between a sale date and payday—this lag needs to be accounted for in your cash flow statements. You'll need to figure out

exactly when you expect to receive payment for your sales, keeping in mind that if you do not receive payment when you sell your product, you will always be waiting for some customers to pay their invoices.

Putting together a cash flow statement will assure that you are always ahead of your expenses, deterring unpaid bills. A clash flow statement should also include your assumptions about loan rates, pay-back periods, and payment amounts. Summarize the initial capital required to start the business, including the funding sources (loans, personal savings, etc.), and how the money will be spent.

As you plan, you'll also need to think about this question: "How long do I keep investing in the company before I can expect a profit?" This is a tough question. For most businesses, you can expect to lose some money for at least eighteen months, and sometimes for twenty-four months or more. If you're not making a decent living within thirty-six to forty-eight months, you should probably consider another venture, or change or add to your products.

These suggestions are simple rules of thumb based on discussions with other business owners. Some people make money much faster. Some invest a bit more time in a good idea, but never work forever on a project that keeps draining their bank account or time. Always have a cut-off point in mind to prevent bankruptcy from your new venture.

Conclusion

The Conclusion section is optional and summarizes all the presented information in the plan and provides recommended actions on the part of your banker or investor. If you choose to include this section, it must directly complement the recommendations made in the Executive Summary but can include more detail.

Appendices

Appendices and supplementary materials contain the facts and details that support your plan. You should refer to them often throughout the plan to substantiate your approach to the business. If you're writing the plan for an investor, the appendices contain the charts, graphs, supporting articles, resumes, and literature needed to convince the investor that you have done your homework.

PUTTING THE PLAN TOGETHER

After you've considered all the sections of the plan and completed all the research to answer any questions about your business, it's time to put the plan together as a cohesive document. Putting an effective plan together is a lot like assembling a jigsaw puzzle. After completing your basic research, you should have all the necessary pieces in order for the puzzle to work. You may need to rearrange various pieces of collected business information for the plan to tell the story of your business.

Once you've developed an outline, you can start to write, fitting all the bits of information together. By its nature, the finished business plan requires you to project the future. Since most of us don't have psychic powers, your plan will inevitably change over time as you attain more information and concrete experience within the marketplace.

HOW FAR AHEAD SHOULD YOU PLAN?

As a general rule, for an "average" business, a three- to five-year plan is adequate. Certain details will drop as your plan develops. The cash flows that are tracked weekly or monthly during the first year of operation may be projected by quarter in the second year and annually in the third through fifth years.

If the assumptions on which you base your plan are sound, the results may be very close to your predictions. Over time, however, small deviations add up, and a plan that accurately predicted your first few months can become increasingly inaccurate. This requires you to keep the plan up-to-date after it's written. We recommend that you review your plan and adjust your priorities and projections each quarter. At a minimum you should update and revise your complete business plan annually. This exercise allows you to anticipate the upcoming year and correct mistaken assumptions from the prior year.

USE THE PLAN TO REAP SUCCESS

You don't get bonus points for the weight of your plan. It's not the quantity of your plan but the quality that counts. These statements are particularly true because a small plan that clearly and concisely addresses all the major points will be more useful than a lengthy plan that drones on about irrelevant information for hundreds of pages. Further, a plan that gets used is of more value than a plan that sits on a shelf.

If you're going to use your plan to get financing or loans, most investors won't take the time to read a plan that is much longer than 40 pages. They also won't try to decipher your plan if you haven't been clear and succinct. For your own sake as well as the investors, don't present an opinion as fact without any supporting information. Investors want to hear facts, not your personal beliefs. If you don't know the facts, research them and make sure the facts are current.

The marketplace changes rapidly. If your data are old, your business concept may not be valid. Don't present conflicting information or trivialize the competition. Don't assume that customers will buy simply because it's your good idea. It is price, quality, availability, service, and competitive positioning that sell products.

WHAT IF IT DOESN'T WORK?

If after drafting your plan you find you that the business just won't work, your original assumptions were not valid. If you had pursued the venture based on those assumptions, you would never have reached your goals. Even worse, you could be bankrupt. A negative outcome on the first round of planning does not negate your idea for the venture. You can now consider a different, potentially more successful approach.

Take a look at your approach to the business. Can it be modified to provide a better, more profitable, strategy? Is the problem with the product, the customers, or the competition? Should you consider different customers for your products, or do you need to change the price to make the product competitive? Do you need more money or time to

achieve the needed market recognition? Are your sales estimates too low? What could you do to increase sales? Are there things you can do to minimize the level of risk or investment?

Remember that creating a successful business plan may take many iterations. You may have many stray facts that need to fit properly before the venture will make sense on all levels. Learn the facts. Rewrite the plan. Be willing to change your assumptions to match new facts. Be realistic about your strengths and weaknesses and the competition.

TURN THE PLAN INTO ACTION

After the plan is finished and the business seems viable, it's time to turn the plan into action. Don't throw away your business plan now that it's done or leave it on a shelf to gather dust. It is a working document that outlines your best ideas on how to create a successful business. The plan is there to remind you of what was important to you when you were just starting out. Use the plan to help determine your performance compared to your estimates (sometimes called performance to plan).

A well-executed business plan determines whether your initial estimates and assumptions were accurate, allowing for midcourse corrections if needed. Use the plan wisely as a reference point to obtain the best return on your initial investments of time and money. If you have investors, you can expect that they will check your performance against the business plan regularly, since they made their investment based on the plan.

CELEBRATE AND BEGIN WORKING

Your plan is the first major milestone in establishing your new home-based business. Before you begin running the business, however, you should take some time to celebrate your accomplishment. Take your family or friends out to dinner at a nice restaurant and trumpet your accomplishment. Enjoy the moment while you can because soon you'll have to make the plan work according to your estimates and schedules if you want to reach that place called "success."

C H A P T E R

7

THE LEGAL REQUIREMENTS OF STARTING A BUSINESS

There are always rules to keep and taxes to pay. This chapter should help you to determine which local, state, and federal regulations apply to your business. In addition, there are sections on choosing a legal structure for the business and information on insuring your business to help you protect your assets.

After you've selected the type of business that's right for you and planned your basic strategy for running the business, the next step is to take appropriate action so that your home-based business is legal and insured. To make sure that you are starting your home-based business off on the right foot, one of your first visits should be made to City Hall to find out what regulations and permits apply to your business. This is as much for your own protection as it is for the public's, since it gives your business a legitimate standing in the community—even though your office is at home.

Before you get your heart set on the business, make sure you can legally operate the business from your home. In some cases, communities and home owner's associations have restricted the operation of home-based businesses altogether. Other communities have developed liberal regulations that encourage home entrepreneurship. Sometimes, you'll have to apply for permission to operate the business from your home. Of course, some home-based businesses that don't bring in customers or use noisy equipment don't need permission because they are unobtrusive. For example, if you work as a writer (as we do) or as an

Internet-based consultant, your business will be invisible to the outside community and probably won't require permits to operate. In any case, you should know the regulations and act accordingly, based on the type of business you intend to run.

If you buy a franchise or get involved in a prepackaged business opportunity, the form of the business may be dictated to you by the agreement you sign to buy or otherwise get involved with the company. Even so, in most cases, depending on what you sell and where you live, different licenses, permits, or other paperwork may be required to operate the franchise.

LOCAL REGULATIONS

Local regulations pertaining to home-based businesses are generally concerned with taxation, public health and safety, and zoning. Each community is different, but the most typical forms of regulation are described in the following pages.

Business Permits

In order to operate a business out of your home, you may have to obtain a business permit, also referred to as a business license. This is usually issued by the state, city, and/or county in which a business is located and is valid for one to two years. The fee for a license is often based on the gross sales of your business and can range from less than $50 to more than $100 per year. In some cases, home-based businesses are charged a reduced rate. You may also have to apply for a seller's permit and other licenses or certifications (as discussed later in this chapter).

Check the White Pages of your telephone directory under your city and county listings. Look under Business Tax Division, Business Licenses, Licenses, or City or County Clerk to determine where you should go and what specific regulations pertain to your business.

Fictitious Business Name Statement or DBA Filing

If your name is Kim Baker and Kim Baker's Consulting is the name of your business, then you probably don't need a fictitious business name statement, also known as the DBA (doing business as) filing, filed for your enterprise. If your surname is not included in the name of your business (i.e., Sally's Sunrise Sauces or Joe's Consulting), then you will probably need to file a fictitious business name statement with the county or state. The purpose of this statement is to protect consumers by making available to the public your identity and the identities of any others who are co-owners with you in the business. Filing the fictitious name statement or DBA also gives your business the legal rights to the name within the jurisdiction of the governing body, which is typically the county. If someone else uses the name within the county, you can ask the courts to order that person to cease operations under your business name. The other business would then be forced to rename itself.

A fictitious business name or DBA statement would generally be required in each of these instances:

- When the business name doesn't include the surname of each owner
- When the business name itself suggests the existence of additional owners unknown to

the public (Staron, Son, and Associates or The Sbraga Company and Friends)

- When the business name (if it is a corporation) is not stated in the articles of incorporation

In the event that it is necessary to file a DBA or fictitious name statement, this should usually be done within thirty days from the date the business commences operations. Filing the fictitious business name statement or DBA filing is a two-part process in most counties. You must file the statement with the County Clerk and have the statement published in a newspaper of general circulation. This second part is to ensure that the public has an opportunity to see your statement. To save time and simplify the process, instead of going to the County Clerk's Office first, you can often go directly to the newspaper where your statement will appear.

Many local newspapers carry fictitious name forms as a convenience to their customers and will often be able to help you complete the statement and fill out the forms for the County Clerk. The total cost for filing and publishing the statement should be somewhere between $25 and $100. If you plan to operate your business under more than one fictitious name, you can save on filing fees by listing all names on one statement (usually up to five names are allowed).

It's a good idea to comparison shop prices for filing the statement. Some local newspapers of general circulation specialize in filing these forms for reduced rates. You can often tell which local papers make a large portion of

their advertising revenue from filing these forms if you look at the classified section of the paper.

Zoning Restrictions

Just as some people are more entrepreneurially inclined than others, so are some communities. One neighborhood might welcome the presence of your home-based business, whereas another community might object to it. Many communities do not permit home-based businesses to post signs or have exterior merchandise displays. There may be zoning restrictions limiting the number of employees you can hire or the level of customer traffic that can come to your door.

The main purpose of zoning restrictions is to protect the rights of people and property. A business that is noisy, smelly, or otherwise bothersome to neighbors can expect to run into trouble when seeking permission to operate from a residence. In general, though, most home-based businesses—particularly nonpolluting, low-profile enterprises—manage to operate alongside their neighbors without major restrictions. To find out what zoning restrictions, if any, will affect your business, contact the planning department for your community.

Other Regulations

Depending on the nature of your business, other local regulations may also apply. For instance, if you are engaged in food preparation, processing, or serving (mail-order salsa, catering, or custom wedding cakes), you must stay within the county health department codes. You may find that a permit from the police department is a prerequisite for doing business that involves many visitors (such as an antique business or other seemingly retail enterprises). Other departments that may have jurisdiction over home-based businesses include the fire and sanitation departments.

STATE REGULATIONS

At the state level, regulations pertaining to home-based businesses center around taxation and the regulation of specific professions. Each state sets its own rules and standards in these areas, but the most common requirements involve obtaining seller's permits (if you're going to sell a retail product) and getting the appropriate state licenses for a regulated profession.

Professional Licenses

As a means of protecting the consumer, most states regulate entry into specific occupations. Obviously, doctors, dentists, and lawyers need special licenses to operate, but other occupations, such as cosmetologists, accountants, marriage counselors, and contractors, also need licenses or certification to operate legally in most states. To find out about any licensing or certification requirements to operate your business, you should check the telephone directory White Pages under "State of—" and the vocational field or licensing department for your field.

To obtain a license, you will need to meet the standards of ability and professionalism set forth by the state licensing agency that has jurisdiction over your industry. Once issued, a license is usually valid for a period of one to five years, at which time it must be renewed.

The costs and requirements vary widely based on the state and the profession.

State Seller's Permit

If your business buys and sells merchandise and you live in a state or community with retail sales taxes (most of them), then it is likely that you will need a seller's permit. This permit (1) exempts you from paying sales tax on the merchandise you purchase from suppliers for resale through your business and (2) authorizes you to collect sales tax from your customers. Moreover, in states, cities, or counties that require a seller's permit, you may need one to be admitted to trade shows or to purchase goods at wholesale prices. Usually, there is no fee to obtain a seller's permit, but, depending on your estimated gross sales for the year, you may be required to post a bond or other deposit. This is to ensure that you collect and remit all sales taxes due.

When applying for a seller's permit, remember that the lower your estimated sales for the year, the less money you will have to post as a bond. Keep a copy of your seller's permit in your wallet or purse so that it's always handy when you need to buy goods that will be resold.

To find out more about the seller's permit and whether or not you should have one, check the state, county, and city listings in your telephone directory White Pages and look for the tax or revenue departments.

FEDERAL REGULATIONS

At the federal level, regulations pertaining to home-based businesses focus on taxation, employer responsibilities, consumer protection, and the registration of trademarks, patents, and copyrights.

Employer Identification Number

If you employ one or more persons in your business, the federal government requires you to have an employer identification number. This enables the government to verify that you are paying all appropriate employer taxes and are withholding the proper amounts from employee pay checks. At this writing, you can obtain an employer identification number (EIN) by filling out IRS form number SS-4 and submitting it to the Internal Revenue Service. There is no fee for getting an EIN.

You should also ask the IRS for its free publication number 454, *Your Business Tax Kit,* which contains tax instructions, forms, sample notices sent to businesses, a checklist, and a calendar of due dates for filing returns and paying taxes. Both the SS-4 form and the tax kit are available at your local IRS office or through the IRS and government Web sites listed on the CD-ROM. To locate the IRS office closest to you, check your telephone directory White Pages under "United States Government—Internal Revenue Service."

Consumer Protection Regulations

To protect the rights of consumers, the federal government regulates business practices, even home-based businesses, that engage in mail-order sales, interstate commerce, or the import-export trade. If your business is involved in these or other types of sales, it may be subject to regulation by one or more of these agencies: the Federal Trade Commission (FTC), the Interstate Commerce Commission, the U.S.

Postal Service, and the U.S. Customs Service. The Federal Trade Commission also oversees safety and honesty in product packaging and labeling, product warranties, and the manufacturing and labeling of textiles, fabrics, and articles of clothing.

You should familiarize yourself with the regulations that apply to your type of business. You can write to the Federal Trade Commission, Washington, D.C. 20580. The FTC can provide the information you need and also tell you which other agencies to contact, should it be necessary. If you have specific questions about the these regulations and how they affect you, you might want to contact an attorney who is familiar with your type of business.

Trademarks, Patents, and Copyrights

In addition to protecting the rights of consumers and collecting income taxes, the federal government also protects your right to use and profit from your own name (or business or product name), inventions, and artistic creations. Before you can take full advantage of this protection, however, you must be aware of the government regulations that apply to trademarks, patents, and copyrights.

Trademarks

A trademark (or service mark) is any word, name, symbol, device, or combination of these used to identify the products or services of a business and to distinguish them from those of other enterprises. The trademark can be one of the most valuable assets of a business, helping to define its image, increase customer recognition, and stimulate repeat purchases. Especially if you sell retail products, it's in your best interest to create a trademark for your business and to take appropriate steps to safeguard it.

In creating a trademark, it helps to keep the name simple, short, and easy to pronounce. For your logo, choose a design or symbol that is easily recognized. Here are some other hints to help you choose a trademark to represent your business or product:

- Avoid using your surname alone as your trademark because anyone else with the same name can also use it.
- Avoid using a trademark that is too similar to an existing trademark or easily confused with other trademarks in your industry.
- If you're going to sell internationally or sell to international clients, make sure that the trademark has positive connotations both in the United States and abroad.
- Avoid trademarks that are merely descriptive (Fast Service) or geographic (California Hot Sauce). Since others can also use these names, the government doesn't consider them legitimate trademarks.

Although you can legally use a trademark without registering it, it is not recommended. To safeguard your trademark, you should register it with the U.S. Patent and Trademark Office. Proper registration helps to strengthen your claim to the trademark and establishes the date on which you first began using it.

Once your trademark is registered, your right to use it extends for a period of ten years, at which time registration is renewable. For more information on the regulations and trademark process, write to the Patent and Trademark Office, U.S. Department of Commerce, Washington, D.C. 20231, or look up the office on the World Wide Web (the links are provided on the CD-ROM).

Patents

Patents are often difficult to get and usually expensive to obtain, but if you have a truly unique invention, then you need to consider the patent process. In granting a patent to an inventor, the federal government gives him or her the right to exclude all others from making, using, or selling the patented invention in the United States. Patents for new and useful products or processes are valid for a period of seventeen years from the date of issue. A design patent, covering only the style or appearance of a product, may be valid 3½, 7, or 14 years, as specified in the patent application. If you develop a product, process, or design you believe has commercial possibilities, obtaining a patent may be advisable, given the protection it affords.

We, along with the government, recommend that inventors not attempt to prepare their own patent applications without the help of a registered attorney or skilled patent agent. When legal fees are added in, the total cost of obtaining a patent usually runs between $3,000 and $10,000, sometimes more.

To protect your claim to an invention prior to the issuance of a patent, be sure to follow these guidelines:

1. Keep good records that detail the progress of your invention from the idea stage to its final form. The records should be in ink, signed and dated by you, and witnessed by someone other than a coinventor.
2. Conduct a search to discover if any inventions identical to or similar to yours have

already been patented. A lawyer or patent agent can help you do this. Your findings will help determine whether you should apply for a patent.

3. Find a good patent attorney or agent if you decide to go ahead and file a patent application.

4. Some actions will prevent you from obtaining a patent, including if, more than one year prior to filing the patent application, you (1) publicly use or sell the invention or (2) allow information about the invention to be printed in a publication. Don't lose your right to your own invention by doing the wrong things.

5. In order to secure a patent, it's important to be informed. Proceed carefully. We recommend getting the assistance of a lawyer. To get the basic facts on obtaining a patent, contact the Patent and Trademark Office, U.S. Department of Commerce, Washington, D.C. 20231, or go to their Web site, which is listed on the CD-ROM.

Copyrights

A copyright protects the right of an individual by preventing others from copying his or her artistic creations. Although most commonly associated with literary works, copyright protection extends to photographs, paintings, graphic designs, sculpture, musical compositions, sound recordings, and audiovisual works. Included within this broad coverage are such diverse creations as catalogs and advertising copy, charts, technical drawings, and computer programs. Thus, whether or not your home-based business is directly involved in

literary efforts or the arts, you may still be able to benefit from copyright protection of your work.

Obtaining a copyright is much easier than getting a trademark or patent. Essentially, it involves providing public notice of the copyright on the item ("Copyright © 1998, Sunny Baker") and filing a simple application form. The fee for filing is currently about $40, and the registration process can usually be completed without the assistance of an attorney.

Once granted, a copyright is valid for up to fifty years after the copyright holder's death. To receive all the relevant information on copyrights as well as the appropriate application forms, contact the Copyright Office, Library of Congress, Washington, D.C. 20551. Again, there is a Web site address provided on the CD-ROM.

THE LEGAL STRUCTURE OF YOUR HOME-BASED BUSINESS

A major aspect of keeping your home-based business legal involves choosing the legal structure for it: sole proprietorship, partnership, one of the corporate forms (C Corporation or Subchapter S Corporation), or a Limited Liability Company (LLC). Each legal form has its own unique characteristics. Your goal is to choose the form that works best for you. In addition to being necessary for government reporting and tax purposes, the correct form can enable your business to operate more efficiently and spare you tax liabilities.

Sole Proprietorship

Sally woke up this morning and decided to begin selling gift baskets for Christmas. Because she decided to make money by selling the baskets, she just became the head of a sole proprietorship. Any business owned by one person (or a married couple who runs the business without developing a formal partnership arrangement), who is entitled to all of its profits and responsible for all of its debts, is considered a sole proprietorship. As a sole proprietor, your business expenses are deductible, all income is taxable, and you assume the liabilities of the business. Providing maximum control and minimum government interference, this legal form is currently used by many home-based businesses. Being a sole proprietorship does not limit whether or not you have employees, although many sole proprietorships are one-person businesses.

The main advantages that differentiate the sole proprietorship from the other legal forms are (1) the ease with which it can be started, (2) the owner's freedom to make decisions, and (3) the distribution of profits directly to the owner.

The flexibility associated with being the only owner is often attractive enough to keep people in business as a sole proprietorship, even after the company grows large in revenues. Still, the sole proprietorship isn't without disadvantages, the most serious of which is its unlimited liability. As a sole proprietor, you are responsible for all business debts. Should these exceed the assets of your business, your creditors can claim your personal assets— home, automobile, savings accounts, and other investments. This means that, if the company were sued for any reason—such as if someone ate some of your homemade salsa and was hospitalized from food poisoning—you would be personally responsible for answering that

lawsuit. As the owner, you could lose everything you personally own if the business-related lawsuit is lost and the damages are high. Sole proprietorships also tend to have more difficulty obtaining capital through banks and investors. Most sole proprietors should be prepared to be generalists, performing a variety of functions, from accounting to advertising.

Partnerships

A business owned by two or more people who agree to share in its profits is considered a partnership. Like the sole proprietorship, a partnership is easy to start, and the bureaucracy involved is usually minimal.

In essence, a partnership is like a sole proprietorship owned by several people. All liability is passed to the partners. A special partnership type, called a limited partnership, provides certain partners with a maximum financial liability equal to their investment. To maintain this limited financial liability status, these partners, called limited partners, cannot participate in the daily operation of the business. The general partner is responsible for the day-to-day management of the business.

Limited partners invest in the company and rely on the general partner to run the business. There are special laws that govern the operation of a limited partnership, and, if those laws are not precisely followed, the courts may hold that the partnership was general, not limited. The formerly limited partner, therefore, may become liable as a general partner for business-related debts. You must complete and file special paperwork with the state to form a limited partnership.

The main advantages of the ordinary partnership form are that the business can (1) draw on the skills and efforts of each partner, (2) offer employees the opportunity to become partners, and (3) use the partners' combined financial resources (if there are any).

However, for your own protection and the protection of your partner, you should have a written partnership agreement drawn up by a lawyer. This should state (1) each partner's rights and responsibilities, (2) the amount of capital each partner is investing in the business, (3) the distribution of profits, (4) what happens if a partner joins or leaves the business, (5) ways in which the business can be sold to others or other partners can be added, and (6) how the assets are to be divided if the business is discontinued.

Partnerships also have decided disadvantages. Who wouldn't want a partner to share the good and bad times in a business? Well, if you have ever been in a bad relationship, you know the damage it can do to your psychological and financial well-being. When two or more people form a partnership, they are essentially married from a business standpoint. Either party can obligate the other via the business, and everything the business and the partners individually own is on the line. The unlimited liability that applies to sole proprietorships can cause even more problems for partnerships. As a partner, you are responsible not only for your own business debts but for those of your partners as well. Should one of your partners incur debts or legal judgments against the business, you could be held legally responsible for them.

Disputes among partners are a common problem. Unless you and your partners agree on how the business should be run and what it should accomplish, your business, not to men-tion your relationship as people, is in for trouble. Before you agree to go into business with anyone—even your best friend or spouse—make sure you discuss the issues and agree on how you'll work out disagreements.

Corporations

A corporation differs from the other legal forms of businesses in that the law regards a corporation as an entity possessing the same rights and responsibilities as a person. This means that, unlike sole proprietorships or partnerships, a corporation has an existence separate from its owners. Upon its formation, the corporation issues shares of stock to its shareholders, the owners. The shareholders exchange money, goods, or expertise to receive their shares of stock. A Board of Directors, elected by the shareholders, manages the corporation. This board then appoints officers of the corporation to handle the day-to-day affairs of the company. In many small, home-based corporations, the business owner is the primary, or only, shareholder and only board member.

There are three primary advantages to the corporate form of business:

- **Limited liability.** In the corporate form of business, owners are not personally responsible for the financial or civil liabilities of the corporation. For this limited liability reason alone, many people choose to change their structure from a sole proprietorship to a corporation. The shareholders only risk the amount of money they have invested in their respective shares of stock.

- **The ability to raise capital by selling shares of stock.** Once the buyer and seller agree to a per-share-of-stock price, the buyer simply purchases the number of shares equal the amount of money needed. For instance, assume you need to raise $50,000 to expand your marketing program. If you find a buyer who is willing to pay you $10 per share, then you sell them 5,000 shares of stock to receive the $50,000. Or, if you don't know anyone with that kind of money on hand, instead of selling 5,000 shares at $10 each to one person, you could sell the 5,000 shares to a hundred different investors and still get the money you need. You now have 100 shareholders instead of one, but you got the money you needed. Of course, it's rarely this simple in practice, but this example outlines the basic benefit associated with funding a corporation.

- **The ability to easily transfer ownership from one individual to another.** Thus, unlike the sole proprietorship and partnership, the corporation has the potential to outlive its original owners through the transfer of ownership to other shareholders and officers.

The main disadvantages of the corporate form of business include taxation, reporting requirements, and expenses to incorporate. The corporation pays taxes on its annual profits and passes the profits to the shareholders in the form of a dividend. In what amounts to double taxation, you must pay taxes on both the income the corporation earns and the income you earn as an individual through the dividends.

A corporation is more difficult and more expensive to start than both the sole proprietorship and the partnership. In order to form a corporation, you must be granted a charter by the state in which your home-based business is located. For a small business, the cost of incorporating usually ranges from $800 to $3,000. This includes the costs for legal assistance in drawing up your charter, state incorporation fees, and the purchase of record books and stock certificates. In addition, since corporations are subject to closer regulation by the government, the owners must bear the ongoing cost of preparing and filing state and federal reports. You don't always need a lawyer, but we recommend that you use one.

Public or Private Corporation?

There is a difference between a publicly held corporation and a privately held corporation. Publicly held corporations are traded on the various public stock exchanges, such as the New York Stock Exchange, the American Stock Exchange, and NASDAQ. The shareholders are typically large numbers of people who never come in direct contact with each other. They trust the Board of Directors to manage their investment for them.

Privately held or closely held corporations are more common—and that's probably the type of corporation you want to set up as a home-based business. The shares are held by a few people, often family members, who also sit on the board and participate as officers of the corporation. The shares are not offered to the general public. If the number of shareholders exceeds 35, you must comply with the Securities and Exchange Commission (SEC) regulations for publicly offered companies or choose to form a Limited Liability Company (described later in this chapter), which permits more than 35 shareholders.

If your company does extremely well, you may want to "go public" someday, but, at the onset, most home-based businesses don't need to worry about this aspect of the company. If you intend to sell stock publicly, you will definitely need legal and accounting services. When a company "goes public," it offers to sell shares in the company to the general public. This is a common way for the founding members of a company to make a lot of money from the large numbers of stock shares they received during the initial phases of the business. The founders often buy or receive this stock at the outset for a nominal price, sometimes pennies per share. When the company goes public, the shares may sell for dollars per share. Thus, several hundred thousand shares sold at a public offering can add up to a lot of profit for the founders.

This opportunity for a large profit alone, despite the associated risks, keeps many people actively working for start-up companies instead of working for larger, more stable companies. If you do intend to become a large company, you may be able to offer stock options in your company to your future employees as a way to lure good employees and underwrite part of the compensation package, but most home-based businesses don't need to think about this at the beginning of their operations.

Subchapter S Corporations

The standard corporate form is often referred to as a C Corporation. But let's say you want the legal protection provided by a C Corporation but hesitate to form one because of the double taxation. Well, there's a way to avoid the double taxes. The IRS and Congress created the Subchapter S Corporation for just

this purpose. In a Subchapter S, or S Corporation, instead of the corporation paying taxes on its income, the business income is passed onto the shareholders (you) who then declare the income on personal income tax statements.

The Internal Revenue Service permits this type of corporation to be taxed as a partnership rather than as a corporation. However, in order to qualify for S status, your business must meet the specific requirements set forth by the IRS. These include limits on (1) the number and type of shareholders in the business, (2) the stock that is issued, and (3) the corporation's sources of revenue.

Subchapter S Corporations retain all of the legal protection provided by a standard C Corporation. So why opt for the S instead of the C Corporation? If you, personally, are in a lower tax bracket than the corporation, then passing the business income to you will decrease the overall tax paid. In addition, if the corporation loses money, you can use that loss to offset personal income earned from other investments you may have. However, if you don't plan properly or if the company does better than you expected, you could find yourself with a huge tax bill at the end of the year.

For more information on forming an S Corporation, ask the IRS for its free publication number 334, *Tax Guide for Small Business*. If you think the S Corporation is right for you, check with an accountant and an attorney before taking the plunge. A little prevention goes a long way to avoid unforeseen problems down the road.

Limited Liability Company (LLC)

How would you like the advantages of a corporation or partnership without some of the restrictions regarding shareholders? That's what a new form of business organization, called a Limited Liability Company, can provide. Limited Liability Companies are now authorized in most states. The reason for their popularity is that LLCs provide business owners with personal liability protection, just as corporations do, and still tax profits at the individual level only, as with Subchapter S corporations. LLCs do not have the same restrictions regarding shareholders as those placed on S Corporations. S Corporations limit the number of shareholders to 35 and require that they be U.S. citizens; non-U.S. citizens, domestic corporations, and co-owners of partnerships may not participate. LLCs, on the other hand, have no limits on the number of shareholders and do not place restrictions on the makeup or citizenship of its shareholders. In addition, LLCs can have more than one class of stock and can own stock in another corporation.

Because of these advantages, LLCs are anticipated to exceed Subchapter S Corporations, regular C Corporations, partnerships, and limited partnerships as the preferred organizational structure. Since conversion to an LLC from another type of business structure can be costly, LLCs are generally recommended by lawyers for many start-up companies.

One concern about LLCs, however, is that there is no unified set of tax laws, since individual states created their own laws regarding LLCs, which were then copied by other states. The IRS has yet to provide a general set of national tax laws for LLCs. Check with the Secretary of State to find out more about the laws governing LLCs in your state. And watch the IRS Web site to see if federal guidelines regarding LLCs change.

The decision to choose any form of business over another or any one form of corporation is heavily based on how much revenue you anticipate your company will generate. This is why the strategic planning aspects of business and your business plan are so critically important.

Professional Corporations: Doctors, Lawyers, and CPAs

There is a special corporation form that addresses the needs of professionals who share a practice, such as doctors or lawyers. (In most cases, professional corporations use the letters P.C. after the company name to indicate the type of corporation.) The professional corporation, as it was initially called, provided special tax and liability benefits to its participants. Many of the benefits have been reduced since 1981, however, and the growth in the number of professional corporations has declined.

If you are a licensed professional who falls into this special category, check with an accountant to determine whether or not a professional corporation provides you with any special benefits.

DOING BUSINESS IN MORE THAN ONE STATE

Since you're starting a home-based business, you probably won't have offices in several states; however, if you do—or if you intend to develop offices in multiple states at some point in the future—your business life just got more complicated. If your home base is in one state and the majority of your business is from that location, you can avoid the multistate problem.

If this is not the case, you will need to perform some filings and registrations to qualify for offices in each state in which you do business.

There are firms that specialize in setting up companies that need to operate offices in several states at once. Contact a law firm and get a referral to one of their suppliers, or simply contract the law firm to perform the needed paperwork for you. Hopefully, most of you will avoid this problem by keeping your operations in your primary place of residence.

WORKING WITH THE TAX MAN

We all hate paying taxes, and most taxes never go away. All you can do is try to minimize their negative impact on your profits. Your choice of organizational structure has an important impact on your tax obligations and reporting requirements. The information we present here about income taxes is only general, so talk to your accountant about your specific situation. Remember, there are many taxes a business will have to pay. You need to learn about all of them in your area—city, county, state, sales, franchise, and the list goes on.

All business entities, except for the C Corporation, pass the income directly to you as the owner or major stockholder. You then declare it on your personal tax return. In corporations, all salary expenses (including the owner's salary) are deducted from the company's revenues prior to determining how much tax must be paid. You then pay personal income tax only on your salary, just as you would for any company. Self-employed individuals really feel the bite of FICA and Medicare taxes, since they pay both the employee's share and the employer's share of these taxes.

In a corporation, however, dividends paid to shareholders are taxed twice. Dividends are paid to the shareholders out of company income after the corporate taxes have been paid. Shareholders also pay tax on the dividends because they are part of their personal income. This "double taxation" can get expensive. Sometimes, corporations will try and come up with creative ways to avoid or minimize the financial bite taken out of their shareholder's dividends as a result of double taxation. Some people get so focused on avoiding paying taxes that they lose track of their primary concern: running a successful and profitable business that fulfills their personal and financial goals. Avoid the temptation to fiddle with your tax planning to the point that you lose focus of your business.

Individuals and corporations do not pay tax at the same rate. You will find that the break points between tax levels differ. Depending on your situation and the company's income level, you may be better off leaving the money in the company and paying corporate taxes instead of paying yourself a large salary and paying personal income tax on that salary. At this writing, for example, if you're a single corporate owner who makes between $21,000 and $50,000, the personal tax rate is 28 percent. The corporation tax rate is 15 percent. That 13 percent (28 percent minus 15 percent) can be left in the corporation for business use at a lower tax rate than a sole proprietor would have to pay. Given that advice, expect things to change. You will need to keep track of the IRS changes in the tax structure.

Your best defense in tax situations is keeping accurate, up-to-date records of your business transactions. Even if you keep the books yourself, we recommend having an accountant to help advise you on the type of records you need to keep—before April 15, when the taxes are due. We talk more about your need for accurate bookkeeping and financial records in the next chapter.

INSURING THE BUSINESS AND YOURSELF

When you start a business, you can't protect yourself against everything, but you should limit your risk by insuring those aspects of the business that are most vulnerable to loss. As a new business owner, your insurance needs will depend upon the type of business you run, the number of employees you have, and the type of space you use at home for your business. For example, a self-employed computer consultant who operates out of her home will have insurance needs that are significantly different from those of a company that manufactures fireworks in the back garage. The cost of insurance, therefore, also depends upon the type of business you operate. Further, if you're self employed and don't have insurance from your spouse's employer, you'll probably need to get a health insurance plan and life insurance to protect yourself.

To find an insurance agent, ask your small-business friends and associates who they use. Another source that may be more focused, more experienced, and less expensive is your industry association. Industry associations usually provide a large, predictable, homogenous pool for underwriters, which generates lower rates. They can often provide one-stop shopping for both business and personal insurance

needs (e.g., liability, property and contents, life, medical, etc.). The CD-ROM lists many of these associations.

When comparing prices, don't look at just one type of insurance to make your decision. Look, instead, at whether or not you can save money by having a single company handle all of your needs. Look for an independent insurance agent who can do the price shopping for you. Obtain bids for a complete insurance package from several different insurance agents and companies. When you are comparing insurance proposals, make sure you are not inadvertently comparing apples and oranges. Make sure the packages have very similar types of coverage and similar amounts of coverage.

Types of Insurance

Below are brief descriptions of the various types of insurance that your new business may need. Remember, no two businesses are alike. Some businesses may require additional types of insurance, and some may require only a few of those mentioned.

- **Property insurance.** This insurance will cover losses arising from physical damage, loss of use of the property, and theft losses. Remember to insure against the losses of the contents of your business, too. It is very possible to have a larger investment in machinery and equipment, inventory, and business records than in the house you own—so make sure your home insurance also covers your business property, or take out additional insurance for the business.

- **Liability insurance.** This type of insurance protects you if you are sued for accidents in your place of business (in this case, your home). It will pay judgments against you, up to the policy limits, as well as the legal fees you incur in defending yourself. Some small businesses, such as doctors, lawyers, and consultants, will also need to carry professional liability coverage, which protects the insured against lawsuits that result from professional error. You may also need liability insurance to cover lawsuits arising from the use of your products. Make sure you have business liability protection as well as personal liability protection when you use your home as an office.

- **Business interruption insurance.** This type of insurance will pay your bills while you are out of operation for a covered loss, such as a fire. Just because your business is shut down does not mean that your bills will stop. This type of insurance will also provide your business with protection from lost profits. Be aware that this type of insurance is often difficult to get when you first start out because you don't have a track record of profits or other operations.

- **Key person insurance.** This type of insurance includes coverage for the owner's death or disability. It is meant to get a company through the tough times following the loss of a key person and includes a buyout of the deceased owner's interest at the time of his or her death. Again, you may need to be a corporation and have a track record to buy this type of insurance, but some insurance companies offer this insurance as part of small-business packages, so shop around if you need this type of security.

- **Workers' compensation insurance.** This type of coverage is necessary for those small businesses that have employees. It varies by state and employee job duty classification. The cost will vary based upon the worker classification.

- **Life and disability insurance.** These policies provide covered individuals or their families with income in the event of death (life insurance) or a disability not related to work (disability insurance). These types of insurance are relatively inexpensive and easy to get.

- **Health insurance.** This type of insurance pays the medical bills for covered illnesses and injuries. Health insurance for home-based businesses can be a major expense and a headache to obtain. Buying insurance through your business can be cheaper than buying an individual policy for yourself. Because of the high costs, most small employers don't offer health insurance as an employee benefit.

If you need personal health insurance as the owner and can't find affordable rates for your home-based business, look into group plans provided by trade associations and clubs. Your membership fees in the association may be well worth the insurance benefits provided to you, even if you don't attend meetings or read the journals.

Planning your insurance needs is just as important as any of the other planning you will do or have done for your new business. It's possible to reduce your overall insurance costs by instituting certain safety procedures in your home, such as smoke detectors and burglar alarms. Ask your insurance agent what steps you can take to reduce your costs.

DO YOU NEED A LAWYER AND AN ACCOUNTANT?

There are many legal and tax-related ramifications in starting and operating a new business. So, you're probably wondering when you should you use a lawyer and an accountant. The best answer is "before you need one." Prevention is always the best cure for legal and tax-related problems. If your business agreements are created and documented in a responsible way with all parties equally involved in the discussions, you can minimize the likelihood of future legal action. If your financial records are complete and accurate, you'll never have to fear an audit by the IRS.

Lawyers will tell you that much of their income is generated in repairing the damage done by people who attempt to economize on legal fees by developing contracts and agreements on their own, only to find out that the documents they developed don't accomplish their objectives. Accountants will tell you that they make most of their money from people who have waited until April to prepare their income tax forms or who have done their taxes on their own, only to need advice before they go to a hearing at the IRS office. If you have the money (or even if you think you don't), have an attorney draw up your corporate filing documents and review any contracts you sign and have an accountant review the records you intend to keep for your business.

If money is a real concern, try taking your best shot at completing important legal documents on your own and then run them past an attorney for review. You can purchase prewritten articles of incorporation, stock certificates, and corporation bylaws from the same companies that supply attorneys with these forms, and there are software programs that automate the process of completing the forms. There are also many inexpensive accounting programs that can help you keep your financial records and even help you with doing your taxes. A CPA can advise you on the best program to use for your business. We've also provided links on the World Wide Web to companies that provide accounting and tax preparation packages.

As always, if any agreement is for a large amount of money and limits you in critical ways, you should consult an attorney before getting too far in your negotiations. If your business changes in size or complexity, a visit to the CPA can save you lots of time in setting up your accounting system as well. A few hundred dollars up front for professional advice can save thousands of dollars and hundreds of hours at a later date.

At the very least, you should know of a lawyer and CPA you can use when you have legal requirements that necessitate professional advice. It's good to have someone in mind, just in case.

How Much Will a Lawyer and CPA Cost?

To find out how much a lawyer and an accountant will cost you, ask your friends and business associates or call some lawyers and accountants and ask them. In most cases, a lawyer or an accountant will not charge you for an initial visit, so you can do some free comparison shopping (but make sure you call and confirm that the initial visit is free before you go).

Once you've selected a lawyer or an accountant, he or she may ask you to pay a retainer fee, which is a lump sum that you pay up front and then draw against every time the lawyer or accountant advises you. This practice is becoming increasingly common because lawyers and accountants are growing wary of providing advice on credit to businesses that may fail before the bills are paid. Be aware that retainer fees vary considerably. Ask around to find out what others are paying. And make sure to get references on the lawyer and CPA you choose before you sign a retainer agreement.

IT'S NOT THAT MUCH WORK, IT JUST SEEMS LIKE A LOT

If everything you've read in this chapter seems overwhelming at this point, don't dismay. Although the rules and obligations just for starting a business in your back bedroom or garage may seem like a lot to consider, you have to remember that you're operating a real business and that you intend to make money doing it. Once you get the permits and set up your business operations, you'll find that there isn't that much to do to keep things safe and legal as long as you remember to follow the guidelines and keep up-to-date on the rules.

8

BOOKKEEPING, ACCOUNTING, AND TAXES: KEEPING TRACK OF PROFITS AND EXPENSES

This chapter won't make an accountant or bookkeeper out of you, but it will introduce you to the basic records you should keep, the accounting terms and methods you should know, and the taxes you'll have to pay. You'll also learn enough to manage an accountant in a way that is valuable to your business situation.

Most business owners treat bookkeeping and taxes as necessary evils, but your financial records are really a godsend. Your records are an important part of your ability to manage your business. Good records enable you to substitute facts for guesswork, and continuity for confusion. In addition to depicting the financial history of your home-based business, your records provide a scorecard that rates your performance. The easiest way to get ready for April 15 is by keeping good records throughout the year. The more accurate and up-to-date your financial records are, the simpler it will be for you to prepare your tax returns.

WHY RECORDKEEPING IS SO IMPORTANT

The purpose of the highly structured world of bookkeeping and accounting is to provide you with information needed to manage the business or evaluate the results of your investment. Not only should you keep good records to satisfy the government, but you also need them for your own benefit. By taking the time to set up and maintain a recordkeeping system for your business, you will ensure receipt of the business-related tax deductions entitled to you. Furthermore, your records are a valuable tool in making business decisions and in helping you identify problems quickly and take corrective action. Instead of having to hunt for financial information or develop it on the spot, you already have it in hand waiting to be used.

An efficient recordkeeping system should be able to provide you with the following information:

- Sales totals by week, month, quarter, and year-to-date
- Taxable income for the year
- Amount of money invested in inventory and supplies
- Customers who owe you money
- Your financial obligations
- Business operating expenses
- Products or services most in demand
- Current orders to be shipped

These facts, which are necessary for tax reporting and management purposes, also may be required by any suppliers or lending institutions with whom you do business.

CHOOSING THE BEST ACCOUNTING SYSTEM

Although the Internal Revenue Service (IRS) does stipulate whether you use an accrual basis for reporting your income if your business has inventory, the IRS does not stipulate what kind of records a business owner must keep. The IRS only wants records that properly identify the business's income, expenses, and deductions. Thus, as a home-based businessperson, you may use any recordkeeping system that meets these criteria and is suited to your business. For the best results, the recordkeeping system you choose should be simple to use, easy to understand, accurate, consistent, and capable of providing timely information.

You need to accumulate information that is timely, reliable, and useful because you don't want to take valuable time away from moneymaking. You can choose from a number of business recordkeeping systems, ranging from simple to complex. If you are publishing financial information to outsiders, you will need to consider an additional set of special rules (called Generally Accepted Accounting Principles, or GAAP), but for managing any business you must have an accounting system that makes sense.

If you don't know the principles and policies in your industry or business, consider consulting a professional who has the necessary experience to help you set up an efficient system. Once a good accounting system is established, keeping the records becomes a clerical task that can be delegated or performed by an outside bookkeeper if you aren't interested in keeping the books yourself.

The information in this chapter provides some basic accounting concepts to help you understand the considerations involved in setting up and maintaining your accounting system. Time spent planning and developing good procedures can save you countless hours of frustration down the road. There are also computers and simple accounting programs to help you prepare your financial statements and other reports and keep records up-to-date.

Many home-based entrepreneurs use a bookkeeper once a week or once a month, as needed, to do their books. One way to find a part-time bookkeeper is to call the colleges in your area and ask if any students majoring in accounting are seeking work experience. Or, perhaps there is a home-based bookkeeping service nearby that can meet your needs.

Always remember that as the business owner, you need to make sure that the records stay up-to-date. The computer can't enter the data for you. Even with a bookkeeper, you need to keep the records in order so the book-keeper can put the numbers in the columns. Thus, you need to make record keeping and financial review a regular part of your work week.

It's always good to know where your sales are coming from and how your money is being spent. It's a good idea to review your company's performance on a regular basis in case of potential problems, such as running out of cash or lower sales figures. Most companies, small and large, look at their basic financial statements on at least a quarterly basis to measure their progress toward long-term goals. Most managers review their cash position on a daily or weekly basis. You should too.

ACCOUNTING PERIODS AND WHY YOU NEED THEM

Your first accounting task is to set up accounting periods. Accounting periods are lengths of time, like months, quarters, or years, that allow a company's financial reports to be compared from one time frame to another. Accounting periods also provide a basis for comparing company performance from one period to the next, from quarter to quarter or from year to year.

In order to file your tax returns, you have to determine what month you want your fiscal year to start and end to report your profit or loss for that year. Unless there is some reason to do otherwise, as recommended by your accountant, keep your fiscal year the same as the calendar year, from January 1 to December 31. This means your quarters will end on March 31, June 30, September 30, and December 31.

CASH OR ACCRUAL ACCOUNTING: WHICH IS BEST FOR YOU?

After establishing your fiscal year, you need to determine when you actually incur an expense. Is it when you use the product or service, or when you pay for the product or service? The answer is different depending on whether you use the cash basis or accrual basis of accounting. One of these two approaches is more appropriate for your business.

The cash basis of accounting recognizes sales and expenses when money is actually received or spent. The accrual basis of accounting focuses on the earning process and matches sales revenue with the period when the earning process is completed. The accrual basis also matches expenses incurred to generate those sales to the period in which the income is reported.

In accrual accounting, when you receive a payment from a customer for work that hasn't been completed yet, for accounting purposes you need to show that payment as "unearned income" until the work is completed. When the earning process is complete, the accrual basis of accounting will report that transaction as income. If the customer can cancel his order, the money really hasn't been earned yet. If you haven't finished earning the money by meeting all the terms of your contract with the customer, you shouldn't consider the revenue from those sales as truly yours. If you have a noncancelable contract along with a nonrefundable advance, then the money you receive is yours. At that point, you can include it as revenue.

If you use the cash basis of accounting, you don't need to know the difference between collections and "earned income." In the cash-based accounting world, everything you receive from sales is considered income when it is collected, and you don't make any special accounting entries to show when it is earned.

Accountants believe that the accrual basis of accounting provides better information on the results of business operations, even though an accrual system may be more complicated and more costly to maintain.

So how do you track money owed to you when you're using the cash basis of accounting? Very simply, you complete work for a customer and you bill them. In some businesses, you'll receive payment right away, such as for products at a flea market. At the end of the day, you total the amount collected on all the sales slips and match them with the amount of money in your cash register. You deposit most of that money in your bank account and keep some in the register to use as change the next day.

Many businesses, however, have to wait to receive payment. You may bill a customer on the first of the month and have to wait thirty days until a check arrives. To keep track of who owes what, create a file of all the invoices sent out to customers. As customers pay, deposit their checks in the bank and take their invoice copies out of the file. You can always check to see whose invoice is outstanding by looking in the file. After thirty days, you'll want to give the customer a call and find out if there is a problem.

Accrual accounting imposes an additional accounting step. You must use the accounting system to track when a customer is billed as well as when the collection comes in, and you may be making accounting entries at times when no cash has changed hands. Furthermore, accrual accounting may report handsome profits while you have no cash in the bank because your customers haven't paid you yet.

When managing your business, remember that "cash is king," and be sure to track your bank balances and your cash flows. Accrual accounting may make it seem like you have more cash than you actually do. Don't run out of money before the bills are paid regardless of how much money you have coming in next month.

Accrual accounting may also impose tax complications. No one likes to pay taxes on reported income before the cash from those sales has been collected, but that is the way accrual accounting works. Your accountant or tax adviser can give you suggestions on techniques to minimize this dilemma.

Again, if your business has inventory, the IRS forces you to use the accrual basis of accounting. However, if you run a service business, especially if you are a small business, you may find that keeping your books on the cash basis is much simpler. Most accounting software programs for small businesses handle both accrual and cash-basis accounting.

Here's an example that illustrates the differences between the two methods. Assume that you run a small consulting firm and that you have only one client. Last month, you spent $200 on supplies and office expenses, paid yourself $1,000 as a salary, and billed your client $3,000 for the month's project. This month, your client pays the bill, and it clears the bank on the fifth of the month. You again pay yourself a $1,000 salary and have $200 in expenses. Under the cash basis of accounting, you show a loss of $1,200 last month since you paid for the supplies and your salary last month, and you show a profit of $1,800 this month since you collected a payment.

Under the accrual basis, you match the expenses incurred last month with the revenue earned last month and show a profit of $1,800 ($3,000 in revenue less $1,200 in expenses) for the first month, even though the income was received in the second month. On the second month you show a loss of $1,200 because you have no income associated with the expenses.

If you have a fairly simple business, with expenses incurred close to the time sales revenues are collected, the cash basis of accounting may give you information that is accurate and timely enough to let you run your business.

Most larger businesses usually use the accrual basis of accounting, however, for some or all of the following reasons:

- They have inventories, and the IRS makes them use accrual accounting.
- There are long lags between the time expenses are incurred and the time sales revenues are collected. Most accountants feel that in these circumstances cash-basis accounting gives a distorted picture of the operations.
- The business sells a small number of large items. If you show earnings based on collections, you'll see dramatic swings in reported performance every month even though the underlying operations may not be fluctuating nearly as much.

RECORDING YOUR INCOME AND EXPENSES

Regardless of the type of accounting you do to report income to the IRS, one of the most important functions of your recordkeeping system is to provide an accurate record of the sources and amounts of income, expenses, and taxes generated by your business. This is important not only for tax-reporting purposes but also for decision making.

If you use a computer program to keep your records, the program most likely provides forms or menus to complete for all transactions. However, if you intend to keep your records by hand, or if you use handwritten records to back up your computer records, the following sections describe some of the basic financial records you must maintain for your home-based business.

Cash Receipts Journal

At the bare minimum, the income records for your home-based business must include a cash receipts journal. If you extend credit to your customers or don't receive payment at the time of sales, you will also need an accounts receivable journal.

A cash receipts journal like the one shown here can be found on the CD-ROM. A journal can easily keep track of your income flow. By recording the date, source, and amount of income earned, the cash receipts journal also indicates which services are preferred. Thus, in addition to providing you with the income figures required by the IRS, a cash receipts journal provides valuable information about your best customers.

After a few months of recording your cash receipts, you should know who your best customers are and which products or services are most popular. This is a good example of what marketing experts call the 80/20 Rule. According to the rule, 80 percent of a business's sales are likely to come from 20 percent of its customers. These customers are your best prospects, also called your "target market." They are the types of customers who benefit most from your products or services. Once you've identified them, you should direct your advertising, selling, and customer relations efforts toward filling the needs of your target market. More information on reaching your target market is located in the Marketing section of this book, Chapters 14 through 22.

Accounts Receivable Journal

If you want to keep your cash flow in good shape, it's best for new companies to receive payment for their goods or services at the time the sale is made. This gives you an immediate use of funds and eliminates the need to collect them later. However, if it's necessary to allow your customers to buy on credit, it's vital that you maintain an accounts receivable journal similar to the one shown in this chapter. This will provide you with a record of each sale and enable you to keep track of the money that is owed. When you receive payment, you can enter the income in your cash receipts journal.

BUSINESS EXPENSES

The recordkeeping system for your home-based business must provide you with a record of tax-deductible business expenses. You will have to determine precisely what expenses legitimately can be termed "business expenses."

Be aware that the Internal Revenue Service regards as deductible only those expenses that are "ordinary in your business and necessary for its operation." Here are some, but not all, of the typical expenses that meet these criteria:

- Advertising expenses
- Accounting services
- Business supplies and materials
- Attorney's fees
- Messenger service
- Automobile expenses
- Business publications
- Postage

Monthly Cash Receipts Journal **Sally's Gift Baskets**

Month of July

Date	Describe the Sale	Customer	Taxable Sales	Sales Tax	Shipping Received	Wholesale Sales	Other	Total Receipt	Notes
1	Basket 21, Inv #331	Sally Field	$100.00	$7.50	$5.00			$112.50	UPS
2	Basket 23, Inv#332	Joe Balooka	$200.00	$15.00	$7.50			$222.50	UPS
3	Inv#334 (10 Baskets)	Remy's Gift Store				$450.00		$450.00	Delivered by hand
4									
5									
6	Basket 23, Inv#335	Ingrid Valentine	$200.00	$15.00				$215.00	Picked up at office
7									
8									
9									
10	Basket 22, Inv #336	George Realman	$100.00	$7.50	$5.00			$112.50	UPS
11									
12									
13	Basket 23, Inv#332	Stan Orton	$200.00	$15.00	$7.50			$222.50	UPS
14									
15									
16									
17	Basket 23, Inv#332	Michelle Sbraga	$200.00	$15.00	$7.50			$222.50	UPS
18									
19									
20									
21									
22									
23	Basket 22, Inv #336	Iver Jensen	$100.00	$7.50	$5.00			$112.50	UPS
24	Basket 22, Inv #336	Anna Sorenson	$100.00	$7.50	$5.00			$112.50	UPS
25									
26									
27									
28									
29	Basket 23, Inv#332	Norma Staron	$200.00	$15.00	$7.50			$222.50	UPS
30									
31									
	Totals for month		$1,400.00	$105.00	$50.00	$450.00		$2,005.00	

Joe's Internet Consulting
Accounts Receivable Journal

1999

Sale Date	Customer	Invoice Number	Terms	Total Sale amount	Date Due	Date Paid	Notes
5-Apr	Mac's Office	442	Net 30	$1,415.00	5-May		Call to remind him.
7-Apr	Jona Whale Supply	447	Net 60	$2,245.00	8-Jun		
4-May	Interware Services	550	Net 30	$3,345.00	5-Jun		More business to come in July.
				$7,005.00			

- Association dues
- Consultants' fees
- Business safe deposit box
- Credit reports
- Salaries
- Depreciation
- Sales commissions
- Business-related entertainment
- Stationery
- Shipping and freight charges
- Supplies
- Business insurance
- Taxes
- Interest paid on business-related loans
- Business trip expenses
- Licenses

In calculating your business expenses, it's important to separate them from your personal expenses. We recommend a business checking account and business credit cards to keep your business separate from your personal finances. For instance, travel expenses on a business trip are deductible, but the same expenses on a vacation are not. Taking a client to lunch is deductible, going to lunch with a friend socially is not. Postage on Christmas cards sent to customers is deductible, postage on cards sent to friends and relatives is not.

In the event that an expense is for both business and personal uses, only the business portion is deductible. For example, if you go on a trip for both business and pleasure, you can deduct only the business portion of the trip.

A form like the one shown in this chapter can help you keep track of your deductible business expenses. Be sure to keep receipts or other forms of documentation for all the expenses or you won't be able to deduct them for income tax purposes.

Cash Disbursements Journal

The best way to keep track of your expenses is to enter them in a cash disbursements journal similar to the one shown in this chapter. When recording disbursements for paying bills or for paying for supplies, be sure to include the following basic information:

1. The date the expense was paid
2. The name of the person or business receiving payment
3. The check number or receipt for payment
4. The amount paid
5. The type of business expense

When you set up your expense categories, it's useful to arrange them in alphabetical order or in the order in which they will appear on your tax forms. You should file the receipts in the same order. This will make it easier for you to locate the information later and to transfer it to your tax forms when preparing your income tax return.

At the end of each month, it's also a good idea to add up the expenses in each category to determine where your money is going. By analyzing your finances each month, you should stay within your budget and keep unnecessary expenses to a minimum.

Home Business Expenses

Because you do business at home, you may be entitled to deduct a portion of residence operating expenses and depreciation. To qualify

Michelle's Weaving

Cash Disbursement Journal   Month of <u>June</u>

Date	Payment type (If by Check, Include Number)	Payee	Description of Expense	Total	Inventory (Merch.)	Supplies and Postage
06/01/98	Check 213	UPS	Shipping, Monthly Bill	$45.72		$45.72
06/01/98	Visa	Wool Supply, Inc.	Wool for spinning	$78.00	$78.00	
06/03/98	Visa	Generations Cafe	Lunch with Spinning Guild	$46.75		
06/04/98	Check 214	AT&T Telephone	Telephone charges	$126.00		
06/15/98	Check 215	Sally Wonka	Labor, weaving	$225.00		
				$0.00		
				$0.00		
				$0.00		
				$0.00		
				$0.00		
				$521.47	$78.00	$45.72

Labor Non-employee	Employee Payroll	Advertising	Rent	Utilities	Taxes and Licenses	Travel & Entertainment	Miscel-laneous	Non-deductible
						$46.75		
				$126.00				
$225.00								
$225.00	$0.00	$0.00	$0.00	$126.00	$0.00	$46.75	$0.00	$0.00

for this deduction, the IRS specifies that a part of your home must be set aside regularly and exclusively for the business. In this regard, the space must be used as either your principal place of business or a place to meet and deal with patients, clients, or customers. There have been some new deduction rulings regarding the use of a secondary office at home when the office is used as a normal place of work (i.e., the home office used by a doctor or other professional who has another office for the practice or the secondary, home offices of telecommuters). Because the laws are changing, refer to the IRS publications on home offices for up-to-date information. The CD-ROM has links to these resources.

If your business occupies a free-standing structure next to your home—a garage, guest house, or barn for example—expenses are deductible if you use the space regularly and exclusively for the business. In this case, the structure does not have to be your principal place of business or used to meet customers.

If you are an employee who works out of your home as a telecommuter, you may be entitled to deduct some expenses for the business use of your home, too. In this situation though, you must work at home for the convenience and by the company's schedule, not just because you want to work at home occasionally.

Most home businesses with a dedicated office space are able to deduct expenses related to mortgage interest, depreciation, maintenance, utilities, and insurance in equal proportion to the amount of area your business requires as a percentage of the total space in your home. Thus, if you have a 1,200-square-foot home and your office takes up 400 square feet, you can deduct 30 percent of all the expenses associated with buying or renting, maintaining, and insuring your home.

Once you've determined the deductible percentage of your home expenses, multiply this figure by each expense in order to obtain the dollar amounts of your deductions. (For example, 30 percent multiplied by $1,500 in home utilities equals a $450 business utilities expense.) Those expenses that only benefit your business, such as painting or remodeling the specific area occupied by the business, are 100 percent deductible.

Expenses that only benefit your home and are in no way related to the business, such as landscaping or remodeling the bathroom, may not be deducted. To make certain you have accurately defined those expenses that benefit both your home and your business, only the business, and only the home, it's advisable to consult with an accountant.

If you decide to sell your home, the expense deductions you've taken for the business will have a bearing on how and when capital gains on the sale are to be recognized. For more information on selling your home when it is also used as a business, check IRS publication number 523, *Tax Information on Selling Your Home.*

The laws on home-business deductions are changing rapidly, and it's a good idea to get advice before you spend money on your home office. Use a form to help you keep track of all home-related expenses and calculate the percentage of allowable deductions for income tax purposes.

Business-Related Automobile Expenses

If you use an automobile or truck in your business, those expenses resulting from the business use of the vehicle are deductible. These include gasoline, oil, maintenance and repairs, insurance, depreciation, interest on car payments, parking fees, taxes, license fees, and tolls. There are two ways to calculate your deductible automobile expenses: using a standard mileage rate or deducting a percentage of the total operating costs.

Standard Mileage Rate

To calculate your standard mileage rate, keep a record of all the miles you drive for business during the year. Multiply your total business mileage by the current rate allowed by the IRS. This, plus any documented amounts for parking fees and tolls, will give you the dollar amount of your automobile expense. The applicable rates are subject to change by the IRS; therefore, research them before you file your taxes.

Percentage of Total Operating Costs

To calculate your automobile deductible by a percentage of your total operating costs, keep a record of the number of miles you drive for business during the year, and keep track of all automobile expenses. Multiply the deductible percentage of automobile expenses by the total cost of operating your car.

Since this method is based on your automobile operating costs rather than on a standard rate per mile, it's especially important to keep receipts documenting your automobile expenses. To make sure that you are claiming the full automobile deduction the IRS allows,

try both of these methods (at least in the beginning). After comparing the totals, choose the method that gives you the highest deduction.

If you use the total cost method, you may also be able to deduct the depreciation of your car if you meet specific criteria. Refer to the IRS publication on automobile expenses or the IRS Web site for more information on the criteria for the current tax year.

Entertainment Expenses

A portion of your business-related entertainment expenses also are tax deductible. To qualify as a deductible item, the entertainment expense must be necessary in carrying on your trade or operating your business. As with your home and automobile expenses, you must separate your business entertainment expenses from your nonbusiness expenditures. Whenever entertainment is for business and social purposes, only the business portion is deductible.

For example, if you entertain a group that includes four business prospects and one friend, you may deduct the expenses for yourself and the four prospects, but you may not deduct the amount spent on your friend. In determining whether or not an entertainment expense is deductible, ask yourself if the entertainment had a specific business purpose. Was it to get new business or to encourage the development of an existing business relationship? If your answer is yes, you should be able to claim the expense as a business deduction. Taking a prospective customer to lunch or dinner is usually a deductible expense if you discuss business at some time during the meal.

To comply with the IRS rules on entertainment deductions, you should keep a record of all business entertainment expenses along with the receipts or other supporting evidence. When claiming an expense as a business entertainment deduction, you must be able to prove:

1. The amount of the expense
2. The date the entertainment took place
3. The location of the entertainment
4. The reason for the entertainment (to discuss a contract or introduce your services)
5. The name of each person you entertained and their titles or occupations

Entering a luncheon date on your desk calendar isn't enough. To be properly documented, the lunch must be supported by a receipt for the meal. The more specific you are, the better. Proof will add to the validity of your deductions if you are ever audited by the IRS.

TAXES, TAXES, AND MORE TAXES

Taxes are an inevitable part of doing business, but if you keep good records, taxes shouldn't be a problem for you. The nature of your home-based business, its legal form and location, will determine the taxes you must pay. Most entrepreneurs probably pay federal and state taxes, and many also pay local taxes.

The two most prevalent federal taxes that home-based entrepreneurs are required to pay are income tax and self-employment tax. If you employ other people in your business or manufacture or sell certain types of goods, you may also be subject to employment taxes and excise taxes.

Income Tax

Every business is required by law to file an annual federal income tax return. The form you use depends on whether your business is a sole proprietorship, a partnership, or a corporation. If you are a sole proprietor, you should report your business income and deductions on Schedule C (Form 1040). Attach this schedule to your individual tax return, Form 1040, and submit them together. If you own more than one business, you must file a separate Schedule C for each one.

If you are a partner in a home-based business, your income and deductions from the partnership should be reported on Schedule K-1 (Form 1065) and filed along with your individual tax return. Each of your partners should do the same, accounting for his or her income and deductions in this way. In addition to this, the total income and deductions for the partnership must be reported on Form 1065.

Corporation

A corporation reports its taxable income on Form 1120. S Corporations use Form 1120S. Any income or dividends that you receive from the corporation should be entered on your individual tax return. However, if you are a shareholder in an S Corporation, your income and deductions should be reported as they would be in a partnership except that you would use Schedule K-1 (Form 1120S).

Self-Employment Tax

Self-employment tax is a Social Security tax for workers who are self-employed. It's similar to the Social Security tax paid by wage earners, but you pay it yourself instead of having it withheld from your paycheck. As a home-based business-person, you must pay self-employment tax if you have net earnings from your business of $400 or more a year. To find out more about this tax, check IRS publication number 533, *Self-Employment Tax.*

Estimated Tax Payments

The IRS requires that you pay your income and self-employment taxes each year on a pay-as-you-go basis. Rather than paying taxes in one lump sum at the end of the tax period, you must estimate them in advance and pay them in installments by certain dates. If you use a calendar year for your fiscal year, you must pay tax installments on April 15, June 15, September 15, and January 15 (of the following year).

Using this method, you generally pay one quarter of your estimated total tax liability on each date until the liability is paid in full. If you discover that in July you paid too much or too little tax, you can decrease or increase the size of the remaining payments. Remember that you are required to prepay at least 90 percent of your tax liability each year. If you prepay less than 90 percent, you may be subject to a penalty.

Beginning in 1998, you won't have to make quarterly estimated tax payments if you expect to owe less than $1,000 in taxes on April 15, beyond any withholding on paychecks or tax credits you receive. If your business is making lots of money, you'll still need to make estimated tax payments every quarter.

If your company is a sole proprietorship and you expect to owe more than $1,000 in income taxes, and if your spouse is already working and having taxes taken out of a pay-

check to account for a part of the withholdings, you can use one of two alternate methods to compute your estimated payments as a family: the total payments (including those based on salary deductions and the profit of your business) should total below 90 percent of this year's tax bill, or 100 percent of last year's tax bill. However, couples with adjusted gross incomes (AGI) over $150,000 and singles with AGI over $75,000 must use 110 percent of last year's tax bill as the second part of the method.

If you do owe something, don't forget to send your tax estimate checks in on time. You'll be fined on the underestimated tax payments for the year, even if you pay the entire amount due by April 15.

Try to make your estimates as accurate as possible to spare yourself the expense of fines and penalties. When in doubt, remember that you will fare better to pay more than the amount you've estimated to ensure meeting the 90 percent prepayment minimum. The form used to estimate your tax is Form 1040-ES, which can be obtained from the IRS.

Employment Taxes

If you have employees in your home-based business, you will probably need to pay employment taxes. These taxes include:

1. Federal income tax, which you withhold from your employees' wages
2. Social Security tax, part of which you withhold from your employees' wages and the rest of which you contribute as an employer
3. Federal unemployment tax, which all employers must pay

4. Any state or local employment or unemployment taxes you must pay or deduct from wages

Report both federal income tax and the Social Security tax on Form 941, and pay both taxes when you submit the forms. Report and pay the federal unemployment tax separately, using Form 940.

For more information about employment taxes and which ones you must pay, read IRS publication number 15, *Circular E,* and contact your state and community revenue offices for information on the employment taxes and withholding required by your state or community.

Excise Taxes

Although it's not likely that you will have to pay any excise taxes, you should be aware of their existence. Any tax that is selective in nature, singling out some products or services for taxation, is known as an excise tax.

Excise taxes come in a variety of categories. Some excise taxes are levied on the production or sale of certain goods, while others are imposed on specific kinds of services or businesses. For example, if your home-based business involves transporting people or property by air, it will be subject to an excise tax. If you are an insurance agent who handles policies issued by foreign insurers, you will have to pay excise taxes on those policies. The subject of excise taxes is clearly arbitrary. To determine whether your product, service, or home-based business is subject to excise taxes, read IRS publication number 510, *Excise Taxes.* This document will give you basic information about

excise taxes, along with an explanation of the procedures for reporting them.

State and Local Taxes

The types and amounts of state and local taxes that home-based business owners must pay will depend on where the business is located. For instance, businesses in New York and California are subject to higher tax rates than those in Tennessee and Texas. Some states have income and sales taxes, others don't. Just as states vary when it comes to taxation, counties, cities, and towns within the states do, too.

Taxes imposed at the state and local levels include business taxes, licensing fees, unemployment taxes, and income taxes. To make sure that your business is meeting its state and local tax obligations, contact the authorities for your state, county, and community to determine those taxes for which you are responsible.

Don't Take Our Word For It

Because things change frequently in the tax law, don't expect our advice about the IRS to be completely accurate. Instead, go to the IRS site on the World Wide Web for more complete information on tax payments, forms, and filing requirements. There are links to the site for the IRS and other tax related Web sites on the CD-ROM.

Be careful about using relatives or close friends as professional tax advisers. Sometimes relatives or friends are not as brutally honest as you need them to be because they don't want to make you uncomfortable, or they simply don't know the laws.

IRS TAX PUBLICATIONS

The publications listed on the CD-ROM can provide you with additional information about business taxation. These publications should be available at your local IRS office, or you can obtain them by writing to the Internal Revenue Service, Washington, D.C. 20224. You can order some forms on the Web site as well.

To save you grief while doing your taxes, here are some basic guidelines:

1. Keep your business expenses and personal expenses separate by using separate bank accounts for business and personal transactions

2. Make all payments by check or company credit card, rather than cash, to keep your expenses clearly documented

3. Keep all business records and supporting documentation (checks, receipts, and other documents) at least three years

4. Choose the recordkeeping system that is most compatible with the needs of your business, or ask an accountant for advice before setting up your system

5. Keep an expense diary in your car and use it to record your automobile and daily expenses

6. Document all business entertainment expenses by writing the business information on the receipts themselves and filing them by type of expense

7. Prepay your percent of estimated income and Social Security taxes to avoid a penalty

8. If you need to obtain tax forms quickly, check with your local IRS office or order a copy of the forms from the World Wide Web site

FINANCIAL STATEMENTS

Even if you intend to use an accountant to manage your records, you still need to understand basic financial terms to make reasonable financial decisions. This section introduces you to financial statements and explains their basic purpose.

There are three basic financial statements: the balance sheet, the income statement, and the cash flow analysis. The balance sheet shows your assets and your liabilities at a particular point in time, usually calculated on the last day of the year. The income statement shows you the amount of money brought in and spent during a specific accounting period, usually a year. The cash flow analysis determines exactly how much you actually received in revenue and how much you spent on a monthly, weekly, or quarterly basis.

While bankers are most concerned with your balance sheet because they want to be sure you will have enough resources to pay off the loan they've given you, you must watch your cash flow carefully. Your cash flow statement keeps you informed about how much money you have to keep your business operating in the black.

The Chart of Accounts

Financial statements usually start with a chart of accounts, making recordkeeping easier and more understandable. In a chart of accounts, similar transactions are grouped together, making financial statements easier to produce. Accounts that summarize the assets and liabilities of the company are grouped together and form the balance sheet. Accounts that summarize the sales and expenses of the company are grouped together to form the income statement. Taken together, the income statement and balance sheet describe the financial condition and resulting operations of your company. If you are using the accrual basis of accounting, you also need a financial statement that details cash flow activity, which is likely to be different from the activity shown on the income statement.

Cash basis companies may not need an elaborate analysis to understand their cash flows (because the money in the bank account is a good indicator), but they should still be aware that lags between billing and collection can adversely affect their cash position. Depending on the size of your business and the complexity of your collections, a cash basis company may also need to develop a full-fledged cash flow analysis report.

The following sections contain examples of an income statement, a balance sheet, and a cash flow analysis. There are also forms for completing your own financial statements on the CD-ROM.

The Income Statement

Your income statement, or profit and loss statement (P and L), tells you whether or not your business is making a profit. The income statement totals the amount of revenue and then subtracts the expenses associated with making that revenue. The result is the pretax profit or gross profit.

Income statements determine how much money you made versus how much you spent during a particular period of time. Most businesses prepare year-end income statements to see how they did during the year. You can also prepare income statements for any period, such as monthly, quarterly, or year-to-date.

Expenses fall into two categories: cost of sales expenses and operational expenses. Cost of sales expenses (also called the cost of goods sold, or COGS) are those directly related to producing your product or providing your service. These costs generally include the cost of raw materials, the cost of labor to build the product, and other expenses required to sell the product or service. For example, if you sold a gift basket for $100 and it cost you $30 in material to make that basket, because you made the basket yourself and didn't receive a salary, there is no labor cost for the basket. Therefore, the cost of sales is $30, which is what you paid for the materials to make the basket. The gross profit calculation associated with this single basket's sale is:

Revenue – Cost of Sales = Gross Profit, or
$100 – $30 = $70 Gross Profit

Because the costs of producing your product will change depending on how much you manufacture at a time, cost of sales are variable expenses. Products usually cost less when you buy them in bulk, and producing a product in large quantities works the same way. The more you produce, the lower the cost per product and the higher the gross profit.

Operating expenses are also called fixed expenses. Operating expenses are those everyday expenses associated with running your business, including your salary, your portion of the mortgage payment, the electric bill, insurance, any employee salaries, and other similar costs for operating the company. No matter how much you sell this month, you will still have these expenses. Fixed expenses should be paid out of the gross profit, if you have any.

The Balance Sheet

An income statement reflects the flow of money in and out of a company during a specific period of time, whereas the balance sheet shows the amount of company assets and liabilities at a particular point in time. The balance sheet is based on the following accounting equation:

Assets = Liabilities + Owner's Equity

Assets

Assets are items of value that the company owns, such as cash in the business checking account, accounts receivables, equipment, and other business property. You have two types of assets: liquid and fixed.

Cash is one of the liquid assets, also called current assets. You obtain cash from liquidating shares, obtaining a loan, or by selling your services or products. Cash is money you can spend on the spot. You can use your cash immediately to pay off a debt or to purchase items for the business. Other common liquid assets include accounts receivable and your inventory.

Fixed assets have a longer life and are more difficult to convert into cash quickly. Typical fixed assets include buildings, machinery, and land. The value of a fixed asset is based on its initial purchase price minus any applicable depreciation. Different fixed assets have distinct depreciation terms, or depreciable lives. Check with an accountant to determine the proper depreciable life of a given item, or read up on depreciation on the IRS Web site.

Liabilities

Liabilities are amounts that you owe. Typical liabilities include loans, credit cards, taxes owed, and other people to whom you owe money. Short-term liabilities, which are paid back within twelve months, are also called accounts payable. Long-term liabilities include mortgages and equipment loans.

Owner's equity is what is left over when liabilities are subtracted from assets. Take what you have, subtract what you owe, and you are left with owner's equity. You want to maximize this number since it reflects the value of your company. The initial investment of your company stock (if you're incorporated) and retained earnings are added together to calculate owner's equity.

The amount of net income determined at the end of the year is added to an equity account named retained earnings. Add the current year's net income to the prior year's retained earnings to calculate the current year's retained earnings. Ideally, retained earnings become cash for the company to finance further earnings, product development, and promotion.

As your company grows, the numbers on your assets, liabilities, and equity line will grow larger and larger. This is due to the purchase of new equipment, increased accounts receivable because of higher sales, or improved cash flow. Companies just starting out will have very small numbers on their assets, liabilities, and equity line. This means that as your assets increase and your liabilities decrease, your equity will increase. The balance sheet precisely calculates this equation. Although your balance sheet may not change drastically from week to week, it's a good idea to review whether

Simplified Income Statement

MyCo

Period Ending Dec 31, 1998

Item	Dollar Amount	Description of Income
Sales revenue	$275,000	All revenue
Cost of sales	$ 65,000	Variable costs associated with revenues (excluding fixed costs)
Gross profit	$210,000	Sales revenue minus costs
Operating costs (fixed) Salaries	$ 45,000	
Overhead	$ 12,000	Costs for electricity, share of house, copier lease, etc.
Marketing	$ 14,000	Costs for promotion, advertising, etc.
Total other expenses	$ 71,000	All costs other than cost of sales
Total expenses	$136,000	All expenses
Pretax profit	$ 74,000	Gross profit minus expenses
Federal & state taxes	$ 8,900	Uncle Sam's cut
Net Income	$ 65,100	The bottom line

you are taking on more debt or increasing the value of your company regularly. Most software packages provide you with a balance sheet and income statement to help you do this.

The Cash Flow Analysis

A cash flow analysis is your most important financial statement because it determines whether you have enough cash to run the business and pay the bills. Although tracking your assets and liabilities is important over the long term, the key challenge is making and keeping a profit. A cash flow analysis, or cash flow statement, looks a lot like an income statement except that your income statement focuses only on earnings from operations, while the cash flow analysis also reflects investments, borrowings, payments on loans, and other balance sheet changes.

Most small businesses know whether their cash flow is okay because they have a positive balance in their bank accounts. However, a look at the bank account balance won't necessarily alert you to upcoming bills or other expenses that you might not have considered.

Cash flow from operations may also be significantly different than reported earnings, especially if you are using the accrual basis of accounting. If you depend on an income statement that looks at a longer period of time, the good months and the bad months even out. You wouldn't know by looking at your income statement that March almost put you out of business, but your monthly cash flow analysis would alert you to potential problems. The reason you need both an income statement and a cash flow analysis is because of the fluctuation in monthly sales. If you determine your cash flow analysis, you can prevent running out of money during the bad months by planning in advance.

HOW TO USE FINANCIAL STATEMENTS

Your business records and financial statements are about more than columns of numbers in little boxes. Those numbers determine your financial and management success. You should use last year's cash flow analysis as a guide to estimate what your sales and expenses will be this year by month. Use last year's income statement to estimate year-end totals for sales and expenses versus today's expenses and year-end expectations. Use your income reports and cash flow analysis as goal-setting tools to improve your company's financial situation as the business grows. Are your expenses growing faster than you planned? Are products costing more to produce than you expected? You need to know the answers to these questions to keep your operations on track.

If you watch your numbers and compare them to your performance over time, you'll be financially sound. The same applies to your balance sheet. Do you want to buy a new computer for your business and pay off some of those loans this year? Create a projected balance sheet for the coming year. Estimate what your balance sheet will look like once you pay off those debts or buy the equipment you need. Your records can only help you if you use them; therefore, learn to use them habitually and review them regularly.

Simplified Balance Statement

MyCo

Period Ending Dec 31, 1998

Current Assets	$ Dollar Amount
Cash in bank	5,000
Accounts receivable	17,500
Inventory	650
Other current assets	1,500
Total current assets	24,650
Fixed Assets	
Office equipment	12,800
Machinery	0
Accumulated depreciation	700
Total fixed assets	13,500
Total assets	38,150
Current liabilities	
Wages payable	1,500
Taxes payable	2,300
Loans, credit lines, credit cards	500
Total current liabilities	4,300
Long-term liabilities	
Business loans	15,000
Equipment loans	7,000
Total long-term liabilities	22,000
Total liabilities	26,300
Owner's equity	
Common stock	5,000
Retained earnings	7,850
Total owner's equity	12,850
Total liabilities and equity	39,150

CASH FLOW ANALYSIS--6 MONTHS

	January	February	March	April	May	June	Total
Beginning Cash Balance	$ 1,250	$ 8,659	$ 9,448	$ 6,898	$ 3,801	$ 3,801	$ 33,857
Income and Other Receipts							
Sales & Receipts	5,400	6,100	4,100	4,500	5,500	4,500	30,100
Shipping Fees Received	125	180	112	115	225	115	872
Sales Tax Received	270	305	205	225	275	225	1,505
Payments on Accounts	350	350	350	350	275	500	2,175
Loan Proceeds	12,000	0	0	0	0	0	12,000
Other:		25			45		70
Total Cash In	$ 18,145	$ 6,960	$ 4,767	$ 5,190	$ 6,320	$ 5,340	$ 46,722
Available Cash Balance	$ 19,395	$ 15,619	$ 14,215	$ 12,088	$ 10,121	$ 9,141	$ 80,579
Cash Out (Expenses)							
Advertising and Promotions	2,250	1,200	1,550	2,000	1,550	1,200	9,750
Bank Service Charges	125	125	130	135	118	137	770
Credit Card Fees	79	85	95	74	95	95	523
Shipping and Delivery	225	180	200	115	117	120	957
Materials for Production	500	700	450	700	500	225	3,075
Business Insurance	125	125	125	125	125	125	750
Health Insurance	350	350	350	350	350	350	2,100
Interest	225	225	225	225	225	225	1,350
Inventory Purchases	750	500	1,000	1,000	750	500	4,500
Miscellaneous			45		72		117
Freelance Labor/Services		250					250
Professional Fees			400			400	800
Percentage of Mortage or Rent	450	450	450	450	450	450	2,700
Subscriptions & Dues	40		25				65
Office and General Supplies	125	21	55	30	28	76	335
Sales Tax Paid	270	305	205	225	275	225	1,505
Other Taxes and Licenses	125		400				525
Utilities & Telephone	132	155	112	113	129	144	785
Other:	65			45			110
							0
							0
Subtotal	$ 5,836	$ 4,671	$ 5,817	$ 5,587	$ 4,784	$ 4,272	$ 30,967
Other Cash Out Flows:							
Capital Purchases	3,400			1,200			4,600
Loan Principal							0
Owner's Draw	1,500	1,500	1,500	1,500	1,500	1,500	9,000
							0
Subtotal	$ 4,900	$ 1,500	$ 1,500	$ 2,700	$ 1,500	$ 1,500	$ 13,600
Total Cash Out Flows	$ 10,736	$ 6,171	$ 7,317	$ 8,287	$ 6,284	$ 5,772	$ 44,567
Ending Cash Balance	$ 8,659	$ 9,448	$ 6,898	$ 3,801	$ 3,837	$ 3,369	

WHY YOU SHOULD CONSIDER PROFESSIONAL HELP

Unless you are one already, you probably don't want to be an accountant or bookkeeper. In addition, you probably don't want to spend your evenings and weekends putting numbers into a computer or paying bills. It's much more fun to talk with customers, make your products, or think of new ideas for your advertising program. Is it in your best interest to spend time doing bookkeeping, accounting, and tax returns when you could be making more sales for the company? Probably not. Instead, you'll probably want to hire an accountant or bookkeeper to maintain your financial records.

There are three areas in the accounting world where you may require help: bookkeeping, tax accounting, and managerial accounting. Bookkeeping involves accurately tracking your money and getting numbers into the right accounts with the proper values. You can hire a bookkeeper to manage your recordkeeping, or you can invest in a computer program to do the same thing. Bookkeepers are not necessarily accountants, although they do help organize your information for use by your accountant.

Tax accounting is a type of accounting concerned with how much money you will have to pay in taxes, allowing you to keep as much of your profits as possible. Tax accountants can help you to minimize your tax bill.

Managerial accountants help you use your financial information to make business decisions. Generally, these accountants are responsible for verifying the bookkeeping records and

financial reporting. If you use a computer program to process your books, you can get the financial reports from the program, but the program won't help you to analyze them. In the beginning, you may not need a managerial accountant. If you understand the implications of your financial reports and can produce the reports on your own, you may never need a managerial CPA. However, most home-based business owners will probably want to consider a tax accountant or bookkeeper.

Bookkeeping is time-consuming, tedious, and relatively inexpensive to turn over to a third party. Tax returns are becoming more and more complex, requiring a significant effort to get the best advantage of legal deductions. An accountant, even the most expensive CPA, will generally pay for themselves by helping you to identify tax advantages for your business. You should ask your accountant if he or she wants do both your bookkeeping and your tax planning. Accountants sometimes throw in free tax-return preparation when they do your bookkeeping, since their software can generate a tax return based on the numbers they've been recording for you.

You may want to act as your own accountant in the early days to save money, but if you're not good with numbers, find someone to handle this for you right away. Otherwise, you may damage the company's financial records and your tax position.

There are a number of easy-to-use accounting packages designed just for small businesses. Some even have modules for home-based business deductions. The programs, such as Quick Books, DacEasy, M.Y.O.B, and others, make the basic bookkeeping process easier. We've provided information for accessing the Web sites for these companies so you can get more information on the packages. Most of them can also produce financial reports based on both cash and accrual accounting. Most small business accounting programs sell for less than $200 and may even include a basic payroll module that calculates how much to deduct from your employees' paychecks.

As your company gets larger and more complex, you'll probably want to employ the services of an accountant, and maybe even a CPA (an accountant with credentials). Here are some suggestions for making it easier and less expensive to work with accounting professionals when you decide to do so:

1. Automate from the beginning. Get a computer and a software package that will track your sales and expenses. Most of these programs will help you set up the chart of accounts, customer records, and other basic information to run the business.

2. Keep your records organized by type and accounting period. File and clearly label everything related to money that has anything to do with your business.

3. If you depreciate your equipment or use the more complex accrual accounting, use an accountant (not necessarily a CPA, but someone who has been certified for tax reporting) to review your tax return the first time you do one (even if you use one of the new, easy-to-use computerized tax preparation programs such as TurboTax or something similar). This will probably pay for itself if you depreciate a lot of equipment.

4. Unless you have only a few transactions each month (common in home-based consulting and service businesses), you should consider getting help with the bookkeeping details. Talk to your accountant because you may get bookkeeping and tax return services as part of an inexpensive package deal. You can also get good bookkeeping services from accounting students at business schools or through local bookkeeping services. You should still file your receipts and invoices in a logical fashion, but you won't have to log them into the forms and ledgers.

5. Consider getting a CPA when you work with external financial companies (such as banks or investors) that will require an independent audit verification. Your bank or other investor will probably need reports prepared by a CPA, including an income statement and a balance sheet for the company. Investors will want to see CPA certified reports based on standard accounting practices. This is why it's a good idea to have your bookkeeping and accounting practices reviewed by an accounting professional from the onset, even if you'll be keeping the books yourself. That way, when you need a CPA certified report, you'll be in a position to provide the appropriate records to get one.

THE BOTTOM LINE

Now that you know about the basic records you need to keep, the taxes you need to pay, and the way to analyze the position of your business with your financial statements, you know all you need to know about keeping the books to run your business from home.

It isn't really hard to do your taxes or keep your books if you keep organized records that are up-to-date. Simply set up your files from day one. That way you'll be ready for the true fun of running your home-based office—counting the money you make.

9

Working with Banks, Investors, Credit Cards, and Other Financial Institutions

In this chapter, you'll learn what banks and investors look for in a business relationship, and you'll get hints on securing credit card services for selling retail goods directly to your customers.

Whether you're asking for approval to accept credit cards or requesting a loan, be aware that your bank will probably look harder and longer at a request from a home-based business. But if the numbers are good (and your credit is in reasonably good shape), you'll have a pretty good chance of getting the approvals, services, and loans you need to get your business venture started (or expanded). If your business proposal looks risky or unsubstantiated based on your experience, consider another way to finance your venture, such as a part-time job, a partner, a loan, or a modified approach to bringing in customers. Don't give up if the banks don't cooperate, just look for alternatives.

From day one, you should establish good banking and financial practices and exhibit sound creditworthiness because someday you may need to ask your bank or another type of investor for money. The only way to do that is to have a documented history to show your credit potential. Bankers are important to you, even if you don't need to borrow money. You'll have to work with a bank for your business checking account, payroll tax deposits (if you have employees), credit card processing, and other administrative tasks. Thus, take some time to absorb the information in this chapter so you make the best banking selection to help support your business activities.

YOUR BUSINESS CHECKING AND SAVINGS ACCOUNTS

Before you choose the bank for your basic business accounts, be aware that some banks are easier to work with than others. Some banks cater to small businesses by offering special accounts, rates, and support services. Before you simply go to the same bank that handles your personal accounts, check out the rates for your business account (which will likely be higher than the rates for a personal account). Shop around for services and value.

Although you don't legally need to have a business checking and savings account separate from your personal accounts, we recommend that you separate your business banking activities from your personal financial activities for tax management and organizational and managerial reasons. A separate business account makes it easier to establish your home-based entity as a true business and helps you produce the financial reports you need to analyze the profitability of the business and to secure loans and other types of business credit. If you accept credit cards in payment for your business wares and services, you'll definitely need a separate business checking account; banks and other credit card vendors won't put the credit card monies into a personal checking account.

Unless you have very large sums of money to invest in a savings account at the bank, business checking accounts are generally more expensive than personal checking accounts. You'll find, however, a much larger range of services (usually at a cost) provided to businesses.

For most commercial checking accounts, you'll be charged for the number of transactions and the average account balance. Expect to pay about $.03 to $.05 for each check you deposit. Yes, the bank bills you for giving money to a commercial account. Rates may vary based on the source of the check (local, in-state, out-of-state, or international). You will also be billed for the checks you write from the account. The transaction fees sound expensive, but, if you keep a decent balance in the account, most commercial accounts also pay you interest on the money in your account. This interest helps offset the fees. You really need to shop around for a commercial account and ask questions about minimum balances required, interest rates, per-transaction fees, and other charges to the account.

Make sure the rules and requirements fit your needs. Banks handle commercial accounts in different ways. It's better to ask a lot of questions before you open the account. Making changes to your business account is more involved than changing a personal account, so spend some time looking for the most appropriate arrangement.

When you find a good deal on a commercial bank account, be sure to ask general questions about loans, lines of credit, and credit card processing. Even though you may not need the services now, its a good idea to be aware of the parameters for obtaining additional money. Smaller banks are usually more flexible with the rules regarding loans, but bigger banks usually have deeper pockets for making the loans. As your company grows, you may want to switch from a smaller bank to a larger bank just for this reason. Remember, it takes as much paperwork and documentation to get a $25,000–$50,000 loan as it does to borrow $250,000. The bigger banks would rather get interest on the larger loan if you can qualify for the investment.

DO YOU HAVE ENOUGH MONEY TO GET STARTED?

Even the best idea in the world won't enable you to get a loan from a good bank. As the old joke goes, "The only way you can get a loan is to prove that you don't need one." Thus, from day one, you'll need to establish yourself as a credible businessperson who can handle money with aplomb.

You have to decide for yourself how much money you are willing and able to set aside to start or expand your business. It may be less than $1000, or it may be much more. Every business is different. Be aware that the type or size of business you start may be somewhat limited by the amount of money you have available—and you can't start a business without enough money, no matter how good the idea may seem.

Even if you are able to squeak by the first month or two, you may be jeopardizing your future by not having enough money to fall back on during the initial phases of the business. If you can't come up with the cash on your own, try getting some financing from a bank or other institution.

Once you've received a loan to get your company started, it will be tougher to go back to your investors and ask for just a little more to keep you going. Make sure you can cover your living expenses for several months (at least six to twelve), and give yourself some

room for making things happen. Sometimes, good ideas just take a bit longer than you anticipate to get going.

If you need money to get started, you have a number of choices for outside investments. You may choose an unsecured line of credit, which is really a personal loan to the officers of the company (that means you and your partners, if you incorporate your home-based business) that is then invested in your company. The loan conditions (interest rates and repayment terms to the bank) should be similar to those you'd find on any normal business transaction. To get such a loan from the bank before you get started, you'll have to have great personal credit, a good history of loan repayment, and usually some other type of ancillary income for collateral. A secured line of credit is the next best option for financing your business. In this case, the bank or other investor will loan your company money but will secure your loan with some sort of asset (often your home, a savings account, or the equipment and inventory in your business). If you can't repay the loan, the assets are sold to recover the investment.

You can also use your (documented) receivables or inventory as collateral for short-term loans. This type of loan is really a secured line of credit. Typically, a bank will only loan up to 80 percent of the value of your receivables or other assets each month. If your receivables or other assets are declining, you may have to come up with some quick cash to pay down the loan. If you haven't planned for this payment, you could quickly be in financial trouble.

Another option is to sell stock in your company. This is called equity funding. Usually, you'll want to sell stock in your company after you have demonstrated success in the business venture, but, with a good business plan, you can sometimes sell stock to private investors or venture capitalists. The downside in this type of investment is that you're selling part of the company to other people, and you'll have to get these people involved in some way with the company—in annual meetings and through communications with the other investors. Sometimes these investors will want a place on your Board of Directors or will want to examine your business operations. This can be a good thing if your investors are sophisticated businesspeople. However, most professional investors tend to be demanding and relatively heartless when your business doesn't perform as promised.

For most home-based businesses, we advise to steer away from the equity type of financing unless you intend to grow your business into a major corporation at a very fast rate. Securing private capital for equity financing and working with outside investors is often more work than running the business. Unless you like working with these investment types, wait until you have a business that's ready for selling on the open stock market for large amounts of money.

Perhaps you have a rich relative or friend who doesn't mind lending you the money. In some cases, you can sell these investors equity in the company without operational control. It's more likely that you'll get a loan from these folks, although most of us don't do too well in finding relatives with extra money to invest in new business ventures. We suggest formalizing the loan or other investment terms in a contract, with interest rates and repay-

ment agreements listed, so your good friend doesn't become a fast enemy. Find a lawyer to help you draw up the papers.

GOING TO THE SMALL BUSINESS ADMINISTRATION (SBA) FOR HELP

When nobody else will help, the Small Business Administration (SBA) may be able to provide assistance. There is now a simple two-page application, as part of the LowDoc loan program, if you need less than $100,000 to get your business started. Be aware, however, that you can only get an SBA guarantee for a business loan when three banks have rejected your requests for traditional financing. If you are approved for an SBA loan guarantee, the SBA does not provide the money; the money is provided by a bank. The SBA simply guarantees that some percentage of the loan will be repaid. This guarantee makes the loan much more attractive to the bank.

You don't necessarily need an SBA approval to get a loan from the bank, but if you fill out the SBA forms at the time you apply for a loan, and, if you don't quite meet the bank's standards for loan approval, the bank can go to the SBA for a loan guarantee.

There are several different types of SBA loans, and they change on a regular basis. Check out the SBA site on the World Wide Web if you want more current information on working with the SBA. The SBA can also provide help in developing your business plan or a marketing strategy, and they offer other operational support. We've provided the links to the SBA in the banking and services section on the CD-ROM.

BE HONEST WITH YOURSELF AND YOUR INVESTORS

If you plan to show your business plan to potential investors (banks, private institutions, or personal investors) before you start your business, be sure to include the assumptions you made when writing the plan—potential risks and rewards and important milestones—to ensure the investor understands the whole picture. Making your situation appear too rosy will make investors skeptical, while making your plan seem too risky may scare them off. By simply being honest about what you see as the strengths and weaknesses of your situation, you allow investors to make up their own minds based on the information you have.

Being up front with yourself (and potential investors) will help you avoid problems down the road if things don't go as planned. Given the right opportunity, you can lead professional investors into a minefield, as long as you first tell them that there is a minefield in the way. Investors bring resources to the table that can keep you from getting into big trouble if and when it arises. However, if they feel you have misrepresented your company, you may seriously damage your working relationship (and your source of future financial assistance).

Investors frequently look at situations in terms of opportunity cost. Bankers and other investors consider the other investment opportunities they are giving up by investing their money in your company. If the return from your business idea is lower than their next-best option, then they will probably not give you the money for your business idea.

THE FIVE C'S FOR GETTING A LOAN

Banks and other investors will evaluate you on the Five C's of lending: character, capacity or cash flow, collateral, condition of the business, and capital (the equity of the company). Make sure your C's are in good order before you ask for money.

To establish your character, you'll need to demonstrate your expertise and confidence to run the business. You do this through your initial meetings with the bank and through your résumé, which you attach to your company's business plan. For the capacity or cash flow of your business, you'll have to document, through financial statements and other documentation, that you can repay the debt. For collateral, you'll need to establish the value of any equity you have to support your business loans (such as inventory, property, or receivables). Make it clear that you don't intend to default but that the bank is covered in any case.

To document the condition of your business in terms of economic potential and to establish the capital requirements associated with your business, you'll need to document the potential of the business through financial projections. Remember, loans come down to the numbers. You need to prove the company's value to your lender, or you won't get the money.

Here are some additional steps to help you ensure your best chance of getting the money you need for your business:

1. Create a track record of your business acumen in advance of your lending request. Keep your personal and business finances

in healthy shape. If your credit is in bad shape to start with, work on improving your reliability. Use credit carefully, and put diligent effort into paying your bills on time.

2. Keep detailed and accurate records of your company's business transactions and be able to answer questions about your financial situation on a moment's notice.

3. Develop good business references through honest relationships with your customers and vendors.

CREDIT CARDS AND APPROVAL

Credit cards are fast becoming a preferred type of legal tender. If you sell retail goods, especially if you choose to sell products on line or through the mail, you should consider giving your customers the option to pay using a credit card instead of by cash or check. Most retail businesses, whether at home or contained in a traditional store, must offer credit cards as a payment option, or the business will lose sales—probably lots of them.

In the ideal world, at least from the home-based business owner's perspective, all customer transactions would be paid up front and in cash. But most businesses are forced to accept one or more of the three major types of credit: credit cards, checks, and credit terms. Credit cards are the least risky, but they will cost you a percentage of your sales.

From the business owner's standpoint, the advantage to accepting credit cards is that your bank account will be credited with the amount of the sale by the end of the business day. The credit card company bears the responsibilities of billing and collection from customers and the risk that the customer will pay later or not at all.

Accepting Credit Cards

If you want to accept credit cards, the first step is to open a credit card merchant account with a bank. If you have an established business reputation or a long-standing relationship with your banker, you probably won't have any trouble opening up an account. If, however, you're just starting out, you have a mail-order business, or you work out of your home, you may have some trouble getting a merchant credit card account. The reason is that banks and credit card companies are scared to death of fraud, so they've become much more cautious about opening new accounts in recent years. In fact, some banks won't even deal with you unless you have a storefront business.

If you operate a home or mail-order business, your best bet may be to start with a medium- or small-sized bank. If possible, find out from other home or mail-order businesses where they have their merchant accounts. When you go to your bank to open a merchant credit card account, you'll need to make a full financial disclosure in the same way that you would if you were asking for a loan from the bank. The likelihood of obtaining a merchant account for the acceptance of credit cards from a bank will depend upon the following factors:

- **The type of business.** Certain types of businesses are considered higher credit risks than others. In general, a home business will have a more difficult time opening a merchant account than will a company with a traditional storefront. No, it doesn't seem fair, but it's still the way things work.

- **The length of time in business.** If you're just starting out, you'll have more difficulty opening a merchant account than will an established business.

- **Your general credit history.** As a home-based business, the bank will want to look at your personal credit history as well as your business history. Your bank will want to know whether you've ever declared bankruptcy or if you have any judgments or liens against you. If your credit is shaky, your chances of getting a merchant credit card account are not good.

- **Any previous merchant account experience.** Your bank will want to know if you've ever before had a merchant account because it's a good way to assess your overall creditworthiness.

You should be prepared to submit all the financial information you can gather about your business as well as information about your personal credit history. Also include the information normally found in your business plan, such as information about how your business is financed, how it is organized, and how you plan to run it.

Take this opportunity to request a credit report on yourself. You can obtain one by contacting a credit bureau, such as TRW or Dun & Bradstreet. If anything on the report is wrong, notify the credit reporting company in writing, and keep following up until the information is corrected. It's important that your report be accurate for all your dealings with banks and investors.

Using an ISO for Credit Card Acceptance

If your bank won't let you open a merchant account, consider using an Independent Service Organization (ISO). You can contract with an ISO to open a merchant account, and the ISO will contract with the bank. The ISO, in effect, bears the risk of doing business with you.

Before you sign up with an ISO, be careful. Although there are more than 1,400 ISOs in the U.S., they are not regulated. Make sure that you understand all the extra charges before you enter into an ISO agreement. Sometimes you can be charged too much for the terminals and other supplies that the ISO provides you, and there may be other hidden charges.

Internet Accounts to Accept Credit Cards

Some banks will now let you open a special type of merchant credit card account for accepting Internet transactions. Believe if or not, in some cases, the Internet transaction processing fees are lower than those of traditional credit card transactions. If you're interested, talk to your local banker, or search on the Web for "merchant credit card accounts" and take a look at some of the offerings. Once again, be careful. Make sure that you understand all of the risks and the costs involved before you sign on the dotted line. There is more information on merchant accounts on the CD-ROM.

When NOT to Accept Credit Cards

If you'll be selling expensive advisory services that cost many thousands of dollars, a credit card probably isn't the best way to be paid. You should request a credit application from new clients and be paid by check. When we work with small companies, we often request an advance on our services to cover our costs. This practice is common with many consulting firms and agencies, so don't be afraid to charge for your services in advance if you haven't worked with the company before (or even if you have).

The Cost of Accepting Credit Cards

The main problem with accepting credit cards is the cost to use the service. If you'll be using electronic transaction processing (which is truly the only way to go unless you only do a few large transactions each month), you'll have to pay for the machine used to process the cards. This small transaction processing machine is often owned by a bank or one of their sales representatives, who acts as a liaison between your company and the credit card network.

The credit card processing company will typically charge you an application fee ($65–$100) and a programming/installation fee ($35–$550) to enable you to use their machine. For these fees, you'll be able to accept payments by VISA, MasterCard, and probably Diner's Club and Carte Blanche but not payments by American Express or Discover Card (which have their own application procedures).

American Express has its own processing network called the Electronic Draft Capture (EDC) network. If you want help with setting up an account to accept American Express cards, call 800-847-8848 for information on their EDC processing and setup procedures. Once American Express receives and completes your request for American Express credit card transactions, you'll need to contact your terminal provider (the folks who are renting you the credit card processing machine, such as CNET or FirstNet) and make sure that they program your machine to process American Express transactions.

American Express will charge you a fee for the privilege of being set up on their network, usually $65–$100. They will also send you a box full of supplies that include an imprinting machine and the sales receipts.

The Discover Card also has its own network and requires actions similar to those employed by American Express. Call Discover Card at 800-347-2000 to start the process and get the electronic terminal to read and process Discover Cards transactions.

Do You Need A Credit Terminal?

If you'll be handling a large number of credit transactions, you may consider buying your own credit terminal. Before you do, try renting a terminal for a few months and see how it goes. If your volumes are high, consider buying a terminal. If your volume is very low, consider going to a hand-approved system that eliminates the cost of the terminal.

After paying the monthly fee for your electronic terminal (around $25 to $40), which is deducted from your bank account by the service company, you'll also need to pay a monthly service fee (about $5–$10 at this writing) for the reporting of your account activity during the month.

Beyond the basic operational charges, the credit card company will charge your company a percentage of the transaction amount for each purchase. This transaction amount is compensation for guaranteeing the charge. The amount you have to pay will vary between service providers, credit card companies, the type of transaction involved, the size and frequency of the transaction, and whether the transaction is processed electronically or manually (using a paper system).

For example, VISA typically charges between 2 percent and 3 percent of the sale and $.20 per deposit. American Express, on the other hand, charges about 4 percent to 5 percent of the transaction, with various deposit charges (depending on the size of the transaction and your sales volume). In some cases, these fees are negotiable among the banks, so make sure you find the best rate possible.

How Credit Cards Work

Here is what you get for your fees and how the process works when you have an electronic terminal to verify your credit card transactions and charges:

1. You run the card through the credit card machine (called swiping the card). The terminal reads the card number and card type off the black magnetic strip on the back of the card.

2. The credit card terminal requests the transaction amount and expiration date of the card. When requested, you type in both and tell the machine to process the transaction.

3. The terminal dials the phone number to the card processing company and sends the information to the computer, which then confirms whether the card is in good standing.

4. If everything is okay, the computer responds with an approval code that you write on the sales receipt. (Never forget to do this.)

5. The credit card processing company then deducts the proper percentage from the purchase amount and deposits the rest in your business checking account. You essentially get the money immediately.

6. Most banks charge businesses a transaction fee for each deposit you make, so you'll also be charged for credit card deposits.

7. Every month, the processing company sends you a summary statement that outlines all transaction dates, sales amounts, credits applied (product returns), discount rates applied, and net deposits. This statement is handy for reconciling your bank deposits, invoices, and receivables when you have customers paying by different methods.

Protecting Your Credit Card Charges

Sometimes things go wrong with credit card processing. What happens if your customer later contests the charge and refuses to pay? Or what if the person using the card isn't supposed to be using it? You could be stuck with a bad debt. Here are a few things you can do to minimize the chance of losing money on your credit transactions:

1. Always verify the expiration date on the card. Make sure that the date is embossed on the card, not printed.

2. Check for the hologram or other security symbol on the card. These emblems are difficult to duplicate. If you can't find one, you may be holding a forged card.

3. Disclose the terms of the sale in advance. Make sure terms and conditions are easily spelled out on the receipt.

4. Get a signature on the receipt whenever possible, although this is more difficult with e-mail and telephone transactions.

5. Run the card through an imprint machine when possible. Make sure your receipt is legible and complete, with all pertinent information included. Make sure the date of sale, the receipt number, and the amounts are correct when you fill out the form.

6. Get an authorization number for each transaction. Run the card, amount, and expiration date through your electronic terminal to receive the approval code. Always write the authorization number on the sales receipt before you have the customer sign for the goods.

If you plan to take orders via the telephone or over the Internet without seeing the person and getting a signature, you can still take a few steps to better protect yourself. Since the chances of getting burned over the phone or by mail are much higher than in person, the credit card company or bank will probably charge you a higher fee for this type of business transaction. When processing a telephone or e-mail transaction:

1. Get all credit card information and repeat all numbers, dates, and names.

2. Verify that the person making the purchase is the person to whom the card was issued. Get some other form of identification if possible, such as a driver's license number or social security number.

3. Always get an authorization number and write it on the sales receipt.

4. Verify the person's billing and shipping addresses and phone number before he or she hangs up or otherwise completes the online sales transaction.

5. Don't ship your wares until you verify the account.

If you are processing a credit card sale by phone, if at all possible, fax or e-mail the customer a copy of the invoice, including all credit card information, to assure that the person agrees with your prices and delivery terms.

Contested Credit Charges

Even if you have a credit card payment approved, you can still run into problems. Credit card fraud is common, and certain people will take advantage of situations if presented with the chance. New customers or those you will never see again can leave you with a contested charge that can cost you money.

Taking the steps outlined here may seem like a hassle, but you will have a good chance of getting your money from the credit card company should the charge ever be disputed by the customer. If the customer signed the sales draft, saw the terms and conditions, and clearly knew what was being purchased and for what amount, you have an excellent case in your favor. The more written documentation you have of the transaction, the better chance you have of keeping the money.

Caution and standard procedures are the solutions to avoiding credit card fraud. Define credit terms and stick with them. Always check the expiration dates on the card. Always get some other form of identification. Be persistent, careful, and complete in your credit transactions. In this way, you'll rarely lose money if you accept credit cards.

THE BOTTOM LINE WITH BANKS

As your business grows, remember that your own personal creditworthiness and financial management skills are your best attributes when working with banks and investors. Regardless of your immediate banking needs, as a home-based business owner, you'll certainly need the assistance of a bank at some point. In fact, the more money you make, the more likely you'll need a bank and other investment firms to help you manage your money. Therefore, take the time to secure good relationships with your banking officers and other investors. It's time well spent in the long run.

PART

3

YOUR WORK ZONE—CHOOSING FURNITURE AND TECHNOLOGY

CHAPTER

10

SETTING UP YOUR WORK SPACE

Now that you have decided to open a home-based business, with financial guidelines and business plan in hand, the challenge is to create a comfortable office in your home so you can get to work. The focus of this chapter is to identify the furniture, supplies, and office space you need to run your business efficiently. This is not as easy as it sounds, unless, of course, you have a home with large areas of unused space and lots of extra money to get started. This chapter provides help in putting together a productive space in your home, even with limited resources.

Most home-based business owners lack the luxury of unlimited space and endless financial resources. It is a challenge for most of us to separate our working areas from our living areas. In many home offices, these areas overlap, but, if you take the time to contemplate questions on furniture and room environments, and play with work flow, you will have the basis for setting up a comfortable, professional-looking office without sacrificing the entire house or your lifestyle. Some checklists on the CD-ROM will help you with this.

Very few office workers (except CEOs and other VIPs) have the absolute perfect office space. Don't expect perfection just because you're now working at home. Space is usually limited, and each furniture and equipment option needs to be examined carefully. Is there enough space to work in a bedroom, den, attic, or basement, or will you have to partition a corner of the family living space? What furniture and supplies are needed? How should the office be arranged for maximum efficiency? The answers to these questions will require a tape measure, a pair of scissors, some time, and a little imagination.

HOW MUCH WORK SPACE DO YOU NEED?

One of the primary considerations in opening a home-based company is the size of the space you need to accommodate your business operations. Before you can determine the size, you need to decide which physical things will go into the office, such as a desk, chairs, file cabinets, storage areas, equipment, a conference table, and a display area. You also want a large enough free area that you can at least stand up and turn around. You should have an idea of the supplies you will use, since everything needed to run the business should have a work and/or storage space.

What type of work you perform will determine the type of furniture and supplies you consider. A writer may need a desk and chair, a computer or typewriter, paper supplies, pens and pencils, and perhaps a filing cabinet, fax, and copy machine. On the other hand, an artist may need a worktable instead of a desk, a stool instead of a chair, a customized filing cabinet, glue, tape, a paper cutter, scissors, and colored pens.

Take the time now to decide exactly what equipment and supplies you think you need, and fill out the Home Office Supply Checklist on the CD-ROM. With this checklist, you can calculate the amount of work space you need, and the checklist can then be used as a shopping list. This will save valuable working time, and you will not be running back and forth to the store when something is missing. Space has been left at the bottom of the checklist so you can customize the office supplies for your business.

Once you know exactly what furniture you want, take the tape measure and start measuring furniture sizes and work surfaces. The size of the space your business needs will be determined by the area taken up by furniture, equipment, storage, the clear work space needed, and you. If there is a choice of areas in your home, this exercise will help determine where the center of operations will be located. If there is no choice, the exercise will indicate if your office plans are feasible, and offer suggestions on how things might be rearranged.

It may not be critical to have all of your supplies, such as a name plate or artwork, before you open for business. Add the "nice but not necessary" items to your supply wish list. The wish list items can be obtained later, as time and money permit. It is also a handy reference list if anyone asks what you need at the store.

The information provided about the physical items to be placed in your home office includes things to consider when selecting your furniture, such as writing surfaces and adjustability. This will give you a reference point when selecting new pieces. (Don't forget your tape measure if you are going shopping!) It will also explain why that old desk and rickety dining room chair may not be the correct choice for your new business.

OFFICE FURNITURE

One of the first things to determine when picking out a desk or table is whether or not you will be entertaining clients in your home office. An old desk or table may work just fine if it is comfortable and no one will see it, but it may be necessary to consider refinishing it or buying something more up-to-date if clients are coming in and out.

Next, decide what is more appropriate for you—a desk or a worktable. A desk gives you the advantage of having file and box drawers within reach. A worktable is advantageous when a large, clear work area is needed to spread things out. It is very common to place a worktable behind the desk. The worktable can be accessed by just turning around the chair. Depending on how much work surface is needed and the size of the space, you may need both.

Desks

Desks come in all shapes and sizes. Not all of them may be right for you. The smallest desk you should consider is 60 inches wide by 30 inches deep. Even though this size desk is used by most businesses for clerical positions, it is considered small. If space is available, consider using a 66-inch- to 72-inch-wide by 36-inch-deep desk. This size is normally given to business officers and managers because there is adequate free work space plus room for the normal desk accessories.

Using your tape measure, determine how high the writing surface of the desk is from the ground. Many desks have a writing height of 30 inches. Some come with an extra work surface at a typing height of 26 or 27 inches for a typewriter or computer. The recent trend is to manufacture desks with a writing height of 28 inches, which is the new standard height for both writing and typing surfaces. Typing for any length of time on a surface higher than 28 inches can be uncomfortable for your wrists, back, and neck.

Whether you use a desk or a worktable, a 30-inch-deep surface is minimum. This is especially true if you are putting the computer and keyboard on the work surface and want the keyboard in front of the CPU. If the keyboard is on a pullout drawer below the work surface, you can get by with a 24-inch-deep work surface, but it will be rather shallow.

If there is no choice but to install a computer on a writing surface higher than 28 inches, a pullout keyboard drawer can be installed to the underside of the writing surface. This will lower the keyboard to typing height. You may want to put the CPU unit sideways on the floor under the desk and place just the monitor on the corner of the desktop. This allows a major portion of the desktop to be kept free for other things.

In choosing an office desk, don't overlook the finish that is used. A dark finish, such as black walnut, may cause too much contrast with white paper, and it is just as difficult to read a white piece of paper sitting on a white finish. If you're buying a new desk, the available finishes are not limited to wood. Desks are also available in metal, and desktops are available in a variety of plastic laminate colors on both wood and metal desks.

Most desks have a box and file drawer on one side and two or three box drawers on the other side. Some desk manufacturers offer several drawer options. Determine what you want to keep in the desk drawers and select the option that works best for you.

Worktable

If a worktable is needed, you can use something as simple as a flat plank of wood over stacked concrete blocks or construction saw horses. If you're looking for something more elegant, a large piece of glass over wooden crates might be more to your taste, but this type of table must be able to hold the weight of whatever project you are working on, in addition to your equipment. If a computer or typewriter will be sitting on this table, you might have to go to a more conventional work table.

Like the desk, when you select the worktable, make certain it is big enough for its intended use, (including any equipment you want to put on it) by using your trusty measuring tape. Also measure how high the writing surface is from the ground. Anything higher than 28 inches can be uncomfortable with this piece, too.

If your business involves drafting, the work surface should be adjustable and much higher, probably 36 inches. With this type of table, another work surface will definitely be needed if you also use a computer or typewriter.

Conference Table

It is perfectly acceptable to conduct business with your clients using your desk and several customer chairs. In less than ideal circumstances, you may have to use your dining room table, your kitchen table, or the living room. If at some point only a conference table will do, decide on the table shape that works the best—round, square, oval, or oblong. That choice may be determined more by the space available than by your preference.

When measuring a conference table, don't forget to include the area that the chairs occupy, usually another 3 to 4 feet. This allows room for the chair to be pulled out and sat on and for someone to then walk around the occupied chair. You do not want to ask a client if they would mind getting up for a moment so you can get around them.

If nothing works out satisfactorily, you may have to make a point of only seeing clients at their place of business.

Display Area

Businesses involving such things as artwork, brochures, or crafts may need a display area. This could be a glass case, a large portfolio, or a display rack, depending on the product. The questions you need to ask yourself are:

- How is the finished product best displayed?
- Does the display area/case need to be in the office, or is there another display area that would be more appropriate?

If you find that you can't fit another thing into your home office, your options are to use another room in your home or to carry the finished product to your client.

The furniture checklist on the CD-ROM will help you determine the types of furniture you'll need in your home office.

Your Office Chair

Whether in a crowded office or your own home-based business, the desk chair is one of the most crucial elements to consider. Without the proper comfort and support from a chair, you'll find yourself squirming and wiggling in an effort to get comfortable. A poor choice of chair will reduce your work output.

When most work was done on typewriters, typists constantly changed positions in the chair—to change paper, go to the filing cabinet, make copies, etc. Now, with personal computers, almost everything is done in one location. We usually don't change our position unless it's to slump over when we get tired. Because of this, there are more back, neck, and shoulder problems than ever before. This also puts more importance on chair design.

When picking out your chair, there is more to be concerned about than just its color. The chair must be designed properly, with the correct ergonomics. Ergonomics is the study of all physical and psychological variables contributing to a person's comfort and ability to carry out a task easily, effectively, safely, and efficiently. Chairs designed ergonomically reduce operator fatigue and discomfort. They provide proper body support and are designed to fit the job.

When choosing a chair, there are several important factors to consider, including the seat, height adjustment, backrest, armrests, and materials used to construct the chair.

The Chair Seat

When sitting, 65 percent of the body's weight falls on the chair seat. If the seat is too narrow, the heavy pressure can constrict the flow of blood from the buttocks to the knee region beneath the thigh. The seat should end 5 inches behind the bend of the knee when your back is against the backrest. If the seat is too long, you will find yourself leaning forward when working.

Because your back is not straight when you lean forward, added pressure is put on your lower back and thighs.

If you're using an older chair, chances are it doesn't have a knee-tilt feature. This mechanism allows the body to be supported while you are leaning forward or backward and reduces the effort required for reclining and returning to an upright position.

The knee-tilt mechanism is designed to have a 3:1 ratio; for every 3 degrees that you recline, your legs raise only 1 degree. This eliminates the tendency, found in nonergonomic chairs, for the legs to be raised off the floor by the seat. When the legs are raised, pressure is put on the thighs as you lean back and cuts off blood circulation to the legs.

Many high-quality ergonomic chairs offer a floating seat pan or seat-tilt mechanism as an option. This is an important item for keyboard-intensive jobs. The seat pan allows you to tilt forward so you can sit upright and get close to the computer or typewriter. To provide proper support when using a seat-tilt mechanism, make sure the backrest is also able to come forward. As the body leans forward, the backrest moves with it, giving the back support.

The front of the seat edge should be rounded. This is called a waterfall edge. This type of edge does not restrict the blood circulation to the legs as does a square-edged front. The seat should also have a firm but giving seat cushion.

Height Adjustment

Most quality office chairs have an adjustable height feature. These adjustments are either static (made by adjusting a screw when the

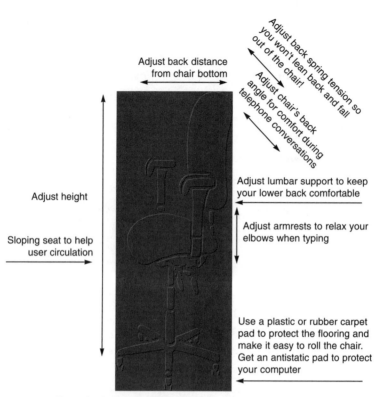

Adjust back distance from chair bottom

Adjust back spring tension so you won't lean back and fall out of the chair!

Adjust chair's back angle for comfort during telephone conversations

Adjust height

Adjust lumbar support to keep your lower back comfortable

Sloping seat to help user circulation

Adjust armrests to relax your elbows when typing

Use a plastic or rubber carpet pad to protect the flooring and make it easy to roll the chair. Get an antistatic pad to protect your computer

Good chairs adjust to your body and physical working requirements.

chair is held upside down) or hydraulic. Hydraulic is preferred. A hydraulic height mechanism allows you to make adjustments while seated. Hydraulic mechanisms also provide a cushion when you first sit on the chair, protecting the tail bone from undue shock.

When adjusting the height of your chair, the seat's highest point should be 2 inches below the crease behind the knee when you are standing. This will support a knee angle of 90 degrees, which will help prevent leg swelling.

Your Backrest

Back support is critical. In an erect sitting posture, the muscles work harder to maintain a natural inward lumbar curve and must overcome the added pull of the now-sloping pelvis. All this work leads to muscle fatigue, which causes slouching. While slouching results in less work for the muscles, it places more strain on the ligaments and causes back and leg pain and bad posture. A properly contoured backrest can eliminate this problem. The backrest should have an inward-leaning lumbar support.

Different tasks require different back supports. The backrest should be from 14 to 21 inches high and should slope back from 5 to 15 degrees. It should also adjust to meet the lumbar curve in your back.

You may prefer an office chair with a straight back if your job is not keyboard intensive. If the chair does not allow the back to recline independently or have a knee-tilt mechanism, your legs will lift off the floor when reclining, which can reduce blood circulation. Look for a chair with the pivot point behind the knees (knee-tilt mechanism) rather than centered under the seat pan. This allows the feet to remain on the floor and eliminates the pressure under the thighs.

Most home-based businesspeople are multitask workers. Multitask means that you perform several functions from the chair, such as writing, typing, and phoning. If this is the case, you need a backrest that reclines, locks in several positions, and has adjustable tension. This way, the chair can be adjusted in the most comfortable position for each task you perform.

For jobs that are keyboard intensive, look for a backrest design that conforms tightly to the small of the back. When the back is supported in this manner, you will have less back, shoulder, and neck pain after a day of intensive typing. Better-designed chairs also have a lumbar support that adjusts up and down.

If you are at a drafting table, use a stool that has a backrest. Several of the better chair manufacturers make a stool version of their standard desk chairs. Several of the stools on the market today also have hydraulic height adjustment.

Armrests

Many jobs today, especially in home-based businesses, are keyboard intensive. As a result, there has been a sharp increase in wrist injuries relating to carpal tunnel syndrome. This is an irritation of the tendon sheaths, which is caused by flexing the wrist in a way that does not allow the user's hands to be in line with the wrists. If the fingers are significantly higher or lower than the wrists, the tendon sheaths can become irritated, leading to a painful swelling in the wrists and hands. Armrests can help prevent this condition by keeping the wrists and hands at the same level. If you are considering a new chair, look for armrests that can be adjusted or armrests that are at the correct level when you are typing.

You must also determine whether or not the armrests will interfere with your desk. If they are too high or too wide, the armrests will bang into the desk every time you move the chair. Not only will you end up pinching your hand or arm between the desk and chair, you will also wear out the armrests very quickly.

Chair Materials

The materials used in your chair are very important in providing comfort and support. The seat pan and backrest must provide firm support and still be comfortable. Today's technology uses multidensity foams that are laminated together. This provides the needed body support while allowing you to sit on a firm but softer surface. This type of construction is found in today's better-quality chairs.

The choice of fabric is also important to your comfort in the chair. Porous materials, such as wool or rayon, allow body heat to dissipate, while a nonporous material, such as vinyl, traps body heat and causes perspiration. The correct fabric also allows you to lean forward without slipping off your chair. Seat belts are not an option.

The Chair Base

Another part of the chair you might want to consider is the base. Most chair manufacturers have switched from a four-star base to a five-star base. The star base refers to the shape and number of legs on the chair base. A four-star base is perfectly fine, but the five-star base gives you more stability.

Most of the chair bases today have casters that are available in different configurations and materials, depending on the floor surface. A chair rolls across the floor better with the right casters. Most chairs today come with dual casters—two wheels on each leg. Dual casters roll easier, are smaller, and offer more stability than do single casters. The caster material is also important. As a rule of thumb, a hard rubber caster is used on hard floor surfaces to provide grip. Hard plastic casters are used on carpet, where you need less rolling resistance. Talk to a chair dealer about the type of floor you have to determine the correct casters for your chair.

When we were children, our parents usually scolded us when we turned around and around in a swivel chair. While we don't advocate turning in circles all day, your chair should swivel. While it's the seat that actually swivels, the mechanism is located in the chair base. This movement gives you maneuverability at the desk. The swaying movement can also induce creative moments when you have run out of ideas.

Used Furniture

Cost can be the largest factor in determining whether you buy a new chair or a used one. You should never scrimp on your chair, because you will spend a lot of time in it, especially if your home-based business involves a lot of work at the desk and computer. With your increased work output, a chair tailored to your individual tasks will pay for itself in a relatively short time. Visit several local office furniture stores and look at all the brands and price ranges of chairs available. Compare adjustability, materials, and quality before making any decisions. Ultimately, the decision should be based on comfort and durability. There are high-priced, supposedly ergonomically designed chairs that are extremely uncomfortable. There are also are quality, low-priced copies of ergonomically designed chairs that are extremely comfortable.

We have talked about many kinds of adjustments that can made to the chair, such as seat pan, backrest, and knee tilt. Be open-minded about the adjustability of the newer chairs, but don't pay for all the bells and whistles if you are not going to use them. The more adjustments a chair makes, the better it will fit your body. Whether you are using an existing chair or buying a new one, learn about all the adjustments and use them. The best chair in the world will be of little value unless you are comfortable. Whatever you decision is, make sure the chair fits your needs and provides comfort and support.

Guest Seating

Not all home-based businesses will require seating for visitors, but a surprisingly large number of home-based businesses do need seating for customers, vendors, and/or work partners. Seating for visitors in your office is not as critical as your desk chair. Even your dining room chairs can fill in for a short time when discussing business in the office.

When purchasing new guest chairs, it is not necessary that they recline, swivel, roll on the carpet, or have padded seats. Armrests, however, do provide a degree of comfort. Client seating does not have to be elaborate or expensive, just tasteful and functional. If space is tight but you still want to conduct meetings in the office, customer seating can be stored in another room when not in use.

If you will be purchasing a conference table, look for matching chairs. The dining room chairs can still be used, but if you put a few of them around a conference table, the office might begin to look like the dining room annex. Again, conference chairs don't have to be elaborate. The no-nonsense customer chairs we just talked about are appropriate in most cases. Before making that decision, however, calculate how much time you and your clients will be spending at the conference table. If long meetings will be the norm, consider conference chairs that recline, swivel, and have castors. Comfortable customers are happy customers.

File Cabinets

Every business has a different need for filing cabinet space. The questions to consider when determining space requirements are: is your work file intensive, what papers do you need to keep and for how long, and what type of filing cabinet will it require?

When looking for filing space, consider the drawers available in your desk. Are the drawers available to accommodate some files? Can the drawers hold the folders your business requires? Can the files be pulled in and out of the drawers without ripping and tearing? If the answer is yes, you may not need to worry about a filing cabinet right away. If this is the case, continue on with this section anyway, especially if a filing cabinet will be purchased in the future. With the needed space already calculated and the File Cabinet Checklist filled out, it will be easy to find exactly what you need.

If the desk is unsuitable for storing files, then it's time to start calculating drawer space and the area needed for the file cabinet. When estimating how much drawer space is needed, keep in mind that the business will probably not start out with 500 files, each 2 inches thick. Also consider how much will be kept on a computer diskette rather than in a file cabinet. If your business is file intensive, closed files or those with information more than a year old can be boxed and stored in another area, freeing up space in the cabinet.

There are two types of filing cabinets, vertical and lateral. Vertical files are usually 30 inches deep and 15 inches wide for letter-sized documents or 18 inches wide for legal-sized documents. This type of cabinet provides 25 inches of filing space per drawer. A vertical file works well when there is limited wall space but adequate space in front of the file cabinet.

Lateral files vary in width from 24 to 48 inches and are 18 inches deep. They work well when there is limited space in front of the file cabinet, but they do require more wall space. Measure the width of the drawer and subtract 2 inches; this is the number of inches of filing space per drawer.

A lateral file allows more flexibility in file arrangement. Legal-sized files can be arranged left to right. If the file cabinet is wide enough, several rows of files can be arranged from front to back by using removable supports. Letter-sized files can also be arranged from front to back by using the supports. A vertical file can only store one row of legal- or letter-sized files from front to back.

If you will be purchasing a file cabinet, look for one with a full-drawer suspension system. If the files are confidential, make sure the cabinet comes with a lock and key. Even though you are in your own office, security can become an issue if clients are in and out or if you don't want the children playing with the file cabinets.

With a full-drawer suspension system, the drawer pulls all the way out, allowing easy access to back files. Many of the less expensive cabinets do not have this feature. Files in the back of full cabinets become very hard to retrieve. It is difficult to read the file names, and you'll find yourself with scraped knuckles trying to pull out the folders.

When the business is first starting out, there may not be enough space in the desk for your files, but only one drawer of a file cabinet will be full. As fast as your business will be growing, that space will be used in no time. For now, use those empty drawers as storage space, keeping in mind that someday soon you will have to find a spot for that storage.

Shelving and Storage Space

During the course of a business day, there are items in use all the time, such as reference books, special tools, or sample inventory. Maybe you need to find a spot for the office supplies that don't fit into the desk. Books can be put in a file drawer or stacked on the floor, but this may not be practical or tidy. If you are at a loss as to where to store things, consider adding shelves or creating storage space in other rooms.

To determine how much shelving or storage space will be needed, go back to the completed Home Office Supplies Checklist. How many supplies and books will you have for the business? Your needs will vary depending on the business. Will there be extra room in your desk or filing cabinet to store all the paper, office supplies, and books you will need? Will they be easily accessible?

If you have some of those supplies and books already on hand, use your handy tape measure and estimate the space you think will be needed. Line up all those books and start measuring. You may be surprised at how much room they can occupy! Also remember that you will continue to purchase materials as the business grows, so allow extra space. Now, where does all this stuff go?

Does the area under consideration for the home office have a closet? The easiest thing would be to convert the existing closet, or at least the shelf in the closet, into office storage space.

Another idea is to use half of the closet and add either an additional small filing cabinet for storage or create a shelving system. If you're not handy enough to build a closet system, check a telephone directory or some home catalogs. Many of the pre-built systems on the market are for clothing storage, but the pull-out drawers, shelves, and spaces can be converted for office use.

No room in the closet, or you just don't need that much extra space? Consider adding wall shelving. An existing wall unit could be used if you have a space large enough. If not, hang additional shelves on the walls themselves. Doors can be added to the shelves to create a cabinet if you need to hide the materials.

Whatever your storage situation, a shelf over the desk is a good idea for the books and/or tools needed in your day-to-day routine. You can save a lot of time and unnecessary rummaging around if everything is neatly placed close at hand.

Additional Space

You've utilized every possible nook and cranny, and there just isn't any more room. This will probably be the case if you keep any type of inventory on hand. The question you need to ask is whether or not the inventory or supplies must be kept in the office area. If there are things not used or referred to every day, there may be space in another room in the house or even in the garage, attic, or basement. Again, take into consideration that your requirements will grow as your business grows. Consider every possibility and measure, measure, measure.

A SPACE ALTERNATIVE

If the available office area is just too small for your work, a modular office system can solve the problem. Modular systems are made up of integrated, engineered components consisting of panels, work surfaces, and file cabinets, which can be mixed and matched in several ways. For instance, a work surface or overhead shelving unit can be hung from a wall or a panel. By taking the very same work surface and adding end panels and a front to it, you now have a desk.

Modular office systems vary in price according to quality and name brand and are used extensively in the business environment. Some of the better-known manufacturers are Steelcase, Herman-Miller, and Haworth. A new middle-of-the-road system for a typical office will range from $2500 to about $4000, depending on the options selected, how the components are used, and how the office is arranged. The end result will be an office that uses less space and offers more flexibility in the arrangement of the furniture. (We've provided links to these manufacturers on the CD-ROM.)

If this seems the answer to your dreams but a nightmare to your checkbook, check around for used systems. You might contact the local representative at one of the companies mentioned above for information on who might be changing or upgrading components.

PUTTING IT ALL TOGETHER

After you've measured work surfaces and calculated the office space requirements, now you'll have to figure out where to put everything. The location of your office in your home is an important decision. Your office should be large enough for your business operations and well lit. It should also be in a room that has adequate potential to accommodate phone lines, electrical outlets, heating and cooling requirements, and general ventilation.

FINDING THE BEST LOCATION IN THE HOUSE

Take a good look around the entire house. If you're lucky, there is a whole spare room (that's bigger than a closet) that lends itself perfectly to serve as a general office space. Most people will choose a spare bedroom to start their businesses, but many find that they must move to the family room or other larger quarters after the business gets going. Some people are lucky to have enough room for a detached office. In less than ideal circumstances, you will be faced with a room in an unfinished basement or attic, actually working in a closet, or partitioning off part of the family living space.

Spend some time in each area of the house you think could serve as the office. There are no right or wrong answers for the best office for your new business. Your answers to the questions in the Home Office Supply Checklist on the CD-ROM will help you find the best location in the house to start your business—that is, if you have any choice. If you don't have a choice, the answers will help you make the best of the situation.

If the area is not large enough to comfortably handle the work space you need, can you get by with less work space? Does every piece of furniture and equipment have to be in place before you open your doors? Start slowly. Everything on the Office Supply Checklist does not have to be purchased at once. Transfer some of the items to the Wish List section of the checklist.

There is a balance you will need to develop to separate your business from your private world at home. You don't want to be cut off from the rest of your life, but you need to separate work from play in order to stay focused on the business. If your children play in the family room next to your office, will you be able to concentrate? On the other hand, can you keep an eye on things, or hear the doorbell if the office is in the attic or basement? Would this situation make you feel totally cut off from the world?

If you have children, you may not have a choice about remaining in touch with the kids. If they are not old enough to take care of themselves, your business hours will not be from 9 to 5. Many older children are able to look after themselves and understand when you need to get work done. Sometimes they will even help.

Whether you have children or not, if the only place the office can be located is in the attic or basement, you don't have to feel cut off. An intercom can be installed at the front door and in any room of the house. The doorbell can also be connected to ring in the office.

If you entertain clients, the possibility exists that people will walk through the entire house to get to the office. They may also need to use restroom facilities. This may influence where you locate the office or if you invite clients into your home. If you don't have the right office space for visitors, you may be forced to do all the traveling between sites.

Before you decide on the office space, consider the future potential of your location. Even if it is more than adequate now, what if the business doubles or triples in size? What if you need to add a full-time or part-time employee? What if you need more and more equipment? Will the space be able to handle it?

Most likely, there is no ideal place to put your office. The answers to the checklist questions should give you a better idea of how good or bad the space really is. What does our ideal home office look like? It's a room as big as a master bedroom suite (with bathroom) that is detached from the home. It has an intercom to the front door, doorbell chimes, and a house phone that rings in the office. There are clearly marked pathways for clients and deliveries and a separate meter for electricity. Ah, to dream!

THE AMBIENT ENVIRONMENT

Hold on, you are not done yet! There is more to consider than just finding a suitable space to put your desk and chair without too many interruptions or a feeling of isolation.

Is the ambient environment suitable to locating your home-based business office in this space? What kind of environment...? The ambient environment is the environment that surrounds you, such as noise, temperature, lighting, and color. Before setting up shop, you need to consider whether these factors are suitable for your office. You wouldn't function effectively in an outside office that didn't have enough light or was too warm. The same principles apply to your home-based business.

Leave the tape measure behind and wander around the office area for awhile. Get a feel for the space at different times of the day, too. Noise levels, the temperature, and light

change throughout the day; you need to understand how these changes may affect working conditions.

Noise Factors to Consider

Everyone reacts differently to noise. One person's noise is another's symphony. Consider how much distraction you may encounter by the everyday noises you will hear from your office. There will always be noise—traffic, children playing, the squeak in your chair when you swivel around. Spend some time sitting in the proposed office to determine what the everyday noises are. If the droning of the television in the next room makes you crazy, consider locating the office someplace other than next to the TV room. If you live on a busy street, traffic, squealing brakes, and horns may distract you from your work every 5 minutes.

Does the office have to be in this space? If you are lucky, there are other options. If not, there are ways to minimize the noise. Panels or partitions may help block out sounds. Heavier window treatments can deflect outside noise. Restricting TV time, or at least the volume, is always an option. Sometimes something as simple as turning on a fan or a radio will calm you down and block out noises.

The noises in your own office can also slow you down. Regularly oil the base of that squeaky chair or door. The bell on the telephone is also adjustable. While you can't cut out noise entirely, nor would you want to, be aware that most sounds can be regulated.

Temperature Control

Temperature is not something we think about as long as we are comfortable. However, if the temperature fluctuates a few degrees, suddenly we can't sit still. It is very difficult to concentrate if you're so warm that sweat is covering your brow or so cold that your fingers are numb.

Where the office is located will affect the temperature. The heat emitted from your dryer or dishwasher will find its way into your office if you are working near these areas. If the office is located on the west side of the house, the room will be warmer in the afternoon when the sun slants through the windows. A computer terminal emits heat equivalent to one person. Each piece of electrical equipment, especially a copy machine, also radiates heat. This could be very uncomfortable during the long, hot summer.

There are several options for cooling down the office area. The first, and easiest, would be to install either an overhead or oscillating fan. This will circulate the air and allow the room to feel cooler by dispersing appliance heat and the extra heat given off by computers. Fans can be turned off and on according to how you feel. They also won't send your electric bill skyrocketing as will cranking up the air conditioning.

While fans will also help lessen the warmth from the sun, it is always better to stop the light rays from coming in at the source—the window. Using heavier window coverings and adjusting them during the day will help keep the temperature regulated. You can also install shade screens on the outside of the affected windows. Keeping the sun from reaching the window is better than having the window treatment absorb the heat directly into the room.

For an office located in an area not centrally cooled, such as an attic, basement, or garage, look into adding a window air conditioner. Don't forget about winter. You may be sweating now, but think about any special heating arrangements that need to be made for the winter months. All that equipment and sun on the windows may not keep you warm enough when the frost is on the pumpkin.

Lighting

The amount of light needed in a room depends on visual preference and the type of work being done. Inadequate lighting can cause headaches and make you see things incorrectly or not at all. When looking at the lighting for the proposed work area, take several things into consideration—your preference for light, what task is being performed, the effects of glare, and computer use.

What is your preference for light—direct natural sunlight, a dark room with bright lighting, or a dark room with subdued lighting? Many people like working in natural sunlight or in a brightly lit room. Bright light tends to keep our spirits up and keep us awake. Unfortunately, too much light can cause glare. Glare occurs when a source of light in the field of vision is brighter than the task materials being used. This can be a major problem in work areas with computers. Computer users need a softer light to cut down on screen glare. Bright lights do not let the eyes quickly refocus when moving from a dark screen with light letters to copy that usually consists of a light background with dark letters. Computer areas work best with an indirect ambient light source. By using a fixture that only directs the light toward the ceiling, ambient lighting is reflected into the room.

When positioning computer equipment, check that direct light from the sun or a lamp doesn't shine over your shoulder. When this happens, you can see everything behind you reflected in your computer screen. Overhead lighting that shines down and reflects off artwork glass on the wall behind you will create the same effect. If you don't use a computer, how you position your desk is still important. The direct light will also cast a glare on the paper you are using at your desk.

Lighting problems are be among the easiest to solve. Adjust the window coverings to the time of day and the amount of natural light shining through. Add task lamps to work surfaces to give additional light as needed. These lamps are usually adjustable and can be positioned to cut any glare. Do not use task lighting at computer monitor areas because of the glare they will cause on the screen. If your major source of light is from the ceiling, add a dimmer switch to make the lighting adjustable.

Dust on light bulbs dims the rays of light emitted from the bulbs. It also makes them burn hotter, which increases the heat in the office. When dusting the office (or the house), give those light bulbs a good swipe.

Color

Color affects how you think, act, and feel. Red may make you feel powerful, while blue soothes and orange makes you furious. We tend to think that colors affect us only in how we dress. Wall coloring also creates moods.

Wall color can make a statement about us and what we do. If no one visits your office, paint the walls in a color or pattern that makes you feel happy and productive. If clients are involved, consider using more subdued tones.

They might get the wrong impression if your profession is a political consultant but your walls are painted fuchsia and covered with cartoon characters. As an artist, the impression created would be very different.

Whatever your occupation, the work area should look professional and comfortable if you are expecting visitors. Does the area need to be repainted or wallpapered? While the color doesn't always have to be white, any light color will make the room look larger, brighter, and more airy. If you can't live without puce in the room, consider an accent wall or a wallpaper trim where the wall meets the ceiling.

OTHER CONSIDERATIONS

While not a direct part of the ambient environment, carpeting, window treatments, and electrical considerations will add to the overall general ambiance of the room, making it much more comfortable and professional.

Carpeting

Carpeting comes in all sizes and colors. It absorbs sound, making a quieter surface to walk on. It is also easier on your feet and legs if your business has you standing for any length of time.

Many homeowners have wall-to-wall carpeting throughout the house. If you are using the attic, basement, or garage, wall-to-wall carpeting is not necessary to convey a professional atmosphere. Area rugs that extend almost to the wall can be used. If the wall-to-wall or area rugs don't match the color in your house, any blatant problems can be minimized with a throw rug in the doorway. These rugs can also be used to brighten up the room. Carpeting or rugs can be any color. As with wall covering, a lighter floor covering will make the area look larger. Be careful with how light the carpeting is, though, because light colors show dirt. Dark carpets hide dirt but show lint.

Many residential carpets have a high pile that mats down after a few months. A definite pattern, where the rug has the most traffic—especially if it isn't vacuumed every day, can be seen. The pile on commercial carpeting is denser and resists matting. Of course, for these benefits, you also pay more.

Whatever type of carpet you decide on, if the pile is too high, chair casters will not roll freely. If this is the case, you may need to use a chair mat under the desk.

If you are purchasing new carpeting, look for a brand that has static control. During certain times of the year, static electricity can build up in the rugs and give off electric shocks when you touch something grounded, like your computer. You may have encountered this in your home. In your office, however, if you touch the computer, you could send it off line or affect the screen. If you experience static electricity, there is a static control spray available in a spray can from most janitorial supply houses. The carpet should be sprayed several times a year.

If you are looking at replacing or adding carpeting, it can be a major expense. The color selection may not be exactly what you want, but good-quality, used carpeting and padding can be purchased. Many businesses, and even some homes, replace carpet that still has a few good years left. Contact your local carpet dealer for information and leads or look in a telephone directory.

Window Treatment

Treatment for windows can range from curtains and shades to blinds and shutters. Shades and metal blinds are the least expensive type of window covering and come in assorted colors to match the decor. Wood, on the other hand, is a natural insulator. Wooden blinds do not get hot like the metal ones. Curtains, wooden blinds, and shutters can range from moderately expensive to outrageous. Again, whether or not clients come to your office may decide which type of treatment you use. The football motif on the curtains in a now-unused bedroom may be fine if you don't see anyone all day, but these curtains will probably not make the correct statement for management consultants counseling clients in their home office.

Whatever type of window treatment you now have or contemplate buying, they must be adjustable. This statement has already been made in several other sections of this chapter, underlining the importance of adjustable window treatment. Window coverings help control the amount of light, heat, and noise coming into the room. In the winter, they also help restrict the amount of heat going out of the room through the windows.

In an attempt to keep the office cooler in summer, especially if it faces west, consider mounting shade screens on the outside of the windows. These screens do not replace window treatment but are in addition to the inside coverings. Shade screens reflect the heat from the sun before it hits the windows. This will keep the office cooler because the windows themselves are not as hot.

Electrical Outlets and Other Power Considerations

Have you ever rearranged the furniture into that "perfect" setting before finding out there was something missing? For example, we don't often think about the location of the electrical outlets—unless we don't have one when we need it. The best layout, design, and work-flow patterns are rendered useless if there are no electrical outlets to plug in the computer, printer, fax machine, copier, and desk lamp. In our office, we have thirty-seven separate electrical devices to deal with. We are always experimenting with better ways to deal with the morass of cords.

When considering the home office work area, examine the location of all the electrical outlets. The placement of outlets could limit how you configure the office. Older homes may only have one or two outlets in the entire room. Similarly, attics, basements, and garages may be limited. Outlets can be added in the wall or floor, but it is better to determine whether you need them before you open for business. Adding outlets can be expensive.

Because of building codes and buyer's demands, many new homes have only one electrical outlet on each wall. Obviously, this may not be enough if you have a lot of computer and office equipment. Since computers, in general, do not draw a large electrical load (check your equipment specifications to determine the electrical load), you do have several inexpensive options. One is to convert your duplex outlet into a four-plex. The other option is to buy a good quality multi-outlet plug strip. These usually have six outlets and an overload protection device. The better ones can also offer some ability to absorb electrical spikes,

keeping them from burning up your computer equipment. Do not use the cheap dime-store electrical extension cords. These cords cannot take a large electrical load and can heat up, causing a fire. The fire prevention codes in many cities have banned them from use in commercial applications.

A circuit is a closed path on which the electrical current travels to a predetermined number of electrical outlets. In residential use, each circuit (except those used for air conditioning, electric hot water heaters, and the electric kitchen range) is limited to 20 amps (amps are the amount of pressure needed to push the voltage, or power needed, through).

Add up all of the load requirements of your computer equipment from the electrical specifications. If it adds up to more than 20 amps, you need an additional circuit. Unless you are an electrician or understand electrical household circuitry, you will need to hire someone.

There is also some office equipment that can cause electrical noise feedback to computers if they are on the same circuit. This can send your computer off line or cause a glitch, losing any information not saved up to that time. This is not a noise that you can hear, but it is real. Some of the culprits of this noise are electric typewriters, calculators, and copy machines. Do not put them on the same circuit as your computer equipment. They may never cause your computer to go down, but it can happen, and you'll never know when. Why take the chance?

Another consideration is that many of today's copy machines and the most important of all equipment, the coffeemaker, usually require their own circuits because of the large

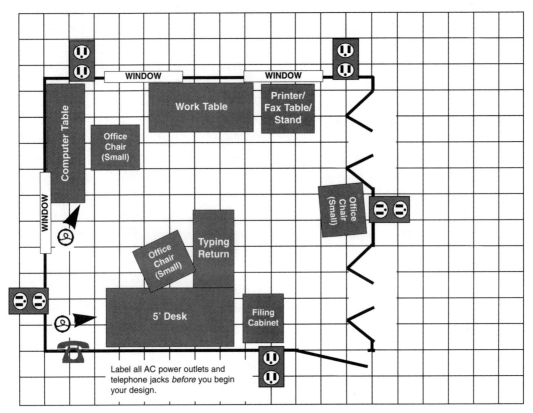

Label all AC power outlets and telephone jacks *before* you begin your design.

A Bedroom Office

electrical load they draw. By themselves, their loads may be below 20 amps, but when they all go on together, you will probably blow a circuit breaker. If you need to add a room air conditioner, it will also need its own circuit.

You may find that by adding all of these circuits, your electrical panel is not large enough to handle the additional circuit breakers. It can be expensive to add an additional panel. You may want to put the coffeemaker and the copy machine in another room, which is on another circuit, where the electrical demand is not an issue.

Personal Touches

Don't forget to include little touches that make your work zone a professional-looking office. Include some plants (silk or real, depending on your green thumb), framed posters or artwork, and a few personal items (such as family pictures). This isn't something necessary only when you have clients coming to the office. Create the environment and ambiance that is most comfortable for YOU to work in. Frame those diplomas and awards, too. Be proud of all your accomplishments, and reinforce your belief that you and your home-based business will succeed beyond anyone's wildest expectations.

We have talked unendingly, it seems, about making your office professional looking, especially for clients. That does not mean that you need to run right out and spend a ton of money on new furniture and fixtures. Carefully evaluate pieces you already own. They may only need some painting, refinishing, or cleaning. Desks and filing cabinets can be purchased second-hand from garage sales, the Salvation Army Thrift Store, or through newspaper ads. Second-hand furniture doesn't have to mean old and run down—think of it as refinished and distinguished.

DESIGNING THE HOME-BASED OFFICE

Whether by choice or default, if you worked through the last pages, you have weighed all the options and staked out your office space. This is it! You're pretty sure all the equipment you need will fit. Now you need to know if the setup and flow of work are compatible. You need to do an office layout before you move into the space. No groaning! This is actually the fun part. Go into the proposed office area, sit down, and relax for a few minutes. Don't forget to take the worksheets copied from the CD-ROM and a pair of scissors!

How do you design work flow? Some won't have a hard time, they'll just put the desk down, hook up the computer, and go to work. For others, it will make a difference if the worktable is behind the desk or across the room. Some will need the file cabinets close to the desk.

There are some questions listed on the Work Zone Design Checklist (OFFICE.doc) for you to answer about work flow and layout, but there are many more questions that only you will know to ask. Space has been provided at the bottom of this checklist for you to write out those questions and answers as you design the office layout.

To determine the questions that are important in determining your best work-flow pattern, just relax and envision what you think will be a typical day. What pieces of equipment and furniture do you see yourself working at the most? Does the phone ring all day or just occasionally? If you spend most of the time at a worktable, is it better to have the phone on that table or across the room on your desk? What can be kept in storage, and what should be near at hand? How close do you have to be to the file cabinet? You get the idea. Keep asking yourself questions about what it will take to get the job done. Some of this work has been done earlier in the chapter when you calculated how much space would be needed.

Remember, nothing is carved in stone. In fact, some things may change as you start laying them out on the layout grid (as described in the next section). Things will certainly change as you start to work.

Laying Out the Space

To lay your space out in an efficient manner, we've provided, on the CD-ROM, a grid and standard office space cutouts to arrange on the grid paper. Note the work-space dimensions you have already calculated on each item and cut them out. If you have specialized equipment, create a drawing for them, too. Remem-

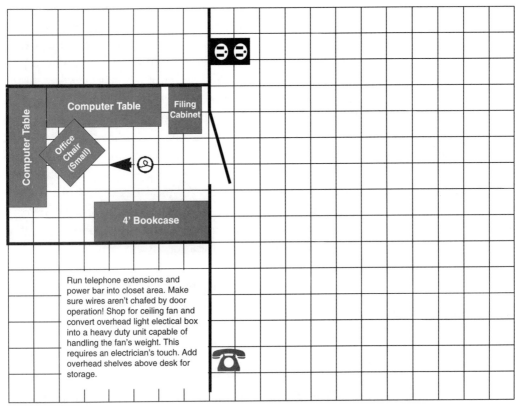

A Closet Office

ber, some things on your list may be slated for another room, like the display case or the storage area.

Work Zone Cutouts

Print out the appropriate desk and chair symbols and draw any other ones you need. Then cut out the symbols and lay them out on the grid paper provided on the CD-ROM (and available from most office supply stores).

Your Work Zone Layout

Now for the really fun part! Using the tape measure, take the dimensions of the room.

Transfer that information to the Work Zone Grid (or use grid paper purchased at an office supply store that uses ½ squares). Each ½ square on the grid represents 1 foot in your room. Add the windows and electrical outlets to the sketch. Lay the cutouts in the configuration you think will work best using the questions and answers from the Work Zone Design Checklist. Does everything fit as you thought it would? If not, arrange and rearrange the cutout furniture until you get the right look and flow to the space. This is much easier than moving real furniture around.

Make sure to leave enough walking space around the furniture. If the space is too small for a productive work flow, go back and figure the requirements again. Reconsider those questions about storage and where things can go. If you are lucky and have more room, don't be too quick to add additional equipment and furniture unless it is really needed. Save some things for future expansion.

OPEN FOR BUSINESS!

If it is at all feasible, have as much of your furniture, equipment, and supplies in place before opening for business. Every last thumb tack is not necessary, but you need to have the big items such as desk, chair, computer, and filing cabinets. This expectation may be unrealistic, but having everything from the start will save time and convey a professional feeling, not only to your family and clients but to you as well. Knowing that you're in business makes a big difference in getting things done.

We spent considerable space in this book on your office because your office space is an important part of keeping you productive at home.

It doesn't really doesn't matter how neat and tidy your office is if you're not productive. If you need help getting your work done, we will talk about organizing your time in order to meet the priorities of your business in Chapter 23.

C H A P T E R

11

TECHNOLOGIES NEEDED TO PROSPER AT HOME

In this chapter, we describe some of the most common uses of office computer equipment and provide guidelines to help you identify your needs and preferences. Keep in mind that the products and functions presented in this book are not comprehensive—a home-based office can take a number of forms and can be used for an infinite number of tasks. After reading this chapter, you'll be able to choose home-based technologies that are just as functional (although perhaps not as unique), specifically tailored for you and your business.

If you are already a computer enthusiast or technology addict, you may wish to skip this chapter. If you are one of those people who knows that a computer is probably looming in your life but are still reluctant to take that first big step into automation, then this chapter is for you.

We urge you to automate. Start simple, but get started. Technology is cheaper and easier to use than ever before. Computers have

become compact objects, and these machines are central when setting up a productive home control center. If you are a hopeless computerphobe, new electronic organizers and personal digital assistants (PDAs) from companies such as Sharp, Apple Computer, Casio, and others are easy-to-use starting places until you feel ready for the computer-based plunge. Some PDAs can even process handwriting and/or take commands when you simply point at the function you want to use. Sharp's Wizard electronic organizers are actually sophisticated computers, but they ask you the questions and require no special computer skills to operate. All it takes is a little practice with these tiny machines while reading the easy-to-understand instruction manuals.

If you would like to take the leap into full-feature computerization, the new generation of computers makes learning how to use a computer almost painless. Whether it's a notebook computer, a PDA, or a full-fledged desktop computer, it is important that you add some kind of computer automation to your home office. Computers are now easy to use and relatively affordable; no legitimate excuse remains for not becoming "computerized."

You don't have to quit using your day book and notepads; take them along. Over time, you'll see how new and old technologies, together, make you a much more productive businessperson. You'll wonder how you ever did it without the electronic tools. Your home-based colleagues who still work without computers will be left in the dust, struggling to keep up with you.

INTEGRATION AND PLANNING

The integration of many tools and techniques, both electronic and manual, is required to get the most from your office technologies. This can be achieved only by carefully choosing the right tools and learning how to put them to work effectively. If the technology and services are properly selected, a mobile office can become more powerful and more productive than a traditional desk-based office.

While many people routinely travel with a cellular phone and a compact computer, the heart of making this technology work is to learn how to combine individual elements into systems. A system is a combination of several tools that accomplishes a business purpose. For example, most people use their notebook computers only for writing a few notes and maybe creating a spreadsheet on the road. Not Bob. Bob considers his notebook computer the "brains" of his mobile empire. Beyond writing reports and taking notes, he uses it for everything from locating new prospects and making sales presentations to entertaining himself when the day's work is finished. Bob also carries a tiny Sony Walkman tape recorder and playback unit. In Bob's hands, this cigarette pack–sized tape unit is used not only to listen to music but also to benefit from relaxation tapes that help soothe him to sleep on the airplane and for taping sales demo sessions for review back at the office. In Bob's home office, every tool performs multiple functions, and all the tools work together. It's this integration of tools that makes an automated office an effective environment for getting work done instead of just a house full of gadgets, wires, and papers that weigh you down.

SEVEN MAJOR BUSINESS FUNCTIONS OF A WELL-EQUIPPED HOME OFFICE

There are seven major business functions that must be performed in any office—home-based or traditional. As you put your technology-enhanced office together, you must consider all seven functions in order to make the office fully functional. The functions include:

- **Communication.** Communication is the central function in business. Almost everything in business depends on communication of some sort. You need to maintain contact with customers and other companies. Office communications are facilitated with modern telephone equipment, online communication services, presentation software, and a variety of computer-based messaging systems, including fax machines, copiers, and the Internet and other online services.

- **Reporting.** Reports of various kinds are vital in order to keep yourself and others informed of the status of your work and finances. A properly equipped office provides the tools for preparing complete reports in all formats, including those required by the IRS, your bank, and your investors. Of course, office communication equipment can be used to submit your reports whenever you like.

- **Information Gathering and Research.** Access to current information is critical to strategic business decisions and profitable sales activities. With an automated office, you can gather data through online research services and review disk-based information directories. Information can be analyzed right on the spot.

- **Analysis and Forecasting.** Data is only useful if it can be analyzed to develop appropriate business objectives. Data analysis now can be performed from almost any computer. Past and present sales figures, for example, can be graphed and future performances extrapolated to show the relative performance of new product ideas and marketing programs.

- **Planning and Scheduling.** Sophisticated planning and calendar functions turn tracking a complicated schedule into an easy task. Many of the new tracking and planning tools are equipped to remind you of upcoming events when you turn on your computer or electronic organizer. Programs are also available to automatically track billable time. Capable of tracking multiple projects and clients, these programs can be used to bill clients for telephone conference time at a different hourly rate than those of other activities. At the end of the billing period, the programs print a complete report of your activities with respect to each client, which can then be used to bill the client or draft your trip report.

- **Project Management.** Software can be used to manage any project, from designing a brochure to redesigning the space shuttle. Because the complete project can be made available on your home-based and mobile computers, the project can be planned at home and updated in the field. Other strategic documents such as marketing plans can be created, scheduled, and tracked as well.

- **Organization and Recordkeeping.** The automated office offers a wide range of options for recordkeeping. The options range from client data stored in easy-to-use handheld organizers from Sharp and Casio to sophisticated database programs on notebook computers that track all operations within a company. For example, you can maintain a contact file of all your customers that shows their account status, purchases, and monies owed. Automated recordkeeping helps when you have to report to the IRS or make business plans for your bank.

- **Education.** Your home-based office can help maintain balance in your life by satisfying your personal need for more information. Many interactive, computer-based products can teach you everything from the basics of investment banking to foreign languages and advanced mathematics. Many of these products mix fun with learning. There are even online university programs, such as the degree programs offered by the University of Phoenix and other accredited schools, that allow businesspeople to finish a degree and still meet their business obligations. Students simply connect to the "electronic classroom" through the modem in their computers. If you need more information about current events, you can connect to many metropolitan newspapers and other news services through the World Wide Web and commercial online services, such as America Online.

With all these options, you can see that an appropriately automated office can make you more productive and can keep you educated and informed to be a better competitor.

EVALUATING YOUR OFFICE TOOLS AND TECHNOLOGIES

We recommend using very specific criteria to evaluate the tools and technologies to be used in your home office.

- **Size and Weight Versus Functionality.** If you have extra space, don't worry about this criterion, but in most home offices, space is limited. Every inch on your desktop counts. This means that a 5-pound notebook computer that can be used for a wide range of office needs is a more reasonable choice than a 5-pound device that keeps only a calendar of appointments.

- **Ease of Use.** If the average businessperson can't quickly put a device to work, then it's not very useful—regardless of the potential for the device. Some of the computer software technologies are very powerful, but they take practice and persistence to learn. Thus, we recommend advanced programs only to those who have a specific requirement for their functionality and the time to learn them.

- **Set-up Time.** Remember, technology is about making you more productive at home. Because you may want to dash off a quick memo or a fax only minutes before a meeting or catching a plane, fast access to the functionality of your office tools is important. For example, if it takes 5 minutes to get your computer ready so that you can send a one-page fax, then in our opinion, the set-up time is unacceptable.

- **Safety.** No component of a home office—be it computer, cellular phone, or spiral-bound notebook—should have fragile or loose parts, sharp edges, or awkward or weak latches. It helps also that, when closed, all components are waterproof enough to resist at least a few drops of rain. Who knows, you might need to pull your organizer out and make an appointment on a Seattle street corner.

- **Life Span Versus Cost.** It's no secret that most technologies expand in capability while rapidly decreasing in cost. You should keep this in mind before purchasing an expensive item that may cost 20–50 percent less within a year. We only consider products that will make an immediate difference in productivity. If the payback is less than the price tag, it's time to ask whether or not you really *need* the tool.

- **Reliability.** Product reliability is of paramount importance. There's nothing more frustrating than losing a week's productivity because your computer or phone or some other device failed to work as promised. This means that the reputation of the manufacturer and service availability should be important determining factors in making individual home office purchases.

Taken together, these criteria provide a framework for evaluating home office products based on their performance in the real world. There are many tools and options for home office use, but we don't recommend that anyone use all of them. Before you go on a spending binge, ask yourself what you really need when you work. For the "fully wired" professional, it is always a compromise between everything you'd like to have and what you can practically use. Not everybody needs a full complement of computers, phones, copiers, scanners, printers, and other gadgets to help manage the business. You must critically evalu-

ate your own work requirements and personal preferences to put together the best home office system for you.

Once you determine your needs, you can match the right tools to your style, work habits, and productivity requirements. Priorities will vary from business to business. For example, an accounting business will likely require more efficient, responsive computing power than a business that makes gift baskets for the holidays.

THE BASIC COMPONENTS OF AN AUTOMATED HOME OFFICE

The basic office automation components for the majority of home-based businesses include the following:

- **A Computer.** Most people should get the most powerful, least expensive machine that meets their needs. In the next chapter, we provide a complete list of options and selection criteria for choosing this premier component in your home office.

- **A Cellular Telephone Or Electronic Pager.** You need some way to remain in touch with the office (or home) at all times and a way for people to keep in touch with you when you're out of the office.

- **A Small Tape Recorder** (preferably with an integrated radio). A tape recorder, such as a recording Sony Walkman or one of the many competitive units on the market, can perform a variety of useful business functions on the road—ranging from simply playing back music when you're jogging around the block thinking about new marketing ideas to recording an important presentation by a competitor at a trade show.

- **A Manual or Electronic Organizer.** Even though you'll use your computer for most recordkeeping activities, there are times when you just need to take notes or jot down a phone number, and this often happens when you don't have your computer with you. Thus, an organizer of some sort is used to take brief notes and to keep your schedule up to date. This is the device you take everywhere with you. It can easily fit in a coat pocket or handbag. If you use a manual organizer, your computer should be able to print pages that fit the configuration you use. If you use an electronic organizer, it should be compatible with your desktop computer so that the two can share information via a cable and linking software.

- **A Printer.** Your printer should be capable of producing quality, business-like output for reports, invoices, letters, and advertising flyers.

- **A Fax Machine.** You can combine the fax machine with the modem or copier to send and receive orders, messages, and other information.

- **An Image Scanner.** If you intend to put pictures into your publications or add them to your business Web site, you will need a scanner to produce a professional image. Scanners are now more affordable and usually recommended as a basic office automation requirement, especially for businesses that use the Internet.

- **A Modem.** A modem or other high-speed connection to the Internet, such as ISDN or a cable modem connection, allows you to communicate through e-mail and use online services and the Internet.

- **A Copy Machine.** If you do not make many copies, this is optional.

You may want to consider an integrated output device that combines the functions of a copier, scanner, modem, fax machine, and printer in one machine. There are many integrated machines available at affordable prices. We like these machines for home offices because they take up a small amount of space and offer a wide range of useful services.

We talk about the criteria for choosing these various devices in the next chapter.

MORE GADGETS TO CONSIDER

Beyond the basics—computer, cellular phone or pager, printer, recorder, and organizer—there are literally thousands of handy gadgets for use in a home-based office, including air purifiers, and burglar alarms. We suggest getting a catalog from one of the large office supply chains (such as Staples or Office Max, listed in the Supplies and Furniture section of the CD-ROM) to check out current prices and options.

Before you buy anything, remember to only purchase technologies that you intend to use. Never buy a technology that intimidates you. While you may learn to use such a device, chances are that it will make you nervous enough that you won't.

Always evaluate the usefulness of each device in comparison to its cost and productivity potential. The best kinds of items to add to your repertoire are those that fulfill more than one function. That's why a computer, cellular phone, and tiny recorder are so useful; each is capable of performing multiple functions for almost any business.

C H A P T E R

12

CHOOSING THE BEST TECHNOLOGY AND SOFTWARE

• •

Choosing a good computer takes time. First, there are so many machines and brands. Second, it's hard to choose a machine because so many technical issues cloud the purchase decision. Third, everyone from friends to salespeople will give you their opinion on the matter, regardless of how much they know about the topic. To choose the best technologies for your office, we suggest that you first read this chapter and then proceed to purchase something that meets *your* needs, not the needs of your friends.

ALL COMPUTERS GREAT AND SMALL

There are literally hundreds of computers on the market. Alternatives to full-sized office computers range from tiny "palmtops," with keyboards that bring new meaning to the words "cramped fingers," and clunky "luggables" that are portable only because they have a handle. In most cases, a desktop computer or a full-featured notebook computer with a large screen should be considered the starting point for computer technology.

To get started in your selection, reread the last chapter on uses for computer technology, and then list the primary ways you plan to use your computer. Then, after testing a few systems at a store, base your final choice of platform on the software you want to use.

After all, it's the work you need to get done that is most important, and it's primarily the software that determines the work you'll get done—in spite of all the other things we talk about in the next pages.

SELECTING A COMPUTER FOR YOUR BUSINESS

There are literally hundreds of computer manufacturers. In addition to producing desktop machines, many companies produce a line of notebook computers suitable for use on the road. The machine that's right for you will combine compact size with adequate performance at a price you can afford. You also want to purchase your computer from a company that makes reliable products and provides a good warranty program and accessible technical support (preferably providing a toll-free number and one-day turnaround on repairs). What good is a computer if it's in the shop all the time?

Start With The Operating Platform

Your first decision is to choose a platform. The most common platforms are Microsoft Windows–based or Microsoft NT–based computers and Apple Macintosh computers. Note that these machines use different operation systems (the software that makes the computer work) and can't share all of their information with programs on other platforms.

Not all programs that run on one platform have an identical version for other platforms, but many products have a version that runs on multiple environments. Select the soft-ware and hardware that best fits your needs, and then make the decision about a platform. Your hardware/software platform choice should be the easiest to use and also offer the most flexibility while remaining within your budget. After you make your platform choice, you can use the following guidelines for selecting a specific machine and model within that platform.

Start With the Right Microprocessor

Depending on your budget and the kind of programs you plan to run, the selection of your CPU or microprocessor (your computer's brains) is a critical decision and a confusing one as well. The current Intel Pentium microprocessors (now called Pentium II and MMX processors) come in many varieties. The various microprocessors used in the Apple Macintosh computers from Motorola are produced in different configurations based on data handling capability, speed, and graphics processing speed.

The microprocessors are produced in various clock speeds—at this point they range from 133-MHz to well over 300-MHz (expect these numbers to increase over time). The clock speed measures how fast data is processed. The bigger the MHz number, the (generally) faster the microprocessor. Faster is more expensive, but faster is more desirable for most applications.

Internal Memory

When you decide on a computer, you'll also need to decide on the amount of internal memory or RAM (random access memory) you need in your computer. The answer to this question rests on the kinds of software you plan to run. If your work is limited to one or two applications that run strictly on Windows 95, 16 megabytes (MB) is probably all you'll need, but most modern computers that use Windows 98 come with at least 32 MB of memory or more. More memory is better and more expensive. Again, expect these basic requirements and recommendations to increase quickly over time. (By the time this is printed, the internal memory configuration may start at twice these memory capacities or more.)

Hard Drive Storage

While at one time computers came with only small hard drives (20 MB or less), basic machines today routinely come with 3 or more gigabytes (GB) of hard disk storage. A gigabyte offers about 1,000 times as much storage as a megabyte. The storage is empty space for data and programs. The amount of hard drive storage that's right for you depends on your needs, but it's best to play it safe and buy a computer with a larger capacity drive than you think necessary.

You will want a large hard drive for reasons you haven't even considered yet. Most modern programs tend to be large. Microsoft Word is a case in point—the program, including all of its files, uses about 45 MB of memory, and even the "minimum" installation occupies about 10 MB. Another space-intensive task is receiving faxes via your modem. An incoming fax is saved as a picture, and these images take up substantial real estate on the hard drive. Should someone send you a ten-page fax, you may run out of room on the drive before you receive it all. Other space-intensive applications include desktop publishing and multimedia applications. The more you do with your computer, the more hard drive space you'll need.

Other Computer Criteria

Buying a computer can be a difficult decision because of the sheer number of machines out there. For a truly confusing introduction to hardware options, pick up a copy of *Computer Shopper*, a tabloid-sized publication stuffed with ads from various mail-order computer companies and resellers. One way to get to the bottom of the selection process is to look only for machines that meet your criteria for CPU, storage capability, and hard drive size. There are several other features you can use to further narrow your choices.

The Display

The first question about the display, or screen, is its size. You must feel comfortable that the screen can show you enough information at one time to do useful work. This is more a problem with notebooks than it is with standard desktop computer displays, which are generally at least 15 inches wide. In our work, the larger the screen the better, although some users don't always need the benefits of a large screen (17 inches or more) that can display more than a full page at one time.

The next decision about the screen involves the resolution. Displays are now in color, but what's really important to you is how readable the display is in practice. To determine this, you must test the machine at a dealer. With notebooks, magazine photos showing machines with crystal clear screens may be misleading or deliberately enhanced. The best machine display is one that is clearly readable in any light, from total darkness to bright sunlight, and that is easy on the eyes.

Pointing Devices

Most computers come packaged with a suitable mouse, but you may want to use a trackball or other pointing device instead. Always try the pointing devices before you buy one.

The Keyboard

When inspecting prospective computers, pay special attention to the keyboard. There are many add-on keyboards with better touch and feel than those packaged with your basic machine. Make sure that the unit has a full complement of function keys. The keyboard should also have the right "touch" for your typing style. On portables, be wary of keyboards with tiny keys close to one another (unless you are shopping for a subnotebook or palmtop machine).

Disk Drives, CD-ROMs, and Modems

On portables, the need for a floppy disk drive is definitely arguable. Still, unless you are shopping for an exceptionally small, lightweight unit, we still prefer a machine with a built-in 3½-inch floppy disk drive.

At one time, a CD-ROM drive was an option. We don't consider it an option any longer. Get the fastest version possible (at least 16X or higher at this point). On some computers, you'll have the option of a built-in Zip Drive, a high-capacity drive that holds about the same amount of information as 100 floppy disks. These drives are great if you'll be moving a lot of data onto multiple machines.

A modem is an integral part of your office. Make sure you buy a modem, either external or internal, with your computer. Get the fastest modem possible (at this writing, at

least 33.6 kbs or 56 kbs, but, again, expect the number to go up quickly). The speed of the modem determines how you can use the Internet and World Wide Web. (We have provided more information on selecting modems and Internet connections later in the chapter.)

Using these criteria together, you should be able to narrow the field of candidate computers to three or four. The last thing to do before making a decision is to find someone who owns the unit you are interested in and ask his or her opinion about the machine. Take anything less than a glowing tribute to mean that the machine is not as useful or easy to use as the owner expected and move on to your next candidate. If you can't find anyone locally who owns the machine, ask the dealer or manufacturer for several names and call a couple of these people. If you can't find anyone who has one of the little jewels you have your eye on, then think twice about getting one yourself.

BUYING A USED COMPUTER

For those on a limited budget, the prospect of saving a few dollars by purchasing a used machine may appear attractive, but unless you're positively broke, we don't recommend it. Here's why:

- Used machines may employ near-obsolete technology. This means they are slower than current models. For example, a survey of the used computer ads in the *Los Angeles Times* revealed several ads for notebook computers that employed 286 and 386 chips— these can't really run Windows or many other large applications. If you want to run current versions of Windows, you absolutely must buy a recent model of the Pentium processor (or whatever replaces it in the future).

- Older machines invariably have a small hard drive, some as small as 160 MB. For today's sophisticated applications, this is simply not enough storage for anyone who will be seriously using the computer in a business environment.

- A used machine may have hard-to-detect problems. These can range from a functional but defective hard drive to intermittent memory failures. You may not find out that the machine is dying of old age until it is too late.

- A machine more than two years old probably needs upgrading in terms of hard drive space, modem, and other features.

- The sellers of used hardware may be completely out of touch with the PC price wars. They may be selling their machine for more than it costs to purchase a new, more powerful computer. People in this position are often difficult to negotiate with in terms of the machine's actual market value, although you can try.

If you must take the used route, try to buy a newer machine. Before buying, take the machine into a service center and have them test it thoroughly. This may cost you $50 or so, but it may save your bank account should the machine prove to have fatal technical problems.

Choosing the right computer for your home office should take some time. Even if you work with computers on a daily basis, with the new models, increasingly compact technology, and changes in the marketplace, you may need to take a week or two just to get a handle on what's out there and how much a good system should cost. Take your time and don't choose a machine until you are absolutely sure that it will fulfill your needs without breaking your budget. If you choose correctly, you can expect some great productivity to help support your home-based endeavors.

Now, let's look at some guidelines for choosing other technology equipment for your home-based office.

CHOOSING A PHOTOCOPIER

Not every home-based business needs a photocopier. There are multiple copy centers (like Kinko's) in every town and city. Even the grocery and drug stores have copiers. These machines, with buy/lease payments for new ones and service contracts for used units, add a significant monthly payment to the business overhead. For home operations that require an on-site copier, with only a few phone calls, you'll have photocopier salespeople lined up at the door.

Inexpensive Copiers

Bare-bones copiers can be purchased for less than $500. You probably don't want one unless your copy volume is limited to a handful a day and a store offering copy services is not located nearby. The most basic machine requires that you not only place the original on the sliding platform (allow room for the sliding), but also manually feed each sheet of paper.

Ultimate Survival Tip

Scan It or Copy with a Fax Machine?

If you almost never need copies, use the fax machine or your computer's scanner and printer. The fax machine is fastest, but if yours uses thermal paper, the copy will fade eventually. The scanner can be used as well, although what takes seconds to perform on a warmed up copier takes minutes on a scanner, and you still have to print it.

These machines are very limited in the number of copies they can produce before the toner needs replacement, and, with copy times of 30–60 seconds, you might as well use the fax machine.

Intermediately Priced Copiers

Generally the choice for home-based businesses, these intermediately priced units are full copiers. Priced from $500 to the low $1000s, options include sheet feeders, collators, resizing, and automatic exposure setting. Most units either require a sturdy table for placement or fit on an optional stand. Go for the stand. It has wheels and paper and toner storage underneath.

The best way to acquire a new copier in this price range is the lease/service contract. In such an arrangement, you choose the model and options based on your monthly budget. (Negotiate the payment!) Included is a fixed number of copies per month and unlimited scheduled maintenance and repairs. Then, when the lease is up and the machine is wearing down, order a new one. That way, you get the best years out of the unit with a minimum of down time.

Expensive Copiers

If your home-based enterprise's core business is copying (such as running a copy center or producing technical manuals), a fast, high-quality "rig" is required. Although priced in the stratosphere, both color and black-and-white machines are available. A quality color unit runs in the $30,000+ price range. A color machine is comparatively slow because four passes—one each for cyan, magenta, yellow, and black—are required for each copy. Much faster black-and-white-only units, used for high-volume applications such as producing book-length documents, are rarely sold. Instead, most are leased, with the price determined by the number of copies run per month. The fee may or may not include paper. Plan on an extensive contract negotiation in the acquisition process.

When considering an upper-end machine, you must have room for not only the machine but also for cases of paper and supplies. Climate control is also required, and you may find that the manufacturer protests to locating a half-million-dollar machine in a home environment.

CHOOSING A FAX MACHINE

There are two options when buying a fax machine: a stand-alone unit or a much less expensive fax modem. The former sends outgoing paper-based documents and receives and prints incoming documents. The latter requires a computer, printer, and scanner to duplicate all the functions of a stand-alone fax but can use computer software to send faxes in bulk. Which is right for you? It depends—some home offices will want both.

A stand-alone fax doesn't slow down the computer while it's sending and receiving. Fax modems are free with almost every computer and send computer-generated documents without the intervention of paper. Both require access to a phone line and are most convenient when that line is used strictly for data transmissions.

The Stand-Alone Fax Machine

The easiest to use is the stand-alone fax machine. You dump what you want to send into the in tray, choose or dial a number, and press send. Incoming faxes are received automatically and print as they are received. Newer machines allow for advanced programming with multiple mailing lists and the transmission of grayscale images, and they print on plain copier paper instead of greasy-feeling and rapidly fading thermal paper. Cheaper units don't even chop the paper from the thermal paper roll, which produces long piles of curled up paper on a busy day.

Look for a machine that uses plain paper and toner or ink-jet technology instead of the thermal transfer medium. Toner machines cost more. Your fax should be easy to program— many aren't or use series of clumsy codes and button procedures. Check the machine's manual to ensure it's easy to understand. You'll also need a built-in line-switching ability or an external device if the same phone line is used for voice, data, and fax. Current machines fax at 14,400 BPS and employ compression to reduce transmission times (and with that, phone bills) for long-distance calls.

Fax Modems

Fax modems are modems accompanied by faxing software. All such modems can send and receive transmissions, but to send documents originating on paper, a scanner is required. Because the fax originates on the computer and most faxing software can read database output, you can set the modem up to fax to a mailing list while you sleep. (Don't fax to home-based businesses or consumer numbers because you'll wake the house!) Fax modems tie up your computer when in operation, and, to automatically receive transmissions, you must leave the machine on and the software active. (You must also have enough extra RAM to accommodate the fax software when applications are open.)

Choose a fax modem with quality software (Windows includes basic fax modem software) or separately purchase a package that meets your needs. Look for a simple interface that operates like a printer selection from inside applications and flexible fax mailing list software. When buying a modem and fax software, get one with line switching if the same phone line is used for voice, data, and fax.

CHOOSING A MODEM AND INTERNET CONNECTION

You can reach the Internet in several ways, not all of which require a modem. Of course, you may need a modem for purposes other than accessing an Internet gateway. Modems can be used for faxing (as described above), for communicating with online services (such as America Online), for accessing electronic bulletin boards, and for transferring files to other computer users. When doing a job for a company, you may need a modem in order to access their e-mail network, using a temporary mailing account they provide.

Choosing a Modem

At this writing, the standard modem speed is 56,000 bits per second (bps) or 56 kbs. You want a modem of this speed. Anything else, will waste your time while you wait for something to happen. With prices for the best modems at only about $100, why buy something slower and save only $50? PC users with an available full-size slot should buy an internal modem board or an external modem connected to an available serial port. Mac users buy external modems that connect through the serial port. (Most external modems work with either platform.)

Choosing a modem is tough. They vary in construction quality, but, unless you are a member of the IEEE, a visual inspection won't tell you much. Instead, concentrate on the manufacturer's reputation and the software included. Does the modem use shunts (tiny black connectors that fit over minuscule pins) to set parameters? If so, skip it and look for one with at least DIP switches (tiny rocker switches). Inspect the instruction manual, too. Is there an easy-to-understand setup section that explains how to determine the IRQ settings for Windows?

Cable Modems

Relatively new on the scene are the much faster cable modems, which use cable TV lines to connect to the Internet or online service. Although they are more expensive than standard units, cable modems can be a real boon for Internet users. By using the cable lines, telephone wires aren't tied up in a home with limited-line access—a problem that's growing around the country as more people require multiple lines. Connections for other uses are limited by the speed of the receiving modem.

Accessing the Internet

There are several ways to access the Internet from a home-based business. A modem is the most traditional. You connect through an Internet Service Provider (ISP), an online service such as America Online or Microsoft Network, or through the fast megabit services and Integrated Services Digital Network (ISDN) or International Business Services Network (IBSN) lines available from many telephone companies.

Choosing an Internet Service Provider

If you don't have a direct Internet connection through the phone company, the best way to choose an ISP is through recommendations of locally based friends who use one. You want a service that's inexpensive, offers unlimited access (no hours limit), never has busy signals, and offers quality technical support with long availability hours. Avoid those demanding annual contracts. That way, if things don't work out, you can try another service.

CHOOSING A PRINTER

Choosing a printer is as daunting as selecting a computer. Most home entrepreneurs will want to purchase both a fast black-and-white laser printer and an inexpensive ink-jet color printer. Use the black-and-white laser printer for routine tasks, such as producing proposals, invoices, accounting documents, and reports. Use the ink-jet printer for promotional materials, let-terhead, and charts, diagrams, and pictures that will be inserted into black-and-white documents.

Black-and-White Printers

You want a printer that is fast enough for your needs (test it—page-per-minute ratings are unreliable), handles the maximum-sized paper you need (and can afford), and has a long warranty (printer repairs are expensive).

Do you plan to produce promotional materials on thicker-than-bond papers? With the kind of paper you have in mind, try the printer's manual feed option. Some printers handle stiff or thick papers better than others do.

Color Printers

All the same parameters for choosing a black-and-white printer apply to color printers, although multiple paper trays are uncommon in the color world. Central to color printing is print quality and color quality. You'll want a color printer with at least a 600 dots-per-inch (dpi) output. When using high-quality paper, expect vivid color and detailed output, but don't expect the printed colors to exactly match the colors on your display screen. Also check the cost of extra ink cartridges or toner replacements.

Compatability

Most readers will want a printer that is both PC- and Macintosh-compatible. (Who knows what the future will bring?) You also want support for Ethernet, with its fast data transfer, even if you don't need it right now.

Modern PC printers use the computer's parallel port or (usually) add-on Ethernet. Pur-chasing a scanner that uses the same parallel port requires the addition of an add-on board.

Mac printers may use the Mac's serial port, Ethernet port, or LocalTalk. The use of the serial port is the least desirable option because the serial port is also used for external modems.

PostScript

PostScript is now standard on all but the least expensive laser printers, which you won't want anyway because they are too slow and are limited in paper tray capacity. What is Post-Script? It's Adobe System's page description language. PostScript interprets the outlines of typefaces and certain kinds of graphics in order to "redraw" them with precision on the printed page. Not all users need PostScript, but pro-grams like Adobe Illustrator and some picture files won't be able to print at high resolution without PostScript. PostScript Level 3 is the current version of the language.

Software versions of PostScript are also available. These work, but instead of utilizing your printer, they require your CPU to pro-cess the PostScript code, which takes CPU time and requires adequate RAM memory and hard drive space for the task.

Memory

Except for basic ink-jet models that use the computer's memory, you will want at least 7 MB of memory for a 600 by 600 dpi black-and-white printer and at least 12 MB for color printers. Make sure your printer's memory is upgradable before you buy.

Choosing a Black-and-White Laser Printer

You can use an ink-jet printer for producing black-and-white output, but it's slow and requires quality paper to keep the type looking crisp. A laser printer, with its faster output, use of inexpensive photocopier bond, and built-in Postscript processor is more practical. Today's laser printers print 600 by 600 dpi and handle letter or legal-sized paper. More expensive models print on 11" x 17" paper with 1200 by 1200 dpi resolution.

Look for a unit with adequate paper tray capacity and, if you can afford it, support for multiple paper trays and envelopes. Name brands are easiest to support, and replacement toner cartridges are available at local office supply and computer stores.

Choosing a Color Ink-Jet Printer

The least expensive color printers are ink-jet models. When choosing one, the proof is in the output quality. Good color output requires the use of appropriate ink-jet papers and the unit's ability to produce at least 600 by 600 dpi output. Compare the output of several models under consideration for speed, color quality/accuracy, and especially detail. Use the same kind of paper and printer settings for the comparison. Study the typeface edges for smoothness and compare the realism of photos. Choose a model with separate black, cyan, magenta, and yellow ink supplies. Otherwise, cyan, yellow, and magenta are combined to make a mediocre black.

Choosing a Color Laser Printer

For those with deep pockets, color laser printers produce excellent output. Most home-based operations won't want the expense of such a purchase unless color output is central to the business. For example, if you produce T-shirt transfers or color page proofs, you'll need such a printer, but otherwise, use your money on something truly useful. Before buying a color laser printer, compare its output with that of a quality ink-jet printer. The ink-jet will be slower, but, considering the price of the color laser and its toner, the ink-jet may be more sensible.

Other Color Printers

When shopping for a color printer, you may also encounter dye sublimation units and thermal wax models. "Dye subs" produce superb photographic output on pricey paper. Most home businesses will be as happy with an ink-jet.

Thermal wax printers use heat to transfer colored wax from plastic rolls to paper. This technology was largely supplanted in the 1990s by color lasers and ink-jet printers.

HYBRIDS—FAX, PHOTOCOPIER, PRINTER, AND SCANNER IN ONE PACKAGE

A growing number of hybrid machines are appearing on the market. Laser printers that receive faxes and machines combining printers, faxes, and scanners are common. Such devices also serve as limited photocopiers. Test all its capabilities before you buy one. For example, a "combo" unit with a sheet-fed scanner is of no use if you want to scan books for optical character recognition (unless you tear the pages from the unfortunate book). Otherwise, we like these machines for home offices because they take up a small amount of space and offer a wide range of useful services.

CHOOSE EQUIPMENT BASED ON YOUR BUSINESS NEEDS

You've heard us say this before: The first element in choosing a computer is to analyze what you plan to do with the machine. The classic mistake is to buy the equipment first and then try to make it work for your needs later. With some equipment, this is like trying to fit a round peg into a square hole. It's impossible or at least impractical.

With all business and computer technologies, the selection process is as follows:

1. Describe your needs
2. Identify the products that meet your needs
3. Test your selections thoroughly before purchase
4. Purchase the product you (not the reviewers) like the best
5. Use it

Only by working from your needs and preferences can you choose the right organizer, personal digital assistant (PDA), computer, and software. Testing is definitely required before purchase. Many times, the claims made in product literature don't, under actual working conditions, pan out as promised. For example, software can turn out to be less capable than the manufacturer claimed or difficult to use because of clumsy design. A notebook computer's battery life may be less than

was promised. Or, you may find that the spreadsheet module for an electronic organizer is as powerful as you were told it was but almost impossible to use because you spend more time moving around the tiny screen than you do getting useful work done.

If you are new to working with computers, you should also carefully evaluate the ease-of-use of each product under consideration. For example, while you may have no trouble using an electronic organizer, some computer systems may be difficult to master because serious computer training is required. That's why you should test each product before purchase by trying a demo in a store (or by ordering from a mail-order company with a sturdy money-back guarantee). Try some of the tasks that you will use the computer for. Also, if you do use both an electronic organizer (also called a PDA) and a computer, make sure the data can be transferred between the two systems with ease. There are third-party network kits for making the transfers between most computers and most of the name-brand organizer manufacturers. The more compatible the systems, the better you will like using them.

CHOOSE WISELY AND GET TO WORK

In the last few pages, you have been introduced to a number of the basic hardware options for empowering your home-based office. Remember, the six functions that every office computer system must accommodate include communication, reporting, information gathering and research, analysis and forecasting, planning and scheduling, and organization and recordkeeping. There are also the personal functions of education, entertainment, and relaxation. It is largely the software you choose that allows you to perform these functions. Thus, we urge you to further explore the hardware options we have already discussed after choosing the software tools you will need—including a word processor, spreadsheet and accounting programs, and a database for keeping customer records.

On the CD-ROM, we've provided contact information for many software and other major technology companies and their Web sites, which you should consider when searching for hardware and software for your home-based office.

PART

4

SALES, MARKETING, AND PROMOTIONS FOR YOUR HOME-BASED COMPANY

C H A P T E R

13

Sales, Selling, and Customer Satisfaction

··

With so much for sale, there's too much competition for products to get up and walk by themselves. Instead, a push is required to hurl them out the door and keep them from returning. That shove is called sales. Sales skills are paramount to home-based success. A sale is the process of convincing a buying party to offer money in return for goods or services that please the customer. This chapter takes you through the sales process and explains sales basics, distribution channels, and how to connect effectively with your customers.

Build a better mousetrap and the world beats a path to your door? Not likely. There are too many products competing for the same business and the same consumer dollar. It wasn't always so difficult to sell things. Until the twentieth century, almost any product brought to market found willing customers because there weren't many products to buy. Today, that isn't the case. Services, too, have expanded greatly, with everything from car rentalships to central-heating-system duct cleaning businesses to singing stripper telegrams.

As a home-based business owner, you're going to add more products and services to the multitudes already out there. So, what do you need to do to sell them? Well, you're going to need to learn how to sell, sell, sell. Your other promotions (which you'll read more about in the upcoming chapters) will help bring the customers to you, but, eventually, you're going to have to get on the phone or make a visit to a customer and actually sell the products and services you've been promoting.

In a home-based enterprise, the salesperson is probably you, the owner, or a partner who handles sales. As you grow, you may have outside salespeople handle some of the selling for you, or you may hire a broker or distributor to complete the task of selling to the ultimate customer. Regardless of your help, at some point you'll have to negotiate and sell to someone—whether that someone is the distributor, the other salespeople, or the brokers. Thus, every home-based businessperson should know something about the sale process.

ORDER TAKING, SELLING, AND THE HARD SELL

If you're new to sales, you may not understand that work and planning are often required in order to complete a sale. Your personal experiences may be limited to retail, in which you pick something off the shelf and head for the counter to pay. With the exception of answering questions, the clerks do not try to talk you into a purchase.

A visit to a car dealership may be your sole encounter with selling. While you wait complacently to choose a car, a salesperson greets you, engages you in conversation, and tries very hard to see that you go home in a car other than the one that brought you. Spending hours with you if necessary, the salesperson answers your questions and attempts to overcome your objections to buying a car today (a better price, adding a CD player, "we already have the financing all approved," etc.). All

your possible reasons for not buying a car are methodically addressed. A few signatures, a check, and soon you're on the road in an unfamiliar vehicle, your head swimming from the dealership's well-honed selling machine.

SELLING AND COMMISSION

The difference between the clerk's and the car salesperson's approach is that one is a passive approach, while the other is proactive and often very aggressive. Why? It's a matter of pay. Grocery store cashiers receive the same pay whether they spend the day stocking shelves or checking out 200 customers. A car salesperson receives a token base pay—usually minimum wage—and earns the bulk of his or her income from the commission on sales. A typical used car salesperson earns 10 to 20 percent of the vehicle's selling price. If you don't buy a car, they don't earn enough to eat, and the dealer replaces them. That's also why, in a car buying situation, you are sold the most expensive vehicle you can afford with as many options as possible. A higher selling price means a larger commission.

The Why of It

Why not just have mellow order-takers on the car lot instead of pushy commissioned salespeople who may alienate some customers? The answer is simple. While you may grab a $2 tube of toothpaste from the drugstore shelf and pay for it without intervention by the seller (except to collect your money), some goods don't sell themselves.

Big-ticket items require selling, especially if the item is complex, highly technical, or a

---

DEFINITION: Big-Ticket Sales

Big-ticket goods are single items with hefty price tags (in contrast to a single sale of a large quantity of inexpensive goods). For consumers, a $1,650 side-by-side refrigerator/freezer is a big-ticket item. For a major electronic manufacturer with deeper pockets than a consumer, a multimillion-dollar assembly line with robots and test systems is a big-ticket item. Big-ticket goods require salespeople to explain their merits and handle the financial aspects of the sale.

---

potential risk. A $20,000 new car is the perfect example. Faced with a major expense, dozens of models in a given price range, multiple options, financing, and title and registration paperwork, few buyers could wade through the maze of decisions. A car lot at which customers walked in, pointed to a vehicle, and paid at the check-out counter would move few vehicles. Instead, a (hopefully) knowledgeable salesperson provides product education and guidance and handles the multiple layers of paperwork. This, at least in part, justifies commission selling. For the selling agent, the commission induces him or her to work harder to close the deal.

Almost All Products Get Sold

On a trip to Home Depot for a pound of nails, no one buttonholes your collar and expounds the merits of a special brand, but it's selling that puts the nail on display: the nails have been sold to Home Depot. You may just grab the pound of nails and pay, but a commissioned sales representative sold them to Home Depot's buyer in a tonnage lot. Your sale may represent 95 cents—hardly worth special attention, but tons of nails might go for tens of thousands of dollars. Such a sale requires a salesperson to not only to detail the benefits of the company's line of nails to the decision maker but also to negotiate price, delivery dates, and contract terms.

The Exception

True factory-direct selling doesn't require a salesperson. In a home-based business, you might offer the sale of manufactured goods via

---

DEFINITION: Close, closing, closed, the closer

When a salesperson gets a buy commitment from a customer, he or she has *closed* the deal. The *close* is a series of steps used to get the commitment. *Closing* is a verb that describes the act of completing a deal. A heavy close is one in which strong pressure (sometimes coupled with ham-handed tactics) is used to force a commitment from a wobbling customer. The *closer* is a special high-pressure salesperson brought in to complete a deal after a less experienced person "warms up" the customer.

---

a toll-free number so that customers can call and order products from your catalog. A home-based mechanic simply hands out business cards that feature an advertisement of low prices for car repairs and waits for the phone to ring. In both of these businesses, little or no selling effort is required. The first market calls and orders. The second has a car that won't start and is short on funds, and therefore needs little persuasion to buy.

THE SALES CYCLE

If your product requires proactive selling, there is a series of steps to follow. These steps take different forms, depending on the product for sale. The length of the sales cycle varies greatly too, depending on the price of the item, the size of its market, and many other factors, including the people involved. For example, selling a big IBM mainframe computer requires a team of sales personnel, technical experts, sales managers, and administrative assistants. On the customer side, a committee composed of decision makers, technical wizards, and purchasing managers usually makes the buying decision.

1. **Lead generation:** Leads consist of contact information for customers who are tentatively interested in your product. Leads are "generated" through response to advertising, direct mailings, telemarketing, and other sources. Leads vary in quality. Some are "hot"—a customer very interested in acquiring the product or one like it immediately. Cool leads are ones that are less likely to produce a sale or ones that may produce a sale sometime in the future.

2. **Contact and qualification:** Telephone contact, from the contact information in the lead, is usually made with the prospect. The salesperson qualifies the prospect. This is the process of asking the customer a series of questions to identify exactly what they're looking to buy, how much money or credit is available, and when the purchase might or must be made. The questions are friendly in nature and often buried in what appears to be genuine interest in the customer, his family, or business.

    The salesperson may close (complete) the deal over the telephone. Telemarketing is a common kind of phone sale in which the process is completed in one or two telephone calls and then the product is delivered and the payment collected.

3. **Contact:** Following one or more phone contacts, physical contact is made when either the salesperson visits the customer (at home or business) or the customer visits the salesperson (in a home-based

DEFINITION: *Prospect*

"A prospect" is sales jargon for a likely customer who hasn't yet purchased the product. "I'm meeting with my prospect at 2 p.m. to try and close the deal." Looking for potential customers is known as *prospecting*.

store or outlet). The salesperson demonstrates the wares and/or offers a presentation to further reinforce the customer's understanding of the product and why it's the brand he or she should buy.

A proposal is then generated. This is either a written document that details feature and pricing information. In the case of a small purchase, the proposal may name the price and explain basic product benefits and why they meet the customer's needs.

4. **The close:** During the same meeting (or later during another meeting, phone call, or contact), the salesperson attempts to close the deal. Sometimes, this takes more contact sessions, depending on the prospect's readiness to commit and overall comfort with the price, terms, etc.

Should your prospect fail to buy or buy elsewhere, you should attempt to ascertain what went wrong. Was the prospect not really the decision maker? Did the competition's solution undercut your price or better fit the customer's needs? Or did the competition simply do a more effective selling job?

5. **Delivery:** The goods and services are provided by the salesperson or other personnel. The delivery may consist of little more than handing an item to the customer, on-site delivery and installation, or providing an on-site service such as furniture refinishing.

6. **Payment:** The salesperson ensures that the payment or contract terms are carried out. Payment may be made by credit card at the time of purchase, or terms, such as a

30-day trial period or multiple installment payments, may be offered. A salesperson (unless that's you, the owner) receives a commission once payment is received.

7. **Follow-up:** The salesperson follows up to ensure that the customer is satisfied and that any problems are immediately remedied. Subsequent quality assurance calls comfort customers and provide an opportunity for selling additional products, add-ons, warranty extensions, services, etc.

The sales cycle is the same in any business, be it small and home-based or conventional. The components of the cycle vary with the amount of time and effort required, according to the nature of the product. A single phone call may be all that's required to move an on-impulse item. (Example: telemarketers employed to get charity commitments under $100.) A carefully orchestrated "presentation and education" process may take months to convince a prospect to purchase a complex or very expensive product. (Example: representing heavy machinery from a home-based office.)

MORE ABOUT SELLING

Selling is a mix of common sense, enthusiasm, and hard work. It's a skill that takes time to build. You have to learn to judge your customers and put the right amount of highly focused effort into closing the deal. You have to learn to infer which prospects are viable and which ones are wasting your time. (It's harder than you'd think.) It's all too easy to dismiss a customer as a "stroker" than to add just the right touch that closes the sale. It's even easier spending days, weeks, and months working with a client on the "Big Deal" that never materializes.

This book can't teach you everything about selling. First, there's too much to learn. Second, you'll learn best by watching other people doing it—in sales seminars and in stores where "pitches" are made for everything from an add-on warranty to skin-care products.

Lead Generation and Analysis

Leads come in all shapes and sizes. They derive from sources including advertising, PR, direct mail, trade shows, customer calls, telemarketing, surveys, and contests, and they differ markedly in quality. The best lead is one in which the customer is already familiar with your product, and with credit card or purchase order (PO) in hand, calls you. The weakest lead is a session with the phone book or a mailing list purchased elsewhere; most of these would-be prospects have no interest in your wares. When following up on leads, always be sure you know where they came from. A bingo lead (see Chapter 15) from Brazil may actually be from a junior high school student who circled all 150 numbers on the magazine's card. You won't want to hop a Varig flight and waste an in-person sales call on such a lead!

Leads are prioritized. The hottest are addressed first, while the kid in Brazil is probably last. The customer who calls you should get immediate VIP attention. The kid in Brazil gets a brochure or price list. (Never completely ignore any lead, no matter how weak. The kid in Brazil might be doing research for Dad, the president of Global Ventures S.A., or he may grow up loathing your operation because you ignored him.) Ultimately, leads are sorted into three categories: Hot prospects (those who may buy *very* soon), warm prospects (those who may buy soon), and back-burner (those who probably won't buy soon or who don't qualify i.e., no money). Salespeople may also do their own prospecting. That is to say, they may look for their own leads and contacts instead of relying solely on ones generated from promotional activities.

Leads are also tracked. That way, you have a list of all contacts and know the status of their contact. Customer tracking is discussed later in the chapter.

Persuasion and Presentation

Persuasion is a two-way street. Instead of you, the seller, providing the prospect with a compelling reason to buy your product, the prospect must feel like they fully understand the product and are making the decision themselves. The most persuasive sales contact is a mutual exchange of questions and answers. You learn more about your client and his needs while he learns more about you, your product, and your company. This exchange builds your credibility, puts the customer at ease with you, and, who knows, you might learn more about the field you sell into.

Presenting Your Company

The key to selling is putting your best foot forward. You should look like you're in the business you sell into (crisp pinstripes for selling to IBM and clean work clothes for selling on a construction site). You must have a friendly demeanor and represent the interested, concerned person that your customer might like to have as a friend. Most importantly, it helps to be mentally fast on your feet to be persuasive and sound credible, especially when it comes to answering objections.

Ultimate Survival Tip

Talk Shouldn't Be Cheap

If you sell by telephone from home, buy a telephone that's of good quality and test its voice transmission quality. Otherwise, if you are difficult to hear, your prospect may give up trying to listen to you. When doing business on a cellular phone, always inform your client that you are using one so they understand why your voice sounds funny or occasionally cuts in and out. For telemarketing, pass on the $15 headset-style receiver. Buy one used by professional telemarketers. These are typically priced at least $100, but they usually last longer than a $25 unit.

Sound Like You Know What You're Doing

In addition to looking like the right person to do business with and involving the prospect in the presentation, you must sound credible to the person at the other end of the line or across the desk. Other than honing communication skills, there's no time used better by a salesperson than the time spent learning more about the product for sale, its market, how customers use it, why they need it, and its pricing. Customers are rightfully negative when dealing with a salesperson who has to ask someone else for information or thumb through a book to answer every question.

Benefits Versus Features

All salespeople are tired of the cliché, "sell the sizzle, not the steak." This is to say that the customer may be looking for a steak, but the true attraction comes from the steak sizzling on the grill, which produces a tantalizing aroma. In fact, the customer is looking for the sizzle, not just a large slab of raw meat.

That's true in sales, too. A customer who is looking at your company's carpet and upholstery cleaning services is not only looking for a clean rug and sofa but also the benefit of a better-looking home environment. Your company's services—deep cleaning, free carpet deodorizing, and optional stain proofing—provide the benefits of a better-looking home. When buying, your customer looks past the features to the benefits.

In a sales situation, you should explain your product's important features and link each one to a benefit. That way, the customer sees how the product will improve his life, business, prestige, etc.

Never Say Die

Persuasion never stops. Even after the sale closes, you must keep customers convinced that they made the right decision. With big-ticket items, there's often a period between commitment and when the goods or services are delivered. A customer, unsure that he made the right decision, or swayed by a competitor, will find a way to keep the transaction from finishing. Organization helps too. If you are presenting your product for the first time, prepare notes if you need help presenting yourself, company, and product.

Qualification and Objections

Arguably, the most important tactic in selling is qualifying customers. This is the process of identifying exactly what the customer is looking for, matching the right product in your line to the customer's needs, and verifying that the customer has the ability to pay for your product. (We once experienced a realtor who, through studied conversation, took our entire credit history except for account numbers.) Mistakes made in the qualification stage usually terminate the prospect of a successful sale. Here's what effective qualification requires:

1. **Be prepared.** Be it a phone call or a presentation to the company's Board of Directors, have all your product, pricing, and specification information at your fingertips. If a question that you can't answer is posed, instead of fudging around it, promise a return phone call with the information. Call the same day, if possible.

2. **Put your customer on comfortable ground.** Assure them that you won't waste their time while maintaining an outgoing stance. If the customer wants to chit-chat, by all means do it. If you're faced with a customer that shows you his watch and ominously states, "You've got just 5 minutes to make your pitch," chuckle softly and launch your most compelling points up front. Do it right, and the 5-minute window will vanish.

3. **Ask the right questions.** You should know what is important to the buyers of your wares. In "Jeopardy" style, turn the answers into questions. Example: If your product's main selling feature is price, then you should certainly ask if your prospect wants to save money.

4. **Listen.** The central tenet of qualification is the ability to listen. Everyone has been faced with a salesperson who talks non-stop ("It slices! It dices!"). These people are annoying because, rather than listening to what you want, they can only tell you what they've got. You can avoid the same mistake by listening carefully to what your prospect is asking for.

5. **Take notes.** Not only will this help you remember all points raised and all questions that need answers, in a person-to-person sales call, it also keeps you looking like you're hanging on the customer's every word and gives those nervous hands something to do.

6. **Respond.** Always ask for clarification of the points you don't understand. Otherwise, you may miss or misunderstand a key customer's concern or requirements.

Objections

Customers can always find a reason not to buy your product. Some are real objections that must be addressed. ("It's a great house, but my mortgage approval leaves me short $15,000.") Others are stalling tactics because they don't want, can't afford, or aren't convinced of the merits of your product. The classic consumer stalling tactic: "I'll talk to my wife/husband about it," is equal in business to: "I'll talk to my boss about it." Another timeless objection is, "I'll think about it." This kind of general objection results from one of the following:

1. You haven't provided a complete and/or convincing argument for a sale

2. You've done a poor job of qualifying and are pushing a product that's a poor match to the customer's needs or budget

3. The customer dislikes you, your company, or has a bad feeling about the transaction

Other objections are grounded in more specific issues, such as price, a missing feature, or a component lacking in the deal. Some customers will come right out and explain the problem when you ask if there is something about your offer that they're unhappy with. Some others will require you to ask probing questions to identify the root of their objection. It could be as little as an additional 2 percent price reduction to match the competition's price, or the problem might be more difficult to address, such as a customer with a $15,000 budget when your least expensive offer starts at $20,000.

By probing, you will hopefully find the real source of the problem and can then set about addressing it and closing the sale.

The Decision Maker

Part of the qualification process is to ensure that you are dealing with a person authorized to make purchasing decisions. The decision maker can be anyone, from someone ordering one of your unique $15.95 T-shirts to a committee made up of managers and purchasing agents in a major corporation. You need to successfully sell to *all* decision-making parties so they achieve consensus on the purchase. A routine part of the qualification process is to identify the decision maker(s) in order to understand your prospect's actual role in the purchase.

Some selling requires different approaches to each part of the buying team. When selling an automatic lawn sprinkling system (complete with hardware and installation) to a family, each decision maker may have their own agenda. One spouse may want easy-to-use controls, but the other, not concerned about ease

of use, wants elaborate timing features for better control of the lawn and garden. The kids may want pop-up heads for easier lawn trimming.

In a big company, your prospect's boss may be concerned about the product's cost and the effect it will have on the company's bottom line. Your prospect's employee, who will use your product, has technical questions about it. Your prospect's concern is the product's long-term maintenance package. Each of these people must be handled appropriately and have their concerns addressed because each has a say in the buying decision.

Closing

The easiest sale is one in which the customer is so fully convinced that they *ask* to buy your product, but not all sales are that easy. Sometimes, you must close the customer, which is to ask *them* to buy. From "would you like one" to "what can I do to get you to buy today," closing takes many forms. Not surprisingly, many salespeople feel awkward about closing and bungle it as a result.

Closing Early

A central part of persuasion is to verify the customer's interest in and comprehension of your argument. This is a type of close because a disinterested customer won't want to waste more time or respond to questions that require an iota of thought. Ask the customer if he/she would like to see a demonstration of your product or to respond to a question asked earlier in the discussion. A customer who is thinking about lunch instead of your pitch will not want to see a demo and won't remember what you said earlier.

FIVE REASONS CUSTOMERS WON'T BUY

1. You have a strong prospect, but you can't seem to get a commitment from him or her. An expensive lunch didn't bring you any closer to closing the sale, and probing questions reveal only evasiveness. What's wrong? You may not be dealing with the decision maker. The decision maker is the one with the authority to approve the sale. Your "customer" may actually be an underling with an impressive title, and your time is being wasted. Adequate and appropriate qualification should bring this matter to light. (In some companies, higher-ups may need to approve the deal, but the primary decision is made by your prospect.)

2. Your customer appears disinterested and yawns a lot during extended conversation. It could be that the classic advertising axiom, "you can't sell a product to people who don't need it," comes into play. Judge for yourself. When watching TV and a tire ad pops up, do you pay attention or ignore it? Most of the time, you reach for the mute button. If the car is due for a new set of wheels, however, the advertisement suddenly gets your complete attention.

3. Your customer appears disinterested and yawns a lot during extended conversation. If it's not Number 2, you may have bored the customer with an incessant presentation style when you should have involved them in the conversation. No one will buy in this state of mind. Instead, they'll look for a place to take a nap.

4. They can't afford the product. If, through the qualification process, you have ascertained your customer's budget requirements, it could be a simple matter of lack of money. They may be stalling in anticipation of next year's budget, a big sale they're about to make, a raise, winning the lottery, etc. Equally common are customers who want to finance the purchase but lack the credit credentials required.

5. Other forces are at work. On the consumer level, a disagreeing spouse may sink a sale. On the corporate level, the normally cooperative senior manager (who must authorize the deal) may balk at the cost, ask that the product be purchased from a company on an approved vendors list (find out how to get yourself on it!), or think the purchase is inappropriate or unnecessary.

One who does, however, is engaged, and you can go onto the next step, the trial close. The purpose of this exercise is to ensure that the customer is still with you mentally. Test for any objections and determine the customer's willingness to buy. A trial close isn't unlike the process from the last paragraph, but it takes a little more work on the customer's part. For example, telephone-based salespeople might ask a customer how he is going to put the product to work. Doing so requires the customer to think and may help him clarify and voice objections. During a sales meeting, you might ask your prospect for specification information, a demonstration of how he will use the product, or something else that requires just a little bit of effort. (Besides, you might really need this stuff.)

The Soft Close

If the preceding steps went well, you can try to close the deal if you've provided all the information requested by your client, clearly discussed pricing and terms, and it seems your client is interested and cooperative. If you're new to selling (that's why you're reading this chapter), try a two-step close. It's easy and even if you sound nervous trying it, chances are your prospect won't notice the close.

Step 1: "Is there anything else you need to know?"

This informs the client that you've provided all the information they need, and it gives them a chance to ask additional questions or raise objections. Should new points come up, address them. Then begin again with Step 1, saving the close until your customer is fully satisfied that he is making the right decision.

Step 2: "Well, I think that covers everything. Would you like to purchase a *YOUR PRODUCT NAME HERE?*"

Step 3: Thank the customer and explain what (if anything) needs to be done to finalize the deal. Hand the product to the customer and get a credit card number, purchase order number, or a contract signature, as appropriate.

This simple approach provides two escape routes for your prospect. The soft-but-direct approach either achieves a commitment or provides you with information you need to complete the deal. Should Step 2 fail, with the reasons the client provides for "No," you can address the problem and begin the close again when the time is right. If the product has a short sales cycle, you can close again during the same phone conversation or meeting. For longer sales cycles (especially if responding to customer objections requires additional research, thought, or information) the closing process may have to wait until the next contact.

The Hard Close

There is a close you can use in certain situations, such as when a customer is about to "walk" (abandon the possibility of a sale). Customers walk when they decide they don't want the product or have tentatively chosen a competitor's. Unlike the softer approach, this tactic puts customers on notice that (1) it's time to buy now and (2) they have an opportunity to get the best deal possible. A typical hard-close line is:

"What would it take to get you to buy right now (today)?"

At this point, the customer is likely either to be mildly offended at your tactics or to explain what's holding him back from consummating the transaction. This tactic is used in businesses when the prices are negotiable, the transaction must take place quickly, and the decision maker has full authority. The hard close is (usually) impossible when a committee decision must be reached or approval by the purchasing department or other higher-ups must be sought before the sale closes.

A home-based business that distributes products to consumers might use the hard close on the phone to sell their wares. Likewise, a home-based appliance repairman might use it to close a deal with a waffling customer. In a highly competitive situation, the hard close can be employed after first attempting the soft close to find out why the customer won't commit.

Customer Satisfaction

Keeping buyers happy is one of the most important aspects of sales. A happy customer buys again *and* spreads positive word-of-mouth advertising about you and your company. The latter often provides easy-to-close referral business.

Customer satisfaction begins the minute the deal is closed, whether the customer receives the product immediately or has to wait thirty-three days to get his house painted because your painters are booked. Through follow-up (most often consisting of phone calls) the salesperson needs to ensure that the product arrives and works as promised. Also be certain that other members of your company treat the customer with respect and provide timely responses to questions, problems, and service. Should a product require on-site delivery and set-up, the salesperson should be there to explain procedures to the customer, answer any ques-

tions, and ensure that set-up goes without a hitch, even if the salesperson doesn't set up the product himself. Complicated products may require hands-on demonstration and training.

For a product with long lead time between the close and delivery, constant, regular follow-up is required. If the customer has or acquires lingering doubts, he'll often find a way to torpedo the deal. Following up with regular contact gives the customer an opportunity to explain anything he isn't entirely satisfied with. This also applies to products that are delivered but have a 7- or 30-day return policy. Your follow-up calls to address questions and problems go a long way to keep the product from rolling back in the door.

SALES CHANNELS

There are many ways to move goods and services through selling tactics. One of the major marketing decisions home-based entrepreneurs make in market planning is how to sell their product. Part of this decision is based on the product itself. Products may be sold to endusers, (the people who actually put it to work), distributors (who sell it to other companies who sell it to endusers), or wholesale distributors (who sell it to distributors who sell it to endusers).

There are five channels of distribution. More than one channel may be employed before a product reaches the enduser. Likewise, a product may be sold through multiple channels to reach a larger slice of the market pie.

- **Retail.** You sell directly to endusers through a home-based store or via mail order.

- **Direct.** A business sells their goods or services directly to the enduser. Your home-based enterprise convinces a distributor (often more than one) to carry a line of goods.
- **Distributor.** A separate business buys the product from you and, in turn, sells it directly to the enduser or to another business, such as a retailer, for sale. You buy the product from a source and resell it at a markup.
- **VAR (value-added reseller).** A business purchases a product, adds features, and then sells the "value-added" product to either a distributor or an enduser. You buy a finished product, add your name and (usually) additional components, and resell the package at a profit. Example: computer motherboards. You purchase computer boards from one source, cases from another, and also additional components. You assemble a finished computer that is ready for buyers who won't want to buy and assemble the separate components.
- **OEM (original equipment manufacturer).** Sometimes bantered about, particularly in the computer industry, an OEM makes the original goods sold to a VAR for "improvement." Many OEMs also directly sell their own version of the finished product through another channel(s).

Services are sold the same way, although the format looks different. For example, if your home-based business offers historical tours of your home town, a larger tour company may be interested. They contract with you to include your tour on one of their package tours. You, in turn, provide the tour to members of each party visiting your town but are paid by the tour company. For their "distribution" services, they collect a markup (the difference between what they collect from package participants and what they pay you).

From a sales perspective, the steps in selling are identical, but selling on the road to distributors is a much longer process than moving a product through a factory-direct retail outlet.

CUSTOMER TRACKING

Part of a salesperson's job is to track leads, prospects, and customers. Although usually done via one of many customer tracking software packages, in a shoestring home-based business, an index card file can be used. Tracking is used to provide salespeople with a list of prospects to call, information on the state of the sale, what the customer has previously purchased, and the customer's credit rating with the company. The company uses this data to produce mailing lists for future promotions, to track sales and success rates, and, if multiple salespeople are employed, to ensure that there's no overlap (when one salesperson calls on another's clients. In sophisticated home-based operations, the tracking database can also be used by others to check a customer's account status and to schedule delivery and service requests.

On a rainy day, a salesperson can use the tracking system to obtain a list of prospects who haven't purchased your product for one reason or another. Calling a customer who wasn't ready for a commitment at the last contact may result in a new sale!

WHAT *NOT* TO DO

People don't like to be manipulated. High-pressure sales tactics, lies, and a bad attitude send customers to your competition. Pressure tactics (even ones that result in a sale) can anger customers. This results in the deal falling through, the goods being returned, no chance of future business, and negative word-of-mouth advertising.

No one has to resort to manipulative tactics to sell effectively. It's an indication of poor salesmanship or lack of faith in the product, or it's a sign that the company needs the money now because they're already in trouble for some reason. (At a car dealership, the salesperson may take the keys to your trade-in or your driver's license, and conveniently, not return them until you buy or they run out of tactics.) This is part of the hard-sell game. Make it hard for unwilling customers to leave, apply pressure, and people cave in.

A hard sell is manipulative and often uncomfortable for both the seller and the buyer. Home-based businesses that rely on repeat-business customers should avoid hard-sell tactics. Fortunately, most professional salespeople can effectively convince a customer of a product's integrity and the customer's need for such a product The customer will then pull out a checkbook or sign a PO, almost on reflex. Now *that's* the approach for you.

14

Promotion Starts With Your Company's Identity

It doesn't matter how small your company is, nor where it's located: you need a company identity to separate your company from the competition. An identity is the look and feel your company has in the outside world. A carefully designed identity will help you to stand out from the competition and to be remembered by customers, the press, and other members of your industry. Your identity as a company is also important in maintaining a positive image. In this chapter, we cover the basics of developing a corporate identity, product packaging, and other identity-related programs to help get your message out to the crowds.

ESTABLISHING YOUR COMPANY'S IDENTITY

Several elements are used to create your company's look and feel. First, there are the overt elements, such as your choice of logo and company colors. Second, there is the overall use of color, the style of typography, frequently used design elements, and the way the pieces of the communications program work together as a family. If you have multiple products, you may have subidentities for brands or product lines as well as an overall company look.

Identity programs should be carefully designed, tested, and then used consistently on all visually oriented communications, from your letterhead to press releases and television commercials. By establishing an appropriate look and sticking to it, your communications are instantly recognizable to those already familiar with your company, and you will easily build an image in the minds of those unfamiliar with your company. A consistent identity also makes the communications process much easier because your audience will recognize you and will already have a positive knowledge of your company.

The Logo

Logos are symbols or marks that are used to identify an organization. Your logo may be as simple as a particular typeface of your company name always printed in a specific color of blue. Or, your logo may be a highly refined mark developed by a professional design firm. Large companies may pay several hundred-thousand dollars for an appropriate logo.

The right symbol consistently rendered in the same color gives an organization a strong identity. It can be legally protected so that other companies can't copy or use a mark that is deceptively similar.

The design of a logo should be handled by an accomplished logo designer, if you can afford one. If not, a strong type treatment of your company's name may suffice until more money is available. The logo should not be created in isolation, however. It should be part

of an overall company look that includes company colors and possibly the selection of a typeface, compatible with the logo, that will be used in printed materials.

The Look

In addition to the logo, companies develop and evolve a look that, together with their logo, makes them instantly recognizable in a crowd of other companies. The look includes, but is not limited to, a certain typeface for use in all communications materials, specific colors, and certain stylistic elements that can be readily associated with other materials from the same company.

This look, for maximum effectiveness, is conveyed through all of the company's communications programs and is usually adaptable to a wide range of implementations. Large companies may put together a style manual that explains the look they have chosen and how to implement it. Since few looks remain inviting and up-to-date for periods of more than a few years, you may need to adjust your look over the years, but modify it slowly, and make sure the old look has some relationship to the new one.

The Tag Line

A tag line is a brief sentence that describes a company's business or philosophy. The tag line is optional, but, if you choose to have one, it should always accompany the logo on major communications and company letterhead. Short, snappy tag lines add identity and can be used to explain your business to the uninitiated. Tag lines evolve with the company, and it is acceptable to change your tag line as long as

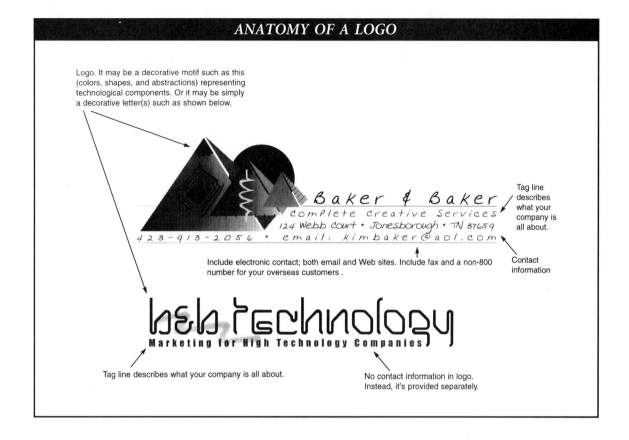

ANATOMY OF A LOGO

Logo. It may be a decorative motif such as this (colors, shapes, and abstractions) representing technological components. Or it may be simply a decorative letter(s) such as shown below.

Baker & Baker
Complete Creative Services
124 Webb Court • Jonesborough • TN 37659
423-913-2056 • email: kimbaker@aol.com

Tag line describes what your company is all about.

Include electronic contact; both email and Web sites. Include fax and a non-800 number for your overseas customers .

Contact information

web Technology
Marketing for High Technology Companies

Tag line describes what your company is all about.

No contact information in logo. Instead, it's provided separately.

all materials that display the old tag line are replaced within six months to a year.

The Color

The most identifying aspect of a company's look is probably the color(s) employed in the logo and used consistently in your company materials. There are design houses that do nothing but choose colors for companies and spend a considerable amount of time (and your money) researching and testing color combinations. For obvious reasons, color is not important in radio, and, in the case of TV, anything goes, but, for print communications, color can be a major identifier.

Here are a few basic tips when you consider your company colors:

- Avoid browns and greens as dominant colors because they draw a negative reaction from many people. Occasionally, they can be used as secondary elements.

- Avoid the obvious use of "business" blue and gray. These colors are certainly the safest route to travel but also the most boring because they are so overused by companies.

- Gray and maroon and maroon-on-creme are color schemes that were popular in the 1970s and are now out-of-date. Using them will make your company appear out of step with the times. Brown–on–creme is equally passé. However, in ten years or so, you may find these colors coming back in favor again.

- Surprisingly, some pastel colors are safe choices and can be very effective when employed by a designer with an eye for color. Because any color can be used as a pastel, this color family offers you a wide range of choices. (Pastels are colors with substantial amounts of white added to lighten them.)

- Signal yellow is a strong attention-getting color. When used tastefully, it can make your literature jump out at readers.

- Gray-on-gray combinations are attractively conservative and, if handled by the right designer, can make a very appealing color combination.

- Bright colors are strong attention-getters, and they excite people. Dull colors tend to relax (or bore) people. If your company is conservative, use relaxing colors. If your company employs new technology or sells trendy products, use exciting colors.

- Use strong reds and red-oranges to draw attention to a logo or tag line, but don't overuse them. The eye and mind are quickly fatigued by too much red stimulation.

- If you make products that compete against or work with products sold by a much larger and more recognizable company, consider adopting a corporate color scheme that is similar to theirs but different enough to separate you. (Note that some color schemes are registered trademarks and that adopting them is illegal).

- Colors go in and out of style in cycles. Adopting today's hot, trendy color may quickly date your literature when tastes later change. Choose something you will be able to live with over the long haul.

- Only consider foil stamping or metallic inks if you can afford to print them on everything from letterhead to brochures, as this is an expensive process.

- If your look involves the use of creme or light tan, consider printing on a creme-colored paper. There are several excellent creme-colored sheets such as Karma Natural available.

- Rules are meant to be broken. A designer with a real eye for color can disprove all of the above suggestions by producing a stunning look that uses passé colors or ones that are overused. Unfortunately, without a lot of shopping and a large budget, you are unlikely to find such a person to develop your company's colors. If you're not sure, play it safe and observe these rules.

MAINTAINING THE LOOK

We suggest that you look at professional design books before you choose your company look, and, unless you're a designer, go to a professional who can help you develop a look and feel for your company. Remember, once a look is established for your company, it must be used consistently in all communications, regardless of how trivial the communication may seem. Using a variation of a logo on the company's checks is a bad idea because check recipients might wonder if it represents a new logo or a different division of the same company.

PRODUCT PACKAGING FOR ATTRACTIVENESS AND UTILITY

If your company sells physical products, you will require packaging in addition to your company's look. Packaging plays several roles, depending on the product and its path to sale and consumption. Packaging is used to protect products during shipping and handling and to give a product shelf appeal if it's sold in a retail store. Consumer products that depend on this appeal (like shampoos and liquid soaps) are usually designed by experts—some with more than 20 years of experience in designing and engineering product packages.

Merchandising, which goes along with packaging, is the display system used to promote products in a retail environment. Examples include cardboard displays that generate awareness of goods and services, neon beer signs, electronic messages on the Goodyear Blimp, and any other awareness-generating mechanism that doesn't physically contain a product.

Packaging Primer

If you need to package a product, the first order of business is to decide what you want the packaging to accomplish and then to choose a format that meets these requirements. If you are currently designing a product that will rely on a potentially expensive package, consider investigating the packaging issues before finalizing the product design. Sometimes, minor changes to a product's size or shape can substantially affect the package cost. Ideally, product specifications and product packaging should be developed in tandem so that both items work together for maximum utility and appeal.

Another factor to consider when choosing a package is the manufacturing process. If your product will be stuffed into its package by a machine, for example, the capabilities of the equipment must be kept in mind when designing both the product and its package.

The packaging for a single product may include one or more of the following packaging options:

- **Containment Packaging.** These packages contain the actual product. Cremes and ointments that require packaging (lead or plastic tubes) to contain and dispense the product. In the case of more durable packaging, such as aerosol containers, the product package is also the shelf package.

- **Utility Product Packaging.** Many products require packaging that has some shelf appeal but is primarily intended to protect the product during shipping. Consumer electronic products, such as VCRs and computers, are packaged inside a minimally decorated cardboard box. They are further isolated from damage by carefully designed foam pieces that keep the outside box from making direct contact with the product during rough handling.

- **Shelf Packaging.** The objective of shelf packaging is to get the product noticed on a shelf of competing products. The packages most also provide protection during transportation to the purchaser's final destination. For example, in the case of toothpaste, containment packaging is used to contain and dispense the product. Then the tube is stuffed into shelf packaging which consists of a printed cardboard box. This additional level of packaging is used to make stacking easy and to protect the tube until it reaches the buyer's bathroom. Most shelf packaging is designed to promote the product, and provides enough information for the buyer to make an informed decision before purchase.

- **Transport Packaging.** Often consisting of corrugated cardboard boxes with little or no printed decoration, this transport packaging may contain a number of shelf-packaged units. Transport packaging not only protects the units from damage, it also makes the product easier to handle. For example, cans of ground coffee are sent in transport packaging boxes to facilitate the handling of a large number of cans and to protect the cans from dings and scratches. Occasionally, two levels of transport packaging may be required.

- **Image Packaging.** Some packaging is actually more important than the product. These are called "image packages." Consider perfumes and expensive cosmetics as examples. Many times, the elaborate packages are more expensive than the contents. These packages must incorporate design, shelf appeal, and identity in order to be effective.

Packaging Your Product

Product packaging, beyond a very basic plain cardboard box or simple shrinkwrap, is best left to experts. In addition to designing packages that are durable, safe, and appealing, a good packaging designer knows where to buy the most cost-effective materials and fabrication labor. These savings quickly pay for the design services and get you a package that meets your objectives.

Look for a designer or design firm with a broad packaging portfolio that includes the same kind of materials you will use. For example, if your product requires elaborate glass bottles, don't hire someone who designs fancily printed cardboard boxes—they won't have the experience you need.

If your packaging needs include custom bottles or plastic containers, you may need to hire both a designer and a package fabrication engineer. Sometimes a designer will render a look for the package and the packaging engineer will then implement the final fabrication. The engineer will work with the designer to take the concept from sketches to reality and will occasionally reject ideas that are unworkable or risky.

Here are the basic steps for creating packaging (these hold true whether you're doing it yourself or working with a packaging designer):

Step 1. Collect samples of your competitor's packaging. If your product must compete head-to-head with someone else's product on a store shelf or retail floor, your product must look at least as good, if not better, than your competition's (unless yours costs less). Your designer should study these samples too.

Step 2. Define how your product will be shipped, displayed, and contained. You need to consider packaging requirements from the factory to your end-user. Adequate protection during shipping and warehousing is vital to maintain product integrity and to keep shelf packaging fresh and compelling. Packaging designs must also take into account transportation after the sale. For example, a customer purchasing eggs that are sold in a flimsy container may arrive home to find them scrambled right in the carton.

Step 3. Approve a design. A competent designer will research your needs and show you several sketches for your approval. If you are designing your packaging within the confines of a budget, there are several sources for ready-made and semicustom packages.

You can find standard cardboard packaging at mailing stores or through a catalog from a local box manufacturer (found under Boxes—Corrugated & Fiber in the *Yellow Pages*). Some cities have stores that only sell packaging on a retail level. They will have a wide variety of box styles available, and the suppliers can special order many that aren't displayed. Many of these boxes can be overprinted with your product name, logo, and other text and graphics.

If you are looking for off-the-shelf packaging ideas other than cardboard, call vendors of special promotional items (found under Advertising Specialties in the *Yellow Pages*). Many of these companies dabble in packaging, and they may be able to give you a solution that requires only a little custom work. These companies also handle a variety of cardboard and plastic items, although they generally cost more than buying directly from the manufacturer.

Suppliers for bubble packs, foam, and custom plastic packages can be found under the several Plastics listings in the *Yellow Pages*.

Step 4. Assemble a sample to see how the package works. Once you have approved the design or selected the materials, ask the designer to assemble a *dummy* from the actual materials. A dummy is a proof that closely resembles the finished package. Study it carefully to make sure that everything looks right and, most important, that your product fits properly. If your project involves packages within packages, check that they all fit together and that the innermost packages are adequately protected by the outside ones. Test your package dummy (or off-the-shelf packaging sample) for:

- **Breakage During Shipping.** Drop the boxes onto concrete several times, if appropriate, to ensure that the product remains intact. In the case of products shipped by truck or the Postal Service, the transport package (with the product inside) should be able to stand about a six foot drop onto concrete without major damage.

- **Crushing.** Estimate the maximum weight of packages that can be stacked on top of your packaging. First, weigh the dummy (with the product inside) on an ordinary bathroom scale. Then place red bricks on top of your packaging until the weight on the scale equals 120 percent of the packages weight. The product should remain intact, and any shelf packaging should remain undamaged.

- **Weather Proofing.** If you product must endure storage outside in the elements, make sure it can withstand the sun, rain, cold, and heat.

- **Containment.** If your product is a powder or liquid and is packaged in self-shipping containers, it should not leak after the above tests are performed nor when heated or cooled within normal environmental ranges.

- **Gluing.** If your package uses glue, it should be tested for failure under conditions of hot and cold. Keep in mind that a product shipped across the desert by tractor-trailer during the summer will be exposed to extreme heat for as long as a week. The area near the ceiling of a sealed truck may reach temperatures of 200 degrees or more in the sun. A glue that's strong and resilient at room temperature may turn to goo in such conditions. Other glues crack when they get too cold.

- **Hazardous Product Testing.** If you sell potentially hazardous products, have an accredited lab test and approve the packaging.

Step 5. Produce and inspect the packaging. Have the packaging produced and inspected for defects before you accept the shipments. The steps for producing many of the printed elements of packaging are similar to the collateral production steps covered in Chapter 18.

Ultimate Survival Tip

There May Be Special Legal Requirements for Your Packaging

There are a number of labeling, declaration, processing, permit, and other requirements you must meet if your package will cross international borders or will be used to transport hazardous materials (pressurized gases and other flammables), foodstuffs (meat and agricultural products), alcohol, and prescription medications. Get expert advice on any such issues before you design and print the package.

MERCHANDISING FOR MAXIMUM IN-STORE VISIBILITY

In terms of breadth, merchandising is a massive area of communications. All signs and displays that promote a product or a company are merchandising. The production steps for most merchandising elements are similar to those covered already for collateral materials. Rather than describe all the merchandising possibilities (that would take a book in itself), here are some effective merchandising ideas that work for a variety of products:

- For physically small consumer products sold in a retail environment, colorful cardboard displays work well. They grab the eye and free up valuable shelf space in stores already jammed with merchandise. Cardboard countertop displays also work well in some markets.

- Brightly colored signs generate strong awareness for certain products. Provide your dealers with quality, attention-getting signs. Bright banners, attractive neon signs, and lighted displays all work well. Make sure that all printed signs are regularly replaced because they easily fade or become soiled.

- For complex mechanical or electronic products, small signs that explain the operation of each part are a powerful education tool. For example, the technological advantages of a new machine can be explained with small signs attached to each important section. This way, even if no salesperson is available, customers can get a good understanding of the product and what it can do for them. These signs, acting as cues, also help salespeople make a more organized sales presentation.

- For feature-laden products, such as consumer electronics, signs that list the features of the product are helpful to consumers as they comparison shop. If your product has a sign that lists its features but your competitor's product doesn't, you have a better chance of getting the sale. This is particularly important for consumer electronics because their product lines are frequently replaced with new models. Few salespeople can keep up with every new product feature.

- For products sold in large quantities to a big chain of stores, custom display signage is helpful. For example, if your company makes homemade soups that are sold through a chain of grocery stores, your product will have higher visibility if you provide the grocery store with elegant signs to accompany the shelf pricing. In this case your custom signs should be made to fit comfortably alongside the store's pricing signs, which usually fit into a grooved shelf edge.

- Posters are excellent merchandising tools for many markets. They work to increase product awareness and to build your image. The best posters end up permanently attached to your customer's wall (even framed). You can use posters at trade fairs, swap meets, retail stores, and other locations.

The best source of merchandising ideas is found where your product will be sold. Watch customers making buying decisions. This will give you some idea of why one product is chosen over another. Study your competitor's merchandising schemes as well. You may pick up an idea or see a new opening for generating awareness.

PROMOTIONAL ITEMS

Also known in the trade as advertising specialty items, promotional items are generally used to complement other promotions or the sales process and help to keep your company's name visible before, during and after the sale. Special promotional items are imprinted with your company's name, address, phone number, and often a message. Examples of common items include imprinted coffee mugs, pens, shirt pocket protectors, and notepad holders.

Special promotional items are available directly from manufacturers, but it is much easier to buy them from a dealer. While dealers often charge a markup over factory prices, they also readily resolve any conflicts you may encounter and are invaluable in getting orders straight.

Specialty advertising dealers can be found in the *Yellow Pages* under Advertising Specialties. A few of the companies in this classification only imprint wedding and party items. Unless you're planning a wedding or party, stick with the firms that handle business-oriented promotional items. Because there are so many items to choose from, many of these companies print a catalog of their wares, or they will have a showroom of merchandise available for viewing. Some are even equipped with computers that can take a word or phrase and then search through hundreds of thousands of items to find a match between idea and product.

What Promotional Items Can Do

Special promotional items are used to remind a customer or prospective customer of a company or product. They can also be used to commemorate an event or to remind employ-ees of a corporate goal or new program. A well-chosen special promotion can have a long life on a recipient's desk or be used routinely in daily life. This category of communications has the longest potential lifespan of any tool in the marketing communications toolbox. Of course, not all special promotions are that successful. Many end up in the trash can with-out receiving any attention whatsoever.

Selecting Promotional Items

When choosing a special promotional item, the goal is to select one that your customers will not only keep but also use or see on a daily basis. That way your name is always on display. What makes this difficult is that many inexpensive specialty items are useless to a wide range of people. Your customers may already have one or more given to them by other companies. Choosing an item of general use is advantageous because more of your cus-tomers are likely to keep it. However, if you consider an obvious item, such as a coffee mug, many people already have a closet full of mugs given to them by various companies. Choosing an unusual item may uniquely iden-tify your company, but fewer of your custom-ers may have a need for an unusual item and it may hit the trash can or be given to their kids.

Good taste is particularly important when choosing these items. Some items are of a sexual nature and therefore destined to be offensive to many customers. Some are simply tacky. Many are obviously cheap, and giving someone a piece of junk will not help boost your image in any way. A common mistake when selecting a special promotional item is to look for the cheapest item possible so that a

larger number can be handed out. The gift must match the recipient's level of importance. Giving the president of a major company a cheap plastic notepad holder is a mismatch—he or she may take offense to the gift rather than appreciate it. Giving a low-level employee in a customer's organization an expensive gift may seem like a bribe.

Here are some suggestions that you can follow when shopping for the right item:

- If your recipients are technically oriented, consider giving them something they might actually use, such as a precision ruler or a mechanical pencil. Neither of these gifts is expensive.

- For management-level recipients, give some-thing that will be useful. Desk organizers that hold scissors, tape, rulers, and other items are an example of something they might use. A leather day book or a notes portfolio is always a good choice. Another appropriate example is a tasteful or unusual clock (not one with an LCD readout). Even if they don't use it at work, they'll probably take it home.

- For recipients in an office environment, consider giving away an inexpensive battery-operated pencil sharpener or an electric letter opener. Small computer tool sets are also appreciated by people who work with personal computers. Tools to take apart and hook up computers are always in short supply in offices.

- If you must give a coffee mug, choose one that is highly unusual in shape or have a designer put together a brightly colored mug. While a recipient may already have several mugs, if yours is especially unusual and/or attractive, it will be the one its owner uses while the others gather dust on a shelf. The same thing applies to t-shirts, another standard give-away. Make the design memorable and use quality shirts.

- Avoid giving alcoholic beverages away, unless you know the person. While, at one time, a bottle of fine wine or imported liqueur was considered a tasteful present, unless you know that the intended recipient enjoys such beverages, this is risky. You might be giving it to a recovering alcoholic or to someone whose religion forbids alcohol.

- Pens and pencils have long been standard giveaway items. People actually do use them. Unfortunately, unless you can afford to give away Mont Blancs or Cross pens, these items don't have a long lifespan in customers' hands.

- For retail giveaways, consider selecting a promotional item that goes along with the sale and is useful as a result. If you sell swimming pool equipment, give away an imprinted inflatable beach ball. If you sell expensive jewelry, give away an imprinted ultrasonic jewelry cleaner. While these may cost you $10 a piece in quantity, if you sold a number of $2,500 rings as a result, then you can afford it.

- Try to match the specialty item to your organization's message or business, if possible. For example, one company makes a product that solves serious computer problems and gives out imprinted bottles of aspirin that say, "Without XYZ products, this is your only recourse for computer headaches!"

Ordering and Producing Advertising Specialty Items

Specialty-item production is fraught with problems, but you can avoid most of them by following the right steps when ordering and inspecting the merchandise. Because many of these items originate in Taiwan and Hong Kong, the quality control often leaves something to be desired. The American and Canadian companies that make custom items and do imprinting are often not very well organized either. Here's how to get the best results when you order your special promotional items:

- When ordering an item from a catalog (or if you have not actually seen the product) ask the salesperson for a sample. This sample will usually be rushed to you and won't slow the ordering process much. The actual product may be much poorer in quality than you imagine so you may want to order something else. If the final order is not of the same quality as the sample (a frequent occurrence), you can point to your sample and say, "This is what I ordered and this is what I want." When ordering custom-made items, such as an expensive gold lapel pin or something encased in a clear plastic cube, ask that a sketch or rendering be done before the work begins. This sketch may be an extra charge, but, without one, you may be very surprised by what you actually receive when the finished order arrives.

- Put all instructions to the vendor in writing, and keep a copy for yourself. Because the information must pass through several hands before reaching the factory floor, there are plenty of opportunities for miscommunication. Written instructions give you a better chance of getting what you ordered. Additionally, if something does come out wrong, your written instructions are a free ticket for getting it fixed or replaced.

- When your order arrives, *check all of it carefully*. Without careful inspection, you may not notice a problem until salespeople are already giving the item away. It is possible for part of an order to arrive as specified and part to arrive with serious flaws (often buried in the bottom of a box and hard to find).
- If your logo is imprinted or embossed on the item, make sure you provide a clean copy of your logo to the manufacturer. The logo should be the same size or larger than the imprinted one. Never provide a small logo that must be enlarged because this will cause rough edges in the imprint.

If you are unsure about the appropriateness of an item for your market, test it. Get a sample and then ask several of your friendlier customers what they think of it. Would they would like one if you were giving them out? Take anything less than a very enthusiastic "yes" to mean that the item is not appropriate, desirable, or of sufficient quality for your needs.

Taken together, the tools presented in this chapter can give your company a physical presence in your marketplace. The corporate or organizational identity you assemble allows you to put your best foot forward, and special promotional items keep your name in front of your customers. Together, these tools can give your company a positive, memorable image and separate you from the "me too" competitors so common in home-based industries and businesses.

Advertising Basics for Home-Based Businesses

Just because your business is home-based doesn't mean that the advertising program needs to be incompetent or unprofessional. Home-based companies can and should consider spending some money on quality advertising, just like large corporations do. Through the right advertising, no one will ever know you build your custom furniture in your garage or make your salsa in your kitchen. In this chapter, a wide range of advertising opportunities are suggested. Some will be more appropriate for you than others, but you should understand how you and your competitors may use them.

The business of selling products is often referred to as a war—a war to beat the competition to market, a war for limited consumer dollars, and a war with increased sales and profit as the victory. In the battleground of business, advertising is the key tactical weapon. The right ad seen by the right people can change a company's position in the sales war almost overnight, which is why companies continue to spend more and more on advertising. Yet advertising is a battle in itself—a battle for recognition and response and a battle between creative concepts and creative minds.

Advertising was defined earlier as *a persuasive, nonpersonal communication paid for by a company or sponsor to be published, displayed, or broadcast with the purpose of promoting a product*. This means that when you advertise you pay to get your message across to your marketplace through print, television, radio, or outdoor advertising media.

Advertising can be used to educate, inform, motivate, and reinforce or change an image. Advertising is generally regarded as the single most powerful tool for getting the word out about a product or service. While often the most costly form of marketing communications, with some advertisers spending more on ad placements than on any other single line item in their budget, the expense of a strong advertising program can result in substantial returns.

All advertising and most other promotions must meet four basic criteria if they are going to do their jobs in the sales struggle:

1. They must be seen or heard by target customers
2. They must deliver an effective message
3. They must be seen or heard often enough to have an impact on a world crowded with advertising
4. They must stand out from other ads for competing products

A successful ad not only catches the attention of its viewer or listener, but it holds their attention long enough to get its message across. If your ad works, people will buy your product or remember you the next time they need what you have to sell. The resulting income is used by the business to build more products and to buy more advertising in an on-going cycle. Effective advertising can profoundly affect a market quickly—turning an unknown product into a major profit maker almost over night.

Today, because of the acceptance and power of advertising, large sums of money may be required for purchasing effective advertising media. Money and media go hand in hand, which is one reason why there are an ever-increasing number of channels for promoting products. Advertising single-handedly supports the very existence of all radio and television stations and networks, with the exception of nonprofit religious stations, PBS, and National Public Radio. Almost every magazine and newspaper is fully dependent on advertisers. Subscription and newsstand revenues barely pay for paper and printing used to produce most publications—it's advertising revenue that keeps them alive and well.

The growth in specialty magazines and newspapers is completely fueled by advertisers looking for better ways to reach an audience with specific needs, interests, and tastes. There has been equally phenomenal growth in trade-specific publications. Where once a handful of magazines such as *Ladies Home Journal* and *Saturday Evening Post* dominated the market, today's publications can be pretty esoteric. Trade magazine titles include *Llamas Magazine— The International Camelid Journal; Your Virginia State Trooper Magazine*; and who could forget the *Mid-Continent Bottler*, which according to *Writers Market* is dedicated to "soft drink bottlers in the 20-state Midwestern area." Everyone from mortuary owners to automobile glass installers has his own specialty trade publication.

Media expansion and targeting is also taking place in television. The cable-only channel, Lifetime, runs shows and ads targeted at doctors and the health conscious. The Travel Channel runs travel videos, which are really long TV commercials to attract tourists. ESPN provides full-time sports coverage and sports-oriented ads. Other cable programs include science fiction, humor, and gourmet cooking. The trend toward targeted programs and channels is new to television, and we can expect more specialized programming as the cable companies scramble to add channel capacity.

This expansion of media and advertising is both a blessing and a curse to advertisers—a blessing because many companies can buy advertising space in magazines or media that clearly appeal to people with specific interests. The expansion is also a curse because companies that sell products to a very broad market without clearly differentiating traits (such as toothpaste and soft drinks) must use very expensive space and airtime in popular media such as network television and major news magazines to reach enough people.

THE FUNCTIONS AND CLASSIFICATIONS OF ADVERTISING

Today there are four general classifications of advertising, including image advertising, consumer product advertising, trade and professional business advertising, and retail advertising. Each of these classifications has specific functions and market appeal.

Image Advertising

To ensure a positive reception in the communities and markets they serve, large corporations develop image ads. The primary function of an image ad is to build corporate awareness and positive associations in a broad marketplace. Sales development is a long-term, peripheral goal of image ads. These ads rarely focus on specific products, but instead highlight a recent corporate success or an innovative new program. Image ads are also used by large, faceless corporations to establish a corporate presence in the mind of the public. Transamerica Corporation, for example, is a financial services company that was publicly invisible before building their now-famous pyramid-shaped office building in downtown San Francisco and spending a fortune on image ads showing the pyramid. Sometimes groups of organizations (The Beef Council, The American Gas Association) use image advertising to jointly promote a cause or interest. Many examples of image ads can be found in upscale business-oriented magazines such as *Forbes*, *Fortune*, and *The Economist*.

Consumer Product Advertising

Consumer advertising is designed to reach and influence the mass market. Consumer ads have the function of making the public at large aware of products used in everyday life. The bulk of television advertising and the ads in popular magazines are consumer advertising. While often placed by the same companies that do institutional and corporate image advertising, these ads focus on a specific product or product line and are trying to persuade you to buy the product. A reverse consumer products ad is one that solicits donations for charities and nonprofit organizations. Examples of consumer product ads can be found in magazines such as *Cosmopolitan*, *Sports Illustrated*, and *Time*.

Trade, Professional, and Business Advertising

For products sold directly by one business to another or for products that are used only in a specific occupation or profession, it would be a waste of money to advertise in mass media because only a small percentage of readers, viewers, or listeners would have any interest in the product. Therefore, a business selling products aimed at another business or profession uses specialty publications and media that appeal directly to their market. The goal of this category of advertising is to be highly focused and well-targeted. These ads are often more educational in approach, with more detail on product features and benefits than normally found in consumer advertising. Examples of these ads can be found in trade or business-specific magazines and newspapers.

Retail Advertising

Retailers, including department stores, specialty shops, markets, and malls, must also advertise to attract customers. Retail ads may emphasize specific product specials ("Iceberg lettuce 59¢ this week only!") or instead may announce a big sale or promote a special event at the store. Retail advertising primarily uses local media to get its messages across. The purpose of this kind of advertising is to make consumers aware of the store's existence, their range of products, and to motivate consumers to buy. Retail ads are the most common type of advertising found in local newspapers.

DEVELOPING AN ADVERTISING PROGRAM

The same basic process is used to develop all advertising, regardless of the type of media employed. The process starts with defining marketing messages and goals and finishes with the published or broadcasted advertisement. The step-by-step path illustrated here should be followed, whether you're developing a small, simple ad for a local newspaper or assembling a major advertising blitz involving multiple media and formats.

From setting a goal for an advertising program to implementation and measuring results, everything should be tracked and thoroughly thought out. A worksheet has been provided to help you make the right decisions while you plan your ads. Let's review the general steps first, then we'll cover media selection and the specifics of print, television, and radio advertising in more detail.

Step 1. Define the target audience for your ad. All advertising programs must be based on an in-depth understanding of who your customers are. For consumer and retail-oriented companies, you need to know what attributes your customers share as a group (if any), where they live, work, and play, and what they spend their money on. For business-to-business ads, you need to know how many companies need your product or service, where they are located, their financial profiles, and how they are structured.

Step 2. Establish the advertising goals and objectives. Once you have a sense of your target markets, you'll need to establish goals for your advertising and decide who will

HOME-BASED ADVERTISING WORKSHEET

Use this worksheet to choose the advertising venues that provide the best return of customers for the least amount of capital.

Choosing Media Types

1. Describe the profile of your typical customer:

   Profile A:_____

   Profile B:_____

2. Which media is your likely customer likely to see, hear, or read?

   _____

   _____

   _____

   _____

3. Choosing specific media.
   After researching the media, list specific media that will reach my customers. (List newspapers, radio stations, mailing lists, trade show events, etc., that will work for you.)

   Contact information:

   a._____   f._____

   b._____   g._____

   c._____   h._____

   d._____   i._____

   e._____   j._____

4. Narrowing the search.
   From the listings in Number 2, choose the three or four best media for your needs that you can afford. (You can choose more or less depending on your needs and budget constraints.)

   1._____   3._____

   2._____   4._____

develop the ads if you don't already have an agency or an in-house staff to work with. (More information on working with an advertising agency is offered later in this chapter.)

There are two fundamental goals, common to all advertising:

First, your primary message must be delivered successfully to the target audience. An ad that fails to deliver its primary message is either poorly executed or placed in media ignored by the intended target market.

Second, good advertising strives to get the maximum response from prospective customers for the least amount of cost.

In addition to these underlying goals, there are objectives that need to be established for measuring advertising effectiveness. These objectives are the specific results you expect to achieve with individual ads and advertising programs. Objective-driven advertising is more likely to be effective than placing an ad without a clearly defined payoff in mind. A measurable objective clarifies all aspects of the process from media selection to concept to final design and production. There are several standard types of measurable objectives for ads. You might:

- Sell a specified amount of product or collect a specified amount of contributions within a set period of time. Almost all advertising has some sort of sales goal attached to it, whether tangible or intangible.

- Position a product within a market. Positioning means defining a place for your product in relationship to the competition. For example, if your company manufactures big-screen television sets with a brighter picture and a higher price than the competitor's less-capable sets, you would position your product above the competition's because the extra price is a result of superior technology that produces a better picture. The competitor would probably position his TVs above yours because they are quality products of good value for less money.

- Educate a market about a product so that people will see a need that they did not recognize before. The personal care products market uses this approach to educate the public about major health risks that they did not know existed, such as plaque build-up on teeth that leads to gingivitis. Through this education process, markets are created for both new and existing products.

- Change or improve the image for a product or company. For example, you might want to reverse the public's perception of your company from one of providing conservative, expensive products to one that delivers innovative, value-packed merchandise.

- Gain a specific number of responses in the form of business reply cards, new customers, or telephone calls. In the case of new companies or new products, it may be difficult to come up with a specific sales goal; therefore product awareness and interest can be used as a success indicator instead.

In addition to the primary objective, an ad may have one or two secondary objectives that can be accommodated, as long as the primary objective is the ad's focus. For example, a retailer of fine men's clothing may have a once-a-year, 50 percent off sale with the objective of moving $10,000 worth of inventory.

However, a secondary objective, to "continue to position the store as a purveyor of fine-quality, expensive men's clothes," can still be accommodated in the ad's copy. Likewise, a television commercial for a radical new electric toothbrush with an objective to "position our product as technologically superior to the competition" might have a secondary objective of changing the company's image from a maker of home-care products to a provider of health-oriented products.

If you decide to work with an advertising agency, give them objectives that help to focus their efforts. As a result, they will make better decisions on your behalf. Most agencies will help you to develop and specify objectives. Realistic objectives are a powerful yardstick for measuring and improving the effectiveness of your advertising and your agency.

Step 3. Determine the marketing message for the ad. In addition to measurable objectives, strong advertising is based on a clearly defined message. In the last chapter we discussed how to define and refine a marketing message for use in ads and other communications, therefore we won't cover the process again here. Remember that a crisp message is key to all of your marketing efforts, especially advertising.

Step 4. Choose the media placement for the ad. After you have determined your target audience, the objectives for your ad, and the message you want to convey, you need to determine which media will best meet your objectives. The standard classifications of media include print, television, radio, and outdoor.

Newspapers and magazines sell space for ads. Radio and televisions stations sell airtime. Outdoor advertising companies sell placements or showings for billboards on highways and posters on buses and in stations. It is the choice of media, more than any other decision, that will determine who will see or hear your ad and thus determine the overall effectiveness of your advertising effort. A great ad running in the wrong media is a waste of time and money.

Your choice of media should answer the following question, "What it the best time and place for ad to run in order to meet the advertising objectives?" The considerations for media selection are covered in detail later, and topic-specific aspects of media selection are covered in the media-specific sections in this chapter for print, radio, television, and outdoor advertising.

Step 5. Customize the ad concept for the target media. To convey your message, a concept or idea is developed that gets the ad noticed, delivers the message with as much impact as possible, is appropriate for the selected advertising media. A good concept is what makes an ad interesting to read, see, or hear. Many advertising people refer to the concept as the "big idea." Rosser Reeves of the Ted Bates advertising agency defines one kind of concept as the USP or Unique Selling Proposition—the idea that every product has unique aspects and that this USP differentiates the product from its competitors. Behind every "big idea" in advertising is always the message.

A raw message is very ordinary and would make for dull advertising copy. That's why a concept is invented to make the message interesting and compelling. A concept is thus an idea that translates an ordinary message into a provocative ad. Creating a concept requires imaginative thinking. If you're not an "idea person" yourself, a talented creative director or a freelance writer are good sources for inventing interesting concepts for an ad. Creating a unique, high-impact, and communicative concept for an ad is the most difficult aspect of advertising. For this reason many ads have little or no concept behind them and rely on flashy graphics or film effects and a laundry list of features to sell a product instead.

Step 6. Test the concepts with advertising research. Advertising agencies and large corporations spend considerable money and time researching the potential impact of advertising concepts before the ads are placed in the media. Although you could employ the focus groups and questionnaires used by such agencies, as a home-based business owner we suggest that you just have some target customers review your ads for feedback on the concept. It won't cost much, and you'll get some idea of what works and what doesn't.

The reality is that most research is less accurate than it could be. It may be incomplete, poorly executed, ask the wrong questions, or present contrived responses to artificial questions. Another reason research can have limited value is because the statistics are often used to reinforce a political point of view within a company or advertising agency. Still, most companies with large advertising budgets like the security a research campaign provides. In many cases research can point out less obvious flaws in an ad before it runs. Think of advertising research as optional in the case of small campaigns and necessary, yet open to scrutiny, when used with larger, more expensive ones.

Step 7. Produce the ad. Equally important to the proper media selection is the production of the ad. Even with the right media

selection and a good concept, a poorly executed ad or commercial will not work. In severe cases, it may work against you. Proper execution is critical to the impact of an ad campaign for large and small programs alike.

The production of each kind of advertising is a process in itself. A section for print, radio, television, and outdoor advertising follows with step-by-step descriptions of the process and the choices required to produce quality ads.

Step 8. Run and verify the ad. After your ad is produced, it will run in the media you have purchased. Wherever possible, check your ad to make sure it ran properly. Listen to the announcer read your ad on the radio, watch it on TV, check out newspapers, and flip through magazines. In the case of ads running in remote cities, ask a friend or associate living there to make sure the ad ran correctly. Mistakes are common, particularly in print advertising. Ads may not run when scheduled, or there may be a serious flaw on the part of the media supplier such as incorrect placement or the wrong use of colors. A television soap commercial caught our attention one day because while the video for the soap commercial was playing, the audio was from the Humphrey Bogart movie we had been watching before the commercial break.

If anything is wrong, such as poor printing, muddled transmission quality, or placement at the wrong time of day, complain immediately to the media supplier. Complain verbally first, and if you are not satisfied with the media supplier's response, write a letter documenting the problem. Depending on the severity of the problem, you should get a free placement or a percentage discounted from your bill. The contract between you and the media works in two ways—they promise to print or broadcast your ad as specified and you agree to pay the bill. If they don't deliver as promised, you deserve an equitable adjustment.

Step 9. Conduct post-advertising research to find out what works. In order to measure your success in meeting advertising objectives, you must do post-advertising research. Again, this can be simple or complex depending on your company's information requirements. By far the most effective kind of advertising research is done after the fact. This is one kind of research every company should do effectively, at a relatively low cost.

Post-advertising research involves reviewing the effectiveness of an ad after it is seen or heard. After an ad runs, or on a monthly basis if it's a continuing program, you should track the number of responses you get from the ad. Depending on your product, ask customers where they heard about you, count bingo leads and business reply cards from magazine ads, or poll customers walking in the door of a retail store. (Bingo leads are the leads generated by circling numbers on a magazine's "reader information card." They are called bingo cards because the rows of numbers faintly resemble game cards from a real bingo game.) If no one mentions or responds to your ad, then you know it isn't being seen or heard.

Post-purchase research involves customers who have already purchased your products and is used to determine satisfaction, demographics, and future advertising strategies. For example, restaurants often have short questionnaires querying satisfaction with the price, food, service, and environment on the back of the bill. By including a question or two about customer demographics and customer media preferences, a restaurant can use this information to improve its advertising effectiveness. The customer warranty cards inside consumer products are often post-purchase research in disguise. They may ask many questions about where a product was purchased, what other products the person has, and what media the person subscribes to.

If your post-advertising or post-purchase research discloses a trend in the customer base—for example, all of your customers live within a certain radius of the store, they are all over 50, or they all have children who watch Sesame Street—you can target your advertising message more effectively to the people most likely to buy your product. Also, if you find that a whole segment of your target market is not represented, you know that your promotional efforts to this group are not working. Most likely the media mix for your ads and other promotions is wrong, or the message is not appropriate for the market.

Identify as many channels and possibilities as you can think of to effectively reach all of your potential customers. Be creative. Consider both major and minor media possibilities. For example, you could advertise an amplified telephone on a television show with closed captions for the hearing impaired. And, because many people over 50 suffer from hearing loss, you could also promote the product in senior-citizen magazines, such as *Senior Golf Journal* or *Modern Maturity*. Many seniors own RVs too; therefore, *Motorhome* magazine, which features RV lifestyles, is another possibility. Because a wide range of potential customers watch television, you could include an ad in local TV programming guides. The potential list is vast. You will narrow it down later, but for the first step don't limit your options.

One way to informally determine what media your customers pay attention to is to ask them. Ask them to complete a questionnaire, check boxes on warranty cards, or chat over coffee. If you take this last approach, it should be done with tact and in an informal conversational setting. Don't tell them that you are conducting research, just casually ask them what they like to do in their spare time or on their job and move on from there. Since most people love to talk about themselves, your problem won't be getting the answers you desire, it will more likely be one of getting them to stop talking.

MEDIA KITS

Get a media kit from each of the media possibilities for your advertising program. Media kits are used by media channels to promote the advertising space or time they have to sell. The kits include the information a prospective advertiser needs before buying and producing ads in a specific publication or station. Media kits vary from poorly photocopied information presented in a wrinkled manila envelope to flashy folders stuffed with colorful brochures.

Ultimate Survival Tip

Study the Media Your Competitors Use
When studying media options, find out where your competitors advertise, because there's a good possibility that they've already done some of the media homework for you by identifying effective media for their product. Don't make the mistake of limiting yourself to these outlets, however. You may be able to locate media they've ignored and reach a market your competition did not recognize or understand how to reach.

Newspapers have the simplest media kits, sometimes consisting of little more than a photocopied rate sheet. A magazine's media kit contains a price list with a description of available formats and positions, a recent sample of the publication, various promotional information, and readership profiles. Many publications also provide an editorial calendar detailing upcoming feature articles or the focus of specific issues during the year. For example, a magazine for backpackers might have an early spring issue featuring articles on camping and camping equipment. Manufacturers of camping equipment may want to use this opportunity to run an ad on their wares because of the issue's specific editorial focus.

TV and radio media kits are similar, providing information on programming schedules, viewer profiles and ratings (how many people were watching at a given time), pricing, a map showing how far their signal reaches, and information on upcoming shows, special features and special deals. Special and new programming is often featured because stations and networks are usually seeking sponsors for their new shows rather than for more established ones.

Outdoor advertising companies also use media kits. These contain rate cards and maps of the target city showing the locations of available billboards, transit stations, and shelters.

Media kits are free, and most sales representatives will drop one in the mail to you.

On the other hand, they will show up with it on your doorstep if they really need the business.

Get to know the advertising representatives or space representatives for your target media. The people who sell advertising space in newspapers and magazines are called space reps in the trade. TV and radio stations have sales or airtime reps. In the case of a small-town radio station, the rep may be the station's owner or general manager. A major television station in Los Angeles may have 20 or more representatives. A good rep will help you get the right placement or airtime for your needs and will negotiate a discount if there are problems. Because reps are commissioned and depend on selling airtime and space for income, they often attempt to sell you more than you need or can afford. Still, because they're knowledgeable and can provide you with "special deals," it is important to establish a good relationship with them.

Choose a combination of media with the right impact and price tag for your needs. Study the readership profile to see how many prospective customers the media will influence versus the cost of the media. Remember that your goal is to *identify the least expensive media channel with the most impact for the dollar.* Don't buy a pricey ad spot on a large, local TV station if a less expensive ad on a local radio station will work almost as well.

Timing Is Everything

Choose media with the right timing. If you need to get the word out quickly because of a hot new product or a newsworthy event, TV, radio, and daily newspapers work best. Some TV and radio stations will juggle their schedules or cut programming to make a space for your paying commercial.

In the case of monthly magazines, it may take as long as three months for the magazine to hit the streets after submitting the ad. Outdoor advertising is also a slow medium when you're in a hurry, with a minimum turnaround time of forty-five days for most placements.

An awareness of these timing factors is key to running effective ads in multiple media

---

DEFINITION: *Demographics*

Demographics is a word you'll hear repeatedly when defining your target markets, researching, and choosing media for your marketing communications. While an unabridged dictionary will disclose that demographics is the science of vital statistics such as births and deaths, it means something slightly different in advertising. Quite simply, a demographic is a personal profile of the kind of reader, listener, or viewer of a media source. For example, a magazine space representative may show you statistics defining his magazine's readers as white males, ages 35 to 45, making $35,000 to $55,000 a year, and working in management positions. If your product appeals to this market, the publication has the right demographics for your needs.

if you want the maximum retention and rein-forcement value that media mixing provides. If you want to reinforce the messages, you need to coordinate the production of the ads to accommodate the different media schedules. For example, if you want to run an ad in the newspaper and in a monthly magazine, you should try to coordinate when the ad will be seen in both places. (This is called reinforce-ment in the advertising trade and is very impor-tant to businesses who do paid-for advertising.)

Ultimate Survival Tip

Start Your Own Media Library! Impress Your Friends!

Every advertising agency has a print media library and you can too. To start yours, make a trip to a well-stocked magazine retailer. Collect spe-cialty and trade magazines important to your market. Subscribe to as many of the publications as possible. Subscribing is easy and it doesn't have to cost anything. All it takes is a phone call to the magazine's local advertising rep. (Look in the front section of most newspapers and maga-zines for the masthead. It will provide the loca-tions and phone numbers for sales offices). When your local rep finds out that you are interested in advertising, he or she can arrange a free subscription for you. Your media library should also contain the media kits from all prospective publications, radio and TV stations, and out-door advertising sources of possible interest to you.

Getting the Most Exposure

Choose the appropriate media frequency for maximum exposure. The more often an ad is run, the better the chance it has to be seen or heard by the target market. The number of times an ad is run in a specific media is called frequency. Establishing the frequency for adver-tising placements is an art of sorts and there are no hard or fast rules. There are a few things you should know when making your decisions, however. Running an ad on a daily program or in a daily newspaper requires more frequency than running it on a weekly pro-gram or in a monthly magazine. Often some-thing seen or heard only once among a myriad of other ads in daily media is quickly forgotten. A magazine is typically kept longer than a newspaper—so the potential life of the ad is expanded. Research indicates that airing or running the same ad at least three times in the same place or publication gives you a signifi-cantly better chance of getting noticed and remembered than running it once or twice.

Running any ad too many times in the same place will bore people and the message will lose its impact as a result. Optimum fre-quency is a balance between recognition and overkill. Don't waste your money by overusing an ad. Instead, spend your money on a fresh promotion to maintain your market's interest.

It's Got to Be Credible

Choose the most credible media for the money. When researching media, it is important to consider the credibility of the media-supplied demographic profiles. Legitimate media are audited by outside reviewing agencies. In the case of television, the Arbitron Company and the A.C. Nielson Company audit viewers and stations. In magazines, the Business/Professional Advertising Association (BPAA) and similar auditing organizations review the readers and publishers. For newspapers, the Audit Bureau of Circulation (ABC) is a reliable, independent source of circulation statistics.

A few media channels claim an impressive number of readers, listeners, and viewers based on questionable accounting. Don't accept self-audited numbers at face value. A way to check up on demographic claims is to study the advertisers that already use the media to get an idea of who they think reads, watches, or listens to the media source. Paging through a magazine with impressive readership claims and very few ads, or watching a commercial-less cable channel, should raise a red flag.

WHAT SHOULD ADVERTISING COST?

There are no rules about how much advertising should cost or how much you should pay for them, but there are guidelines you can use to determine the appropriate price tag for an advertisement versus the effective promotional value of the ad.

First, if the cost to produce an ad is more than the media charges to run it, you are either producing an ad that is too complicated for the market, placing the ad in the wrong media, or not placing it enough times. For example, if your book-selling business produces a one-shot commercial for use on a local TV station, and the media charge is $5,000 and you've spent $18,000 getting the ad produced, then you've clearly violated this guideline. You should either air the commercial more frequently or spend your advertising dollars elsewhere.

Another way to look at advertising charges is to calculate how many potential customers will be exposed to your ad through the chosen media. Divide the cost of the ad placement by the total number of people who fit your demographic profile to give you a dollars per exposure ratio. This is a handy tool not only for evaluating media but also for getting rid of pesky media sales reps. If a single placement costs $25,000, excluding production, and the publication's media kit shows 2,500 readers with the correct profile for your market, then $25,000/2,500 = $10 per exposure, a figure that justifies looking for another media source if you are selling a $20 product; however, if your product sells for $100,000 each, then the ad might be a good choice.

For some products and industries, there is an established optimum percentage of sales and revenue dollars that should be used for advertising. You can get this kind of information from Dun and Bradstreet reports and from advertising research organizations. If you are a retailer, your distribution source or major product line provider can provide you with ratios that have worked in the past for other companies.

While grumbling is commonplace when the cost of advertising comes up during a planning and budgeting meeting, advertising still remains the most powerful tool for building companies and increasing revenue. Well-chosen ads wisely placed have helped to build most of today's largest corporations and successful charities and have established a new wave of up-and-coming entrepreneurial companies. If you want to stay in business, you must advertise. If you do it right, the cost is worthwhile.

USE OTHER PEOPLE'S MONEY TO PAY FOR YOUR ADVERTISING

Depending on the nature of your company, there may be money available in the form of co-op dollars from your distributors or manufacturers. The way co-op dollars work is that if you advertise someone's product in an ad or catalog, the co-op program will reimburse a percentage of the advertising media (and sometimes production) charges to you. All co-op programs are different, and some are better than others because they pay a higher percentage and have fewer rules and restrictions. (Be sure to follow all the rules and observe all the guidelines and restrictions carefully.)

One warning—don't count your co-op dollars until they arrive. In most programs, you collect co-op funds after-the-fact by submitting copies or tapes of the ad with copies of placement orders and bills. Some co-op programs pay promptly, knowing that you will keep up the good work with reimbursement money in hand. Others take months to write you a check or waste time quibbling over the interpretation of rules and restrictions before paying you. In some markets manufacturers provide co-op dollars as a discount on the next order. Be sure that you are aware of the form of repayment before making a commitment.

Sometimes you can use a joint-promotion or a cross-promotion to stretch your budget. For example, a paint manufacturer might join with a paintbrush manufacturer and a major chain of paint-supply stores to run ads touting paint, paintbrushes, and stores in one ad. This way, each company spends only one third of the cost.

Cross-promotions can be used by large companies to advertise more than one product at the same time, which saves money. For example, if one division of a toy company builds scale model toy trains and another division makes model car and airplane kits, then advertising them together saves money over advertising them separately.

Sometimes joint-promotions and cross-promotions result in ads that are collectively stronger because they provide a more complete solution and a stronger message.

THE PRINT ADVERTISING PRIMER

Print advertising is the general term used for ads placed in magazines and newspapers. Effective print advertising begins with an awareness of the strengths and weaknesses of both magazine and newspaper media. In understanding the advantages and disadvantages of the media, you can make better advertising decisions and won't expect unrealistic results.

Newspaper Advertising Strengths and Weaknesses

Newspaper media are classified by the size of the paper (standard or tabloid), the frequency of the paper (daily, biweekly, weekly), and the publication's reach (who gets the paper and where). The general strengths of newspaper advertising include:

- Newspapers quickly influence large markets because newspaper ads can be produced quickly and be published almost immediately.
- Newspapers are an excellent local and city-specific media.

- Newspapers provide special interest sections that focus a message to specific target markets.
- Newspapers offer a variety of ad formats and sizes to accommodate budgets limitations.

The weaknesses of newspaper advertising include:

- Newspaper ads have a short contact life span.
- Newspapers are a one-shot affair and require frequent or multiple insertions for adequate exposure. If someone doesn't read the paper one day, they'll miss your ad.
- Newspapers offer you little control over the placement of ads on a page. You can specify a location in a special interest section, but you usually can't specify the position on the page, and this strongly influences the impact of the ad.
- Common to all print advertising, newspapers relay only static events; therefore, a dramatic television commercial showing a new, high-technology lawn mower chopping down giant weeds to clear land will be more effective than print.
- Limited print quality dictates the use of simple ads and visuals.

Magazine Advertising Strengths and Weaknesses

"Consistency and continuity—that's the secret for magazines if you want to be visible. For us, that's the way to use print. It's a slow-building medium."

—Dick Costello, President and CEO, TBWA Advertising Agency, as reported in the Wall Street Journal

Magazines are classified by content, geographical reach, and audience appeal. There are consumer, business, local, and special interest magazines. The strengths of magazine advertising include:

- Magazines have the longest potential life span of any of the advertising media. In addition to their longevity, magazines have a high pass-around or secondary readership in addition to the primary subscribers.
- Magazines are the most selective media for targeting specific demographic profiles. There are many general interest and specialty magazines that offer excellent opportunities for targeting advertising to just about anyone.
- Most magazines provide high-quality printing and support for special treatments such as metallic inks, fold-outs, and even microencapsulated fragrances.
- Magazines offer flexible advertising formats (sizes and colors) and usually allow specific placement within a section of the magazine.
- Magazines have a high credibility and authority factor. Therefore they are good for image advertising and complex messages.

The weaknesses of magazine advertising include:

- There is a long lead time before the ad is seen. It can take one to four months to get an ad into print after delivery of the artwork.
- Media costs in well-read national magazines are expensive. A full-color ad in *Better*

Homes and Gardens or *National Geographic* costs approximately $100,000 an issue. Many home-based businesses will look to specialized, small circulation publications instead to meet their advertising needs.

- The ad competition in popular magazines is high, making it difficult to stand out from the crowd.
- The frequency is relatively low—typically only once a month. This means that other media need to be used to reinforce the messages if more frequency is desirable.
- Like newspapers, magazines can relay only static events.

To be effective, print ads need to catch the reader's eye long enough to deliver their message and to be remembered. To see what works and what doesn't in print advertising, collect several newspapers and magazines targeted toward your customers and look through them to see what grabs your attention. Consciously study the pages for ads that don't look good and don't get noticed. Examine the ads to understand why they worked or why they didn't. You may want to buy a notebook and start a collection of print media ads and make notes on the page margins about each one. Collect ads you dislike too and keep them in a separate section of the notebook.

KEY ELEMENTS TO SUCCESSFUL PRINT ADS

When you look at print advertising samples you'll notice some similarities among the good ads. The two main elements in an effective print ad usually include a strong visual element and a short, succinct headline. Ads that use a powerful or catchy visual (illustration or photo) coupled with a potent headline are consistently the most noticed and read. There are some type-only ads and other formats that work if done well, but the best print ads use the headline-visual combination. Good advertisements also make a complete sale—the ad gets the message across and includes all the necessary information for influencing the purchase decision.

Avoid cluttering up your ad with too many elements that detract from the main photo or illustration. Simple formats work better than complex ones in most media. Keep in mind that your ad is competing with many others in most publications. You have less than half a second to catch a reader's eye. Once you attract a reader's attention with a strong headline and visual, the next task is to get them to read the copy. Keep it short, easy to read, and interesting. If the reader pauses while reading your copy because of an ill-chosen word or a convoluted sentence, you've lost him. Good copy carries the reader along like a moving sidewalk to the end of the ad.

The other elements that improve the recognition and readership of print ads include:

- Color—It's very important to print advertising, especially in magazines. Readership studies show that full-color ads get noticed by the most readers, followed by two- and three-color ads. Black-and-white ads attract the least attention. Black-and-white ads require great concepts and exceptional design to create the same response that a color ad does.

- Size—Obviously a larger ad gets noticed more than a smaller ad.
- Position—Some pages get read more than others, so the effectiveness of an ad varies depending on its location in the publication.

SELECTING AND PLACING NEWSPAPER ADVERTISING

Newspaper advertising is usually the simplest because it rarely employs complicated color. Newsprint stock seriously limits printing quality, therefore detailed designs and high-resolution photography are not appropriate. Your local advertising space representative can help you with questions on placements and rates.

Rates for newspaper advertising are based on the following combination of factors:

- Circulation—Increased readership increases the cost of advertising.
- Size of the ad in pages or column inches—Some newspapers charge by the agate lines, a system for measuring depth that measures $1\frac{1}{4}$ inch deep and one column wide.
- Color charges—Ad rates are usually quoted for black-and-white standard ads. Additional charges for color are applied to this base rate.
- Special placement or preferred position charges—If you want your ad located near the front of the paper, in a special section, or in a guaranteed place on the page, you'll usually pay an additional charge.

There are often different rates for national and local advertisers. National advertisers usually pay more for ads than local advertisers. Special reduced rates are often available for frequent advertisers. Advertisers willing to take any position in the paper—called a run of paper rate (ROP)—are also provided discounts. Combination rates are available for advertisers who place ads in morning and evening editions or on consecutive days or weekends.

The best place to run ads in a newspaper are (in order of preference):

1. Pages 2 and 3 of the news section
2. The back page of any section (except classified ad sections)
3. The first three pages of any section (except the classified ad section)
4. Pages 4 and up of the news section
5. Features pages including comics, sports, entertainment, etc. These pages have a higher priority if you are selling a directly related product

When you decide on the size, color, placement, and frequency of your ad, you will make an insertion order to specify the dates and other details.

If you want to do extensive out-of-town advertising, this may be a good time to look up an advertising agency with experience placing out of town advertising on a national scale. If you want to do it yourself, locate a bookstore or newsstand that carries major papers from cities across the U.S., Canada, and sometimes even Europe. The newspapers contain telephone numbers and addresses for you to obtain a media kit. If your advertising plans include small town papers out of your area, find the annual *Gale Directory of Publications and Broadcast Media* in your local library's reference section and make a list of the papers you might consider. (Doing this with a detailed map is helpful for understanding the size and locations of towns and cities.)

Guidelines for Placing Newspaper Ads

Here are some guidelines to help you get better placements and better value for your newspaper advertising dollars:

- One opportunity that works well for local services is the TV section of the Saturday or Sunday paper. Unlike the bulk of the Sunday paper, which gets trashed, the TV section usually stays in readers' homes for a week, and household members who don't read the rest of the newspaper may still read the TV section.

- While the price is attractive, avoid running your ad in the regional section of a newspaper that runs midweek. Several different regions or outlying cities will have their own section assembled into the paper and is delivered only to that region. These sections usually contain news from local organizations and clubs. Many readers don't give this section more than a cursory flip-through on their way to the comics. Although the price may be right, you won't get good value for your money.

- If you're advertising a product purchased by both men and women in a newspaper, avoid running the ad in the sports or cooking section for obvious reasons.

- Newspapers frequently run "special interest" sections of ads and articles pertaining to a particular product line such as cars, boats, home entertainment, and other consumer goods on an annual basis. Before signing up for one of these sections, study last year's version of the special. If it contains solid ads but a limited number of poorly written articles, spend your media dollars more fruitfully elsewhere.

- Adding a second color will get you noticed on a page of black and white ads, but since many newspapers reserve only certain pages for second colors, you may get poor placement or be surrounded by ads with the same second color. Check this out in advance with your space rep.

- Many newspapers will insert your independently-printed flyer or catalog into the papers during binding. For some products and markets, especially supermarkets and department stores, this works well and is less expensive than multiple full-page ads.

Selecting and Placing Magazine Advertising

If your magazine advertising plans include multiple placements of four-color ads, you may want to consider using an advertising agency or a design firm to help produce and place your ads. Remember, if your ad doesn't look good, it won't get noticed. If you don't have experience with design and production, spend the money on someone who does.

Rates in magazines are based on the same general factors as newspapers—circulation, size, placement, the number of colors, and the frequency of insertion.

Color is more important in magazine advertising than in newspapers. When advertising in a magazine, the largest color ads usually get priority placement. Depending on how many color pages the magazine has and how it's assembled, some color ads may end up in the middle or back of the magazine. Your best shot at a good placement in a magazine is to request "a space as close to the front of the magazine as possible surrounded by or across from editorial (articles)." This (hopefully) will buy you a placement away from competing ads and near the front of a magazine, a section which gets read more than the less important articles in the back. In most publications, the smaller your ad, the less chance you have of getting a good placement.

The best locations for ad placement in a magazine are (in order of preference):

1. The inside front cover
2. The back cover
3. The first few pages of the magazine
4. Across from the issue's feature article or cover story
5. The inside back cover
6. The first 25% of the magazine's pages
7. The next 50% of the magazine's pages
8. The last 25% of the magazine's pages

Of course, the preference list varies from magazine to magazine and some publications such as *National Geographic* have no advertising in the middle, so the above list doesn't apply.

After you make your choices, you will place an insertion order with your advertising rep, as you would for newspaper advertising, specifying all the details for location, frequency, color, size, and insertion dates.

Guidelines for Placing Magazine Advertising

Thoroughly investigate all prospective magazine channels before buying an expensive ad in a general-interest magazine—even if you need to employ an ad agency to help you. There are so many special interest magazines, you may find several that will do an excellent job for your needs at a fraction of the price of a major publication.

A tear-away business reply card (BRC) will make the magazine pop open to your ad's page when readers casually flip through it. It may also bring you more leads than just an address and phone number.

In some publications, a well-orchestrated one-page ad located across from an important feature story will get more notice than a more expensive two-page spread. Talk to your rep well in advance to secure this kind of placement.

STEP-BY-STEP PRINT ADVERTISING PRODUCTION

Print advertising is generally the simplest kind of advertising to implement. As with all ads, the print ad starts with a defined goal, message, and selection of the appropriate media. The message is then translated into a concept. If you use an agency, your account representative and the creative director will come up with the initial concepts for approval. After these initial planning stages are completed, print ads go through the following steps:

- A writer drafts headlines or an outline for the copy based on the general concept. Producing headlines usually gives you and the designer a better idea of how the ad will go together than an outline, but some writers prefer one method over the other.

- At the same time the writer is drafting the copy, the designer produces sketches for the ad. These sketches may take the form of simple drawings done on tissue, or they may be rendered as thumbnails, or miniature renderings of an ad. Depending on the project, budget, and time available, the designer may provide several different versions of the ad for you to choose from.

- Once the headlines and thumbnails have been approved, the writer rewrites the copy until reaching a final draft. Depending on the project and the number of people involved in the approval process, a final draft may take as few as one or as many as ten or more revisions, especially in the case of an inexperienced writer or a large, bureaucratic organization.

- In parallel with the writing, the designer takes the approved sketch and renders a comp (for comprehensive). The comp shows the final look of the ad with sketches substituted for photos and illustrations and the headlines drawn in. Since the copy is probably not complete, the text is greeked, which means that a block of dummy text is set in the correct style and size to substitute for the actual words so that you can see how the text looks in the design. Depending on the designer and the project, the comp will vary from a crude photocopy to a piece that looks almost exactly like a finished ad. You should carefully review the comp and specify in detail any changes you want made.

- If the project requires illustrations or photos, they are usually completed after the comp. If a photo session is required, you may want to attend so that you can look at the Polaroid test prints of the shots and approve them. In the case of illustrations, ask to review the pencil sketches before the final illustrations are started.

- The designer takes the approved copy and sets the type while preparing a mechanical of the ad. The mechanical is the final assembly of the ad, usually on a cardboard art board. The copy, illustrations, and other elements are mounted on the board, ready for the printer or color separator to work from. Once the mechanical is finished, the writer and client proofread it one final time for any errors that may have crept in (common). If you have the opportunity, ask the designer to explain the various elements of the final mechanical, such as the color overlays, art paste-ups, and marked color breaks on the tissues. You should review and approve the mechanical. Even if you don't understand how all of the pieces fit together, at least reread the copy and ask questions.

- Depending on the complexity of the ad and the number of publications in which it will run, duplicates of the ad materials may be necessary. If the ad uses complex color, a color separator (an outside service company) will be used to produce final negatives for the publications. In cases where the same ad runs in multiple publications with different physical requirements, several mechanical adjustments to the final ad may be required.

- In most cases, a proof will be produced for your approval before publication. You and the designer (or agency) should review the proof to make sure no errors were made in assembly.
- When the ad runs in the selected media, the production cycle is complete. After your ad runs, the media should provide you with tear-sheets, or samples of the ad as it ran in the publication.

THE RADIO ADVERTISING PRIMER

Most radio advertising is local in nature, even on nationally produced programs such as "CBS News". Radio advertising consists of announcer-read or prerecorded commercials for use on commercial radio stations. Sometimes a radio commercial will also be used as a part of the background music programming in modern supermarkets and other stores.

Radio advertising is divided into three categories: local, spot, and network. Local is used by most local advertisers and focuses on promoting local products and services. Spot advertising is sold to national advertisers who buy airtime on individual stations. Spot time should not be confused with radio spots, another term for a radio commercial.

Radio Advertising Strengths and Weaknesses

Believe it or not, radio advertising can be an effective and affordable way to promote the services and products of many home-based businesses. Before you try radio be aware of the strengths and weaknesses of radio as a media for advertising. The strengths of radio advertising include:

- Radio can reach and influence a large audience in short order. There are more radios than there are households, and people have them in cars and take portables with them on vacations and picnics. Radio has the broadest reach of any of the media, meaning it is heard by the widest range of people.
- Radio ads are less expensive to produce and place than TV commercials. Like TV, radio is quite an effective media for promoting a variety of products.
- Radio offers the lowest media cost per thousand (CPM) contacts.
- Radio stations have formats that appeal to specific market segments, making it easier to target groups of potential customers.

Radio advertising's weaknesses include:

- Unlike print advertising, once a radio commercial airs, it no longer exists to be referred to.
- The creative options on radio are limited, since you cannot rely on visual impressions to emphasize your message.
- A large number of competing stations can make it difficult for an advertiser to choose among stations, and most listeners are loyal to only one kind of station.
- Because radio reaches a very broad range of listeners, many will have no interest in your product.
- The sound quality is difficult to control and some commercials may be half-heard. Many people use radio for background music, so they don't pay attention to the messages.
- The audience size and composition varies over the period of a day or weeks.

If you don't frequently listen to the radio, you should start before putting together a radio ad. Get your hands on a media log of local stations (usually found somewhere in the Saturday or Sunday paper). This log will give you a list of stations, their place on the dial, and a one- or two-word description of their format (adult contemporary, jazz, rock, easy listening, etc.). Spend time listening to various stations and studying the commercials. Note what kind of companies advertise on each station. This will give you a better idea of the kind of commercial that works with each station. Unlike reading the local newspaper, choosing and listening regularly to a radio station is a very personal matter; thus the listener profile for a mainstream country and western station is very different than for a classical music station.

The Key Elements of Successful Radio Commercials

Your radio advertising must get and keep the interest of a listener frustrated with yet another commercial break in his favorite program or music show. You must hold his attention until your message has been delivered and remembered. Your audience may be listening on a car radio with handy buttons for changing stations if they don't like your ad. Remember that you are painting a picture in the listener's mind. This requires quality writing, professional delivery, and as much creativity as you can muster. Concentrate on getting your message across. If the listener only remembers one thing from your commercial, it should be your message. Elements that help a radio commercial capture the attention of listeners include:

- Interesting, provocative, or unusual sound effects and/or music

- A story or testimonial

- Particularly impressive or unusual voice

- Combining elements to tell a story that is interesting and compelling

- Humor. Comedy can be a powerful tool, but tailoring it to make a commercial work well is best left to talented professionals. People's perception of what's funny varies considerably based on age groups, intelligence, and geographic regions. What's hilarious to you may be offensive or simply dumb to your audience, and your commercial will get the raspberry.

The common element in all successful radio advertising is a compelling conversation, joke, debate, story, or the now largely obsolete commercial-length radio jingle. The narrative must appeal to the audience you want to reach.

A standard structure for radio commercials, and one that works well if it's properly executed, includes the following: an introduction to get attention, a middle section where the main message is delivered, and conclusion and/or call to action ("Buy today!"). The use of a simple, provocative sound effect or statement at the beginning of a commercial is an excellent tool for getting a listener's attention. Immediately deliver your message right after the effect. Follow up with more detail, ending with a conclusion that reinforces the message one more time and may include a call to action. Music can be used in the background to provide continuity from start to finish.

Selecting and Placing Radio Advertising

When you receive a radio station's media kit it will specify the demographics of the listening audience and the reach of the station. Now is the time to decide whether you want an advertising agency to assist you in creating and placing a commercial. Choosing radio media is usually easier than selecting TV media, but expertise is required for producing and placing the commercial; therefore, you may need to employ an experienced agency or production firm.

There are two basic steps for matching a radio station to your target market:

1. Determine when your audience is most likely to be listening. *If you're selling a cure for insomnia, late night and early morning hours are obvious times when your market will be tuned in and receptive to your message.*
2. *Match your product to the station's programming and listener profile.* For example, if your commercial promotes luxury cars, running a radio spot during a popular show on investing money is a good idea.

A fairly high level of frequency is required for radio spots to have much effect. Unlike print media, which is usually subscribed to or purchased by people interested in reading it, radio is more scattershot in its success attracting and keeping regular listeners. Running the same commercial on a variety of stations, several times a day is the best way to ensure that a large audience has heard it.

Buying radio time and the rates you will pay for the time slots is based on the dayparts (time of day), average quarter-hour audiences, and cumes (cumulative audience measurements). The frequency of your advertising commitment will also affect your rates. Obviously, the more people who listen to the station at a particular time, as audited by the station and independent auditors, the more money you will pay for the spot. Advertisers can also buy reduced-rate spots on a run of station (ROS) basis. These are aired at the station's discretion (much like ROP ads in newspapers). The best times to run radio ads include:

1. **During drive time.** The drive time is the morning and evening commute, when many people are stuck in traffic listening to their car radios for entertainment and diversion.
2. **Saturday and Sunday mornings.** Many radio stations have special programming on weekend mornings.
3. **During work hours for certain kinds of radio stations.** "Light", classical, and jazz radio stations are used as background music by stores and companies.
4. **During a specialty show that applies to your product.** For example, the "Gardening Today" show is an obvious possibility for ads about nursery or gardening products.

Guidelines for Placing Radio Advertising

Running a commercial frequently over a two-week period is more effective than running less frequent spots over several months. Many stations run several commercials sequentially. If you must settle for this arrangement, ask to be the first commercial aired in the sequence so that the audience is still paying attention. People tend to tune out during commercials, and if yours follows a particularly obnoxious ad, it will have less chance of being heard.

Ultimate Survival Tip

Test the Script for Readability by Reading It Out Loud

A very harried announcer reading your commercial live may have not even glanced at the script until it shows up on his work log as the next task. If your script is too long or short for the allotted time, disaster can ensue. Test read your ad several times while timing it. Also, avoid tricky words or tongue-twisting phrases for obvious reasons. If your organization's name is hard to pronounce, spell it at the top of the script with phonetic symbols like those used in a dictionary.

Commercials that run in the middle of a show often work better than ads at the end or beginning of a show. This is particularly true in the case of radio specialty programming. For example, a popular talk show on politics may command a very specific audience who only listens to the station during the show. Your commercial at the end of the show may air after this listenership has turned the radio off.

Radio fans quickly tire of the same commercial airing over and over, so it's important to produce fresh commercials on a regular basis.

An inexpensive and common practice for radio commercials is for the announcer to read the commercial live. Before agreeing to this practice, listen to the announcer(s) who will be handling your commercial. If he or she

sounds bored, insincere, or mumbles, forego this opportunity.

If you intend to run radio spots in multiple cities, spot selection is more complex and should probably be left to an advertising agency experienced with national radio media placement. If you must do it yourself, you can get station names and addresses from the annual *Gale Directory of Publications and Broadcast Media* and/or *The Broadcast Yearbook* from The Associated Press. National network advertising is somewhat easier to use than individual local spot placements because it offers one-stop shopping for the entire country.

Step-by-Step Radio Commercial Production

Many radio stations offer two kinds of commercial formats: announcer-read and taped. An announcer-read commercial has an announcer or disk jockey reading the commercial on the air from a script. There are some stations where the announcer does a personal testimony describing how wonderful the product is and claims that he or she personally uses it. (If you've never heard one of these, count yourself lucky). Announcer-read commercials are pretty straightforward because they rarely employ special effects or background music and require no recording sessions or voice talent. All you need is a good script.

The second format is a recorded commercial produced in a studio and distributed on perpetual loop tapes called carts (short for cartridges). The announcer puts the carts in a machine with several others and touches a button to start the tape rolling at the appropriate time. When the commercial is finished the tape automatically stops, ready for the next use.

Even if you write the script yourself, other people will be involved in developing your radio advertising. Radio spots use actors and actresses to provide the voice talent or use announcers and disc jockeys to read every commercial. Complex radio ads require the services of an experienced producer to create and edit the voices, supply the music and various special effects, and effectively assemble the pieces into a finished commercial.

Again, every radio commercial starts with an objective, message, media selection, and concept. After a writer or creative director comes up with the concept, the steps in producing a radio commercial include:

- The script is outlined by a writer and a producer is hired if one is required. The script outline demonstrates how the commercial will be structured. A production budget is also produced for your approval.

- The writer (and producer) generate a final version of the script for your review, possibly revising the production budget again if necessary.

- In tandem with the final script development, actors and/or actresses are hired as the voice talent to read the script. They are usually found through an agency that handles a wide variety of talent, or freelancers may be used. (If the script requires a well-known voice, this is negotiated well before the script is written.)

- The voice talent rehearses for the part after studying the script. Most radio spots require little rehearsal unless the reader is not a professional actor such as the owner of a company talking about his firm.

- Special effects and music are chosen from an existing library or arrangements are made to record them. Many large libraries of sound and music are available, so it isn't often necessary to record new sounds unless a big budget is available for production. You should approve the choices in advance of a final mixing.

- The voice talent (and often the producer and you, if it's an expensive ad) make a trip to the sound studio to complete the recording. The narrators or actors read their lines onto tape, completing several takes if a line is flubbed. Some professional voice actors have their own in-home sound studios, but most of the time an independent studio or the radio station's facilities will be used.

- Special sound effects (SFX, as they're known in the trade) and music are recorded if required. This may call for the hiring of professional studio musicians.

- After all of the separate sounds and voices are recorded and approved, the radio spot is mixed to a master tape. A recording technician or sound engineer edits and mixes all of the individual sound elements together while adjusting the volume levels. In some cases the sound engineer may also manipulate the sound quality through equalization and other sound processing systems. You should carefully review the finished master tape before it's duplicated. Note that major changes at this point may be expensive, so avoid making them unless absolutely necessary.

- The master tape is duplicated for distribution to radio stations and the finished commercial runs according to the media contract.

Be Aware of the Technical Differences Between AM and FM Radio

AM radio is less clear and more subject to noise and interference than FM. AM radio tuners are also far more limited in sound capability than their FM counterparts. AM stations have a longer range than FM transmitters. In fact, some clear channel AM stations have ranges of hundreds of miles. Stations also vary in transmitting power, and the presence of natural barriers (hills and mountains) can seriously affect the clear transmission of a given station's programming.

THE TELEVISION ADVERTISING PRIMER

When most people think of advertising, they think of television commercials. Television is the most pervasive, persuasive modern medium for advertising. Television advertising has grown faster than any other media and continues to grow and develop in influence and reach. There are affordable ways for home-based businesses to advertise on television, including public information channels that run short ads for almost nothing and affordable, local TV channels that produce 30- or 60-second spots for less than you'd imagine. You've probably seen these ads used by car lots and real estate companies in your community already, and for many small businesses, these channels actually help build awareness and sell products.

Not all the news about television advertising is good, however. The *Wall Street Journal* recently reported a study by Video Storyboard Tests Inc., a company that tracks advertising popularity among consumers, that claims that the percentage of people who can name an outstanding TV advertising campaign has plummeted recently. In 1986, 64 percent of the people polled could, unaided, cite favorite campaigns—a statistic that was down to only 48 percent in 1990. This decline may be a result of more channels and more ads. It may also be because ads are of such high production quality that they don't stand out from the crowd anymore. It may also be that the ads lack enough substance or creativity to make an impression upon viewers. In the same *Wall Street Journal* report, Martin Puris, president and CEO of ad agency Ammirati & Puris, stated, "It's hard to find a really badly executed piece of [TV] advertising any more, but it's very easy to find a lot of irrelevant, rotten ideas."

At the same time that television advertising's memorability seems to be waning, print advertising's memorability has consistently hovered in the 26 to 31 percent range. Even though many consider print advertising a stable medium and a relative bargain for this reason, print remains a tough sell to national, consumer-oriented companies. Television is still too glitzy and alluring to ignore.

Like radio, most television advertising is classified as either local, spot, or network. Although local ads are run for restaurants, appliance retailers, car dealers, attorneys, and private schools and colleges, they make up the minority of commercial programming in terms of media dollars and are found mostly on less expensive, nonnetwork stations. Most television advertising is regional or national because it consists of ads for consumer products or nationally distributed products.

Another kind of commercial option that has evolved primarily on cable channels is the program-length commercial also known as an infomercial. Often consisting of an expensive production, complete with professional acting talent and a large and endlessly enthusiastic studio audience, infomercials are used to promote weight-loss programs, life improvement tapes, make-up kits, skin-care products and "magic" cleaners, to name a few. Debates continue on regulating the infomercials because the best ones look misleadingly like regular programming. Some stations and cable networks run them with the word "advertisement" prominently displayed at the bottom of the screen during the entire program.

Since most people watch a fair amount of TV, you may not need much additional study of the medium or its commercial formats to become familiar with the advertising options. However, if you rarely watch your local PBS station, study the format and ads of the commercial channels one by one.

If your foray into television advertising includes cable-only channels, you should install cable if you don't already have it. Many of the cable channels such as The Discovery Channel and The Nashville Network are viable media, but their ads and advertisers are somewhat different than on familiar local and network channels. Unlike radio, where listeners primarily tune into only one station or one kind of station, most television viewers will watch any channel offering something they wish to see and will change channels frequently. The advent

of remote control TV and fifty-station cable has exacerbated this effect.

Television Advertising Strengths and Weaknesses

Though television is by far the most powerful of the media in getting its messages across to a wide range of viewers, like all media, television has its strengths and weaknesses. Its strengths are:

- Television can reach and influence a larger audience faster than any other media.
- Television can persuasively demonstrate a variety of action-oriented products and processes.
- Unlike radio advertising, which depends solely on hearing, and print advertising, which relies on sight to deliver a message, television uses both sight and sound, making it a potentially more persuasive medium than either print or radio.
- While large segments of the population don't read magazines or newspapers, and others rarely turn on a radio, almost everyone in the United States watches television on a regular basis.
- A wide range of creative options is available, allowing advertisers to create strong image and brand identification.
- A strong empathy with the television actors can be created, which causes people to identify quickly with a particular product.

The weaknesses of using television advertising include:

- It's very expensive to produce commercial spots, the cost of television advertising is prohibitive for many small businesses and organizations.

- It takes considerable time, money, and experience to produce and place effective television ads.

- Unlike print media, once a television commercial airs, it's gone forever unless videotaped by a viewer along with a program or movie.

- It requires a high level of frequency to reinforce a message.

The Key Elements of Successful Television Commercials

To produce effective television commercials, you must create an ad that's at least as interesting as the program it airs with. Because most Americans watch a lot of TV, they have become connoisseurs of the medium and subconsciously know when a commercial is not up to snuff for any reason.

Elements that help a television commercial get noticed include:

- Dazzling, provocative, or unusual visuals, sound effects, and music.

- A complete story line. Television is a visual medium that lends itself to storytelling formats.

- A high human interest factor. You know how popular the human interest shows are; the same principles apply to advertising.

- Action and movement in the ad to keep people's attention.

- Advanced computer-based animation. Though currently very expensive, animations can be spellbinding. They will become increasingly commonplace and less effective as prices for computer animations decline.

- Famous acting talent to attract attention. Not all people are swayed by this trick, and some actors and actresses do so many commercials and promotions that audiences respond negatively to their image (and your message).

- Humor. Comedy can be a powerful tool, but tailoring it to make a commercial work well is a job for professional comedy writers experienced with writing commercials. Comedy can also be a big flop, so it is usually risky to use humor without substantial testing first.

Many television spots are structured much the same way a good radio spot is constructed. There is an introduction to get attention, a middle section where the main message is delivered, and a conclusion or a call to action. Instead of a simple, provocative sound effect or statement at the beginning of a commercial, as used in radio, a television commercial may use a stunning visual image for the same purpose. This image may deliver the commercial's message or it may immediately follow the message. The middle section of the commercial provides more detail on the product to reinforce the message. The conclusion reaffirms the primary message and may include a call to action.

Not all commercials stick to this format. Television ads may be structured any way the writer and director see fit, and many deliberately break the rules in order to get noticed among television commercialdom.

Selecting and Placing Television Advertising

Normally, your advertising agency should make the television media recommendations for you.

They will know how to negotiate the rates and choose the best frequencies and placement. Consider purchasing television media on your own only if you will be using local stations. It's not that choosing television media is necessarily more difficult than buying media for print or radio, it's just that television is so pricey that even one mistake can be costly.

There are three ways a television advertiser can purchase television airtime for advertising:

1. Companies can sponsor an entire program and secure all the advertising spots associated with the program. For many programs, sponsoring a network program or special requires paying for the program production and the media charges; thus, it is prohibitive for most companies except for the largest.

2. It is less expensive and almost as impressive to buy advertising on a participating basis with a group of advertisers buying a number of national 30- and 60-second spots within the same program.

3. The least expensive form of advertising is spot advertising, which can be purchased nationally or locally. With spot advertising, the advertiser can request various commercial lengths, frequencies, and time periods for each station.

You may not always be able to secure the spots you want for local commercials because some advertisers purchase time far in advance. When you contact your television media rep, they will research the spots that are available (called requesting avails).

The actual rates for television advertising are based on the size of the audience, the rating of the programs, and the length and frequency of the advertising commitment. Most television advertisers compare advertising costs in terms of cost per one thousand viewers.

Before you place your ads you will need to match the television stations or networks and programming to your target market. Here are two guidelines:

- Determine when your audience is most likely to be watching. If you are promoting a college that trains unskilled high school graduates in new careers, advertise it during the weekday, daytime hours when the unemployed will be watching and receptive.

- Match your product to the programming and to the station itself. For example, if you advertise children's products during prime time, a show such as "The Simpsons" is a better choice of media than reruns of the "Lawrence Welk Show".

You may be offered airtime as a package of commercial spots. Study alternatives carefully to identify the package that gives you the best coverage for your product at the best price.

If you are planning on running your commercial on local stations not affiliated with a network or a national cable channel, you'll have to pick and choose compatible stations and programming for your message. If you're considering a major campaign on out-of-area channels, it requires a lot of research and thinking to get your message to the target market. Who knows whether a large percentage of Duluth viewers tune into "60 Minutes" on a weekly basis or whether female Bostonians between the ages of 35 and 55 working in senior management watch reruns of "Gilligan's Island". This is definitely advertising agency territory unless you have a lot of spare time and money to research such pertinent issues.

If you do decide to place the ads in remote cities yourself, you can get a list of stations and their ratings from the library in the *Gale Directory of Publications and Broadcast Media* or *The Broadcast Yearbook* from The Associated Press. However, unlike print media, you cannot get a copy of the publication for inspection along with a request for a media kit. In fact, you'll find little information about the look and feel of remote stations and viewer idiosyncrasies.

The best times to run television commercials include:

1. During prime-time programming—the period beginning at 7 p.m. and running until 10 or 11 p.m.

2. During news programs, particularly during the early evening and late evening news.

3. During sporting events such as "Monday Night Football", but not the local bowling championship unless you sell bowling balls.

4. On news channels during times of crisis (obviously hard to predict).

5. During movies with commercial breaks of no more than three spots in a row.

6. During specialty shows that pertain to your product. If you are soliciting donations for hungry Third-World children, a documentary on poverty in the Third-World is a potentially good place for an ad.

7. During soap operas and daytime programming. While not appropriate for every product, household cleaning and baby-care products work well during this period.

Like radio, frequency in TV advertising gives your commercial a better chance of being seen by a larger share of the target market. Running and rerunning your ad is the best way to ensure that a maximum number of prospective customers have seen it. Also like radio, television is scattershot. While an enormous number of people may see your ad, it's unlikely that more than a minority of viewers will be immediately interested in your product.

Guidelines for Placing TV Commercials

As with radio, running a TV commercial frequently over a two-week period is more effective than running the same number of placements over several months.

Many stations group four or more commercials together, giving the audience time to get up and grab a snack or head for the bathroom. Attempt to avoid these kinds of placements.

If your product appeals to a very up-scale audience (i.e., educated, high income), statistics show that these people watch a lot of movies. In many cases, a well-chosen local-channel movie can be an inexpensive place for your ad, but choose *Casablanca* over *Conan the Barbarian*. Commercials running in the middle of a show often work better than at the end of one show and the start of the next.

Viewers tire quickly of repeated commercials. Produce three or four different commercials or variations on one and rotate them to keep the message and the look fresh.

It's important to get noticed, but particularly loud or brash commercials send TV viewers for the mute button. Use common sense and discretion.

STEP-BY-STEP TELEVISION COMMERCIAL PRODUCTION

Television ads are the most complex to execute because there are so many elements that must work in harmony to make an ad effective. Television advertising is not something you should do on your own. Instead, you should hire an advertising agency or a professional commercial production house. Don't write your own script and have the station produce it, unless you want your ad to look like the laughable, late-night commercials on local UHF channels.

Producing television commercials requires expertise, experience, and a practiced eye that take years to fine-tune. If you are interested in learning more about producing television commercials, a good overview is *How to Produce Effective TV Commercials* by Hooper White (NTC Business Books, 1986).

If you plan to do anything more than display a picture of your product with a quick message for a local access channel, producing TV advertising is a complex process involving a variety of skills, including writing, preproduction, filming, and postproduction tasks. Depending on the nature of your commercial, as many as fifty people may be involved in assembling a complex commercial from start to finish. Only the major steps and the primary personnel involved in television production are listed here.

Television advertising starts with the advertising objective, message, and concepts. Concepts are particularly important in television advertising for highly competitive products, which is why advertising agencies get paid a lot for their creative services. The format for the ad must also be determined—is it a 30- or 60-second spot, or will it be designed to be run in multiple formats?

Ultimate Survival Tip

Don't Use TV Station Talent to Produce Your Television Commercial Unless You Have To

Unless you are running a commercial in a very small market where competing ads are not produced professionally, avoid using the station's production staff to put your commercial together. While the price and convenience is there, the talent isn't. Occasionally you'll find a creative gem, but this is the exception. Most people working inside a station specialize in getting things done fast and cheap but have little concern for your image or your message. If you're competing for the eye of viewers already accustomed to watching commercials that cost more than $100,000 to produce, your ad will look cheap and incompetent in comparison.

Once the agency and client agree on the concept, the production begins. Here are the steps all television ads go through before they air:

- A writer assigned to the project by the agency will produce a script and storyboard for your approval. The storyboard is a sequence of small, captioned drawings that illustrate the flow of the commercial.

- The storyboard and script are sent out to bid at production companies interested in producing the commercial. If you are working with an ad agency, before the production company is hired, the agency will produce a semifinal script and storyboards and send the ad out to bid at several production companies. Most agencies hire outside production companies and their directors to work on the commercials— the agencies provide the management and creative input for the process.

- A production company is selected based on bid responses and experience. Talent is usually more important than price, so it is not always the cheapest company that gets the project. A rough cut production budget is also produced at this point for your approval.

- The script, in theory, was finalized before being sent out to bid, but in practice changes are often needed for a variety of reasons. The writer and director may go over and fine-tune the script where necessary. At this point, usually in tandem with the next step, the final budget and script is worked out between you, the agency, and the production crew. Because commercial production is expensive, sometimes even minor changes to a script can substantially impact the production budget.

- The commercial is master planned in a preproduction meeting, and a shooting schedule is established. Depending on the complexity of the commercial, several meet-

ings may be required to iron out the details with various production units involved. For example, if 50 percent of your commercial is shot in the studio and 50 percent is shot on location in Europe, several preproduction meetings will take place.

- Sets, if required, are constructed, and props are rented or built. All studio shots require set construction because most studios consist of little more than a big room with a concrete floor. Props are rented from prop companies that maintain large inventories of both ordinary and unusual items.

- If the filming is to be done on location (not in a controlled studio environment), suitable locations must be identified and permission must be sought to use the sites. Sets and props may also be required for location shots.

- In parallel with establishing the locations, sets, and props, a cast for the commercial is selected, usually through a talent agency with a wide variety of actors and actresses to choose from.

- While all the other preparations are being made, the special effects and music are planned. These include titles, speeding cars, animated sequences, special video treatments, and more. The commercial's music may come from a library of available music, or in the case of a big budget production, it is performed by professional musicians. If special music or jingles need to be written, then a song writer must also be screened and hired through an appropriate agency.

- All of the planning and preparation steps need to be reviewed prior to the final shooting of the commercial. Typically there are several review meetings between the agency and the client to go over the progress of completing a commercial.

- Once the script is cast in concrete and most of the preparations are well underway, the cast rehearses their parts and costumes are prepared for them. Because few commercials show an actor on stage for more than 60 seconds, rehearsals rarely require more than 2 hours.

- Finally, the filming takes place and studio shots are completed. Location shots and special effects are filmed. Voice-overs, sound effects, and music are recorded. The results of these separate filming and recording sessions will be reviewed and approved by the advertising agency, although the client won't see them until the next step.

- Film rushes for the commercial (the results of the individual filming sessions) are roughly edited and put into sequence. The rushes are a rough approximation of the commercial, not yet edited for final production. You should review the rushes, although it takes experience to understand how the pieces will look once assembled as the finished commercial.

- After the sequencing is complete, the sound is mixed and assembled into its final form as a master soundtrack, ready for incorporation into the master tape.

- Both sound and video images are integrated, edited, and combined on one tape or film master. You should carefully review and approve the commercial before the final edit and duplication. Note that changes become more expensive the further along they are made. Make them at this point only

if absolutely necessary. Prior to final duplication, the finished commercial may be tested on an audience to ensure that it delivers its message as planned.

- Finally, the finished commercial is duplicated and ready for distribution to the television stations.

THE OUTDOOR ADVERTISING PRIMER

Many home-based entrepreneurs have made their fortunes using outdoor advertising—those ads you see on billboards, the seats at bus stops, and on kiosks at the mall. Outdoor advertising, or just outdoor as it is known in the trade, is a very specialized field. Outdoor includes billboards, signs painted on buildings, and transit posters (both inside and outside buses and trains). Major advertising agencies often have complete divisions dedicated solely to outdoor. If you don't use an agency, outdoor advertising suppliers can be located in the telephone book under "Advertising, Outdoor" although some listings may be for ad agencies that handle outdoor rather than direct suppliers. Outdoor advertisers will gladly send you their media kits, which include location maps, viewer statistics, and rates.

Your outdoor advertising objective is to place an ad where it will be seen by the largest number of people in your target market as possible, catching and holding their eye long enough for your message to be understood and remembered.

A drive around most cities reveals a variety of billboard and transit ads. Study them to see which ones grab your eye and why. Notice also how some outdoor ads are placed in better locations than others in terms of being easy to notice and read.

The Key Elements of Successful Outdoor Advertising

For billboards, where your ad may only get a brief glance, a short headline with large type and a strong visual are important to visibility and appearance. Billboards that work are never cluttered. The design must be crisp and clear. Billboard readers passing in cars simply don't have time to sort out a complicated message from myriad images along a highway or street. In the case of transit posters, simplicity is also important. Outdoor advertising should have very little copy, because drivers passing by at 55 MPH won't be able to read many words.

A highly effective approach to billboard and transit ad design is the "T" principle. The headline represents the top of the T and the visual represents the perpendicular line that meets the top of the T. Easy-to-read outdoor ads usually look like a T with the visual moving off to the left or right in some instances. This is a very easy format for a glancing reader to digest in a fraction of a second. The T can be used upside down, with the headline on the bottom and the visual above it.

Outdoor Advertising Strengths and Weaknesses

Most outdoor campaigns are used to reinforce other communications or to build broad awareness for a new product or service.

The strengths of outdoor advertising include:

- Reaching and influencing a large, broad audience quickly.

- A potentially long life span.
- Quickly building name and product recognition for mass-market products.
- Targeting very specific geographic locations even better than newspaper advertising.
- Offering one of the lowest "cost per message" rates of any of the major media.

Outdoor advertising's primary weaknesses are:

- **Geographics.** Although the reach is broad (encompassing many kinds of people), outdoor advertising is geographically limited. This can be both an advantage and a disadvantage, depending on your product.
- **Time.** Outdoor campaigns are time-consuming to produce and must be produced eight weeks or more in advance of placement.

Selecting and Placing Outdoor Advertising

Purchasing outdoor advertising normally requires the expertise of an agency familiar with the issues of location, demographics, and visibility. If your outdoor media plans include only your own city or town, you can avoid the agency expense by taking advantage of the knowledge from a rep who sells outdoor media. A good rep knows what works and what doesn't when it comes to locations. If your outdoor media plans include multiple cities, use an agency experienced with outdoor advertising on a national scale.

Local transit advertising is easier to manage on your own than billboard media. The transit companies can provide you with statistics on readership and package prices for various options. A ride on the bus or a drive around the city will give you a good indication of the package you should choose.

Billboard media are usually purchased as a package of more than one installation, called showings. There are several sizes of billboards and transit ads available, the largest and most visible being the most expensive. Billboards and transit shelters with lights for night viewing are more expensive than shelters without lights. Most outdoor media providers offer rotation programs where your ad can be moved to more prominent areas of a city.

Billboard media rates are based on the length of commitment and the number of placements or showings. The rates are also based on the size of your display, demographics, and location. The best outdoor ads are located where a maximum number of people will see and have time to read them, and these ideal locations are priced accordingly.

The best placements for billboard ads include:

1. Along major highways and near major intersections.
2. Along heavily commuted freeway routes, preferably with few other competing billboards.
3. In cities with limited public transit options that force people to drive their cars (Los Angeles for example).
4. During warm weather, when people are out walking and driving.
5. Painted on walls in districts with no competing billboards.

Transit media consists of poster ads placed in transit shelters, stations, in transit vehicles, and on the outside of vehicles. Ads can be purchased for showings inside or outside the vehicles, in the stations, or in some combination of showings. Like billboard media, transit ads are purchased by number of showings, size, location, and time commitment. A full-showing means that there is one ad on each vehicle in a fleet. There are also package rates known as a run rate or a service rate.

The best places for transit ads include:

1. Inside or on the outside of transit vehicles in cities with a significant public transit ridership. The frequently bored passengers read every ad, even the ugly ones.
2. In lighted shelters located on major arterials where the ad can be clearly seen by approaching motorists.
3. At the end of station corridors, stairs, and escalators where approaching pedestrians walk toward the ad.
4. In airport walkways, especially if you offer products and services to travelers and businesspeople.

Producing Outdoor Advertising

Because outdoor ads are frequently used to reinforce advertising in other media, their production rarely requires more than a redesign of a print ad used in a magazine. In most cases, the steps for producing an outdoor ad are virtually identical to those used to assemble a print ad. The only exceptions are that the writing process is considerably shortened and some billboard ads are painted (not printed) by either a billboard painter or by a computer. Of course, you should use vendors who specialize in outdoor media to supply the production services.

THE ADVERTISING PLAN

Before you place or produce any ads, an annual advertising plan should be created as a part of a total marketing communications and promotional plan for your business. The plan should detail the advertising production schedules, budgets, and media placements. Because advertising can be expensive, it's important that the plan shows not only an event calendar but also cash flow requirements to support the plan. The components of an advertising plan include:

- **An advertising calendar that shows ad production and media for all ads.** It should also show which ads run together as a part of a complete program. Do this by grouping like ads together by line.
- **Objectives for each ad.** Your plan should contain a short note on the objectives for each ad. This is particularly useful for keeping the plan up-to-date, because priorities shift over time in most organizations. If you wrote your plan in December, by the following October some of the objectives may seem out of place, and you should update the plan at this point.
- **The advertising budget by month and by quarter.** This provides an instant cash flow analysis for tracking advertising expenditures.
- **Major event markers.** New product launches, seasonal activities, store and sales office openings, and other important scheduled activities should appear on the plan to ensure that advertising supports these events when appropriate.
- **Personnel responsible for each advertising activity.** If the projects are big enough to involve several people, or if freelancers and multiple vendors will be employed, these names should be plugged into the plan as they are selected.

If you work with an ad agency, they will provide this kind of planning for you. When presented with an agency plan, spend time away from the agency personnel to study it. Most agency plans have elements that can be taken out while still accomplishing your objectives. The worst of these efforts is an agency wish list of ads and media they would like to sell you rather than a working document. In the end you'll benefit from knowing your own priorities, markets, and media choices.

Once your advertising plan is complete, you can produce your ads according to the steps already presented. Of course, as powerful as advertising is, it is only one of the marketing communications tools you will use for publicity about your product or company. In fact, some home-based business may never use or need traditional advertising. Other promotions may be more important. Read on to learn more.

16

Home-Based Publicity—Getting Noticed Without Spending a Fortune

Do you have a new product to announce? Have you developed an innovative technology or process that makes your products or services special? Are you making a special discount offer to senior citizens or to the kids down the street? Have you made a significant contribution (in time or money) to an arts group or local charity? These and many more home-business accomplishments or announcements are opportunities for free publicity. In this chapter, you're going to learn how to master the publicity process by getting your news in the right places.

Of the hundreds of successful home-based entrepreneurs we interviewed, almost all of them cited some sort of publicity or public relations as a central part of their success. Publicity is one aspect of a broader communications category called public relations. Publicity is defined, for the purpose of this book, as free news coverage by the media. Public relations, on the other hand, is a more expansive term that encompasses media coverage and self-generated events and activities that promote your company or products without paid advertising. Public relations events include seminars, special promotional events, articles in magazines, and more. This chapter concentrates on publicity, the mainstay of any home-based public relations program. The next chapter focuses on special events and other public relations activities you can use to generate interest and awareness in your home-based business and products.

Publicity efforts are generally used, in conjunction with other communications tools, as one part of a complete home-based promotional program. Some home-based entrepreneurs who are adept at managing their publicity programs can rely almost entirely on their publicity and other public relations efforts to develop sales.

You don't need a public relations agency or a publicist to implement a powerful publicity program. In fact, with no outside help, you can easily handle your own professional publicity campaign from your home-office, if you know the tricks of the trade revealed in this chapter.

PUBLICITY IS INEXPENSIVE, POWERFUL, AND CREDIBLE

Publicity is a way to get your message out to the world without incurring the expense of advertising or spending the time involved in face-to-face sales. In fact, publicity is one of the least expensive forms of promotion, and requires only paper, envelopes, stamps, and a telephone to get started. It does, however, take time, organization, and persistence.

Many home-based business owners, believing that only the big players or big stories will get mention, fail to realize the potential power of the press and the influence the press can have on their businesses. Any organization, from a restaurant with a new menu or a nonprofit company announcing a fund-raising event to a giant corporation with a major product roll-out can use publicity to get the word out about their products and events.

Unlike advertising, which is obviously self-serving, if a review about your company appears in a credible news medium, readers often feel that the editorial opinion and articles are independent and objective. Thus, publicity can add credence to your advertising messages.

If you have to pay for a review in a magazine or newspaper, this is not publicity in its true form, this is just a disguised form of advertising called advertorial. However, in some industries, buying an ad also buys placement of your news release. Don't be surprised if you get more publicity in a magazine or newspaper in which you advertise frequently. This is true more of trade and industry publications than of major media. Although there may be ethical issues concerning the independence and objectivity of the press, remember that magazines and newspapers are businesses. You can't expect them to ignore their customers any more than you can ignore yours. In most cases, you can get adequate press coverage without paying for it, but you will need to know how to make yourself, your products, and your events newsworthy.

There are many benefits to actively developing a publicity program for your company or products:

1. Publicity can be completed on your own, without the help of agencies or other professionals.
2. Publicity can reach a relatively large audience for a low cost.
3. Publicity and public relations activities, in general, develop positive relationships with the community at large.
4. News is more believable than ads; therefore, people are more likely to use your product or service based on publicity than they are if they only read fliers or other advertising.
5. Publicity reinforces the messages of your other marketing efforts.

If they know how to present news stories with credibility, home-based businesses have the same access to publicity channels as do large corporations. Because your news is as good as anyone else's, you should take advantage of every opportunity to use publicity to promote your business.

HOW PUBLICITY WORKS

Publicity works by making editors, reporters, journalists, or writers in the media aware of your news so that they can write about you in their publications or mention you on the air. If the press people are interested in what you have to say, they will print or broadcast your announcement.

Why do some companies get written up in the business press so frequently, while other similar companies are rarely mentioned? Because companies that get regular, positive publicity make themselves available to the press, and they make their everyday events sound like news. Another new line of canned goods may not sound exciting, but, if the announcement goes along with the right photos and explains how the brand employs a new can technology with environmental advantages, it's news.

When implementing a publicity program, you always need to think in terms of news value. Who would want to know about it? What do they want to know? When should they know about it? Which media do the interested people come into contact with? Which media would be interested in telling the news? Most important, what can you do to make your news interesting or, better still, exciting?

Almost any event has news value to someone. For example, people in business are always interested in promotions and new positions. They read the new employee announcements, even though they don't know the individuals involved. It is a good opportunity to get your name and the name of your company in print.

Publicity is best when it is used to:

1. Develop name recognition, industry presence, image, and positive associations with the customers and public in general
2. Support advertising programs, promotional efforts, and other communications tools

Don't expect publicity to do all of your promotion and selling for you. While there are stories of public relations successes that made home-based entrepreneurs rich overnight, these are very much the exception rather than the rule.

The goal for every home-based publicity program is frequent mention of your company and your products or services in media that your customers are likely to come in contact with. The idea is to keep your name in front of the people who buy or influence the purchase of your products. Repetition over a long period of time is often more important to successful publicity programs than the one-time headline news event. Everyone wants front-page mention, but don't assume you have to wait for a major event before you can begin your publicity program. Send out a news release for everything that is even vaguely newsworthy.

Publicity requires persistence while you build up "share of mind" on the part of the editors, and it may take several news releases before you get noticed. Publicity is less valuable as a one-shot attempt to get your name in print. Sometimes, one-time publicity works if you have something spectacular to tell, but advertising or more direct communications tools are usually better for immediate sales development.

Unless you or your home-based business is particularly controversial or well-known, the media won't know if you've done something newsworthy unless you tell them. Of course, if your organization is a large, influential company, the press may come asking for quotes or opinions about industry trends or news developments. Over time, if you work with the media, you will become a source of information even when you don't send out news releases, but until you become a household name or are recognized as an industry guru, this won't happen without a substantial effort on your part. In most cases, if you want stories, articles, or mention in newspapers and magazines or on radio and TV, you must go to the press yourself.

STEPS FOR A HOME-BASED PUBLICITY PROGRAM

The steps in executing a basic home-based publicity program are simple. If handled with persistence and professionalism, you will get the publicity you want and need for your home-based enterprise. The steps to managing a successful publicity program include:

1. Define the objectives for your publicity. Do you want to create general awareness or to announce a specific product? Do you need to support your advertising messages? Do you need to reach a wider audience? The objectives will help you to identify the media best suited for your publicity efforts.

2. Identify the press and media that will be most useful to your publicity programs. Develop positive relationships with the most influential people in your business. Sometimes, businesspeople set up breakfast meetings or lunches with members the press just to meet them and let them know what is going on, even when there isn't a specific news story.

3. Clearly state the news you have to tell and develop an angle for presenting it to the target media. For your story to be regarded as newsworthy, it needs to fill one or more of the basic news criteria:

   - The participants or companies must be significant or recognized. If the people or company is well-known, the story has a better chance of being mentioned.
   - The news must be important in some way. The news needs to be interesting

and relevant to the individual readers, even if it is not national or international in scope.

- The news should have local appeal whenever possible. People want to know about their own communities and local successes and events.
- The story must be timely and current. Nobody reads yesterday's newspapers, so they won't want to hear your old news either.

4. Write concise, professional news releases or presentations. Follow the standard formats accepted in the industry. Schedule news releases on a regular basis. There is more information on developing news releases and press plans later in the chapter.

5. Mail or distribute the news release to the appropriate media lists. Sources for your media lists are detailed later on, but also include regular newspapers, magazines, and even the World Wide Web.

6. Follow-up on your news releases or media proposals to see if the editor or writer is interested. At one time, letters to editors and cover letters on press releases were quite common. Today, it's better to use the telephone to follow-up with the press.

Keep a file of all resulting press clippings and articles. Use the clippings to learn about ways to improve the next round of news releases. The clipping file is the traditional, tangible way of measuring publicity success because coverage in other media is harder to track and capture. Some companies keep logs that list the date, station, and subject of the coverage to track television and radio coverage. If you don't have time to maintain the clip-

ping file, you can hire a clipping service to do it for you (listed under Clipping Services in the *Yellow Pages*). Some public relations agencies also provide clipping services.

Ultimate Survival Tip

Persistence Is Key

Because editors are inundated with news releases of all kinds, it's important to build and improve press relationships over time. The best way to build a "news channel" is to maintain a helpful attitude and to send out regular news releases. Even in the busiest markets, once an editor remembers you and your product, you'll find that the editorial coverage for your product becomes easier to get. Most important, don't forget to say thank you for even the most banal coverage because that keeps the door open for better press coverage next time.

Keep complete clipping files on your competition. Compare your competitor's publicity to yours as you develop your publicity efforts.

A knowledge the press and their support of your company. A thank you note or a telephone call and the occasional lunch or dinner, when appropriate, can do wonders to build relationships with the media. Don't look like you're bribing them, just treat them with respect.

TOOLS FOR THE HOME-BASED PUBLICIST

Every form of marketing communications has a bag of tricks that makes it work. Publicity is no different. The following is a list of the tools available for your publicity program and explanations of how each is used by experienced publicists and public relations professionals.

The News Release

If there is one tool that is most important when trying to get publicity, it is the news release (also called a press release). News releases are the primary source of information for editors and journalists when they create the stories they publish and broadcast. News releases should be clearly written and should always include the who, what, where, when, and why of the news story. They also need to be produced in a professional, standard format that allows editors to get the gist of the story by scanning only the first few lines of the release. A step-by-step process for producing a quality news release is presented later in the chapter.

Company and Product Backgrounders

Company and product backgrounders provide more information about your company and products than news releases can. They are used to provide general background information for the press, and are often kept by editors in their permanent file on your organization. A backgrounder can be a simple typed narrative on your company or product, or it can consist of an attractive folder with photos and other marketing communications materials, including brochures or product datasheets.

There are two basic kinds of backgrounders—a company backgrounder and a product backgrounder. A company backgrounder typically includes the following information: company history, biographies of key

employees, company goals and positioning, financial information, and descriptions of key company successes. A product backgrounder includes the following information: product features and benefits, design and technology information (when relevant), specifications, pricing, and competitive positioning. A list of key customers, if available, is useful for both kinds of backgrounders. Some companies with only one or two products combine the company and product backgrounders into one document.

Whether you have news to tell or not, a company should always have company and product backgrounders ready to distribute on request. When editors first receive your backgrounders, they set up a file on your company. When you send a news release to these editors, the filed backgrounders are used by editors as a source of general information for adding depth to press releases. You should periodically send updated backgrounders to the media members you work with.

Press Kits

Press kits, also called media kits (not to be confused with the kind of media kits provided by the media to potential advertisers), are an assemblage of current stories and press clippings published about your company, current press releases, and a backgrounder on your company and products. Media kits also include photographs and biographies of your key employees and executives, and may include brochures and information sheets on each of your products. These materials are usually packaged in an attractive folder for easy distribution. Simple folders for this purpose are available at any office supply store. Because they are a primary tool in presenting the company's image to VIPs in the industry, media kits for large corporations are often elaborate affairs that employ custom folders and expensive printing.

If you frequently work with television contacts, you may also want to include videotaped clips as a part of your media kit. These might consist of a product demonstration video, a plant tour showing off your manufacturing technology, or a brief, narrated biography and speeches.

Every company, no matter what size, should have media kits ready at all times to hand out to customers, industry and financial analysts, and press people who want more information before completing a story. In addition to being an important tool for informing the press, an attractive, complete media kit can also be an influential tool for persuading a bank or investment firm to make a loan or investment decision for your company.

Interview and Program Proposals for Television and Radio Shows

News programs on network and local television, cable television, and public-access channels offer many opportunities for gaining publicity. If you want a television or radio station to do more than just make an announcement on the air, then you will need to write a proposal to go along with your news release and backgrounder. The proposal can be as simple as a cover letter on top of a news release that suggests that you are available for an interview. The proposal may suggest a complete program special on your company, which you believe would be interesting and suitable for a particular show. If you have previously had programs aired on your products or company, you should mention these in your proposal, and, by all means, find out the name of the person who makes the programming decisions for the station or the program before you send in your proposal. (This is often the producer of the show.) An unsolicited program proposal without a source name will usually go directly into the trash.

News Conferences

When news is important or timely and you want more attention than a news release can provide, putting on a news conference (also called a press conference) is one way to get a number of media folks together at one time. News conferences allow you to cover more ground than you could through new releases alone. News conferences should only be scheduled when you have something important to announce. If the press feels that your news is not important, you will give a press conference to an empty room. How you determine what is important enough to justify a news conference is based on each individual situation and your organization's visibility. There are no hard and fast rules—just use common sense.

To schedule a news conference you simply invite the press to the conference (over the telephone, if the news is immediate, or with invitations mailed several weeks in advance, if the announcement is planned). Sometimes, advance news releases are mailed out with the invitations. It is advisable to call the press within forty-eight hours of the news conference to verify attendance.

If you do schedule a news conference, make sure it's well organized. The operative word for a successful news conference is preparation. In addition to making your formal announcements to the press in a prepared speech, you should have printed news releases and backgrounders available for the press at the event. If the event includes multimedia materials, such as videotape or slides, copies of these should also be available to the press so they can better remember what you said. The person who makes the presentation should be well prepared and well informed. There should be ample time for questions and answers after the announcement (and the person presenting the news should prepare for tough questions from the press). It is also traditional to have some refreshments for the press, such as coffee, juice, and snacks at the very least.

The physical facilities are very important to the success of a news conference. The room should be large enough to comfortably seat everyone, and the lighting should be adjustable, if possible. If television representatives will be in attendance, the room should have adequate power outlets and be convenient for TV crews with heavy equipment. Ventilation and air conditioning should also be a consideration in choosing a location. A large number of people, hot lights, and electrical equipment can raise the temperature to uncomfortable levels in just minutes. Excessive heat will make your presenter sweat, which looks unprofessional.

Make sure there are no distracting noises in the vicinity of the news conference, such as overhead planes or noisy machinery in adjacent areas. Microphones are sometimes sensitive to picking up irritating background noise.

During the presentation, the use of visual aids, including colorful slides, flip charts, or videotapes to augment the news announcement is often advisable, especially if the news involves multiple announcements or topics. Make sure the microphones and visual-aid equipment are all in working order before the presentation. Disorganization on the part of the company making the announcement wastes press members' limited time. If you want positive treatment by the media, it's important that you and your company look professional at all times.

Press Tours and Press Events

If you have a home-based product or service that is distributed in multiple states or locations, a useful tool for handling complex and important news events (like new product announcements) is to take a "traveling news conference" around the country. Otherwise known as the press tour, your traveling news conference can be one-on-one meetings with individual press people around the country or multiple news conferences held simultaneously in different cities. As always, when trying to get publicity, make sure you have printed press materials and backgrounders available for all of your contracts, and verify all of your appointments in advance. All the considerations for news conferences also apply to press tours. If your press tour involves taking your contacts to lunch, make sure you make reservations, check out the menu, and verify the facilities in advance.

Press Photos

Pictures, illustrations, videos, charts, and photos can help get your news releases read and published. They are an important part of your publicity toolbox. Include photos relating to your news story whenever possible. Editors are always on the lookout for images to jazz up a story, so good ones are of immediate interest to them. Newspapers and trade magazines are always looking for interesting photos to liven up their pages. When including photos in your news releases or media kits, follow theses guidelines:

1. Use a professional to take the pictures, unless you have someone on your staff with equivalent skills and equipment. Refer to the chapter on hiring vendors if you haven't done this before.

2. Make sure your people look natural. Announcement photos and head shots can be posed, but make sure the character of the person comes through. If possible, show people in their work environments. If you take pictures of people during an event, ensure that they don't look posed or uncomfortable, even if they are.

3. Use action shots, if possible. Action in a photo always gets the reader's attention. For example, in a simple product shot of an expensive pen, you might show a handsome hand writing a letter in beautiful, flourished calligraphy. Or, if you are selling a new line of frozen yogurt, show happy children eating the product and have the package clearly displayed. Readers favor attractive product photos with real people in them, even if the photos are of everyday products or mechanical equipment. However, if the people look posed or contrived, it is better to leave them out. Be as imaginative as possible and you'll have a better chance of getting the photos published.

4. Use interesting backgrounds and props, but don't use the portrait studio's "Fall Scene" or anything like it. These artificial backdrops look like cheap sets and should be avoided. If you can't think of something interesting, use something simple.

5. Use 8" x 10" black-and-white photo reproductions for newspapers. For magazines that carry color pages, submit 35mm transparencies (slides) in addition to the black-and-white photos. If you are unsure, include both black-and-white and color photos. Make sure the photos and transparencies are clearly captioned with the subject, company name, and telephone number. Date them on the back or on the slide frame. Photos and the news release materials often become separated, and you don't want another company's photo going into your news story. There are photo houses that specialize in duplicating public relations photos, and they will add the captions to the photos for you. If you can't find one in your area, call a public relations agency for a recommendation.

BUILDING YOUR MEDIA CONTACTS

In publicity, understanding the tools won't help if you don't know who to tell. Develop positive relationships with key editors, industry writers, journalists, analysts, and other VIPs (politicians, authors, etc.) who have influence in your market. Your media lists and media files should include the names of all the people you will be sending news releases to and making contacts with in order to get publicity.

Developing your press contacts and media lists are critical to getting your publicity tools to work for you. You should include the following information for each contact in your media file:

- Name and title of the contact
- Publication, station name, or other affiliation (such as a Web site)
- Mailing address (including zip code)
- E-mail address (if available)
- Information on this contact's news interests and specialties
- Readership profile and circulation information, if you have it available
- Deadlines for publication, if any
- General notes. Include the dates and details of previous discussions and meetings with this person. Include any personal information you may discover about the person, so that you can personalize your conversations with this contact over time.

Ultimate Survival Tip

Use Photos and Illustrations to Get Attention

The majority of news releases received by publications and the media consist only of a news release. In today's world of visual media, a handsome photo, illustration, or even a chart gives editors the chance to print something more interesting than just another block of copy. Particularly unusual pictures, even those of mundane industrial processes, have a better chance of being used than just mere words. For example, if you have a new carpet cleaning method, include some "before" and "after" shots of your work and a flowchart of your process. If you have an important client you have previously worked with, have a photo taken with the client. Be creative.

Keeping the media files and mailing lists up-to-date is an important and ongoing process.

Press people move around, and some change positions frequently. Magazines and newsletters come and go. If you use a publicity professional or agency, they should maintain current lists for you, but you may want to periodically verify them. You may also have names that you want to add to the lists.

Using a simple computerized database program, the mailing lists and contact files are easily maintained. The database program allows you to sort mailing lists for specific releases, and most programs let you print "personalized" letters automatically. If you don't use a computer, keep the file information on alphabetized index cards. The mailing lists themselves can be typed on preformatted forms, ready for duplication on mailing labels designed for the copy machine. There are forms for creating photocopy-ready mailing lists at any local stationery store. If your mailing lists are long, however, use a computer or a local mailing list service for tracking the names and printing the labels.

Customizing Media and Contact Lists

Your media lists should be targeted specifically for your company and industry. Most companies, even small ones, use a number of media lists, each one centered around a specific kind of news or interest. For example, a large electronics company may have a national news list, an industry-specific publications list, a local list for each city the company has a presence in or other geographically targeted lists, an industry analysts list, a key customers list, a political and government officials list, an international list (targeted by country or continent), and a news services/wire services list.

Ultimate Survival Tip

Get the Names of Editors from the Masthead

All publications include a masthead in the first several pages to show who publishes it. In addition to the publisher, most mastheads list the senior editors and the contributing editors. The masthead also includes the publication's mailing address and phone numbers, an instant mailing list! Note that managing editors and advertising people may also show up in the masthead. Neither concern you for publicity purposes because the managing editor is usually a financial business–oriented person, and the advertising people sell advertising and don't write articles.

News releases are sent to the list or lists that are most appropriate for the specific announcement or story. A news release of general importance goes to everyone, while a specific announcement may be sent to only one list. A small company, like a local restaurant, may also have segmented lists, including restaurant reviewers, newspaper contacts, trade press, community associations and clubs, a VIP list, a television list, and a radio list, that target news releases for maximum exposure.

Almost all libraries carry a number of standard list sources. In these references, you can find detailed information on local, national, and industry-specific media for creating your media lists and files.

In addition, there are other sources to use when compiling lists of VIPs and industry contacts, including state government directories ("blue books"), research reports by major industry and financial research firms (Dataquest, Infocorp, Dun & Bradstreet, and Reuters, for example), the *Congressional Directory*, Chamber of Commerce directories, and professional association and club membership directories. Of course, don't forget the local telephone book.

The CD-ROM included with this book lists the addresses and links to these sources and many others.

PUBLICITY SOURCES AND HOW TO WORK WITH THEM

There is a wide range of media sources available for publicity programs. Your publicity efforts should include as many media sources as possible. The major media sources for publicity and the ways to effectively contact them are described below. Remember that almost every one of these sources has a Web site or other online contact information (such as e-mail). Even so, we suggest using ordinary mail to follow up on your e-mail contacts (at least until you get to know the editors).

Newspapers—Daily and Weekly

Though newspapers have lost some of their dominance in the news arena to television in recent years, most media lists and publicity programs still start with the papers. New York City alone has more than forty regularly published newspapers. Even in small communities, there is usually more than one: a daily newspaper, weekly community papers, and, perhaps, an entertainment tabloid or two. As your company, market, and news interest expand, you can add newspapers across the country to your media files.

Newspapers have a number of editors who cover news for specific topics, and there is at least one who covers your subject area. It's always best to get the correct editor's name, if you can, by calling the newspaper. If this isn't possible, send your release to the topical editor or news desk most likely to be interested in your news, such as the business editor, food editor, city desk editor, or national desk editor. If the newspaper is very small, you will probably send your news releases to the Editor-in-Chief, who is responsible for the entire publication, but never do this with larger papers. The Editor-in-Chief in larger papers has topical editors to handle the news and doesn't review the individual press releases.

Newspapers you will want to add to your media list, depending on the size and interest appeal of your news include:

- National newspapers (i.e. *Wall Street Journal, USA Today, Investor's Daily, Christian Science Monitor, New York Times*), but only send your releases to these newspapers if you have something of national interest
- Local newspapers, including general-interest and business papers. These are great sources for home-based businesses

International Newspapers

Local news and entertainment tabloids are other great sources for home-based businesses. Many of these papers need news and will gladly print your well-written news release.

Magazines and Trade Journals

As was already covered in the advertising chapter, there are thousands of magazines published in the United States and thousands more published internationally. Magazines can have a tremendous impact on a target market and,

therefore, on the success of your company (if you receive positive coverage in them).

Many magazines publish general news, so you should include as many relevant magazine editors in your media list as possible. Relevance is the key word in getting magazine coverage. As you did with your advertising, match the magazine demographics to your target market and your news messages.

When sending news releases to magazines, use a specific editor's name. If you haven't updated your mailing list lately, verify by telephone that the editor is still with the magazine before you send out a news release. Sometimes, it is useful to include more than one editor from a publication on your list, because they may not necessarily share information with each other. In addition, some magazines use freelance editors and writers for their articles, so you will want to put these people on your mailing lists.

When you contact a magazine editor over the telephone, ask what kinds of material and in what format the magazine prefers for submission of news materials and releases. Editors for the key magazines in your industry should be sent updated backgrounders and media kits regularly.

The list of specific magazines and related publications to use in a publicity campaign is too vast to include in this book, but here are some general publication types you should consider when developing your media lists:

- National news magazines—weekly and monthly
- International news magazines
- Industry-specific magazines and trade journals

- Popular and special-interest magazines
- Local interest magazines
- Industry newsletters

Special Interest Newsletters and Company Publications

Because of easy-to-use, affordable desktop publishing technology, newsletters are cropping up from almost every company and organization. These include Chamber of Commerce newsletters, insurance company newsletters, the company newsletters in with your monthly power bill, software company newsletters, and others. Large, local homeowners' associations even have newsletters. Since many of these publications are consistently short of article ideas, there is a good possibility they will mention your local business and its products and services. Many of these new publications need fresh news (more so than other media), so make sure to search them out and include them in your publicity campaigns.

Television

Based on many recent studies, both the general public and frequent readers prefer television over newspapers as their primary source of news. With the growth in cable television and public-access channels, there are more and more opportunities for small companies to be interviewed or featured on television, if they have something of potential interest to present.

Before you send off news releases to television stations, however, become very familiar with television programming—the program schedules, the program contents, and the focus of the programming. Once you know the shows that are potentials for your news, you will need to call the station to find out the contact person who reviews news releases and program proposals. Mail your news release and program proposals to this person and, as always, follow up to get their reaction to the news. If your news is of national or regional scope, the wire services (covered later) will send news releases to all the pertinent television stations.

If the contact person is interested in more than making a brief announcement on the air, he or she will usually set up an information interview to discuss your program proposal. Sample programming ideas include a feature presentation of a new technology on a science program, such as Australia's widely syndicated "Beyond 2000". If you sell Chinese woks, you might suggest a Chinese cooking segment that uses your products on a specialty cooking TV show. If you've just started a new training program for your employees, you might suggest a feature on the positive benefits the program has had in stabilizing local employment.

General program sources for your media list for television include:

- News programs—local and national
- Talk shows—local and national
- Public-access stations
- Public television stations
- Cable channels with specific business and news orientation, such as CNN or Financial News Network

At the very least, volunteer for the fund-raising campaigns on public television channels. It's a good form of secondary publicity, and the channel often mentions your support on the air and displays your company's logo in the background.

Radio

Creating radio contacts is much like working with television. Again, start by becoming familiar with the programming. In general, radio stations make general announcements of local events and news more readily than television stations do. There are also opportunities for interviews and general publicity. For these, you will again need to produce a program proposal in addition to a news release and send them to the appropriate program coordinator who is responsible for selecting the people to be interviewed. The major wire services also send news releases to radio stations. General program sources for publicity on radio include:

- News programs—local and national, both AM and FM channels
- Talk shows—local and national
- College radio stations—community colleges, four-year colleges, and universities

Wire Services and News Syndicates

Wire services and news syndicates (companies that specialize in gathering and distributing news for use by the media) can be used to send news releases to a large number of publications and stations at one time. They are best for news that has national, international or broad industry appeal. Wire services are especially important as a source of national news for small newspapers and television stations.

Wire services generally have the reputation of being objective news-gathering sources. The wire service reporters and editors will modify and summarize your release as they see fit, in an attempt to balance the news they send over the service. It is worth the effort to develop good relationships with the wire services and their reporters, but remember that they are usually only interested in major news or stories that are particularly odd or humorous. The positive impact of having your product or company mentioned over the wires is immeasurable.

The largest wire services include the Associated Press (AP), United Press International (UPI), and Reuters (business news). There are both general news services and industry-specific services available. There are also local wire-service bureaus. Wire-service bureaus can help you identify the correct services for your news release, if you haven't sent one to a wire service before. You can locate these in the telephone directory. In addition to wire services, there are also special news and feature syndicates and services for specific industries and topics that supply information to the media.

If you have news of national or international interest and you intend to send it "over the wires", make sure to send the release to both the AP and the UPI wires. Don't play favorites. These agencies are very competitive, and one hates to see "breaking" news that the other one doesn't have. As a policy, it's not good to alienate one of the major services, because you usually need them much more than they need you.

Miscellaneous Sources for Publicity

In addition to the standard media, you should make contact with and be aware of the following potential sources for publicity (if they are applicable to your industry and business):

- Consulting Firms, Data Research Firms, and Industry Analysts—These are crucially important in some industries because many of the influential firms produce newsletters and industry reports that are widely read by investors and customers alike. The analysts working for these companies can also provide the names of other contacts and financial resources you should know in your business or industry.

- Professional and Political Organizations and Associations—There are hundreds of these, and some of them can be helpful to your organization. For local organizations, watch the activities columns in the local newspaper. For names of national organizations, read the announcements in the major industry publications.
- Special-Interest Clubs, Sports Groups, and Fraternal Organizations—Sending a news release about a special offer or a new product to a local club or organization can often result in immediate business. For small and large companies alike, it is a good idea to know which clubs and organizations are most active and influential in your community and to be a part of them, if possible.

With all the sources available, which ones you include in your publicity efforts largely depends on the news you have to tell. If your news is local, then you'll probably stick to local sources. As the size and influence of your company increases, you'll branch out. If you are part of an industry with specific journals and newsletters, include these no matter what size your company is. Some industries have columnists and other VIPs who frequently write about companies and their products, and these people should also be among your contacts.

On the links provided on the CD-ROM, we've provided a general list of many possible sources for the publicity of home-based businesses of all shapes and sizes. If you search, you may find more. There are always new magazines, newsletters, and television programs starting out. Many of these new media need your news as much as you need their publicity. Always keep your eyes out for new sources.

PRODUCING A HIGH-QUALITY NEWS RELEASE

A good news release is the bread and butter of positive publicity. If you are a small company, it's okay to prepare your own news release as long as your writing skills are up to snuff. If, however, you aren't confident in your writing abilities, hire a freelance writer or a public relations agency to help out. If you work in a large company, you will probably have easy access to publicity professionals—use them.

Editors expect news releases to be in a standard format. Even if yours is the story of the century, if it's not in proper format, it won't be read beyond the first few words. The diagram provided annotates the generally accepted format for a professional news release.

The first step toward getting your news relayed in the media is to get your release read in the first place. In a large newspaper, editors may get hundreds of releases every day. In order to get the editor's attention, your news release must be interesting and easy to understand. If you use a handsome format, quickly spell out the importance of what is contained in the release, and specify all the

The Anatomy of a Press Release

Use your letterhead for page one

Staple pages together

Provide contact information.

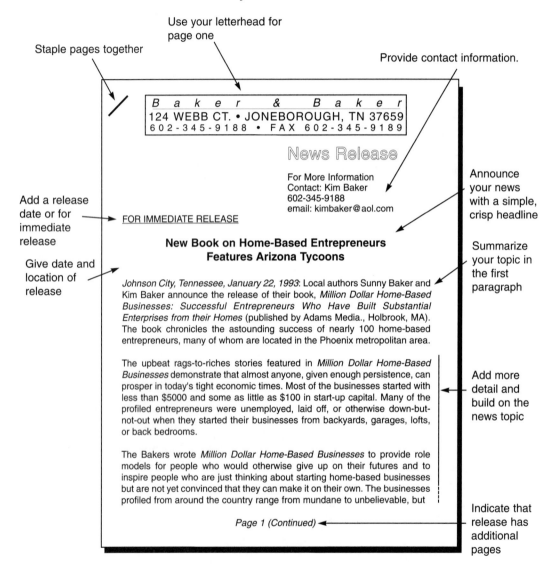

Baker & Baker
124 WEBB CT. • JONEBOROUGH, TN 37659
602-345-9188 • FAX 602-345-9189

News Release

For More Information
Contact: Kim Baker
602-345-9188
email: kimbaker@aol.com

Announce your news with a simple, crisp headline

Add a release date or for immediate release

FOR IMMEDIATE RELEASE

**New Book on Home-Based Entrepreneurs
Features Arizona Tycoons**

Summarize your topic in the first paragraph

Give date and location of release

Johnson City, Tennessee, January 22, 1993: Local authors Sunny Baker and Kim Baker announce the release of their book, *Million Dollar Home-Based Businesses: Successful Entrepreneurs Who Have Built Substantial Enterprises from their Homes* (published by Adams Media., Holbrook, MA). The book chronicles the astounding success of nearly 100 home-based entrepreneurs, many of whom are located in the Phoenix metropolitan area.

The upbeat rags-to-riches stories featured in *Million Dollar Home-Based Businesses* demonstrate that almost anyone, given enough persistence, can prosper in today's tight economic times. Most of the businesses started with less than $5000 and some as little as $100 in start-up capital. Many of the profiled entrepreneurs were unemployed, laid off, or otherwise down-but-not-out when they started their businesses from backyards, garages, lofts, or back bedrooms.

Add more detail and build on the news topic

The Bakers wrote *Million Dollar Home-Based Businesses* to provide role models for people who would otherwise give up on their futures and to inspire people who are just thinking about starting home-based businesses but are not yet convinced that they can make it on their own. The businesses profiled from around the country range from mundane to unbelievable, but

Page 1 (Continued)

Indicate that release has additional pages

Use second letterhead
sheets for additional pages
or substitute white bond

all of the entrepreneurs share common traits of perseverance, fierce need for
independence, and a willingness to take risk. The 260-page book retails for
$9.95 and is available at most major bookstores.

Finish with
background
on your
company
and its
principals.
Keep it brief

Background on the Bakers

Sunny Baker and Kim Baker have published 20+ books with major publishers
in the last five years. Other recent titles include *College After 30* (Adams
Media.), The RVer's Bible (Simon & Schuster/Fireside), *How to Promote,
Publicize and Advertise Your Growing Business* (Wiley), and the best-selling
Color Publishing on the Macintosh: From Desktop to Print Shop (Random
House). When they aren't writing books, the Bakers operate their home-
based consulting firm, Baker & Baker, where they specialize in developing
marketing programs for high technology start-up companies. Sunny Baker
Ph.D. is also a professor at Eastern Tennessee State University.

The Bakers welcome opportunities for book signings. Call the publisher to
schedule yours.

See us on the Web at: http://aol.com/aolusers/kim_baker/kshome.htm!

Priced at $8.95, the book is available from all major bookstores. If the book
is not available from your favorite distributor, copies can be ordered directly
from Adams Media. Call 1-800-872-5627. The ISBN number is 1-55850-246-
8.

Provide
pricing and
where/how
to buy
information

Indicate end
of release in
case pages
get lost or
rearranged

→ *Page 2 (Last)*

vital information, including your name, the name of the company, dates, and contact telephone numbers, your release will have a much better chance of being read.

Steps for Preparing a News Release

Step 1. Know what you want to tell the world and be able to explain why it's news. If you can't explain why your news is important, it may not be. Remember that news should be timely, significant, and straightforward in order to clearly communicate a message.

Step 2. Determine who you should send the release to for maximum news exposure. Using your targeted media files and lists, determine the best contacts for each release. Do this before you write the release because you will want to tailor the news for the intended audience.

Step 3. Draft a one- to two-page (three pages maximum) news release. A news release that is longer than this is probably too long-winded, and the editors will probably not bother to read it. (The exception to this rule is a scientific or technical release, which may be lengthy in order to explain a complex premise or theory.) If you need to provide additional information to the press, provide a backgrounder as supplementary material.

Step 4. Releases for radio and television require a special style for reading them over the air, which doesn't apply to news releases intended for publication. Sentences should be simple and varied in length, and the writing should use a strong, active voice. Attribution should precede the quotations in the release, never following. If you don't have experience with writing for broadcast news, hire a professional to help you.

Step 5. When you are ready to draft the final news release, it should include the following:

- The date and location of the news release. This is obvious but sometimes forgotten.

- A concise, strong headline. The headline should explain exactly what the news is and intrigue the person to read on.

- A strong lead paragraph. The first paragraph, called the lead, should provide the salient information about the release. This first paragraph is the paragraph you want printed should only one paragraph from the release be "picked up" by the media (publicity talk for published or aired). It should arouse the curiosity of the reader or listener.

- Answers to the who, what, why, when, and where questions of the news story in the body of the release. Who is responsible or involved? What happened? Why is it important, and why did it happen? When did things happen? Where did things happen? These are the supporting details, and, if the release doesn't answer all five questions clearly, it is unlikely that an editor will pursue the story. Make sure that the body of the release supports and substantiates the lead paragraph.

- Quotes from key people, if appropriate. Quotes from a company executive or industry VIP add interest and weight to a news release. Use them, but don't over-use them.

- Clear, concise writing. Avoid vague, meaningless, or excessively superlative language.

Every word counts, so use them wisely. Be honest, complete, and simple in your explanations.

- Name, phone number, and address of the person who should be contacted if there are have any questions about the story. You would be surprised how many news releases cross an editor's desk without a contact name or phone number.

- Decide if a photograph, diagram, or illustration would be appropriate to support the release. Even a basic photograph of a key person or product from the company never hurts. As mentioned, news releases that include a photo are more interesting and more likely to get "picked up". Make sure you allow enough time to shoot and reproduce the picture for inclusion in the release mailing.

- Have the release reviewed by an objective outsider. It's always a good idea to have someone else read the release to make sure the message is clear and that no typographical errors have been incorporated.

- If you work inside a large company, have the release approved by the appropriate managers. News releases can have sales, legal, and personal ramifications, so it is important that everyone affected by the announcement approves of (or at least knows about) what is being released to the media. The corporate lawyer or legal department (in companies big enough to have one), should be a part of the routine sign off on all communications, including news releases.

- Duplicate the news release with quality photocopying or printing. Use original letterhead for each release. Do not photocopy the letterhead. Copied letterhead looks unprofessional and lacks impact. You can photocopy onto the original letterhead if you have a quality photocopier available. If not, and your mailing is quite large, consider using a competent quick printer or copy center to duplicate the release on your blank letterhead.

- Mail the release by first class or by priority mail. Splurge on the postage! Press materials sent bulk rate have less chance of arriving on time. If you include photos or other fragile materials, make sure they are appropriately protected from bending, crushing, and other mishaps.

UNIVERSAL PUBLICITY RULES

Beyond the ability to write a good news release, there are some general rules for handling publicity that every home entrepreneur should know. These guidelines are applicable to businesses of all kinds—not just home-based businesses. As a businessperson, you will be expected to know them. As you begin to work with the press, media, and industry representatives, follow these time-proven principles and you'll consistently get more and better publicity.

Rule 1. Always treat the press people and analysts with appropriate respect and deference. Be aware of their heavy schedules and demanding deadlines. Be cognizant of the fact that you are not the only person they need to talk to. Most important, even if you disagree with a press person's opinion, be professional about it. Yelling at a key editor of an influential magazine never helps, even if you are right.

Rule 2. Don't demand anything from the press. It is true that you are entitled to consideration by the press when you have news, but the press doesn't owe you anything unless you convince them that you really have a story. It is their prerogative to choose how they cover your news and where they place it. That includes cutting the contents of your release, changing positive information into negative, including your news in a larger article that also covers your competitors news, or giving you a write-up on page 417. This is one of the downsides of publicity, but, if you treat the press with understanding, they will usually treat you the same way.

Rule 3. Be as influential, knowledgeable, and charming as possible. If you aren't particularly articulate, have someone do the leg work for you or get coaching on the answers. Professionalism is a must in all relationships with the press. Most PR agencies or publicists will help draft answers and provide basic media training for inexperienced managers. Every staff member who has any contact with the press can benefit from this training. Expect that many people in your organization will come into contact with the media over time if your publicity efforts are successful.

Rule 4. Prepare everyone on the staff for dealing with the press and VIPs. People who may possibly come into contact with the media should know the names of the key people on your lists, and, if your employees do not know the names of your media contacts, they should at least be able to identify the apropriate magazine or newspaper. This means receptionists, secretaries, and any other person who may answer the phone when someone from the press calls should know how to respond and what to say. They should know where the media kits are and how they should be distributed, in the event that no one else is available to handle them. Even in small companies, you should let the staff know that you are expecting calls from media representatives or VIPs, and your staff members should know how to answer the questions and take messages. The staff should also know who to refer the caller to and when not to make comments.

Rule 5. Anticipate questions and have answers prepared in advance. Have someone who knows the answers readily available for questions. If you or your representative to the press don't know the answers, check and then get back to them quickly. Prepare answers, in writing, to the obvious questions in advance. That way, you won't stumble when an editor from *Business Week* calls to talk to you.

Rule 6. Follow up with the press, but don't bug them. After sending out a news release, follow up to see if the editors or writers have any questions about your release. With magazines, make the follow-up within a couple of weeks. For daily media, follow up in a couple of days. You may want to ask the contact's opinion of your release so that you can improve it next time. Invite them out to lunch or breakfast just to chat, but don't call every day to see if they have seen and read your release yet. Keep in mind that they get hundreds—if not thousands—of releases every month. Yours is just one of them. Be persistent and consistent in working with the press and media representatives, but don't waste their time.

Rule 7. Never send out a press release or let the news leak out until you are absolutely ready. Advance publicity can be the undoing of a company or product line. If you let people know about your new products too soon, the competition can beat you to market. If you don't deliver when promised, you can lose credibility and customers in the process. Sometimes it seems compelling to let the press in on a "secret" in advance, but, in most cases, this will deflate interest when the announcement is finally ready for the press. News has a way of leaking into the wrong hands, no matter how careful your contacts are. So, if you're not sure the timing is right, don't let the cat out of the bag.

Rule 8. Always know what the competition is doing. This is as true for publicity as it is for advertising. You should know which stories are being published about your competitors. You should always be ready to talk to the media about how your products differ (positively) from the competition. When you talk with media representatives, you should never be derogatory about your competition, but you should be knowledgeable. Be honest, truthful, and put your own products in the best light. As you become known for your knowledge, ethics, and trustworthiness, the media will come to you more often for your opinions.

YOUR PUBLICITY PLAN

As with all marketing communications, positive publicity programs start with planning. As already emphasized, publicity is best when treated as an ongoing process rather than as a one-shot event to be brought out of the closet when deemed necessary. The primary goal is to be positively mentioned in the press as frequently as possible, but publicity also needs to be coordinated with advertising and other marketing communications to be most effective. Thus, a long-term publicity plan that dovetails with the rest of your marketing communications efforts is required.

Publicity efforts should be started before you begin a new advertising campaign, for example, so that the press and your advertising support the messages and announcements you want to make. Since publicity may take longer than ads, begin the publicity program days, weeks, or months in advance so that it will catch up with and support the ad program. If the overall plan is executed with consistency and professionalism, your company will get positive publicity.

In addition to planned publicity, you need to be ready for unplanned events and notices. That's why you produce backgrounders and media kits and have them available at all times—just in case you need one on a moment's notice.

Usually a one-year publicity plan is adequate, although some companies have five-year goals for their publicity efforts. A publicity plan, which is a subset of a complete public relations and marketing communications plan, should include the following:

- A clear statement of your company's mission, corporate objectives, and product sales objectives. Every marketing communications plan, including the publicity component, starts here. We've mentioned it again because it's so important.

- Easily measured publicity goals that relate to the company's mission and objectives. This should include a prioritized list of people you want to reach and the image you want to project to these people. You should also specify goals for how frequently your company or product is mentioned and ways to measure your publicity success.

- A calendar of media events and news releases for each news event. Limit your "big" stories to one or two a year and have lots of "little" stories to fill in the gaps. If you know you have specific events during the year, such as new product announcements or holiday events, mark these down first and do your planning around them.

- A clearly defined primary audience for each news event or announcement. This is done so you can target the mailing of your news releases for maximum exposure. The audience should be defined by geographical and lifestyle or industrial interests. Answer the questions: Who would want to know about this, and where would they most likely read or otherwise find out about the news? This is much like determining the target market and demographics for an advertising campaign.

- A list of all the potential story angles for each news event or announcement. The stories will ultimately become your news releases. Most events have potential for more than one release. Specific releases may be tailored for each of the target audiences and media sources you intend to use to gain publicity for the event.

- Assigned contact people for each story and publicity event. The people who will be involved with a publicity program should know well in advance that they will be called upon to work with the media. Give them ample time to prepare. Get the most

experienced, most knowledgeable people in the organization involved. The more important the person is who speaks with the press, the more important the media will regard the news.

The central idea behind the publicity plan is to determine a strategy and particular tactics for an on-going program with the media in advance. At the very least, a small company should send out one news release or initiate one public relations event a month. Two is better. Large companies have a publicity plan that involves weekly activities, and someone should be doing something involving public relations and publicity every working day—whether its taking an editor out to lunch, speaking at a seminar, phoning editors to touch base, writing an editorial thank-you response to a magazine, or sending out news releases. Your home-based plan probably won't be this complicated, but you should try to pack in as many publicity opportunities as possible to promote your business.

The publicity plan should be reviewed for completeness and impact at least quarterly, and it should be revised, as necessary. If you aren't getting enough publicity (measured by the clippings and announcements in your clipping file) do two things: Beef up your efforts and review your past efforts to make sure that the material was properly presented and newsworthy.

Between reviews, there may be ideas that just occur to you, and that is to be expected. Just make sure that all spontaneous publicity activities complement the rest of your communications strategy.

POSITIVE AND NEGATIVE PUBLICITY

Even the best-planned publicity campaign can go wrong for a number of reasons. You then receive negative publicity, the kind you don't want. In all your dealings with the media, you should be aware that publicity has two sides— the positive and the negative. On the one hand, public relations and its tools can be used as a important component of your overall marketing communications program. Publicity gained from public relations activities can have significant promotional, image development, and general communication value. However, publicity also serves companies when they need to handle negative announcements, the recall of a new product because of manufacturing defects, for example.

The media thrives on conflict and controversy, and they're always looking for an angle. Your image in the news, whether positive or negative, is partially established by how you execute your publicity efforts.

If, in your attempt to gain publicity you alienate the press, or if they feel that your products lack value or features, you can do serious damage to an otherwise well-executed marketing communications program. This generally won't happen if you follow the steps and rules presented in this chapter, but beware that every company has bad news at some time. Learning how to handle both bad and good news with the press can make all the difference in the future of a company. If the relationship you have developed with the press and media over time has been generally good, the treatment you get in the media when you are dealing with negative announcements will generally be better than if you have no relationship with the media or a negative one.

There are a few simple rules to follow to keep your dignity intact:

1. Be honest and straightforward. If you don't know the answer or can't comment, state this—but don't sound evasive.

2. Prepare a written, formal statement as quickly as possible to distribute to the appropriate media representatives.

3. Don't go into more detail than is necessary when asked questions, especially if all the facts are not yet available. You might end up with your foot in your mouth.

4. Without looking insensitive or dishonest, develop an angle on the story that emphasizes the many positive aspects of the news to offset the negative ones.

5. A backgrounder on the history of the situation should be provided if there is time, and it should emphasize positive company accomplishments as much as possible in order to put the problems in the proper perspective.

If you are adept at handling a potentially damaging situation, you may even be able to turn the press around to your side. Planning, honesty, preparation, and positive, ongoing relationships with the media and the community are always your best tools in any publicity situation. As a home-based business person, use these tools frequently and diligently.

C H A P T E R

17

Special Publicity Events

Press releases are great if you have news to tell, but, often, they don't allow direct contact between you and your audience. To make your public relations efforts and advertising pay off, you need to produce your own special events so that you will be recognized. This chapter provides ideas and implementation advice for a number of special events and activities that a home-based company can use to promote its products and enhance its image. Special public relations events and tools include seminars, conferences, community activities, presentations and speeches, and related promotional opportunities—occasions you can use to your advantage.

In addition to advertising and public relations, some businesses can promote and sell their wares through special events, such as speeches or seminars, books, parties, fairs, and community activities. Special events are the best way to make the public aware of you and enhance your image and standing in the community. Sometimes an event and a special promotion are combined for maximum effect. For example, you may offer a training seminar for free *and* give a coupon for a reduced price on your product to people who attend the seminar.

Simple events can be handled by almost any organized, detail-oriented person in the company. Complex events with large audiences or events held in multiple cities will involve many people and considerable coordination. Sometimes your public relations agency or an agency that specializes in coordinating events will get involved, and, other times, someone in your organization will be assigned as the project manager for a special event. Like the other marketing communications tools, special events should become part of your overall marketing communications plan and goals and should be well coordinated with your other marketing communications activities. As always, careful budgeting and clear objectives are central to their success.

SPECIAL EVENT POSSIBILITIES

Though every company should try to generate publicity through news releases and press contacts, not every company will use special events. Many small companies, including small manufacturers and home-based service companies, can use special events as a primary tool for promoting their products. Some companies use events to complement advertising and other promotional efforts. Other companies won't need to use them at all, concentrating instead on other methods to generate awareness. The decision to use special events depends on two primary factors:

1. If you need direct contact with your potential customers in order to sell products more efficiently, then use special events as much as possible. For example, if your market needs to be educated about or trained on your product before being likely to buy it, special events will play a role in your marketing communications strategy.

Products that are likely candidates for the strategic use of special events include technology products, products that replace traditional products or are designed to save time, and many kinds of services and educational programs.

2. Even if your customers don't need a demonstration of or education about your product, special events will play a role if your long-term image and community relationships are important to your company's strategy. Large companies almost always have public image goals that can be best supported by special events and community activities. For smaller companies, this is usually not as imperative, but many small companies support events because they are community minded and they get involved in improving the community as a matter of conscience.

Based on these factors, special public relations events are most often used to build awareness, improve corporate image, establish standing in the community, or educate a marketplace about a new product or technology. In addition, there are some unique benefits of using special events to make the public aware of your company and products:

1. Many events can be produced at a relatively low cost compared to commercial trade shows and advertising. Of course, they can also be very expensive, depending on the type of event you want to produce.

2. People remember a positive event longer than ads or other marketing communica-

tions tools. Thus, events can have long-term impact on a target market or community.

3. Because you are in contact with the audience and potential customers, special events provide you with an opportunity to gather direct feedback on product ideas and programs, which other promotions do not provide.

4. Events can be used to develop positive relationships with the community at large. This positive relationship with the community can have many benefits, including an enhanced image for your company, positive attitudes of potential customers, and the acquisition of new employees.

5. If your company doesn't receive other news coverage, special events can be used to generate publicity in the media, which have a broad impact on public awareness. Thus, hosting an event draws attention to your company and directly exposes customer to your product.

The downside of using events concerns their risk. There is no guarantee that the "right" people will attend or see your event. Of course, this is also true of other marketing communications in general. There are also a number of things that can go wrong when coordinating events, and simple problems, like equipment failure or a speaker with laryngitis, can destroy the impact of an otherwise well-planned activity. However, overall, the commercial benefits of a well-executed event far outweigh the risks.

There is a broad range of possibilities for public relations events. The rest of the chapter describes the most common special events used to promote companies and the steps and procedures for making them successful.

PUBLICITY FROM WRITING ARTICLES AND BOOKS

Having a major article about your company or product published in an important magazine or—even better—a complete book can often do more for sales than can an expensive advertising campaign. One of the added benefits of articles and books used for publicity is that the magazines and publishers often pay you for writing them, although you won't make much unless the article is for a major national publication. Usually, the bigger personal reward is having your name in print as the author.

The process of getting an article about your product or company published is very similar to getting publicity about your product—the difference is that you develop a contract with one specific magazine rather than sending news releases to everyone on your list. You then develop the article within a specified schedule and actually write the article for the magazine (or contract a professional to write one for you).

Articles can be written about a new technology, a major business success, an innovative approach to doing business, customer applications of your product, and the lives and personalities of important people in your company. Pick up the magazines you use in your publicity activities and look at the articles; they frequently focus on specific companies, key executives, and new products. If you can suggest stories like these (or even better ones) to the editors, then you may be able to get similar articles published for your company.

Like a news story, a feature article must have a specific angle. It must be relevant, and it must be well written. Most articles should be accompanied by illustrations and photographs with descriptive captions.

Occasionally, editors will be so intrigued by a simple news release that they will come to you for additional information so they can write a feature article on your product or company. When your company is really in the "big time," the media will come to you regularly in search of articles and feature stories—just like they come looking for news. Until then, the process of getting a full-length feature article published usually involves the following steps:

1. **Know your media options for articles.** Be familiar with the editorial coverage (articles) in the specific magazines and papers that are of interest to your business.

2. **Know the editors.** Use the same process as the one for gaining publicity, which was discussed earlier.

3. **Know the magazines' publication schedules.** Be aware that articles are written two to three months (or more) in advance of the magazine's publication.

4. **Tailor the article idea to a specific magazine.** Make sure the article fits into the format and focus of the magazine. Make sure it is written to the magazine's primary market. The central idea or topic should be relevant and informative. An article should be more than just a glorified press release; it should inform and fascinate the readers.

5. **Before you write the article, send a query letter for your article idea to the appropriate editor.** Send the letter to one magazine at a time, unless you tell the editors that you are making multiple submissions of the idea. A query letter is a special letter to an editor that describes the article you would like to sell to the magazine. It should explain why your idea will be of interest to the readers and why you are the right person or company to write the article. Include a title for the article, specify a proposed delivery date for the article, and specify the length of the finished article.

Most trade industry articles are about 1,000 to 1,500 words, although some are longer. Use past issues of the magazine to guide you. It is not necessary to submit the finished article. If an editor is interested, he will ask to see part of the article or will offer alternate approaches for covering the topic.

Writing a book about your product or company is a process similar to publishing articles, but it takes longer. Most of the time, books are proposed to publishers before they are completely written. If you don't have the expertise or time to complete a book, it is possible to hire professional authors to coauthor or ghostwrite a book on a contract basis, just like it is possible to hire people to write articles for you.

If you want your book published and distributed by a major publisher, books about well-known companies, interesting corporate histories, or products with a large customer base (usually technical products) will normally have a chance of finding a publisher. An alternative is to publish a book yourself through a publisher that specializes in self-published projects. To be effective, you will need to promote and distribute the self-published book.

Before you decide whether or not to use a book to promote your company or product, pick up one of the many reference books about writing and selling books, which are available in any bookstore or library. The good ones will explain how to write a book proposal and find an agent to sell your book idea to a publisher and will also explain the ins and outs of self-publishing.

EDUCATIONAL SEMINARS

Educational seminars can be used to promote a wide range of products—from computer software to heavy industrial equipment and from cleaning products to weight-loss programs. Any product or service that involves technology or a process can be promoted through educational seminars. Educational seminars are especially useful for introducing new ideas and new products into a marketplace.

Educational seminars can be smaller local presentations or larger presentations scheduled throughout the country in key locations. For products with only local appeal, a half-day event is usually adequate. For major new technologies, a two- or three-day event, such as a conference, may be more appropriate. The key aspect of making educational seminars successful is to actually educate the attendees. In other words, teach them something they didn't know before they came. You will be using your product or process to educate your audience, but it is important that the audience members feel that they get value from the seminar without

needing to buy your products. Educational seminars should be more than mere product demonstrations and should be perceived as such by the attendees.

COMMUNITY EVENTS

Community events are implemented to make apparent your support of the local community. Community events promote the positive image of your company, but they rarely have direct sales appeal. Most companies have discovered the long-term benefits of sponsoring community events, which is why there are so many corporate-sponsored car races, golf tournaments, and other special athletic events. Small companies can realize the same general advantage by sponsoring a Little League or local softball team and then promoting the games with ads, flyers, and invitations to customers. A bicycle shop might consider sponsoring local bicycle races. A sporting shoe store could support a marathon or 10-k race.

The possibilities for community events encompasses more than sports, however. McDonald's has opened several Ronald McDonald Houses and has supported other related activities for the families of critically ill children. Rock concerts for saving the rain forest or feeding the homeless are sponsored by major record companies. In the same vein, a home-based law firm may want to hold debate contests between local high schools and offer college scholarships to the winners. Other companies can support art shows or park improvement projects and debut them with gala dinners or barbecues. The possibilities are endless. Whether or not you sponsor community events is a matter of your image objectives, your budget, and your desire to be a benefactor in the community. Community events should be sponsored for the long-term benefits, so don't spend your entire budget on one if you need immediate revenue.

COMPANY-SPONSORED CONFERENCES AND TRADE SHOWS

If there isn't a commercial trade show or conference that meets your promotional needs, then you may want to sponsor your own. Even home-based businesses can do it. You can actually promote your company through these events and make some money in the process. Many small companies have annual user conferences and trade shows designed to train people in the use of their products or to announce future new products.

The difference between a conference and an educational seminar is mostly one of scale. Seminars are usually given to small audiences on a single day. Conferences are large-scale educational events that last more than one day and are typically geared toward audiences of more than 100 people. Conferences usually incorporate a capstone event, such as a speech by an industry leader or the president of a company, and almost always have a major social event, such as a banquet, in addition to the educational sessions. Very large conferences may be held multiple times in a number of cities and involve thousands of participants. With the exception of handling large crowds, the preparation needed for conferences is very similar to that for seminars.

Conferences often go hand in hand with company-sponsored trade shows. The trade show is usually given in the ballroom of a large hotel or in a conference center. A company-sponsored trade show provides an opportunity to display and demonstrate products in a controlled trade show atmosphere, complete with booths and elaborate displays. In addition, companies that produce complementary products used either with your product or in support of it in some way may be willing to pay for some of the expenses and booth space in exchange for the opportunity to display their products at your show or conference. This revenue can be used to offset the price of the total trade show and conference.

The same planning and preparation involved in seminars and conferences also applies to trade shows. We have provided more information on trade shows in general in Chapter 20.

PRESENTATIONS AND SPEECHES

If you or your company has a recognized name, you may want to promote the company by booking yourself at trade shows or important industry conferences. An alternative approach involves inviting a well-known person to speak on behalf of your company at a public event. Almost anyone with a title or an interesting job is a potential speaker at the meetings of community and trade organizations, graduation exercises, awards banquets, and so forth. As the owner of your business, you should add your name to the lists of the speaker's bureaus, which are sponsored by the local Chamber of Commerce and most industry and professional organizations. In addition, most universities maintain speaker's bureaus that provide a wide range of speakers for graduations, community organizations, rallies, and other events.

Be careful not to overdo the speech routine, however. We have seen home business owners overbooked to the point where general business operations suffer as a result. It takes time to write, practice, and present a speech. If you make frequent presentations, make sure that the time you spend preparing and presenting the speeches is worth the effort.

HOLIDAY EVENTS

Holidays are always a good excuse to have a special event, but you have to make sure your event doesn't get lost in the crowd. Some common types of parties include Christmas celebrations, Halloween haunted houses, St. Patrick's Day bashes, Cinco de Mayo festivals, and Easter egg hunts. The events can be coupled with special customer promotions or used simply to promote community awareness and to create positive impressions of your company.

The trick to making holiday events successful is to stick to the theme, make them creative, and ensure that they are truly festive. Sticking a Christmas tree in the middle of the room and calling it a party isn't enough; you need to create an entire environment and atmosphere that is special. Use ample decorations. Music is a must. Wear costumes if appropriate. Always give away a theme-oriented gift (even if small) and serve ethnic or holiday food, as appropriate. A festive party can have a lasting

impression on a wide range of people, so some creativity and a few extra touches can make a big difference on your promotional impact.

PRODUCT DEMONSTRATIONS

If you have a consumer-oriented product with interesting features or capabilities, try to schedule and publicize demonstrations of your product at local malls and department stores or even in hotel lobbies. If your product is more technical, it is often possible to schedule a presentation and demonstration of your product at the meetings of relevant professional groups and societies. It is only a matter of asking; if they say "no" you haven't lost anything for trying. Many store managers and professional organizations are looking for something to attract more people or make their meetings more interesting.

Demonstrations should always be carefully scripted and diligently practiced. If you're giving a demonstration in a store or a mall, you should have a prominent sign, a microphone, a speaker's platform or podium, and something like a small trade show booth to act as a backdrop for the presentation (if there is space). Demonstrations at a professional meeting should employ colorful slides, professionally lettered flip charts, or other images to enhance the presentation. Offer some kind of incentive, such as a discount coupon, a free sample, or a special trade-in incentive (if they're using a competitor's product), to buy your product to the people who have seen the demonstration.

PLANNING AND IMPLEMENTING SUCCESSFUL PUBLICITY EVENTS

There are some basic steps that are common to managing any successful special event. These include:

1. **Define the objectives for the event.** Do you want to build general awareness or announce a specific product? Do you need to support your advertising messages? Do you need to reach a wider audience? Do you need to educate a new target market? Events without clear objectives are events that probably don't need to happen.

2. **Define the target audience for the event.** Before you decide on an event, be clear on who you are trying to reach and where they are.

3. **Determine a realistic budget for your special events.** Based on your overall marketing communications budget, determine the importance of the events in relation to your other marketing communications. If directly reaching your customers is of high priority, this should be reflected in the budget allocation for events. The scale of your event will largely determine the budget. All the small details that go into planning events have costs, so don't underestimate the budget you will require to pull off things professionally. Here are the standard expense categories for most events:

   - Facilities rental
   - Equipment rental, including audiovisual equipment, lighting, and furniture
   - Honoraria and fees for speakers, special guests, and performers
   - Decorations and flowers
   - Promotion
   - Entertainment
   - Travel and lodging for guests and employees
   - Food
   - Hospitality costs for guests or presenters, including meals, limousines, and special gifts
   - Presentation media, such as slides, videos, or background music

   To avoid surprises and panic when managing your event, always put together a small contingency budget for the last-minute details that are inevitably overlooked in even the best-planned affairs. The costs for putting on events are often hidden. Costs that people often forget when planning an event include:

   - Producing and printing the invitations and press releases. If professionals have to design and write these, don't forget to include their fees.
   - Speeches and presentation materials. Again, if someone is going to write the speech or presentation for you, include the costs for the writer and the slides or video production.
   - Postage charges. It is surprising how many people plan the mailings but forget the cost of postage, which can be considerable.
   - Telephone calls and travel expenses for arranging facilities and food, following up with invited guests, and working with the media that will cover your event.
   - Special construction costs for stages, signs, special lighting, or booths.

- Fees for the special services of the facilities staff, including food servers, bartenders, and even carpenters (if you'll be building a stage or speaker's platform).
- The most frequently underestimated expense is the cost in time and money when your personnel works on the event. While people are working on the event, other work won't be getting done. This needs to be considered; otherwise, your personnel won't have enough time to prepare and support the event appropriately. If people resent working on an event or feel overburdened, it will be reflected in the quality of the event. If the event will negatively impact other aspects of your business or there aren't enough resources (people and money) to pull it off effectively, consider another form of promotion.

4. **Select the appropriate type of event for the objectives, the target audience, and the budget.** Your objective and target audience will determine, to a great extent, the scope and nature of the event. If you want to educate a new target market, then a seminar, conference, or product demonstration are all possibilities. If you simply want to make your local community aware of your existence, a holiday party might meet your needs. If your funds are limited, you may want your events to consist of limited presentations and demonstrations. By all means, be creative if you have it in you.

5. **Identify the best timing for the event.** After you decide on the kind of event that best meets your needs, be careful to select the appropriate timing. The times for some events, such as holiday parties or anniversaries, are pretty much predetermined. However, the scheduling of other events can and should be controlled. The availability of facilities, the weather, and the number of competing events should all be considered before you select a date.

6. **Don't schedule events too close to major conferences or trade shows.** Avoid overlapping your events with those of your competition. Avoid times of the year when the weather in your area is undesirable (unless you hold the event in another location). Although you can't forecast the weather, always be prepared for the worst-case scenario—no matter where you decide to hold the event—and make sure there is enough time to prepare the event before you finalize the date. It won't matter how good the date is if you are unprepared when it arrives.

   In addition to choosing the date, you will also need to consider the time of day for some events. If it is an all-day affair, choose a day when the largest number of people will be able to attend. Don't schedule a family event on Sunday morning during church hours. Don't schedule a business event on a Saturday. If you plan an after-work event, allow for commute times and give the people a few minutes to relax with a drink or refreshments before getting started.

7. **Identify the best location for the event.** The location of the event is critical to its success. If you don't have appropriate rooms or facilities in your own company,

rent them. The location should always be accessible, easy to find, and comfortable. Hotels, conference centers, club facilities, and even some well-appointed restaurants are all possible locations if your own company facilities aren't appropriate.

If you are putting on a large-scale event, hold it somewhere close to a major airport, if possible. Make sure adequate hotel and transportation facilities are available. The rooms for the event should be a major consideration in your choice of a facility. They should be able to accommodate your best-case attendance estimate. Make sure the seating is comfortable. Avoid gaudy, brightly colored, or cluttered rooms. Neutral environments that you can dress up with your own decorations and signs are best—unless you are giving a formal dinner in a gala ballroom. Look at many possibilities before choosing the location. Consider things like electrical facilities, air-conditioning and heating, proximity of the rest rooms, and the general services and equipment provided by the facility.

8. **Establish a team for coordinating large events.** For a small event, a competent, organized person can probably handle most of the planning and coordination, but, for a large event, no single person has enough time to plan, organize, and implement a special event. In this case, even small companies form event committees, where one person acts as the project manager for the event and other people (often family members) are assigned specific aspects of the events, such as publicity, decorations, presentations, and logistics. The skill of the project manager in coordinating and managing the team is the key to an effective committee.

9. **Publicize the event well in advance using standard publicity techniques.** You should treat your special event as news and should follow all the guidelines for gaining publicity that were covered in the last chapter, including sending out press releases and following up with your media and press contacts. Timing the press releases is crucial. You want adequate coverage before the event, but you don't want to send your press releases so far in advance that your event is forgotten before it happens. There are also community calendars in most newspapers that you should use for public events. Listings in these are usually free, so it is worth the time to send the editor-in-charge a notice of your event, even if you don't send out formal press releases. For large-scale events, you may want to do some advertising in newspapers or trade journals.

10. **Invite people in advance and follow up whenever appropriate.** In addition to publicity, you will probably want to invite people from your mailing lists, including customers, press and media representatives, prospects, or community leaders, as appropriate. These invitations should be mailed about three weeks before the event, and, if there are people whom you really want to attend, follow up with a personal call to remind them of the event.

11. **Make sure you and all other company participants (if any) are trained and clear on their responsibilities.** If numerous

people will be involved in an event, keep them informed about the progress of the event and the planned activities. All participants should have agendas in advance. All speeches and presentations should be practiced in advance in the actual room (if possible) using the lights, audiovisual equipment, and microphones you plan to use during the event. For large events, it is advisable to have a meeting the day before the event to brief the participants on protocol and their responsibilities. Each person's responsibilities should be clearly specified in a list that is provided to the entire event team.

12. **Follow up after the event to get reactions from the participants.** To improve your events, call selected attendees or send out questionnaires to determine what they liked and disliked. What topics should have been added to or removed from the conference or presentation? Which activities were too long? Which activities were too short? What did they think of the food? Was the location and facility appropriate? The more you learn from your event, the more success you will have with another one in the future.

THE SUCCESS SECRETS BEHIND SPECIAL EVENTS

Why is it that some events go so well and others flop? So that you don't find yourself in a room without an audience or on a stage listening to boos and hisses, here are some simple secrets to making special events work for you instead of against you.

- **Welcome the attendees at the beginning.** Use people's names whenever possible. Provide name tags for the attendees so you can do this without the stress of trying to memorize everyone's name. The power of calling someone by name is immeasurable.

- **Prepare contingency plans for every possible problem.** Try to anticipate everything that could possibly go wrong—bad weather, a sick speaker, or nonfunctioning equipment. Without contingency plans for late speakers or other predictable mishaps, an event can quickly fall apart. The more problems you can imagine and plan for, the more likely the event will go without a hitch. Of course, there is always the problem that no one anticipates, like the time a TV celebrity with a reputation for being a friendly, easy-going guy turned out to be a completely uncooperative jerk who ruined an expensive event put on by a major corporation. If you're otherwise prepared, havoc can be kept to a minimum.

- **Remember the details.** The details that make events special. Things like boutonnieres and corsages for the speakers add a touch of class. Printed agendas, including the names of key speakers, are a must. Tasteful decorations and flowers on the dinner table or on the stage can turn an ordinary event into a gala affair. Quality signs that make rooms and activities easy to find are considerate and help reinforce the importance of the event. Pencils and note pads on the tables are a thoughtful and appreciated addition.

- **Make the event entertaining and informative.** If your event includes presentations, use speakers who are lively and entertaining instead of dry and monotonic. Limit formal speeches to 15 minutes. Use a variety of media in your presentations whenever possible. In large-scale events, like conferences or company-sponsored trade shows, have multiple activities scheduled simultaneously.

- **Remember that the way to a customer's mind is through his or her stomach.** Many special events should have some kind of refreshment. It doesn't have to be haute cuisine or even expensive; it should, however, be something of quality. Snacks are fine for seminars but are inappropriate for conferences. The more elaborate the event, the more elaborate the food.

People often remember the event by the quality of the refreshments. The quality of the food reflects on the quality of your company and your product—so be picky. The food budget may turn out to be the single largest expense when putting on an event, but it will be worth it if the food is memorable for the right reasons.

- **Give the people something by which to remember the event after it is over.** Little gifts, such as a small box of candy at the end of a dinner, an embossed notebook at a seminar, or a carryall bag at a conference, provide positive reinforcement of time well spent. The remembrance doesn't have to be expensive. Imagination and utility often count for more than the cost.
- **Time the activities and presentations for maximum effect.** The key to keeping people interested in your event is timing. Make sure the capstone speeches occur when people are most receptive—between 10 a.m. and noon for daytime events and before 8 p.m. for evening events. Late evenings and early mornings are best for social interaction and introductions.

- **Always know what the competition is doing.** If your rival is giving a one-week all-expense-paid training seminar in the Bahamas, then you know what you are competing against. You shouldn't necessarily mimic the competition, but you must take them into consideration when you develop your event strategy. Sometimes it is appropriate to be a copycat, but it is usually better to do something of equal or better quality that incorporates a much different theme and approach. If you can't afford to put on an event that competes in content, creativity, and organization, sometimes it is better not to put on an event at all. Or, as an alternative, put on a number of smaller, more personal events of high quality as opposed to one colossal event that drains your budget and your resources.
- **Always thank the guests for attending.** For most events, the "thanks-yous" should be done twice—at the event and in a note with a personal signature that is sent after the event. (The note may be printed, but the signature should be personal. A printed signature is tacky.) In large events with hard-to-identify audiences, make sure you personally thank as many people as possible for coming. If people feel special at your event, they will appreciate you and your company, and that's the whole point of special events, isn't it?

18

COLLATERAL MATERIALS—A STAPLE IN THE HOME-BASED MARKETING PORTFOLIO

Your prospective customers may need more information before they can decide on your product, so you hand them a colorful brochure. This example illustrates an important and very powerful marketing communications tools available to home-based businesses—collateral materials, also known as brochures, catalogs, and flyers. In this chapter, you'll learn which collateral material to use and how to produce it.

When you use collateral materials, you are in control of the message, the production, and the distribution of the materials. These tools can have significant advantages over other forms of advertising and publicity if you want to control a message and target a specific marketplace. Further, you can produce collateral materials on your own and promote them on your own schedule.

Collateral materials include brochures, catalogs, reports, data sheets, price lists, newsletters, and other printed materials that work with other tools to enhance and complete the sales process. Collateral materials are used to provide customers with details and information not included in an ad or news release. Most collateral is distributed in person or through the mail in response to direct inquiries made by a potential customer.

Direct mail is specialized collateral that is mailed to prospective customers instead of being handed out by a salesperson. Direct mail in its simplest form consists of a letter or postcard. More complex direct-mail projects use a mailer designed specifically for this purpose or consist of a product brochure sent with a personalized letter to customers. Because direct-mail programs often use materials created in a manner identical to collateral materials, the production of both of these marketing communications tools is covered in this chapter. The way to set up a direct-mail program using collateral materials is covered in the next chapter.

COLLATERAL MATERIALS—THE BASICS

Advertising and publicity create awareness and need for a product and are potent tools for getting the word out. However, since ads and press coverage can't always present all the information customers require when they make a buying decision, a "follow-up" tool— collateral—is needed to add detail and better explain the product and its benefits. Collateral is used to build and enhance a prospect's awareness of your product, an awareness that was initiated through media-based tools and direct mail. It can also be used as a powerful image-building tool to enhance a company's credibility or technological prowess.

Collateral is always used to support the sales process, although this support may take a number of forms. In the case of products sold by an outside sales force, the collateral may include presales brochures and price lists. In the case of a mail-order company, a catalog is usually the major force in moving products. A charity may support a door-to-door soliciting program with a small brochure that adds weight and credence to the solicitor's message.

Collateral can also be used to support future sales. Many consumer goods manufacturers include literature in their product packages to support the buyer's belief that he or she has purchased a "quality product." This postsales literature is provided in the hope that it will motivate customers to buy more of the company's merchandise in the future.

Brochures

The most familiar collateral format is the brochure. A brochure is a multipage booklet that ranges from 4 to 24 pages in length. (More than 24 pages is usually considered a catalog.) The size of the brochure depends on how it will be distributed and the whims of the designer. We've seen brochures as small as 4" × 4" and as large as 2-feet square.

Brochures are best for delivering strong benefits and sales messages. They are also a good choice for enhancing overall corporate image. Product specifications and technical details are best covered in another kind of collateral called a data sheet or white paper or they may be relegated to a back page of the brochure. There are several categories of brochures, including:

- **Corporate Capabilities Brochures.** These typically expensive brochures are designed to convince customers and investors of the stability and integrity of the featured company. Corporate brochures expound the company's advanced technology, financial resources, and customer base. These brochures cover the company's full spectrum of services and resources and the value the company offers its customers. They, along with specific product brochures, are typically used as "leave behind" pieces by a salesforce, or are included as one component of a complete media or literature kit distributed to VIPs and the press.

- **Product Sales Brochures.** Product sales brochures are benefits-oriented promotional pieces for a product or product line. They are usually (but not always) less expensive than corporate brochures and are used directly in the sales process. Product brochures are used at trade shows or as a "leave behind" pieces in the field. These brochures may also be display materials in retail environments. Costs permitting, these brochures can be mailed as part of a direct promotional campaign.

- **Educational Brochures.** These are designed to support other collateral by providing customers with information about competitive product issues or to explain a new technology employed by the company. The purpose of a well-crafted education piece is to show customers what to look for when evaluating competitive products or reviewing similar technology. Of course this "education" is inevitably self-serving and portrays aspects of the company's product as more important than those of a competitor's. Sometimes, educational brochures can be simple "white papers" produced to look like scientific reports. Other times, they are as elaborate as a product or corporate brochure. Again, it's the audience and the

budget that help you decide how much to spend on producing any piece of collateral material.

- **Internal Promotional Brochures.** Large companies often promote themselves or their programs to their employees. They do this by creating brochures for use inside the company. Examples of internal promotional pieces are elaborate human resources brochures used to attract new employees and company benefits brochures.

Price Lists and Data Sheets

Price lists and parts lists are some of the simplest collateral pieces. Taking a variety of formats, they may consist of tiny stand alone booklets or quick-printed black-and-white pages to be inserted in a three-ring binder.

Data sheets are also simple collateral pieces and are typically 1 to 4 pages in length. Unlike a brochure, which focuses on delivering a product sales message, data sheets generally focus more on product features and specifications. Data sheets are usually less expensive to produce than product brochures. They typically employ one- or two-color printing and simple photos and illustrations. The inexpensive format allows for frequent updating at minimal cost as a product changes and evolves. Product brochures should work together with data sheets. The brochure creates the image and expounds the overall benefits message, while the data sheets summarize the brochure's message and add the in-depth technical specifications and operational details.

Catalogs

Catalogs are used to display a wide range of products for immediate and direct sale to customers. Catalogs typically make copious use of photos and illustrations to display the goods. They come in various sizes, although standard 8½" × 11" and 9" × 12" formats are most common. Catalogs are familiar to almost everyone, and include those produced by Sears and Best Products. Manufacturing companies also produce catalogs of products, parts, and equipment.

Recently, catalogs have again become a popular direct marketing tool for a wide range of products, and home-based catalog companies are thriving. Catalog-based companies have sprung up for all kinds of unique and not-so-unique product lines, including clothes, specialty foods, business products, exercise equipment, and leisure time products. We even received a catalog of portable wine cellars, with prices starting at $3,500. We still wonder which mailing list targeted us for that one.

STEPS FOR PRODUCING COLLATERAL MATERIALS

While collateral includes a long list of diverse materials and encompasses a wide range of sales and marketing objectives, the basic steps for creating all collateral tools are (fortunately) nearly the same. The basic steps are:

- Establish objectives for the piece
- Define a format for the piece
- Determine a budget for the piece
- Hire the right vendors to produce the piece
- Develop the concept and write the copy
- Design the piece for visual impact
- Complete the preprint production

- Print the piece
- Distribute the finished collateral piece.

In the next few pages, these steps are covered in depth, and tips and hints for making the process go smoothly are provided so that your collateral materials will have maximum effectiveness in getting the word out about your products and company.

Step 1. Establish objectives for the piece. The process of creating cost-effective and persuasive collateral material begins in the planning stages. More so than other tools in the marketing communications toolbox, collateral materials must be carefully orchestrated to work with other promotional programs and the sales process in order to be fully effective. Many collateral pieces must wear several different hats to meet an organization's needs. Of course, some companies create individual pieces for each need, as can you, but this uses money that could be better spent elsewhere.

Selecting the right format for a collateral piece and setting and sticking to a budget for the project are central to the success of collateral projects. Since outside vendors are often required to write, design, produce, and print collateral pieces, the development of clear objectives and guidelines is crucial. Like most other communications efforts, the process of creating effective collateral material requires a careful balance of the need and function of the piece against the price tag and physical requirements of the format. While a full-color brochure with 24 pages of expensive photos and expressive text is useful for almost every kind of product, it may be cost prohibitive. Instead, a simple two-color 4-page piece may cost substantially less, work just as well, and take far less time to execute.

Be very clear on what uses and functions the collateral material will have. You should be able to explain in two sentences why each piece in a collateral strategy is needed and how the pieces will work together in the sales process. Unless you have a lot of money, avoid the several-level "grand scheme" recommended by income-seeking design firms and agencies. Consider tiered literature schemes only if each piece is justifiable and useful on its own without the rest of the scheme. Remember, the only people who will bother to understand your literature strategy are you and your agency.

You can establish specific objectives for your collateral materials by answering questions like the following:

- Who is the audience for the piece? As always, this is the first question you need to ask.

- How will the piece be distributed?

- What is the expected lifespan of the piece?

- Who in your organization will distribute or use the piece? Salespeople? The public relations department? Executives? The personnel department?

- What functions will the collateral piece perform that other marketing communications will not?

- At what point in the sales cycle will the piece be distributed to the potential customer or other audience?

- What messages will the piece communicate? (Refer to Chapter 2 again for a list of the possibilities.) Be careful to keep the messages focused. One common mistake in collateral materials is an attempt to say everything about a product or company in one piece.

Be open-minded as you define your collateral requirements. The project that you originally defined as one brochure may turn out to be more cost-effective in the form of several less expensive product brochures, or the reverse may be true.

Step 2. Define a format for the piece. After careful review of your objectives, you must determine roughly what kind of piece you need in terms of format. Format includes specifications for size, the number of colors, and the paper quality. What makes this a bit tricky is that the format dictates your budget, yet, at the same time, your budget dictates the format.

Here are some things that can help you determine a rough format for your next collateral piece:

- Collect copies of your competitors' materials to see what format they use (number of colors, size, complexity of design, number and quality of photos and illustrations, and quality of paper and printing).

- Assemble the collateral projects used by your company in the past and review them for effectiveness. Pile the ones that worked best in front of you and put the others aside.

- Make a list of the major topics you want to cover to get some idea of the page count. If the number of topics becomes excessive, delete the less important ones or combine them, if it makes sense to do so. Effective collateral contains one major focus per page. This focus might be to showcase a single product or product line or to describe what makes your company better than the competition.

- Choose a physical size format for the piece based on the number of uses for the piece. Most brochures, catalogs, and data sheets use a standard 8½" × 11" size because it fits conveniently into file folders and provides a lot of room on each page. A slightly larger size sometimes works for a corporate brochure because it sets the piece apart from smaller product brochures and gives it more presence. For consumer products, a smaller size may work, depending on how the brochure is to be used. For example, a brochure promoting an expensive line of cosmetics might be sized 4" × 4" to fit easily into a woman's handbag. A brochure used in a retail store might measure 8½" × 3" to fit in a mounted literature holder. If a brochure will be mailed, it must fit into standard envelopes and floor displays, if used.

- Select the approximate number of colors for the piece. Study your competitor's materials and your pile of "effective" literature to see how many colors were used. If the budget is tight, use as few colors as possible to keep your costs down. Use more if your company has relied on a colorful look in the past or if your competitors use them. Why? Because your one-color piece will look uninteresting to a customer reviewing your literature alongside a competitor's. However, in the case of a charity or not-for-profit organization, the opposite may be true. Your competitor's four-color piece may look like

an imprudent use of donations when it is compared with your simple one- or two-color piece.

- Select any special "extras" required by the project. Examples of extras include business reply cards (BRCs) and special print treatments, such as foil stamping, varnishes, embossing, and coil binding.

- Select a paper type appropriate for your project. You should discuss this with prospective designers and printers if you're new to marketing communications. We've also put some basic information on papers in Chapter 8 to get you started.

- What quantity will be printed? Normally, allow enough collateral for a six-month to two-year supply, depending on how the piece will be used and distributed. The more you print the first time, the less each individual piece will cost.

These specifications will help you set limits on the budget for the project and will provide guidelines for the vendors you hire. After the concept and design are proposed, the vendors might ultimately make a few changes and recommendations to improve your rough specifications, but your initial format will establish your expectations so the vendors don't blow the budget on a design that you can't afford to execute.

Step 3. Determine a budget for the piece. With your format decisions in hand, you can now solicit estimates for writing, design, production, and printing. Based on your format decisions, construct a worksheet that includes the design specifications and send a copy to prospective vendors for each of the primary services required to produce your collateral project. As a control factor, look up last year's projects to see how much was spent for a similar piece.

Step 4. Hire the right vendors to produce the piece if you can't do it on your own with your computer. After getting bids from appropriate vendors, you will need to make a decision as to who can best help you bring the project to fruition. You can hire a full-service agency or design firm that specializes in collateral materials or use freelancers to write, design, produce, and print your collateral projects. In addition, you will need to choose a printer with the appropriate level of skill and equipment required to print your piece.

Be aware that vendors who specialize in the development of print collateral materials have different skills and portfolios than do advertising specialists. Your selection is critical to producing an effective piece that is on time and within budget. For example, the writer who is capable of creating a lengthy brochure is often a different animal than is an advertising copywriter. A few writers can do both, but usually someone who is good at knocking off a 1-page ad will become bored when writing a 24-page brochure that requires several drafts before completion.

Step 5. Develop the concept and write the copy. Unless you're a very good writer, we recommend using a professional writer to produce ideas and copy for your projects. The process of writing a collateral piece starts with a concept (idea) and headlines for each page or spread. The concept for a collateral piece includes a theme, a style, and suggested visual imagery. The person who writes the collateral piece (or the creative director at an agency) is responsible for creating the overall concept

with your assistance. Writers will have meetings with you to ask questions and verify details to be used in the copy.

After specifying an overall concept and organization for the piece, the concept should be reviewed and approved. Then, the writer will create a first draft of the copy while coordinating ideas with the designer to make sure the design and the copy fit together. The writer should also describe and caption all the visuals in a manner that reinforces the messages in the copy.

Ultimate Survival Tip

The Endless Too-Much-Copy Problem
Many collateral projects suffer from the too-much-copy problem. It is a problem that often begins with you. If you have too much to say on a page of a brochure or data sheet, you end up with too much type or you resort to setting the pages in tiny 7 or 8 point type, which is extremely hard to read. If you hire a writer, he or she may be guilty of the same problem. He or she may become unusually prolific on a given topic and include a lot of secondary detail, obliterating the key messages. A designer's advice may be to cut the copy, but keep in mind that if your designer had his or her way, there would be no copy used whatsoever because it clutters up the design. Ultimately, it's your job to make sure the message gets across in the right number of words.

Depending on you, the writer, and your organization, the copy may be accepted nearly verbatim at the first draft, or it may continue through as many as ten rewrites before acceptance. Strong, concise writing and clear, unambiguous organization are the keys to making a piece enjoyable and easy to read; that's what you should look for when you read the draft. If the draft goes through more than three revisions, then the writer is wrong for the project, your review process is not productive, or there are internal political problems in your organization that need to be resolved before work on the piece continues.

After the final draft of copy is approved, the writer's final contribution to a project will be to proofread the ready-to-print mechanical assembled by the designer.

Step 6. Design the piece for visual impact. After the concept is approved, the designer's work begins, although sometimes the designer and writer will work together on a concept for a piece. Designers are used to create the look and feel for most collateral projects. Many designers and design firms specialize in collateral only, taking on other communications projects, such as advertising, only if times are tight. The designer or design firm is usually responsible for taking the project from tissues all the way through print.

Well-designed collateral is a pleasure to view and read. Captivating photos catch and keep the eye, and their captions provide just enough detail to get the reader to read the copy. Charts explain concepts that are difficult to explain in words alone. Color makes the piece vibrant. The choice of type, visuals, and space on the page result in overall cohesiveness.

There are a number of clichés to avoid when planning collateral materials. The more obvious ones to steer clear of include:

- Avoid pictures and images that don't say anything. For example, almost every computer software brochure has a picture of an anonymous person sitting in front of a computer. Photos likes these convey no message.

- Skip themes that use puzzle pieces, children's building blocks, and board games. Thousands of others have already beat you to these tired themes, and in the case of board games, the manufacturer may sue for copyright infringement if you show their game in a photo without permission.

- Unless you're selling baby products, don't use your baby or child in photos. You may think he or she is completely adorable, but your readers may not share your view. If you must show a child or young person in a photo, let the designer select one from a modeling agency.

- Choose something other than shots of underclothed models to sell your products, unless you sell bathing suits or lingerie.

If you use a professional design firm or ad agency to help you out, the design process for collateral is similar to that of print advertising. First, the designer creates tissue drawings of the piece. A tissue may be a miniature thumbnail sketch or a full-size sketch. Most designers draw these sketches using pencil or colored pencils (in the case of a multicolored piece). With your approval of these sketches, the designer will prepare a comprehensive (or comp for short). This is a full-size color mock-up of the piece that shows greeked copy, headlines, and sketches of all photos and illustrations. Before a final comp is produced, it is important that the designer and the writer communicate on a regular basis to make sure they are clear on the concepts and to ensure the space allowed for the copy is adequate.

After the comp is approved, the designer sets the type, has photos taken by a professional photographer, and has illustrations produced in order to create the components necessary to produce a printer-ready mechanical. At this point, the job is ready for the production step.

Step 7. Complete the preprint production. Production is the term used for getting a project ready for printing. This starts with assembling the type, photos, and illustrations into a mechanical. The mechanical is then sent to the printer for stripping (the process of converting the mechanical into film that will be used to create plates used for printing). The printer completes halftones and color separations of the illustrations and photographs and strips them into the film. Then, the plates are "burned" for printing the piece. We have included more information on prepress production in Chapter 8. Most designers oversee these production steps or they do them themselves. Designers use two methods, depending on the nature of the job and the designer's preferences, to complete the production steps— traditional drafting board methods or desktop publishing systems.

With the advent of desktop publishing, you and professional designers can produce ready-to-print film with the aid of personal computers and desktop publishing software. The designers hire an outside service bureau to output the film or resin-coated paper used to produce printing plates. One piece of film is used for each page, and in the case of multi-colored pages, one additional sheet of film is required for each page. This output usually includes all elements of the page, including images, type, and color information. Get a current version of PageMaker, QuarkXPress, or Microsoft Publishers if you want to do this on your own. Most desktop publishers use one of these page layout products for creating professional quality materials.

Step 8. Print the piece. The final step in producing collateral materials occurs when a print shop locks the finished press plates onto a press and prints the job. After printing, many jobs go to a bindery for trimming, folding, stapling, and special effects (such as foil stamping or embossing). Usually, your designer will attend a "press check" at the print shop to verify that everything is correct before the entire job is printed. If the designer won't go to the press check, you should.

Step 9. Distribute the finished collateral piece. Finally, after delivery from the printer, the project is complete and ready for distribution. Most collateral material is stored and distributed as needed or sent to a distribution center. A distribution center may be part of a department within a large corporation or may be an independent business that handles materials from a number of different companies. The key to distribution, whether it is done from within the company or by an independent organization, is making the collateral tools easily accessible to those who need to use them.

Some collateral materials are sent in response to phone inquiries, bingo responses from a magazine ad, or business reply cards. In these cases, the requestor's name and address (along with a special code number identifying the request) should be quickly forwarded to the literature distribution center. A well-equipped center uses the special code to produce the appropriate form letter on your stationery and pick out the right brochure and

THE ULTIMATE HOME OFFICE SURVIVAL GUIDE

envelope from inventory. After stuffing, addressing, and adding postage, the center drops the package into the mail. These centers may also be used to distribute packages of literature to sales offices and retail locations.

GETTING THE MOST FROM COLLATERAL PROJECTS

In order to be effective, collateral must be noticed and read. The following paragraphs outline some guidelines that will help.

If you provide collateral to your dealers or distributors, make it free or inexpensive to use. After reviewing last year's budget, many companies decide to charge their retailers or distributors for all the brochures they "waste." It is not uncommon for these companies to charge inflated prices for the collateral, too. The rationale is that dealers will only hand out literature to serious customers. The reality is that, in many cases, the dealer will resort to handing out muddy photocopies of the literature in order to avoid paying a bill for it. In extreme cases, a dealer or distributor will stop using your materials at all and essentially stop selling your products. If you can't afford to distribute a piece of collateral for free, don't produce it at all.

Make the ordering process easy. Many companies suffer from bureaucratic inertia. If the process of ordering literature is clumsy and slow, your sales force and customers will stop requesting it. A busy distributor who is forced to spend an hour on the phone with a manufacturer in an attempt to get literature will probably not bother to repeat the process in the future. He may also drop your product

as sales fall off. Other companies make the mistake of locking all of the literature in a closet and rationing it out piece by piece because it costs so much to produce. Like the distributors, your sales team will resort to ugly photocopies and leave the literature locked in the "vault."

Some companies use a combination of collateral materials in a folder called a literature kit (known as a lit kit in the trade) as a sales tool. Just because you're a home-based company doesn't mean you shouldn't have a lit kit. Lit kits can include a capabilities brochure, product brochures, and perhaps a white paper or clippings of significant press materials. Make sure your kit contains all the information required to educate customers and nothing more. We know of one company with a lit kit that contains sixteen nonrelated items! Busy customers who receive this package can't determine what's important and what's superfluous and may miss the important material as a result. Keep your lit kit organized and hone the items down to five or six important ones—no more.

Make sure that all your collateral looks like it came from the same company. Cosmetically different collateral confuses customers and reduces the overall effectiveness of your image-building efforts. This is sometimes difficult to control because each time you work with a new designer or design group, they will attempt to create their own look for you after tactfully criticizing the work done by others. Insist on keeping the look you already use. If you must change it, do it slowly and progressively, unless you are entering a completely new market where few customers will have seen your existing materials.

Color Brochures

Brochures are powerful (and expensive to produce) promotional tools for providing key product and company information to prospective customers. A full-color brochure's text and pictures explain and convey a message, and the look of a well-designed brochure can be used to provide a tangible image for your home-based company. Even the paper texture and weight subconsciously communicate something to the reader.

Because brochures tend to have a much longer lifespan than expected (typically three times longer than planned—a brochure that is expected to last only a year may be used for three), try to avoid including references that will quickly date the piece. Instead of focusing a corporate brochure on today's hot new product, talk in more general terms about the product's unique technology. Likewise, don't focus exclusively on any one individual in your organization because, one year down the road, that person may be working for your competition or have left the field all together.

When embarking on an expensive brochure project, select a writer and design house with extensive experience producing brochures. While both your advertising agency and PR agency will be happy to take on a brochure project, designers in ad agencies are rarely up to the task and most PR writers lack the expertise necessary for this kind of document.

Like annual reports, brochures can be complex, long-lived projects and can have numerous political entities involved in the review process. However, unlike annual reports that usually have a legal deadline for completion, a really troublesome brochure project can drag its feet for years. Careful scheduling and skillful project management are important to keep these projects on track.

Large Catalogs

Catalogs vary considerably in scope and complexity. Obviously, assembling the Penney's Catalog is a much bigger job than putting together a seed catalog for a small mail-order company. A small catalog is very similar to a brochure project, although the printing budget may be substantially less for a catalog than for a flashy, six-color brochure.

Ultimate Survival Tip

Check Large Catalogs One Last Time!
Because many big catalogs are printed in signatures that consist of several pages produced at one time, you should always recheck the entire catalog as each signature is completed. If you find an error you absolutely can't live with, have only that signature reprinted. Then, when everything is satisfactory, have the signatures bound into the final catalog. While it's true that replacing a signature is expensive, it's still far cheaper than replacing a finished catalog.

Large catalogs are a logistical nightmare in many ways but are often very important for home-based businesses. There is more work involved in producing large catalogs than in creating a brochure, and the possibility of making serious mistakes is greater. Even the printing of a catalog is different. Catalogs are usually run on a web press (a big press with high-volume capabilities), which involves different production considerations when designing and producing the pages. Make sure your design firm is experienced with catalogs; if it isn't, the catalog is sure to cost you more than it should.

The key to producing catalogs is organization, including assembling a realistic schedule with extra time built in for the surprises that inevitably occur. If you are responsible for producing a complex catalog and you tend to be a scatterbrain, involve someone who is intensely detail oriented to monitor the project and watch out for hidden mistakes. Check everything twice and then once more. Organization is also vitally important because running the wrong photo, adding the wrong caption, or including the wrong price will materially affect the usefulness of the catalog. Reprints aren't cheap if the catalog must be replaced to fix a serious error.

If you lack the manpower or time to handle your own catalogs, consider hiring an outside firm that specializes in catalog design and production. Depending on your needs, a firm can either help with one step of the process, such as mechanical preparation and print supervision, or take the entire project off your hands. If you choose this route, note that some of these firms are highly creative and fully capable of creating an exciting catalog full of bright colors and lively copy. Others are simply assembly mills with little creative capabilities. Depending on your needs and budget, you will want to choose one kind of catalog house over the other. For more information on catalog particulars, look up the book *How to Create Successful Catalogs* from Maxwell Sroge Publications.

19

Direct Mail—A Powerful Promotion for Almost Any Market

This chapter covers the ins and outs of direct-mail promotional programs, one of the most common and most important promotional tools for home-based businesses. You'll learn how to buy mailing lists, design your mail program, and respond to the inquiries you receive.

Direct mail is frequently referred to as the world's largest promotional channel. Because a mailer can contain considerably more information than an ad, you can generate product awareness, and, in most cases, you can provide all of the information necessary for completing the sale in one promotion. Direct mail, whether you use traditional mail through the post office or e-mail on the Internet, is a powerful tool. To invoke participation from recipients, you should have your mailers ask for a response and provide a means for making it.

Make your direct-mail programs timely so that people want to respond immediately.

Once a recipient shelves your mailer or turns off the e-mail, it's unlikely that he or she will get back to your message. Because many recipients receive a large volume of direct mailings, it's likely that, without a means for immediate response, your offer is destined for a nonstop flight to the waste disposal facility.

DIRECT-MAIL FORMATS MEET DIFFERENT OBJECTIVES

Whether done through e-mail or traditional mail, there are two important components to direct-mail promotions: the mailer itself and the mailing. The mailer consists of the physical piece of material that will be sent to prospects. The mailing process consists of selecting a mailing list and sending the mailers to prospects on the list (using the most expedient mailing method within the project's budget). Direct mailers can use a number of formats, including letters, postcards, e-mail messages, and brochures.

Letters and Postcards

The simplest form of direct mail is a letter, on company stationery, that makes a pitch for a new product or special offer. Letters and postcards are the rock-bottom option, but they can be effective if the letter is well written or if the postcard is unusually compelling. For some markets, such as fund-raising, this inexpensive tactic works well when you include hand-addressed envelopes and actual signatures because it makes the effort appear all that more personal.

Use a letter approach if your budget is extremely tight and if the personal appeal of a letter is appropriate for your market. Don't use the letter approach unless you can make it look personal. Note that printing your signature in blue ink, as is often done, won't fool a 6-year old. Use the postcard approach only if you can afford to print the card with at least a second color and, preferably, use an oversized card for better impact. Postcards work well for advertising hotels, property, new model cars, and grand openings of retail outlets. Put a four-color picture of your product on one side of the postcard and the details in two colors on the back. Don't use this format if you can only afford is a small black-and-white postcard—

you may alienate more customers than you gain, and you certainly won't attract their interest.

Brochure–Letter Combination

The brochure–letter combination is a very effective mailing technique that uses an existing brochure accompanied by a letter to personalize and introduce the product. The letter calls the customers to action by making a special offer or by asking them to respond in some way. This is a straightforward technique that works well for almost any product, particularly if you overprint the envelope and have an especially well-designed brochure that's ready to mail.

Use this approach if you have a very sales-oriented brochure already printed and can afford to mail the quantity required for your market. If you are selling very upscale products, such as luxury cars or palatial homes in the country, this is a tasteful approach, although it may take a while to get a noticeable response because of the long sales cycle associated with such products.

There are three weaknesses to consider before you choose this format:

1. If your brochure is expensive to print and your mailing list is long, it may not be economical.

2. Unless your brochure is very buy-me-now–oriented, you may not get the response you intended, even with a strong letter. (Many recipients don't read the letters.)

3. Lengthy, full-size brochures can be heavy to mail and the postage charges may swallow your budget.

Custom Mailers

For maximum impact, a custom mailer is usually the best bet. A custom mailer can be designed in any shape or size that can be easily mailed. It may be a dazzling six-color piece that stands out among the contents of the mailbox. It may be a minibrochure produced exactly as detailed in the collateral section. The total package may consist of an envelope packed with information, a catalog, coupons, or all three. Because a custom piece is planned as a mailer, you can include plenty of "buy-now" information and also provide as little or as much product detail as appropriate.

Use a custom direct-mail piece whenever possible because you can impart a timely message to your customers and create just the right look to get noticed. Brightly (but tastefully) colored pieces work best, but if your budget is tight, consider doing a one-color piece with a striking color such as bright turquoise. Surprisingly, gray sometimes works well for this kind of piece because it doesn't offend anyone and still looks different than all the brightly colored designs. To get maximum impact, choose a designer with a real eye for design and an understanding of color and don't skimp on paper quality.

Hop-Along Mailers and Card Packs

Hop-alongs, also called "hook" mailers and other less attractive names, are promotions sent with other mailings. These include advertisements stuffed in the same envelopes as credit card bills and stacks of postcards mailed as a block by magazines in technical industries. These can be effective promotions, but since they are usually going along for the ride, you will have little control over who receives your mailer. More important the format (usually a tiny insert produced on a lightweight paper to keep mailing costs down) may be extremely limited. In addition, your insert may get buried in a pile of similar promotions for other products.

Since many of these mailers are stuffed in monthly billings, recipients may not be in a hurry to open the envelope. They also may have a negative mindset when they finally do get around to opening the bill. Hop-alongs are best used if you need to reach a large group of prospective customers and you aren't too choosy about timing or readership. This tool works well for selling perfume through department stores and for selling magazine subscriptions through established channels, such as Publisher's Clearing House. "Postcard packs," assembled by magazines and targeted to technical markets, often draw a strong response as well.

Don't use hop-alongs if your target market is comparatively small and focused because it won't be cost effective. Don't rely on this tool for making short-term offers, such as a two-day sale or a limited-time price reduction, because you will have little control of the timing.

You can find out about hop-along possibilities by contacting an advertising agency that specializes in direct mail. Look in the telephone book under Advertising—Direct Mail. An alternative is to contact specific companies directly and talk to their advertising departments.

Online Direct Mail Through E-Mail and Newsgroups

Once you subscribe to an online service (such as America Online or the Microsoft Network) or an ISP (Internet service provider) you automatically get an e-mail address that you can use for sending and receiving electronic mail. If you can buy, rent, or otherwise create a credible mailing list of qualified e-mail addresses, then consider trying online mailing programs as part of your direct promotion program, but don't just send junk mail (called "spam" in the industry). If you have someone's e-mail address, you can send messages 24 hours a day (although we don't suggest doing this too often). We've provided an entire chapter about online marketing to give you more options and guidelines for making online direct mail more successful.

Newsletters—Online and Traditional

Primarily due to the ease of use and low cost of desktop publishing technology, a growing number of organizations are mailing regular newsletters to customers and prospects. Electronic mail enables you to send the newsletter via the Internet as well. While a newsletter may appear similar to a newspaper, its real purpose is to keep the company's name and products under the recipient's nose. The most effective newsletters offer special promotions and/or provide useful advice.

Newsletters are a different kind of direct-mail tool; the best ones advertise products and services under the guise of education. They are effective for generating repeat business from existing customers, but generally are not good for soliciting new customers. A well-assembled newsletter sent to the right person will be read and may be saved for future reference, which gives it a longer lifespan than other kinds of mailers.

If you sell products that require substantial customer education, such as computer software or expensive kitchen equipment, newsletters are good tools for maintaining customer loyalty. Use this tool only if you can dedicate the resources (people and money) to produce the newsletter on a regular basis—a minimum of four quarterly issues to be effective.

Keep in mind that the most effective newsletters require an established mailing list of customers. If you are contemplating such a project, be sure that such a list is available or initiate a program to build the list from inquiries or past purchases.

On the down side, newsletters require a lot of work on a regular basis, and once you begin a newsletter program, your customers may take up arms if you suddenly cancel it, mail it on an irregular basis, or let the editorial quality slip. It only takes one or two sub-par issues for your customers to stop reading your newsletter, so you must be able to guarantee quality stories and writing in this long-term commitment.

Don't use newsletters (whether mailed through traditional mail or sent by e-mail) for inexpensive products sold to mass markets. No one wants to read a monthly newsletter on a new type of everlasting light bulb, and you'll spend a lot of money on production to service the user base. By the same token, some products are simply not very interesting, even though customers could benefit from customer education. It's likely that a quarterly newsletter about getting the most from a new type of washing machine detergent will hit the trash can, unread by the majority of recipients.

INTEGRATING DIRECT MAIL WITH OTHER PROMOTIONS

Some companies thrive solely on direct-mail promotions, including catalog houses and specialty product manufacturers. Other companies spend a large portion of their promotional budgets on direct-mail promotions because of the controlled targeted distribution and the relatively low cost. Other companies expand their online marketing efforts to complement their direct-mail advertising efforts. For most companies, direct mail alone is most effective when integrated into a balanced marketing communications mix. For example, focused advertising and publicity can be used to generate awareness and then direct mail (whether using traditional mail, electronic mail, or both) can be used to close deals by building on the media-generated interest. Direct mail is also good for special offers and announcements that are not appropriate or effective when promoted through other advertising media.

THE DIRECT-MAIL PROCESS

Direct-mail promotions follow a logical set of steps that start with objectives and concepts and end with the customer response—the desired end result of all mailing programs.

1. Establish objectives for your direct-mail promotions. Like all forms of home-based

marketing, direct mail works best when goals for a program are set and the mailing program is designed to fulfill these objectives. By setting an objective for the direct-mail campaign, you not only have a yardstick with which to measure its success but also objectives to help keep the project focused throughout its implementation.

As is the case with other promotions, successful in direct-mail advertising depends on getting the right message under the right noses. This is accomplished by creating a mailer or promotion that appeals to and educates your market and by mailing your promotion to members of your target audience.

As in other advertising, the frequency of your direct mailings is also important. If you run a shop that sells flower arrangements and you send out a bimonthly mailing to residents in the area, your message may fall on deaf years most of the year. When one of these people decides that she needs a present for Mom, however, suddenly your mailer will get read and responded to. That's why, depending on the nature of your business, you need to create a complete direct-mail program with multiple mailings and a mailing schedule for the year. Some businesses send weekly mailing but use more then on mailing in order to keep their message fresh and to reach a broad range of prospects. Other companies mail rarely but regularly—every time a special sale or offer is planned or when a new product is introduced. Most direct-mail programs are planned on an annual basis and allow for a mid-year review to accommodate market changes, surprises, and new promotional ideas.

2. Establish the mailing list sources (whether e-mail, traditional mail, or both). After establishing your objectives, which include the target audiences you want to reach, you should choose a mailing list or lists that meet your audience requirements. The mailing list is central to the success of any direct-mail program. You must choose the lists now because you can't assemble a budget without knowing how much postage will be required and how many mailer units must be printed or otherwise created. Rental lists vary considerably in price depending on the degree of accuracy, the size, and the quality—this cost should go into your budget. There is a section with detailed information on selecting and using mailing lists later in this chapter.

3. Budget your direct-mail program. After you know the objectives and mailing list options, the next step is to establish a budget for individual mailers and for the entire direct-mail program. The budget will include the costs for producing the mailers, the rental costs of commercial mailing lists, and the fees charged by the fulfillment house (if you use one) for handling your direct-mail responses. Use the steps from the collateral section and Chapter 10 for determining your direct-mail budget. Don't forget the charges for the postage. If you use a business reply card, remember that you have to budget for the return postage as well.

   For a large mailing, a success is typically a 2%–5% response from the people on the list. If you are selling expensive products, the success rate may be less. There are some programs that generate a response as high as 25% or more, but these are rare. Before you finalize the budget and decide on the number of mailers to send out, consider the return on investment in your program. If you get a 2%–5% response in the form of new sales, will this generate enough revenue to justify the cost of the promotion? If you are not sure what the response rate will be, conduct a pilot mailing to a well-targeted but small list to determine what you can expect.

4. Define the selling propositions for your direct-mail piece. The propositions will be the focus or hook for the promotion, so the product and company messages you incorporate in the mailer will have a chance of being read and acted upon. Effective direct-mail promotions relay a sense of urgency and require immediate response from customers. To get customers to respond, you must establish a proposition that will motivate them to take action. Some common propositions that work well in direct-mail marketing include:

   - Special pricing, including discounts, rebates, and introductory pricing
   - Combination offers—buy one product, get one free or buy this product and get another kind of product for free
   - Contests or sweepstakes
   - Free gifts for trying out a product
   - Product trials and trial subscriptions

   In most direct-mail propositions it is also important to emphasize guaranteed satisfaction, risk-free offers that encourage prospects to buy with confidence. In addition, the offer should be easy to implement. Whenever possible, take all forms of legitimate payment, including checks and credit cards.

In addition to the proposition, you must always plan the desired response before you create any direct-mail promotion. Unlike advertising, which can be used to establish awareness or to build image and credibility over the long term, mailings that don't call customers to action have little impact and are usually forgotten. The only exceptions to this rule are newsletters, which often include useful product information and may be kept longer than other mailings.

Means of response vary from product to product and from company to company. If you run a retail store and you promote a big 2-day sale (preferably starting the day after the mailer arrives), you have provided an intriguing special offer and an immediate means for customers to respond. If you are introducing a new product, include a business reply card (BRC) in your mailer and a prominent toll-free phone number for customers to call for more information. Your sales force can then follow up on these leads directly.

Coupons are also viable tools for direct response. The mailer may not last more than seconds, but if the product is of interest, the coupons will be saved and used— even if they get passed to Aunt Hattie down the street. For some products, offering a trade-in on a competitor's product is a powerful response generator. After taking (and, most likely, junking) the trade-in, you sell your product with a discount based on the trade-in value of the product. Another feasible tactic is to provide a key or magic code that can be used to open a trunk of prizes or to claim a numbered gift. This is a good way to get customers to visit a store to test their luck.

5. Establish a format for the mailer. The format you choose for your direct-mail campaign must match the objectives, the audience, and your budget. Consider the standard options discussed earlier and see how they relate to your market and product image. If you decide that a custom mailer is right for you, follow the steps for establishing a format and design, which were covered in the collateral section of Chapter 18.

   As part of making a format decision, collect your competitor's materials to see what approaches they use. Consider imitating the format and improving on it. If your competition sends out a cheap black-and-white mailer with minimal design, hire a competent designer and print yours with two colors! It's also helpful to find out which mailing lists your competitors use, but short of espionage or sheer luck, this is difficult.

6. Produce your mailer and any peripheral components, such as giveaways, coupons, mailing envelopes, and dots, to seal self-mailers. If you are creating a custom mailer, follow the design, writing, and print steps that were presented for collateral materials. If your project includes a giveaway item, such as a pen or other geegaw, keep in mind that these products typically

take five to eight weeks to produce. Make sure they will be ready in quantity by your mailing date.

7. Arrange postage for your mailer and the business replay card, if used. If you are using bulk mail rates or postage-paid BRCs, allow several days for this process. For BRCs, you will need to get a permit and a bar code, which must be printed on your card. You will also need to make an advance deposit with the post office for the return postage. Always review the final mechanical art for BRCs with the Postal Service; there are myriad specifications and requirements for BRCs, and one "expert's" advice may differ from another's. It's a good idea to write down the name of the person who approves your reply card in case there's a problem down the road.

If you're using a bulk e-mailing program (check out the CD-ROM for links to sites that offer electronic e-mailing programs), make sure you're working within legal limits. Make sure people have a way of getting OFF your list if they don't want to receive your promotions. This is just courtesy, and it allows you to hone down your e-mail lists to those with interested readers.

8. Get ready for responses in advance of the mailing. If your direct-mail program is worth implementing, assume it will be successful. This means you will get more orders, phone calls, or customers than you can count on one hand. You must plan for handling these responses and inquiries well in advance of the mailing. Define an organized response system or hire an out-

side fulfillment house (again, look under Advertising—Direct Mail in the *Yellow Pages*) to handle high-volume inquiries, purchases, e-mail messages, or phone calls based on the direct promotion. If you are simply providing literature, make sure it goes out no more than 48 hours after the request is received. These requests must be serviced quickly so respondents don't forget what they asked for.

For mailings that generate sales leads that require personal visits, return calls quickly and efficiently and document the customer's status after the phone call. There are inexpensive sales-tracking programs that work on many personal computers. (Check out the CD-ROM for some of these.) Such programs will automatically schedule a sales call next week, document long-term interest, or put the lead in a "dead" file along with other unqualified prospects.

In the case of return BRCs, don't be so eager that you call respondents the minute their cards cross your doorstep. This implies that you are desperate for business or that you use high-pressure salespeople—something experienced buyers have learned to avoid. Be responsive but not overly zealous.

If the mailing included BRCs, sort your incoming mail to handle the BRCs as a priority. All incoming BRCs should be logged in a computer program of some sort to help you build your own mailing lists for future use and to make sure that leads are followed up, instead of forgotten.

If you're using e-mail to respond to your inquiries, make sure you have developed in advance a system for answering each question as quickly as possible.

9. Mail the materials. When using traditional mail, get ready for your mailing by adding address labels and postage to each mailer. This may be done by you, a temporary employee(s), or an outside mailing house (most of these companies can help with fulfillment after the mailing too). If you have the funds available, consider hiring a charity organization for this chore—every city has several organizations that will handle mailings efficiently at the right price—and it helps the organization raise money for worthwhile programs.

Ultimate Survival Tip

Getting Noticed Amid the Peas and Carrots in the Mailbox

Because there is such a high volume of direct-mail activity, your first job is to stand out from the crowd in a prospect's mailbox, whether at home or at the office. Bright colors, unusual shapes, intriguing statements, or the use of hand-addressed envelopes are all excellent tools for getting your mailer noticed. Try using color in your e-mail pieces as well or attach attractive files in full color. If you are putting a mailed piece in an envelope, get the packaging over-printed with bright colors or captivating statements. At the very least, stamp it with a large red rubber stamp that says something along the lines of "IMPORTANT INFORMATION EN-CLOSED!" To get a better idea of what your competition is doing and how to look different, just open your mailbox.

If your requirements demand mailing labels presorted by zip code, most mailing list providers will provide labels or lists arranged in this order. Just be careful to keep them the proper order.

For high-volume in-house mailings, an automated postage machine speeds the process, but it takes some of the personal quality out of the mailing. If you are attempting to target your mailer to arrive on a certain day of the week, consider staggering a national mailing to give farther-traveling units more time to arrive.

If you're using an e-mailing program (there are many available by searching for e-mail products on the World Wide Web), you can address thousands of mail programs at once and let the e-mailer run while you deliver the promotion. Just make sure that you use a qualified mailing list so you won't be accused of "spamming" the readers with junk mail.

The timing of your mailing is also important. Time the mailing so your promotion arrives on a good day—a day when your prospective audience will be the most receptive to your message and there is less competing mail. For business-to-business mailers, Monday is usually a tough day at the office. Tuesday through Thursday are days when business people are in their most receptive moods. Friday is usually a poor choice because, while your audience may be in an upbeat mood, they may forestall action until Monday and subsequently forget your offer. If you are mailing to large companies, your mailing may waste a full day in the mail room or internal delivery system before it arrives at its destination. That means that your Thursday arrival may turn into a Friday delivery.

Mailings to residences require different timing. If your product sells to homemakers, any weekday is a good possibility because people who don't work outside of their homes have time to read their mail and act on it. If your product is a consumable likely to be purchased by working spouses, a Friday delivery is a good date because many of these particular consumers do their shopping on Saturday or Sunday. Weekends are also "home-improvement" and "fix-the-car" days, so Friday or Saturday is a good arrival time for promotions that appeal to these activities.

10. Manage the responses expediently. The response mechanisms covered in Step 8 should already be in place, so now it's time to aggressively deal with all the leads and sales you'll receive. If you've done it right, you shouldn't have long to wait! You can't rest yet. If your direct promotions schedule is aggressive, it's time to start work on the next direct-mail program!

GETTING THE MOST FROM DIRECT-MAIL PROMOTIONS

Here are some ways to make your direct-mail promotions reap more positive responses:

- Keep your copy short, tight, and easy to read. If your customers need a lot of information before purchasing the product, consider providing this information during follow-ups to phone inquiries and returned BRCs. You can also include the information in a separate document sent in the same envelope, but make sure that the first thing recipients notice is your primary proposition, not the details.

- Display your address and phone number in more than one place on the mailer so people can't miss them. If your mailing is sent to non-English-speaking countries, include a fax number so people can place orders or get information quickly without having to cross the language barrier.

- Avoid mailing the same mailer or letter to the same people more than twice. Don't print a three-year supply of a printed mailer and expect it to be relevant that long. The same mailer has almost no impact the third time around.

- Avoid the deluge approach. This is when an organization mails to the same list as frequently as once a week. While becoming more common for highly competitive local promotions that offer specials for pizza delivery and a variety of supermarket coupons, there are far too many of these in circulation to be effective. Recipients may enjoy the attention initially, but quickly become annoyed with the constant clutter in their mailbox (whether online or traditional). This is particularly true of mailers that look basically the same from week to week and repetitive mailings from companies in which recipients have noøinterest.

- Avoid adding gift items to your package unless they are properly packaged. For example, if part of your mailing includes a free pen, even if the pen survives the postal machines, the printed surface of your mailer will be damaged if you don't package the gift appropriately.

Ultimate Survival Tip

How *Not* to Get Noticed at the Mailbox

An increasingly popular technique for getting noticed is to create mailers that look like they contain a check (made visible through a small window on the envelope). Other variations on this are mailers that appear to contain stock certificates, money orders, or even cash. Sure, these techniques work to some degree, but we still recommend against them. If the mailer is produced in a convincing fashion, it will certainly get noticed and opened, but once the recipient sees that it's really just junk mail, it may get torn in two in frustration. People don't like to be manipulated, and they may remember your name and product and deliberately avoid future dealings with you. Sending one of these phony offers to a genuinely poor household is downright cruel and insensitive.

- Try to avoid mailing during the Christmas season (from Thanksgiving to after New Years Day). Mail volume is horrendous at this time of year, which means that your mailer will have more competition than ever at the mailbox. In addition, with the number of Christmas cards and parcels delivered during the holiday season, you have no guarantee that your mailing will arrive in a timely fashion. Business-to-business mailings during this period suffer, too. While most companies don't receive the number of Christmas cards and packages that residences do, many people don't really get their mind back to work until mid-January. This means that recipients may be interested in your offer but shelve it for later response and then forget about it.

- Just because you're home based doesn't mean you can't promote yourself internationally. Many home-based businesses thrive on international orders for their products. Before you do a mailing to international shores, however, be aware of the international mail regulations! If you are mailing from the United States to Canada or vice versa, postage rates are different, and bulk rate and BRC permits are not valid across international borders. If you use e-mail, make sure you adhere to local e-mail regulations, and, when using printed mailers, make sure that your mailer plainly displays "Printed in [country]"; otherwise, postal inspectors can rightly refuse to accept it. If you are mailing to Mexico, you should send pieces by airmail if you want them to arrive within a lifetime. Mark the mailer with a large red "AIRMAIL" stamp, preferably one with a picture of a plane for postal clarification. Always put the name of the country prominently on all international addresses. One of our letters to a relative spent most of a month in Ontario, California, before being forwarded to Toronto, Ontario, because we forgot to add the magic word, Canada!

- If you are addressing your own mailings and the list is sorted alphabetically, look for duplicate addressees and weed them out. Recipients who receive twelve of your "limited special offers" will not take your offer seriously. Quality rented lists rarely have this problem, but if you are using several related lists, this is a common occurrence. To avoid this problem when renting multiple lists from the same mailing-list provider, ask them to do a "merge-purge" on the lists to identify and eliminate duplicate names. This means that, with the help of a computer, they will merge all the lists you rent into one master list to find and erase the duplicates. If there is substantial duplication, you should not have to pay for the names that were removed. If you buy your lists on disk, you can use a "merge-purge" program to help eliminate duplicate names.

• If you are mailing a "price-reduced" mailer to prospects, try not to send it to your existing customers. Few things irritate purchasers more than receiving notification that the product they shelled out $350 for two weeks ago can now be had for only $99. If your company has a return policy, you may see your existing customers return merchandise (and then repurchase it at the lower price) more than you see new sales.

CREATING OR BUYING A MAILING LIST

There are five categories of mailing lists to consider for your direct-mail needs. These categories apply to e-mail lists as well as traditional addressees. The five categories include: *compiled lists* based on compilations of names from telephone books, product registrations, memberships in associations, or other sources; *response lists*, which are compiled from customers who have responded to mailings in the past, *business lists*, which are based on business-to-business marketing and include names, titles and, company locations; *house lists*, which are lists compiled by individual companies for their own needs; and a variety of *electronic mailing lists*, which include people's e-mail addresses.

The best lists for your direct-mail project are the least expensive ones that reach the maximum number of recipients who are potentially interested in your product. For example, if you are looking for money for your not-for-profit community action group, you would do better if you mailed to a list of people who have contributed money to similar causes in the past than if you mail to a list simply culled from the telephone book. The latter list will cost you less to rent, but your "hit rate" will be substantially lower, and a larger percentage of your mailers will fall on deaf ears. Response lists, whether you rent these or create your own, are generally more effective (and more expensive) than arbitrary compilations because the people on these lists have a qualified history of buying products similar to yours through the mail.

If you choose to rent a list, it may be available in a number of sort formats. For an additional charge, the recipient's e-mail address, mailing address, and phone number may also be available. You might rent a list of male homeowners who live within three specific zip code areas and make more than $35,000 per year. You then pay the small extra charge for the phone numbers so that your salespeople can follow up on the mailing with a timely phone call.

Where to Rent Mailing Lists

Mailing lists are available from a number of commercial sources. You can go to a mailing list broker to find mailing lists or have lists created for you by compilation companies. Look for both of these services in the Yellow Pages under Mailing Lists or Advertising— Direct Mail. The most common source for locating mailing lists is the reference section of a well-stocked public library. There you'll find the standard *Direct Mail Lists and Data* and *Guide to Consumer Mailing Lists* produced by the Standard Rate and Data Service (SRDS).

Ultimate Survival Tip

Compile Your Own Response Lists for Custom Targeting

Many home-based entrepreneurs fail to track inquiries or responses to their mailings and lose the repeat business possible from these names and addresses. With the help of a computer database program or an index card system, you can easily maintain information on all customers and prospects who have done business with you or inquired about your products. In addition to their names, addresses, and phone numbers, include information on what they bought, how much they paid, and when they purchased. If you sell an expensive product or service that is personal in nature, add a depth to the database by including background on spouses, children, personal preferences, and interests. Then, when you contact these people for repeat business, you can recall something personal about them. The personal touch works, and this little bit of personal contact can make the difference.

The directories published by SRDS and Gale include descriptions of the lists, rental rates, and restrictions. These descriptions apply to traditional addresses and e-mail addresses.

There are also scam e-mail list providers for who simply put together every mailing address available in no particular order at all. These lists are used by spammers. We suggest avoiding this approach and getting a properly compiled mailing list from a reputable provider.

The listings for each source from a quality list provider offer detailed information on the demographics of the list, market segmentation criteria, and prices quoted in dollars per thousand names. Companies and sources that compile and sell their mailing lists through SRDS publications and list brokers include:

- Magazines
- Mailing list companies that develop mailing lists based on a wide variety of sources
- Credit card companies and banks
- Direct-mail advertisers or companies that sell their own list to make a few extra dollars
- Clubs, not-for-profit groups, and professional organizations
- Trade show companies that track participants
- Catalog companies
- Phone company listings (Yes, an increasing number of regional and national phone companies and long-distance suppliers will rent mailing lists of telephone service subscribers. It's faster than copying the phone book.)
- Special interest groups and clubs on the Internet

When you consider a list in an SRDS reference or through a broker, look at the buying history of the list being offered for rent. There are three things to consider: recency, frequency, and unit sale. The recency of the list is based on the time between the date the list is rented and the date the people sent in their last order or inquiry. More recent is better. The frequency is the number of times a prospect has purchased from the company that rents the list, the length of membership, or the amount of time someone has been a subscriber. The more frequent, the better. Unit sale is the highest dollar amount the customer has paid for a product through the mail. If your product is expensive and the amount is low, consider a list with a higher unit sale.

Most list providers guarantee list accuracy by setting a maximum percentage of dead labels—recipients who have moved, changed jobs, or fled the country. Most commercially available lists are 95% valid. The list provider will reimburse you for excessive returned mailings. Read the fine print in the rental agreement to see how this works and what the guarantee percentage is for a given list before renting it.

If you plan to use the same list more than once, buy it for all of your mailings at the same time so that you can receive the multiple-use discount. This can save you a substantial sum of money when renting a large, high-quality list for several mailings spread out over a year or more.

Note—Most commercial mailing lists are rented, not purchased. Renting mailing lists can be expensive, especially if you find a quality list and want to do repeated mailings to the same people. You may find yourself tempted to copy the names for future use without paying the rental fee. If so, be forewarned that mailing list providers protect their interests by imbedding test names in each list. These test names are actually conduits back to the list provider so he can check to see if list renters are reusing it without paying. Since these names usually look like everyone else on the list, they are impossible to separate. So, if you reuse a list without authorization and the company gets tipped off, expect to receive a bill and hope that a deputy doesn't appear at your door. A safer, legal alternative is to negotiate a fair price for multiple uses of the list in advance.

Compiling Your Own Mailing Lists

There are a number of free sources for creating mailing lists, but with many of these sources no zip codes are included. You can get around this with a copy of the inexpensive zip code directory from the Postal Service or one of the computerized zip code search programs available for personal computers. While looking up names in a directory is tedious, particularly if you are attempting to assemble a long list, you can't beat the price and you own this list rather than having to pay a rental fee every time you use it! Common sources for compiling your own mailing lists include:

- New business listings and vital statistics columns in newspapers
- Chamber of Commerce listings
- Industry guides
- Names collected from a contest or drawing
- Telephone books
- Product registration and warranty cards
- Trade show attendees
- Sales leads
- Visitors to your Web site, if you have one

Ultimate Survival Tip

Use OCR to Save Time When Entering Names

If you are entering lists of typed or printed names into a computer, you can save substantial time by using optical character recognition (OCR) technology to turn the printed pages into word processing text capable of direct manipulation by a computer. OCR uses a scanner to read the page and the power of the computer to turn this picture into editable text. Many affordable desktop scanners (under $200) include OCR software in the package. Do some shopping before settling for second-best or older technology because the poorer the OCR system's accuracy, the less useful its results will be.

Mailing List Problems

Mailing lists suffer from five major problems that can negatively affect the results of your direct-mail promotions.

1. **Too stale.** Mailing lists are dated quickly as people move, change jobs, get married, are born, and die and as companies open and close their doors. The stalest lists are usually the cheapest. Avoid this problem by using criteria other than price to choose your list. Demand a list that is regularly updated, tested, and verified. Magazine subscriber lists are particularly fresh because people are paying to get the magazine and will transfer the subscription as they move around on the home or job front. Don't confuse these lists with ones from throwaway magazines sent free or unsolicited. These lists may be years out of date or contain names of people who regularly trash the publication unopened.

2. **Inappropriate.** Mailing lists must closely match the profile of your intended market. Sometimes, only a small portion of a list may really qualify as prospective customers, although you may be led to believe otherwise. Avoid this problem by carefully reviewing the credibility of the list provider and the demographic data and by choosing well-targeted segments of the list when you place your order. If you are using a magazine mailing list, look through the magazine to see what kind of companies and products are advertised. If they don't match your market, keep looking. If you are considering some other kind of list, ask for references who have used it before to evaluate its success rate. If a list provider won't cooperate to assuage your concerns about his pricey list, find another list provider—there's no shortage of them.

3. **Inaccurate or sloppy.** Lists are often compiled by bored data entry clerks who make numerous mistakes. Misspelling a name or mistaking sex is offensive, even when it's not deliberate. For years, Ms. Sunny Baker received irritatingly misaddressed mailings based on a master list that had her down as Mr. Sony Baher—three mistakes in one name. Who knows what the rest of the list looked like! Avoid this problem by asking to look the list over. Obvious and frequent misspellings of standard names, like common cities for example, points to a serious compilation error rate.

4. **Shallow.** A single list may not include enough names relevant to your needs, forc-

ing you to buy several other lists to get adequate coverage and penetration. This costs more and may mean mailing to a large number of people with absolutely no interest in your product. Avoid this problem by either considering another list source or forgoing the direct-mail route and using advertising to get the word out.

5. **Overused.** Some lists are used so much that the recipients receive a wheelbarrow full of mail each day. As you can imagine, the bulk of this mail never gets opened. Avoid this problem by rotating lists and list sources. While you will inevitably encounter an oversubscribed mailing list, through rotation you will avoid encountering this problem on every mailing. Better still, you may reach people who don't appear on other lists and subsequently get little competing direct mail.

MAILING LABELS FOR TRADITIONAL MAIL PROGRAMS

Unless you address your mailers by hand (always more work than it seems it will be), you will probably resort to mailing labels. The most common format for labels purchased from a mailing list provider are Cheshire labels. These are nonperforated ungummed listings printed four abreast on a sheet by a computer. The labels must be cut apart and glued by a machine designed for this purpose.

Increasingly common (but slightly more expensive) are peel-off labels that can easily be affixed by hand. If you plan to do your own mailing, this is the format for you. If you are

working with your own mailing lists, these labels can be purchased by the box and run through a computer-driven dot-matrix, daisy wheel, or laser printer to imprint the names and addresses. Make sure the labels you buy are designed for the printer you use because some kinds may leave a label stuck in your printer's mechanism, which can result in a potentially expensive repair.

When renting a list, it is important to specify (in writing) what format you want it to be in. Most lists offer Cheshire labels, gummed labels, and computer tape or disk formats. If you aren't specific, your list may appear as unwieldy Cheshire labels or as a useless line listing on a ream of computer paper.

POSTAL CONSIDERATIONS FOR DIRECT MAIL

At first glance, the most obvious approach to postage is the cheapest route—bulk rate. For many reasons, this is not always the best decision.

First of all, mail that trumpets a "special offer reserved for you only" is going to lack credibility if it is obviously sent bulk rate. Many people look through their stacks of mail and drop all bulk-rate material in the trash without opening it. Second, if your promotion is of a timely nature, you can't be assured of delivery dates with bulk mail. So, you must either mail early and risk people forgetting about an event or opportunity or mail late and risk your proposition showing up after it's over. (It happens occasionally and frustrates interested recipients.) Third, a recent test showed that almost one quarter of bulk-rate mail with deliverable addresses never reached its destination.

If you have spent $1.50 per mailing for the contents and the mailer doesn't make it to the intended recipients, does it make sense to save a few pennies per mailer? Can you afford to send 25% of your mailing to the Twilight Zone? Note that this waste is in addition to the bulk-rate mailers with bad addresses, which simply get tossed by the Post Office. Since these don't come back to you, you can't use this information to update your mailing lists.

Instead of bulk rate, consider using pre-sorted mail. It's still cheaper than First Class and your mailing will arrive looking fresh and credible. If you have the money and are short on time, use First Class, with its speedy and timely delivery. With First Class, you don't need to spend time sorting by zip code, and there are no permits to obtain or extra trips to the Post Office. You also get undeliverable mailers returned so you can update your mailing lists (you don't with bulk rate), and First Class mail generally gets the best treatment from the Postal Service.

To get the maximum impact from First Class, don't use a postage meter because your recipients may not notice the rate. Instead, use stamps—handsome commemorative ones work best. Your mailing house (if you use one) may charge a little more to apply stamps, but the positive impression is often worth it, especially if you are inviting a customer to attend a special event or special promotion.

Weight is another consideration for your mailing. Assemble a dummy composed of all components in the package before you produce the pieces. Weigh it carefully on a prop-erly calibrated scale, and estimate the postage. A mailer that is extremely close in weight to the upper limits of a weight category may occasionally go over after labels, stamps, and ink, especially if a faulty postal scale weighs it. This could result in a substantial increase in postal charges.

MASS-MAILING PROGRAMS FOR E-MAIL PROMOTIONS

There are a growing number of e-mail programs and e-mailing routines for sending your promotion to masses of people. The trick is to find a list of e-mail addresses of true value to you. Most junk e-mail is thrown away before it's read, so make sure your message has some value to the readers.

Programs for mass e-mailing can help you sort through the addresses and send thousands of promotional messages in a few minutes. Just set up the system and let your e-mail run while you sleep. There is a list of mass e-mail programs and e-mail providers (along with links to their Web sites) on the CD-ROM.

If you don't want to be accused of spamming the marketplace with e-mail, we suggest using mass e-mail to promote your company's Web site. Keep your e-mail message short. The link to your site provides people with a fast way to get more information about your product. If people don't want more info, they simply won't visit your Web site.

TESTING LIST AND MAILER EFFECTIVENESS

Direct-mail programs are measured by the responses they generate. One of the biggest factors in the success of your program will be the quality of the mailing list. If you are unsure about the demographics, integrity, or appropriateness of a mailing list, do a test mailing with the list first. Most companies will let you purchase a small subset of a list, called a pilot list, for doing this. Mailing to a stale or inappropriate list is like throwing money down the drain. You may get money back on a percentage of returned mailers from the list provider, but nothing will be returned by a list with valid addresses and uninterested recipients. In either case, you may miss a one-time market window opportunity or have to rerun the program all over again.

If your pilot test doesn't give you the desired response rate, before you dismiss the mailing list, consider also that something is wrong with the promotion itself. The message may be wrong or the mailer may lack impact. This can be tested in the same ways that you test for advertising and collateral materials. While you may spend money on the tests, the bulk of your budget remains in the bank while you identify and fix the problems.

Between collateral materials and direct mail, there are a lot of choices and plenty of options. The good news is that you control what you get; the bad news is that you also get what you pay for. Both collateral materials and direct mail play an important role in an overall marketing communications strategy, a role that is often overlooked by your advertising agency (if you have one). It's important that you are able to define your own needs in these areas.

THE DISADVANTAGES

As potentially persuasive as direct mail is, there are some serious disadvantages to consider. For products with target customers who are impossible to identify by address, it won't work. For low-cost mass-market products, such as shampoo, an extensive direct-mail program may be too expensive to be cost-effective, although in recent years, mailing samples has proved effective for some consumer goods manufacturers. Expensive custom goods, such as custom home-made furniture, are difficult to sell directly with mail promotions. You can use direct mail effectively to announce a sale or special promotion for these products.

One of the biggest drawbacks of direct mail is its overuse. In an attempt to keep advertising expenses at a minimum, many companies resort to large direct mailings. Few people go more than a day without receiving a pile of mailings both at work and at home. Some of these mailings offer nothing of interest and have no compelling appeal to respond. People get tired of junk offers, so they stop opening or responding to any kind of direct mail. As a result, direct-mail marketing efforts must be especially well executed to stand apart from the trash.

20

SUCCESSFUL TRADE SHOWS

If you want the larger world to notice your business but still don't want to move outside your home office or play on the Internet, then consider attending trade shows to promote your services and wares. Almost every industry has shows where you can promote your products. This chapter explains how to find, equip, and manage trade shows in order to reach the best customers for your products.

With a credible booth at the right trade show, you can generate leads for new business and make a large segment of an entire industry instantly aware of your products and organization. Of course, if you attend the same show manned only with a couple of wrinkled signs pinned to the backdrop and a rental table people will also be aware of you, but their perception of you and your products will most likely be negative rather than positive. The tools described in this chapter are important image builders. Used incorrectly, they can do sizeable harm. Done right, they can go a long way to building or reinforcing a positive image, and some of them can be used to generate immediate sales. The chapter provides advice that can help you effectively use the tools to get positive results at the lowest cost.

TRADE SHOWS BUILD AWARENESS AND SELL PRODUCTS

Trade shows are organized events attended by large numbers of people who share similar interests. Shows and conventions come in all sizes and cover almost all products and services imaginable. There are industry trade shows, consumer trade shows, recreational trade shows, conventions for professional organizations that incorporate product displays, and even special-interest shows, such as the ones for Star Trek fans. Trade shows may be international, national, regional, or local in appeal. Like advertising media, every trade show has a target audience and definable demographics.

Many trade show attendees are prospects who may consider purchasing goods or services displayed at the show. Other people who attend include the press, job seekers, consultants, industry analysts, and at some shows, pick-pockets and thieves. Depending on the show, a narrow range of closely related products may be featured, or a wide range of vaguely related wares may be displayed, as is the case at "home improvement shows."

Attendance at a trade show requires three basic things—a booth (be it a folding table or a multimillion-dollar colossus), a rented display space on a show floor (be it a dusty area in a dirt arena or the precisely measured concrete floor space of a massive city convention center), and a staff of enthusiastic, knowledgeable people (probably you and your family members) to talk with show attendees about your products.

TRADE SHOWS PROVIDE VISIBILITY

Most companies choose to attend trade shows to supplement other communications activities because, by themselves, trade shows are not always effective selling tools. While it's true that some products get sold at shows, few expensive purchase commitments will be made by attendees who are unfamiliar with an exhibitor's products. Trade shows are best used for:

- Building company and product awareness among prospective customers
- Building industry presence
- Generating sales leads
- Closing sales on inexpensive "impulse" purchases
- Keeping an eye on the competition
- Building press awareness
- Announcing new products

Attending a trade show is a lot of work, and it can be costly in terms of money and time, but for many home-based businesses, the rewards substantially outweigh the effort and expense. Because trade shows can provide immediate, targeted visibility, a growing number of companies are exhibiting in as many shows as they can afford. This, in turn, has spurred more and more shows, which have become increasingly specialized along product and interest lines.

Even cities are getting into the act by building bigger convention facilities capable of housing several large shows simultaneously and by spending considerable sums to attract shows of all kinds. What better way for a bored middle manager to take a three-day vacation with the company's money?

On the downside, with the burgeoning number of shows, it is becoming difficult to choose just the right one(s) to participate in as an exhibitor. Attending all prospectively useful shows is cost prohibitive for all but the largest corporations.

TRADE SHOWS IN YOUR INDUSTRY

How can you find out about trade shows in your industry? If you read the standard trade journals and publications for your industry, you will find out about them because the important shows and conferences are reviewed and promoted in these sources. The Chamber of Commerce is often a good starting place for finding out about smaller, local shows. A full-service advertising agency will also be able to advise you about the shows in your industry that work and the shows that are duds. Ask people who have been in the industry for a while. In addition, industry associations and clubs are good sources of information about trade shows. In fact, many of them have their own conferences and trade shows that you may want to attend.

If you want to look at a wide range of trade show possibilities that cross industries, an annual guide, (produced by Meetings Data-bank in New York) *Trade Shows and Exhibits Schedule* lists the locations, dates, and producers, among other information, about a wide range of shows, conferences, and exhibits around the country.

THE TRADE SHOW PROCESS—GETTING THERE IS HALF THE FUN!

Trade shows can be bewildering because of the sheer amount of detail required to obtain and outfit a booth, ship it, and then effectively man the booth during the show. Here is a summary of an effective step-by-step process for maximizing your results:

Step 1. Educate yourself about the shows and then establish your objectives. Like all marketing communications activities, attending a trade show should start with planning. If you plan correctly, you can choose the shows most appropriate for your company. Start by requesting the show kits and reading them. Then, go to some shows to learn about them. Evaluate each show's effectiveness—does it draw the right customers for your market? Some shows get much lower attendance than the literature claims. You certainly don't want to go through the expense and work to reach a show that no one attends.

Visiting shows also provides an excellent opportunity to study your competitors' booths and booth traffic. By watching their booths, you will get an idea of how successfully they sell goods, take orders, or get leads for future follow up. Your competitors' successes (or lack thereof) demonstrate whether or not the right kind of customers are at the show. Some shows will be more precisely tuned to your market than will others, and by watching how the competition fares, you can decide whether or not your participation is justified.

Use this review process to get a jump on your competition's booth designs. Study their displays to see what works and what doesn't. When studying a competitor's booth, evaluate:

- **Booth Size.** Measure booth size by casually counting your steps as you walk by a booth. Booth spaces are sold in square or rectangular sizes: 10' × 20', 20' × 20', and 40' × 60' or in metric sizes in Canada. In a convention hall, you will quickly become adept at judging booth size because most halls put all of the small booths of the same size together in rows. The large booths get premium placement in the center of the show and by the entrances.

- **Booth Position.** In all shows, the prime locations sell out first, and there may be a surcharge for them. Most trade show companies offer the best spaces to last year's attendees. While you can't compete with companies who have rented space in the same show for ten years and, subsequently, bettered their position on the show floor, you may be able to get a better placement than your competition by renting a slightly bigger space.

- **Construction of the Booth**. Is it simple or ornate? Does it look old and dirty or fresh and new? Identify the size and kind of graphics used. Are they lit with floodlights or back lit? Does the booth make use of the space above it? If so, how? Some booths take up two stories of vertical space or have banners hanging from the ceiling. Is it an inexpensive prefab model that folds up into a suitcase? Do they have a display area, seating, or a stage? What is unique about the booth? With this information, you can design a booth that will match or improve on the look used by your competition.

Consider taking a camera with you on your trade show outings and snapping shots of booths you particularly like or dislike for future study when you get home. Snap pictures of your competitors' booths, too. This will be useful when you begin to build a booth. Your booth designer can add on to your competitor's example and avoid repeating their mistakes. (The lighting in trade shows is often a problem for photographers. Use a camera loaded with fast film and a flash with a "long throw" that requires minimal setup before and between each shot.)

After you educate yourself on what shows are available and what your competitors do, you need objectives for the trade shows you will attend. They can be simple long-term goals, such as "continue to build awareness of our company and the new XYZ product line," or short term goals as specific as "introduce the new ZXY 1000 as a superior solution to the competition's." Having these objectives in mind will allow you to review design drawings or to step back from a nearly finished booth and ask yourself, "Does this booth meet this goal or not?" Your objectives will help you evaluate a booth's overall effectiveness at delivering a strong but simple message. Yes, even trade show booths deliver messages.

After establishing your objectives, you can decide which shows you want to attend, based on the attendance demographics, timing, and location of each show.

Step 2. Determine the right show and reserve your space well in advance. First, call the show's producer (either a private company that specializes in trade shows or the club, professional organization or company that sponsors a particular event) for more information and to receive a show kit. This kit consists general information about the trade show, including time, place, featured speakers and educational events, available space, and rental prices. The kit should also discuss attendance projections and audience demographics.

If you find that the show matches your needs, then you will want to see about reserving space. Remember, the earlier you decide to attend, the better space you will be able to rent. The kit will include a space reservation form and the show's (often extensive) rules and regulations. The kit also provides you with a floor plan for the show, with the committed major exhibitor's spaces marked by name. Study this layout carefully to select the best space for your needs. A call to the show's coordinator (his or her name and phone number will accompany the kit) will inform you of which spaces are available and which are booked. Reserve space verbally and then complete the form and send it along with a check to "seal the deal." Reserve as early as possible because shows sometimes sell out. If you don't book early, you may end up in the show's equivalent of Siberia.

Step 3. Design and construct the booth. A basic prefab booth may be bought, rented, or borrowed. Booths may also be custom designed from scratch or purchased used and rebuilt. You will need to have your booth ready to ship at least two weeks before the show. Along with the booth itself, you will need graphics to decorate the booth, display tables, carpet, chairs, and other peripheral items. Many of these can be rented directly from the convention hall (if you are attending that kind of show) but you must settle for functional and ugly choices rather than attractive choices.

Even the simplest booth needs the following:

- An attractive, readable sign with the company's name and logo

- Graphics that explain key features of your product or message

- Display area for the products

- Room for literature to be handed out to interested people

- Room for people to stand and move through the booth

If you are going to a large industry show, you will also want to create a giveaway of some kind, ranging from plastic bags with your logo to elaborate gee-gaws, as discussed later in the chapter.

When you visit the trade shows you will see the possibilities and the appropriate kind of design for your space. Booth space is always smaller than it seems in the floor plans, so don't clutter your booth with too many elements. Simple is better in booth design. There are companies that specialize in designing and manufacturing trade show booths; they can help you review the costs and possibilities.

The least expensive booths are portable, prefab backdrops for small spaces (up to 10' × 10'). The graphics are attached with Velcro fasteners. These are best for small local and regional trade shows. These portables come equipped with shipping cartons with wheels and a handle. They can be assembled by one reasonably tall person. Beyond that, the booth possibilities are endless—again, limited only by budget, audience, and objectives. Companies spend as little as $3,500 for an attractive portable booth and graphics and as much as $1 million or more on booths for major industry extravaganzas. More information about buying and renting booths appears later in the chapter.

If you are doing a custom booth, remember that they take lots of time. And always assemble the booth once at a warehouse or at the company to see how it goes together and how it looks in final form. You will almost always want to make changes to the booth once you see it assembled—so allow time for this.

Step 4. Ship the booth and other materials to the show. In the paperwork provided with the show kit, you will find a schedule that details when your booth must arrive at the show and that specifies time restrictions for setting it up. Ship all components together and ensure, in writing, that the shipping company knows and understands the delivery schedule. In addition to your booth and furniture, you need to include the materials to assemble the booth, carpeting for the space (unless you rent this), and bulk shipments of literature and other booth supplies. Ship air freight if you can afford it—your booth and other materials will suffer less handling and the chances that they will arrive on time are much better than if you shipped them by truck or rail—especially if time is tight. Inspect your arriving shipment for losses and damage and file any claim immediately, both verbally and in writing.

Ultimate Survival Tip

Get Yourself Insured Before the Show
Make sure your shipment and your company are properly insured. Your regular business insurance rarely covers trade show damage or liabilities. Ask your agent to provide you with the correct policies for trade show equipment and liability. Most large trade shows demand evidence of liability coverage before you can attend the show.

Step 5. Prepare anyone who will help you man your booth. Before you get to the show, make sure the people who will be manning your booth are trained in booth etiquette and procedures. You should develop a printed booth schedule if multiple people will be manning the booth. In addition, a briefing session the night before the show opens is a good idea, perhaps over dinner or drinks. The idea behind the briefing is to create rapport among the booth team members and to assure that everyone has the same answers to the questions the prospects are likely to ask. In addition, you can clarify the schedule and make sure everyone knows their responsibilities. A list of people to contact in case of booth problems should be provided to everyone.

Step 6. Set up the booth and equipment. All shows will provide a setup time for you or the show's staff to put your booth and equipment together. Typically, setup must be completed at least 12 hours before the show opens—your paperwork will specify the times. If you are doing it yourself, prepare for the labor involved by wearing light clothing that is suitable for lifting, hammering, and moving heavy objects. Keep in mind that some halls are neither heated nor air conditioned during setup times, and massive doors may be open to the outside weather. As an alternative to getting grimy and sweaty, you can hire professional setup crews to assist you. Each show has different restrictions concerning outside labor, so read the show agreement in advance. Even if you do hire others to assemble the booth, be sure you are there to supervise. Their interpretation of a layout may differ significantly from yours.

Step 7. Man the booths, talk to prospects, and soak your feet at night. How you and your staff members physically appear at the show can make all the difference to its success. You should be energetic, smiling, and accommodating—no matter how tired you are or how much your feet ache. Working the booth floor in a busy show is hard work. Make sure that all staff members working in the booth are properly fed and not worked to death. Even in the busiest shows, breaks must be arranged and refreshments kept on hand.

Unfortunately, there are unscrupulous people who attend trade shows for the quick pickings. Keep an eye on all valuables during a show and consider leaving purses back at the hotel or locked in the trunk of a car for safekeeping. Don't put anything of value in the space behind your booth or in a quiet corner, because it may not be there when you attempt to retrieve it.

Any prospects who come by your booth should be offered literature, and you should query to see if they have any questions. In most trade shows, you will be able to take names and addresses by running show identification badges through a credit card imprinter, which you can usually rent or purchase from the show's producer. If these are not available, ask for the prospect's business card or have forms available for prospects to fill out.

You should also have a clearly defined way for dealing with members of the press who will inevitably come to your booth. Usually, they should be referred to the most senior person in the booth at the time, given a media kit, and generally treated as VIPs. Most large shows also have a press room that you should stock with copies of your media kits and news releases for the show. The show's producers may also offer times and rooms for news conferences, which can be scheduled in advance of the show by companies with major announcements. The steps for scheduling a press conference at the show are usually spelled out in the show's information kit.

Ultimate Survival Tip

Bring Plenty of Extra Supplies

If your booth uses power bars or extension cords, bring extra ones because, for reasons unknown, they seem to disappear between shows. You can rent supplies at the show (if they have any left), but they'll charge you $35 to rent a power bar that you can buy for $8. Also, bring extra bulbs for all the lights in your booth. In many cases, the convention or exhibit hall may be miles from the closest store and bulbs often break during shipping or burn out in the middle of a show. Extra pens are also a good idea so that you can quickly jot down the questions from prospects. Make sure you have plenty of literature and press kits available. It's better to have extra than to run out at the show.

Step 8. Disassemble the booth and pack for shipping. Once the show closes, you must take down your booth and get it ready for shipping as soon as possible. Usually, this must be done within 12 hours after the show closes. Be aware that, in many shows, this is prime time for theft, so keep your eye on all expensive equipment. Assign someone from your organization to monitor the take-down process. Even empty packing crates may disappear if another participant is one short. Consider carrying out any item of extreme value, particularly if it's small and easily lifted. Many shows will require you to get a property pass to carry anything more than a purse out, but it may be worth the effort. Once boxed and inventoried, your goods will be taken directly to the shipping docks by show personnel. If you didn't make arrangements for return shipping in advance, the show's producers will assign their own shipping company for you.

Step 9. Ship the booth back home or to the next show. When your booth and equipment arrive back home, count the boxes to ensure that they all made it and inspect them for external and concealed damage. File any claim immediately. Use this opportunity to replace anything damaged, burned out, broken, or lost so that, on a moment's notice, the booth will be ready to use for the next show.

Step 10. Follow up after the show. All the leads you get from the show should be immediately distributed to the correct sales regions and appropriate follow-up literature should be mailed as soon as possible. A timely "Thank You for Visiting Our Booth" letter, sent to each visitor, is recommended. In addition, you should have a meeting to evaluate the effectiveness of the show.
To determine what you accomplished and what can be improved for next time, ask questions like:

- Were you adequately trained to work the floor?
- Was the booth space and design effective? You may want to modify the layout or design for better traffic flow next time, or you may want to upgrade the size or image of the booth to be more competitive.
- Were there things the competition did that you should do next year?

In evaluating the overall show results, consider things like:

- The quality and number of leads generated
- Press activity during the show that will gain publicity for your company
- Industry contacts made at the show that may be valuable for joint ventures, investments, or future promotions.

After considering these factors, decide whether or not the show was a success. If you decide it was worth the time and effort, book your space now for next year's show. If not, spend your communications dollars on something else.

TRADE SHOW BOOTH SPACE

More than any other decision, your booth space will determine the traffic you get at your booth. More traffic is definitely better, so when reserving space, consider how people may be drawn toward each prospective location. This is important for a tiny 10' × 10' booth as well as a 60' × 60' colossal space. Some areas in a show floor are going to get substantially more foot traffic than others, no matter what the show people tell you. Your show rep may convincingly explain that attendees will find you simply by consulting the map on the show-provided program. This is true if someone is deliberately looking for you, but many attendees don't even open the program and explore only those aisles that grab their attention.

Booths located near the front door get the most traffic for obvious reasons. Booths located near concession stands, restaurants, and the restrooms also get more notice because people must walk by the booths to reach frequented places.

If you are looking for space for a small booth, keep in mind that a corner booth gets more notice than one in the middle of the aisle. People can approach from four directions instead of two, and a corner booth can have two open sides rather than just one, which makes the booth seem larger. If you are using a larger, island booth (a booth open on all sides), try to get space near the largest booths in the show because their openness will make your booth easier to see, and these locations are usually the best for foot traffic.

If your small company sells add-on or peripheral products that work with products made by a larger company, try to get as close to the larger company's booth as you can. When people head for the big booth, they will see you and they may be interested in your product because they are interested in the big company's products. For example, if you sell computer software that runs on Apple Macintosh computers, a booth located next to Apple's is a good location.

In shows that are not sold out, one location to avoid is near the unsold space. Convention halls screen off the unrented areas. If you rent near this space, your booth may end up in an empty isle surrounded by unsightly drapes.

As we mentioned earlier, you will be able to select from a larger number of spaces if you commit to attend as soon as possible. If you find that there's little space left and that the show's sales rep is trying to talk you into a poorly located spot, weigh how important the show really is before giving in. A really lousy spot may put you in a dark corner miles from the front door, or you may have to pick a location among booths that feature products completely unrelated to yours. These poor locations may neutralize the impact of your attendance at the show.

A last-ditch tactic that often works in a case like this is to tell the show's rep that unless he or she can find you a better location, you simply won't be attending. Keep in mind that these reps are paid on commission, so they won't want to lose you if they don't have to. If this fails, you can usually change your mind. Always ask for a discount if you find that you do need to attend even though your space is poor. If the show is especially popular, the reps will try to charge you a premium for just about anything. However, if it's near the closing date for the show and space is still left, you may get a substantial reduction in the space rental.

Booth Considerations

After selecting a space with adequate traffic, designing the right booth is the next critical decision. Booth options range from a rented table surrounded with pipe and drape (that ugly fabric mounted on pipes that you see dividing smaller booths at most shows) to multimillion-dollar affairs that employ motorized decorations, big-screen TVs, and laser lights and consume a city block on the floor of a large convention hall.

To acquire a booth of your own, you can buy a prefab model, purchase a used booth, or build your own from the ground up. You can also rent or borrow a booth, but the limitations of most rental arrangements make this unworkable for many companies (unless you just want to get your feet wet to see if you want to make a major investment in trade shows).

Most shows rent standard booths in addition to tables, furniture, and carpeting. These standard booths are identical in size and construction and cannot be customized by your company. Usually arranged together in long rows, these rental models are chosen on the basis of long-term durability rather than on good looks, so they tend to be cold-looking affairs that attendees skip over instead of visit. They do little to establish an identity for your company and are often the least-visited booths in the show.

Prefabricated Booths

By far, the most popular booth for small companies and small budgets is the prefabricated booth. These are available in many formats and from a variety of vendors. Many of the models are completely portable and can be assembled by one person in less than an hour. If your company is doing well and wants to grow from a 10' × 10' booth to a 10' × 20', many prefabs will allow you to hook two 10' × 10' units together to create a larger display.

If you decide that this is the route for you, ask the salesperson to pack the entire unit away and then guide you through the steps, from unpacking to complete assembly. Look for a model that is easy to assemble and one that is extremely sturdy, stable, and rigid once put together. Make sure your choice can accommodate small shelves and the weight of sales literature without swaying or leaning. (There are few experiences that rival the embarrassment of talking to a trade show visitor and having your booth suddenly collapse or fall over behind you.) Pass on models that seem wobbly or that use fragile plastic parts for load-bearing locks, struts, and hinges.

Ultimate Survival Tip

What If I Can't Afford a Booth?

A common practice in many industries where show prices and space availability have become prohibitive is to skip the show altogether, rent a swank hotel room close to the convention location, and organize what's called a hospitality suite. There, attendees can see product demonstrations, meet the salespeople, and enjoy a relaxed party atmosphere with free drinks and food far from the hustle of the show floor. This usually costs less than attending the show and requires far less logistical management. Plus, because the atmosphere is informal, prospective customers are potentially more receptive to sales pitches and persuasion. The key to making these suites successful is getting enough invitations out both before and during the show—and the better the food is, the more "uninvited" guests you'll have coming around.

Though prefabs are convenient and inexpensive, when you proudly set up your new prefab at a show and stand back to admire it, you may notice that all of the booths around you are similar or identical models. Because of price, weight, and shipping size limitations, most small prefab booths look very much the same. This is fine if yours is a small company or if you attend shows where most of the competing booths consist only of a rented table and a couple of signs, but for larger companies or those in highly competitive markets, the prefab sends a message of "new, small, and not very financially secure", which is not the kind of image companies desire.

You can, to some degree, get around the look of a prefab by adding flashy graphics, custom tables, and lighted columns, but using this approach to dress up your booth adds to the cost, shipping weight, and setup time. Before you know it, you might have been better off with a custom design.

Buying a Used Booth

A very workable tactic for acquiring a fancy booth at the right price is to purchase a used one. Because companies go out of business, close divisions, or replace existing booths with new models every couple of years, you may find a used booth that's just right for you—at a price that's right too.

To find used booths, spread the word though your network's rumor mill, run a classified ad, or visit local companies that specialize in outfitting booths. (Look for companies in the *Yellow Pages* under Display Designers and Producers.) Business-to-business classified ads are also an excellent place to locate used booths of all sizes.

After identifying several likely prospects, visit the sellers (even out of town if necessary). You will always have to make compromises in booth design, color, and possibly size, but with the money you save, it may be worth it. When shopping for a used booth, have the seller set it up and look for:

- **Suitability.** The booth should already meet your size requirements and should be easy to ship. The shipping cartons should be part of the purchase price. Make sure the booth is attractive and not visibly worn. Verify that whatever modifications your company will need to make can be easily accommodated at a price you can afford. If you need to make too many changes, then it's best to design your own booth from scratch.

- **Lifespan.** When shopping for a used booth, look for solid, quality construction that can withstand the punishment of frequent and abusive travel. If the used booth appears slightly saggy, this points to either poor construction or a unit that has circumnavigated the globe already. Keep looking!

- **Cosmetic Limitations.** A used booth that incorporates striking or unusual designs such as large columns, an animated mechanical apparatus, or a huge replica of a product may be impossible or expensive to disguise. If, even after repainting and remodeling the booth, visitors instantly recognize the booth as having formerly belonged to someone else, then it won't help you.

If you find a booth that looks like it will work, have an estimate worked up for changes and repairs and then add that number to the cost of the purchase price. If the total is more than 50% of the cost of simply building a new one, the price is too high. Since it's a buyer's market for used trade show booths, ask for a better price after showing the seller your numbers. There's a very good chance you'll get it, even if you have to wait a month for the seller to cave in.

Designing and Building a Custom Booth

While undoubtedly the most expensive road to travel, building your own booth can get you exactly what you want and also keep the road open for future expansion needs. Building your own booth usually means hiring a specialist to design it and to coordinate the construction effort with several subcontractors. Everything from the booth to peripheral tables, seating, graphics, displays, and even shipping cases must be either bought or built.

Ultimate Survival Tip

The Used Booth Weigh-In

Before purchasing a custom-built used booth, either have it weighed (with all components and shipping containers included) or ask for and verify documentation of its shipping weight. A booth built of heavy materials, such as particle board or steel, will be extremely expensive to handle and ship. This may be why the seller is dumping it—because it costs too much to move it from show to show. If the booth uses unusually large or awkward shipping containers, find out from a trade show booth shipper if there will be an extra charge for the size and weight of these monsters.

As an alternative to "from scratch" construction, there are a number of modular booth systems available that offer semicustom construction and may save you substantial time. Since these systems were designed with show use in mind, they are already constructed from lightweight, durable materials, and some systems are extremely flexible.

To get started in the custom booth process, you need to locate a suitable specialist for the project. This person is usually a designer who specializes in trade show and exhibit booths. Look for one through referrals or in the *Yellow Pages* under Display Designers and Producers. These listings will include a variety of freelancers as well as large companies that can handle the entire process for you.

When selecting this kind of talent, keep two additional points in mind:

1. Many designers will take on a trade show booth project at the drop of a hat. Hire only designers with a proven portfolio of trade show booth design and production. While many designers can create a beautiful booth design, they may know little about building one that is lightweight, durable, and easy to ship.

2. When searching out a booth design firm, look for one with creative prowess. Many of these firms are simply order-takers with little or no creative expertise.

CONTROLLING AND MANAGING BOOTH CONSTRUCTION

Trade show booths can become a company's hot potato because of their cost, visibility, and complexity. The most senior person in your organization should be the one to give approvals; otherwise, you'll be surprised how many "experts" your organization has when it comes to booth design.

Careful project management is also vital. A large, elaborate booth project can quickly spiral out of control without careful supervision on your part. Avoid the classic "last month" problem (when companies first begin to design or build a booth only a month before the show). Trying to construct a booth in such a limited time frame results in a poorly executed project overburdened by a fortune in rush charges.

BOOTH GRAPHICS

Graphics are often treated as a separate project, especially with prefab booths. The graphics are used to make your booth attractive as well as to deliver a message. Graphics should be treated as an integral part of booth design, whether you are retrofitting an existing booth or building a new one. For many booths, the graphics are the prime attention-getters.

Booth graphics come in a variety of formats—from simple, poster-like graphics, which mount to booth fabric with Velcro, to complex back-lit signs and neon lettering. What's right for an individual booth should be up to your designer and you. In general, graphics should be as big as possible. Use a few well-chosen, descriptive words. Use bright colors. Simple, strong designs are best.

When evaluating graphics in a booth layout, answer four basic questions:

1. Will they grab a casual trade show attendee's attention from competing exhibits?

2. Is your company's name and basic message apparent?

3. Does your eye instantly land on an important graphic, or does it jump from element to element before finally settling somewhere?

4. Do the graphics explain, in several seconds or less, what your company is about and what your products do?

5. A negative response to any of these questions means adjustments are in order.

Ultimate Survival Tip

Beware! Booth Renderings Are Deceptive
As part of the booth design process, you may be shown a rendering of the finished booth. A rendering is a detailed drawing of the booth done with colored markers or an airbrush. These renderings are idealized and show the booth in isolation. The perspective used in these drawings is extremely deceptive if you're not experienced at looking at them. While a 10' × 10' booth is too small for more than two people and a small table, a rendering of this same booth may make it look large enough to display a 1959 Cadillac with its doors wide open. Once you see the rendering, you may be tempted to add more elements to the booth or more displays and tables to the foreground. In a word, don't!

To get a real-world conception of your booth's space, tape off the dimensions on a concrete floor or parking lot. After laying out the rented space, mark where the booth will go, keeping in mind that all booths have a thickness to them and that many designs waste substantial space behind the booth. Now, add any peripheral elements, such as tables and chairs. Block off the areas taken up by each element by adding stripes of tape across them. Then, assemble the number of people who will man the booth at one time and stand in the remaining area. This will give you a realistic estimate of available space. Don't be surprised if it turns out to be substantially less than you thought.

PUTTING IT ALL TOGETHER—THE ENDLESS DETAILS

Once the booth and schedules are all in place, there are more details to be handled. First, you will need people to man the booth during all hours that the show is open. This means that they must be on hand before the doors open and until after the shows closes. In most organizations, getting participants for booth duty is like pulling teeth. Prospective booth workers suddenly come up with the most surprising reasons why they can't attend ("I can't go to the San Francisco show because I'm allergic to cable cars").

For small companies, the best booth workers are the company founders and/or executives. For larger organizations, experienced sales and marketing people can manage. Entice your salespeople to work in the booth by showing them how last year's booth duty generated substantial leads and resulted in big sales and increased commissions.

In addition to conscripting booth workers, you must make transportation and accommodation arrangements for these people. You can save money by booking airline tickets and hotels in advance. Most shows offer substantial discounts through local hotels, but the best deals are taken up early, as are the best booth spaces.

If you are introducing an important new product at the show (trade shows are an excellent place for such introductions), you may want to arrange a press briefing or editorial lunch with to discuss the merits of the new product. If this is the case, provide the press with plenty of notice because you may be competing with a large number of other announcements.

If you want to make an impact with the industry at a major show, sponsor an after-hours party. They're pricey, but they can make a lasting impression. Most large companies will have parties at which key customers and company representatives mingle for the evening. If you want to compete with these guys, then you should think about a special event, but you will need to plan it and announce it well in advance. Cheese Whiz on crackers and beer will not draw a big crowd. Do something with some panache and imagination if you want results from a trade show affair.

Last, when going to the trade show, treat yourself well by booking a trip with the fewest possible stopovers and hassles. Provide yourself with comfortable accommodations and make sure the expense account is adequate. If you don't, you may have an expensive booth in an important show staffed by a cranky, zombie-eyed business owner who is more interested in sleeping than in talking to customers.

21

Marketing Mechanics and Techniques—The Basics of Type, Design, and Printing

One of the most intimidating issues people new to home-business promotion must face is understanding the technical aspects of producing printed communications. Buried in jargon and the subtleties of aesthetics, this is a world of almost imperceptible nuances and never-ending details. This chapter explains the basics to get you started so that you can at least talk to the people who will be designing and producing your promotions, but becoming an expert on your own takes years of practice and experience.

When you first begin to work on promotional projects, you may feel intimidated by the jargon used by designers and printers. Most communications professionals are as comfortable bantering phrases such as "right-reading negative emulsion down at 133 lines per inch with stripped in screen tints from the amberlith" as they are ordering a tuna salad sandwich from a lunch menu. Intimidating? You bet!

Worse, vendors from different companies often engage in one-upmanship with each other (in your presence) by hurling jargon around to test each other's depth of knowledge. They may do this to you to see if they're dealing with a pro who knows the business. Not surprisingly, the less they think you know, the higher the bills will be.

Your first line of defense is this chapter and the glossary provided on the CD-ROM. Covertly study the words to get some idea of their meaning and use. The glossary entries consist of either jargon (words that in communications mean something other than their standard English counterparts) or technical phrases that mean little without a definition. Your second line of defense is to ask the vendors exactly what each phrase means and then further question the explanations until you have a clear picture. A few lengthy question-and-answer sessions will provide you with a free education, and the vendors will cut out the jargon because it extends the meetings.

TYPE AND TYPOGRAPHY

Typesetting is the process of converting typed or written words into headlines and body copy for use in print ads and collateral. Type is also set for billboards, packaging, TV commercials, signs, and even Web sites.

Beyond the words themselves, type is important because it conveys an impression to the reader through its shapes and its position on the page. Typefaces convey intrinsic feelings or style. Strong type design gives headlines more impact and makes the copy inviting and easy to read. Poor-quality type is difficult to read, forcing the reader to work at getting the message. Most readers won't bother to decipher a cryptic message, so clean, easy-to-read type is important.

There are probably millions of typefaces available in the world today. The majority of faces support Indo-European languages, such as English, French, and German. The remaining percentage support the world's other languages.

Language is supported by character sets. Each typeface has a set of characters that comprise all the needs of the language it supports. These complete sets of characters are called fonts. A font may contain a complete set of letters, punctuation symbols, and even fractions as part of its character set. One font may have a large enough character set to handle English, German, French, Spanish, and Slavic languages or it may be limited only to the support of basic English characters. All fonts have names to identify them. Many are named after the designer. Others are named for the person or company that commissioned the design. For example, the popular font Times was named after the *Times of London*, the publisher that commissioned Stanley Morrison to design it for use in their newspaper during the 1930s.

Typefaces are designed by specialists. These typeface designers are extremely knowledgeable about type and can precisely name a face after only a brief glance. Once, type designers had to carve characters out of wood, but today's type designers work entirely on computers to create new fonts.

Some type design is done to further refine the readability of an existing type family or to enhance the style. New versions based on older designs also reflect an improvement in printing technology. Today, because of higher resolution printing capabilities, more subtle changes in a type's shape can be perceived. Other typeface designers are working to create entirely new families of type for specialized purposes.

Meet the *Times* Typeface Family

Here is a partial demonstration of the versatility of the Times' character set. This example is based on the "free" fonts available with both PC and Apple Macintosh computers.

Times

abcdefghijklmnopqrstupwxyzABCDEFGHIJKLMNOPQRSTUPWXYZ`12
34567890=[]\;',./~!@#$%^&*()_+{}|:"<>?`¡™£¢∞§¶•ªº–≠Œ∑´®†¥ˆØπ"'
«Åß∂ƒ©˙Δ°¬…ÆΩ≈Ç√∫˜µ≤≥÷⁄¤‹›fifl‡°·‚±Œ„‰ˇÁ¨˙Ø∏''»ÅÍÎÏ˝ÓÔÒÚ
Æ¸Ç◊ı˜Â˜

Times New Roman

abcdefghijklmnopqrstupwxyzABCDEFGHIJKLMNOPQRSTUPWXYZ`12
34567890=[]\;',./~!@#$%^&*()_+{}|:"<>?`¡™£¢∞§¶•ªº–≠Œ∑´®†¥ˆØπ"'
«Åß∂ƒ©˙Δ°¬…ÆΩ≈Ç√∫˜µ≤≥÷⁄¤‹›fifl‡°·‚±Œ„‰ˇÁ¨˙Ø∏''»ÅÍÎÏ˝ÓÔÒÚ
Æ¸Ç◊ı˜Â˜

Times Bold (synthesized by computer)

**abcdefghijklmnopqrstupwxyzabcdefghijklmnopqrstupwxyz`123456789
0=[]\;',./~!@#$%^&*()_+{}|:"<>?`¡™£¢∞§¶•ªº–≠œ∑´®†¥ˆøπ"'«åß∂ƒ©
˙Δ°¬…æΩ≈ç√∫˜µ≤≥÷⁄¤‹›fifl‡°·‚±Œ„‰ˇÁ¨˙Ø∏''»ÅÍÎÏ˝ÓÔÒÚÆ¸Ç◊ı
˜Â˜**

Times Italic (synthesized by computer)

*abcdefghijklmnopqrstupwxyzabcdefghijklmnopqrstupwxyz`1234567890=[]\
;',./~!@#$%^&*()_+{}|:"<>?`¡™£¢∞§¶•ªº–≠œ∑´®†¥øπ"'«åß∂ƒ©˙Δ°¬
…æΩ≈ç√∫˜µ≤≥÷⁄¤‹›fifl‡°·‚±Œ„‰ˇÁ¨˙Ø∏''»ÅÍÎÏ˝ÓÔÒÚÆ¸Ç◊ı˜Â˜*

Most types can be categorized in one of four groups and then in families within each group. The four main type categories are:

1. **Serif Type.** The most common kind of typeface, serif typeface is widely used in books, ads, newspapers, and anywhere a high degree of readability is important. Type designers are constantly working to perfect and improve this large group of type families. Most serif fonts have a variety of thick and thin strokes used in each letter. Study the T in "This is a serif font." Note that not all of the lines (strokes) are of the same thickness. The serif shapes originally derived from the way monks completed their hand lettering of religious manuscripts with ink pens.

2. **Sans Serif Type.** The word "sans" means without, so these fonts are without serifs. Unlike serif fonts, most sans serif characters are drawn with a line of equal thickness. More modern designs, sans serif fonts are strong and effective when used for headlines. Many technical companies use sans serif fonts because of the modern simplicity of the fonts. A well-chosen sans serif font is almost as easy to read as a well-chosen serif font.

3. **Script Type.** Familiar as the form of type used in wedding invitations and official certificates, script type is a typeface representation of handwriting shapes. Scripts are usually reserved for very formal documents, and because they are difficult to read, brevity is important. Script faces convey elegance and formalism. Scripts may be either connecting or nonconnecting, which means that the letters may actually join or that each character, while still looking like handwriting, may not touch its neighbor.

4. **Display Type.** Display type consists of fonts that don't fit into the above three categories. Usually designed with a particular purpose in mind, display type gets attention and is unique. It can vary, from letters that look like broken glass pieces to fonts in which all of the letters are shaped like cats. Display type possibilities are limited only by imagination and skill, but never use them for anything other than a short headline because, like scripts, they are very difficult to read and ultimately tiresome on the eye. They are best for creating moods, feelings, and style in a communication.

THE FOUR GROUPS OF TYPEFACES

Serif Type

Sans Serif Type

Script Type

Display Type

Type Specification

Basic type specification is part of every communication that uses type. A designer specs type by marking the raw copy so that a typesetter can see how to set it. The spec shows how the type should appear on the page and how much space to put between the lines, type sizes, faces, and more. After "specing" the type, the copy is sent to an outside typesetter who then assembles the copy into a finished form. In the case of desktop publishing, this step may be skipped because the designer/desktop publisher ca spec and produce the type on the screen as he works.

Advanced typography is a subspecialty of design. A handful of designers create only artistic typesetting, type specification (or specs) and hand-drawn scripts. These type specialists take another designer's type specs and fine tune them to the point of near perfection for maximum impact. This kind of service is used for large billboards and expensive ads in which everything has to be just right.

Occasionally, a design may demand the use of a hand-drawn headline or logo. Elabo-rate or crude, this work is highly studied. It typically takes years to fully develop the hand-eye coordination skills necessary to complete competent script designs. Many script artists and calligraphers have more in common with illustrators than they do with designers.

Type Alignment

Type can be aligned several different ways, depending on the demands of the job at hand. Left justification means that the left edge of the type aligns vertically. The right side, however, doesn't. As the typesetter reaches the right margin, he or she "bumps" the next word onto the next line (computers do this automatically). What happens is that the right edge is "ragged," with the edges of the lines rarely lining up. For this reason, this technique is also called ragged right.

TYPE ALIGNMENT EXAMPLES

Justified

Type can be aligned several different ways, depending on the demands of the job at hand. Most frequently, type is left justified (ragged right) or (right and left) justified. Left justification means that the left edge of the type lines up vertically. The right, however, doesn't. As the typesetter reaches the right margin, he or she "bumps" the next word onto the next line (computers do this automatically). What happens is that the right edge is "ragged" with the edges of the lines rarely lining up. For this reason this technique is also called ragged right.

Left Justified

Type can be aligned several different ways, depending on the demands of the job at hand. Most frequently, type is left justified (ragged right) or (right and left) justified. Left justification means that the left edge of the type lines up vertically. The right, however, doesn't. As the typesetter reaches the right margin, he or she "bumps" the next word onto the next line (computers do this automatically). What happens is that the right edge is "ragged" with the edges of the lines rarely lining up. For this reason this technique is also called ragged right.

Right Justified

Type can be aligned several different ways, depending on the demands of the job at hand. Most frequently, type is left justified (ragged right) or (right and left) justified. Left justification means that the left edge of the type lines up vertically. The right, however, doesn't. As the typesetter reaches the right margin, he or she "bumps" the next word onto the next line (computers do this automatically). What happens is that the right edge is "ragged" with the edges of the lines rarely lining up. For this reason this technique is also called ragged right.

Centered

Type can be aligned several different ways, depending on the demands of the job at hand. Most frequently, type is left justified (ragged right) or (right and left) justified. Left justification means that the left edge of the type lines up vertically. The right, however, doesn't. As the typesetter reaches the right margin, he or she "bumps" the next word onto the next line (computers do this automatically). What happens is that the right edge is "ragged" with the edges of the lines rarely lining up. For this reason this technique is also called ragged right.

Justified text is text that runs all the way from the left margin to the right margin, and both the right and left sides align with their respective margins. The text in this book is justified. Since few lines of copy will be composed of exactly the same number of letters, the justification is accomplished by adding a small amount of extra space between words and letters to make up the difference. If the type has been properly set, the reader will not notice the extra space.

Right-justified text is simply the opposite of left-justified. The right edge of the text lines up with the right margin and the left edge is ragged, depending on the individual length of each line. Often called ragged left, this format is used for design impact, but it is very difficult to read and follow.

Centered text is just that—each line is centered between the margins. Unlike justified text where each line touches the margin, centered text floats in the middle of the page. Reserved mostly for headlines, poetry, and menus, centered body copy, like right-justified text, is hard to read.

Leading

Leading refers to the amount of space between each line of text. The expression comes from the old hot-type process, where a typesetter would insert a thin layer of lead to separate the metal rows of type from one another. Leading is used to make type more readable because it adds white space to the printed page. Notice in the example how different the printed lines look even though they use the same typeface and size. The difference is their leading.

How Type Sizes Are Specified

Type is specified by how tall it is, which is usually measured from the top of an ascender to the bottom of a descender.

The height is measured in points or, in the case of really big type destined for a billboard, inches. A point is $1/72$ of an inch. Here are examples of several sizes of the Times font. Note that as the characters get bigger, they also get thicker and appear more solid.

Type is usually specified with two dimensions—the size of the character and the size of the white space between the lines of text, which

---

TYPE SIZE EXAMPLE

Times 9 point

Times 12 point

Times 24 point

Times 48 point

LEADING EXAMPLES

Tight (9 point)

Leading refers to the amount of space between each line of text. The expression comes from the old hot type process, where a typesetter would insert a thin layer of lead to separate the metal rows of type from each other. Leading can be used to make type more readable because it adds white space to the printed page. Notice in the example how different the printed lines look using the same typeface and size but with various degrees of leading added.

Normal (10 point)

Leading refers to the amount of space between each line of text. The expression comes from the old hot type process, where a typesetter would insert a thin layer of lead to separate the metal rows of type from each other. Leading can be used to make type more readable because it adds white space to the printed page. Notice in the example how different the printed lines look using the same typeface and size but with various degrees of leading added.

Extra (15 point)

Leading refers to the amount of space between each line of text. The expression comes from the old hot type process, where a typesetter would insert a thin layer of lead to separate the metal rows of type from each other. Leading can be used to make type more readable because it adds white space to the printed page. Notice in the example how different the printed lines look using the same typeface and size but with various degrees of leading added.

means that the character size and leading are specified together. Typically, this specification takes the form of "¹²⁄₁₅" or "12 over 15." The first number is the size of each character and the second number is the leading (in points) plus the size of the character, so "12 over 15" means 12-point type with 3 points of leading. The type and the leading, together, take up a combined 15 points of vertical space.

Most book and ad copy is set in 10- to 14-point type because it is the easiest to read and yet still allows a lot of information to fit in a limited space.

Bolds and Italics

In addition to the variety of typefaces available, each face can be rendered as bold or italic (also known as "itals"). Bolds thicken each letter and, on a busy page, can catch the eye first. Bold is an effective eye-grabber but don't overuse it. Like the exclamation point in writing, a little goes a long way.

ASCENDERS AND DESCENDERS

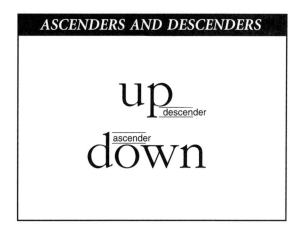

TYPE AND LEADING SPEC EXAMPLE

This example is
10 point Garamond
with 12 points of leading.

This example is

12 point Garamond

with 20 points of leading.

This example is
14 point Garamond
with 14 points of leading.

This example is
20 point Garamond
with 13 points of leading.

Italic is characterized by the slanting of each letter to the right. There's more to italic that just the slant, though. Each character is a redrawn version of the original, with thin diagonal components and other subtle changes made. Study the comparison below between the standard character and the italic version.

Italics are used to set words off from the rest of a paragraph. They are used for emphasis, for the titles of books mentioned in the text, and for secondary headlines. Because italic type is visually lighter (the lines that make up the characters are thinner than normal characters), it appears lighter on the page.

Use italics sparingly. They become tiresome for the eye if they are used for more than a few words here and there.

Proportional and Fixed Type

Type can be set either proportionally or with fixed spacing. This means that since an "m" takes up more room than an "i," the "m" should be given more space. In the case of fixed spacing, all characters have a fixed amount of horizontal space they must fit into. Most type is set using proportional spacing because it looks better and is easier to read.

Kerning, Spacing, Compression, and Expansion

In addition to making characters larger or smaller, characters can also be made wider or narrower, and the spacing between them can be adjusted. Adding or subtracting space between letters can change readability and make copy fit into smaller or larger spaces in a design. Kerning is like spacing but is slightly more complicated. Since many characters, when put side by side, don't match up well because of their shape, kerning allows a typesetter to improve readability by moving them closer

BOLDS AND ITALS

Plain Garamond

Bold Garamond

Italic Garamond

Bold-Italic Garamond

Drop Caps and Raised Caps

Since cloistered monks illuminated their manuscripts by making the first letter in a paragraph or story larger than the others, drop caps and raised caps have been employed as a decorative element in designs of all sorts. Use these type treatments to enliven long passages of copy in which there is little visual relief (pictures or diagrams).

Pull Quotes

Much like drop caps, pull quotes are used to enliven copy-heavy pages. Pull quotes are simply a one- or two-sentence excerpt from the surrounding article. Usually, a particularly strong or controversial statement works best because the idea of a pull quote is to get the reader interested in reading the story. That's why they're called pull quotes—they're pulling in the audience.

together or farther apart. "T" and "L" are examples of characters that don't mate well, but by kerning them, they look just fine (see example). Kerning can also be used to carefully adjust each individual letter in a headline for maximum readability.

The spacing between characters can be adjusted too. Condensing characters makes them thinner so that more characters can fit on a line. Expanding characters makes them appear larger without increasing their vertical size. Super condensing characters is a useful design practice for creating an unusual look for a company name. Expansion can be used the same way.

Special Effects

There are a variety of special effects that can be used to enhance type and make it work for special purposes. While many of these techniques once required expensive handwork or special lenses and equipment, most effects can

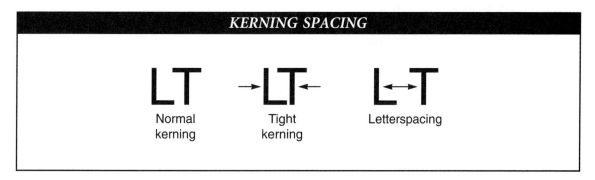

KERNING SPACING

LT — Normal kerning

→LT← — Tight kerning

L↔T — Letterspacing

DROP CAPS AND RAISED CAPS

Since cloistered monks illuminated their manuscripts by making the first letter in a paragraph or story larger than the others, drop caps and raised caps have been employed as a decorative element in designs of all sorts. Use these type treatments to enliven long passages of copy where there's little visual relief in the form of pictures or diagrams.

Raised initial cap

Since cloistered monks illuminated their manuscripts by making the first letter in a paragraph or story larger than the others, drop caps and raised caps have been employed as a decorative element in designs of all sorts. Use these type treatments to enliven long passages of copy where there's little visual relief in the form of pictures or diagrams.

"Drop cap"

PULL QUOTES

Usually a particularly strong or controversial statement works best because the idea of a pull quote is to get the reader interested in reading the story. That's why they're called pull quotes— they're pulling in the audience.

today be easily and inexpensively rendered with the help of a computer.

Headlines, Subheads, Eyebrow Heads, Captions, and Body Copy

There are several terms for elements on the printed page that you should familiarize yourself with because in the process of writing copy and designing a print project, these phrases will come up. Basically there are three kinds of headlines: main heads, subheads, and eyebrow heads. The main head should be the central focus on each page or spread and should work to reinforce the message of the primary visual. It may convey the one idea you want readers to remember more than anything else. Subheads are used to break up copy into readable chunks and should be noticed only after the headline and the main visual. A good subhead draws readers into the copy and conveys important secondary messages. The third kind of head is an eyebrow head. These are used to "orient" readers to the contents of a page. A brochure that covers the Model 100, the Model 200, and the Model 300, respectively, in three spreads might have these names used as eyebrow heads on the top of each page to show the reader which topic will be explained on that spread. Eyebrow heads are most often used in brochures and ads and are optional in all print projects.

Captions are used to explain a visual. Often, a reader will look at the pictures before reading anything. An interesting visual will attract the eye. The reader will then read the caption.

Body copy is simply the text that goes into a print document or ad. Body copy adds detail and explanation to the topics introduced in the headlines and caption. Body copy may be set in one or more columns, depending on the size of the type and the requirements of the document. Avoid very narrow columns because the type may break in undesirable places or become hard to read. Also,

ROTATED TYPE, INLINE TYPE, STRETCHED TYPE, RUNAROUNDS

There are a variety of special effects that can be used to enhance type and make it work for special purposes.

Rotated type

There are a variety of special effects...

Stretched type

There are a variety of special effects . . .

Inline type

There are a variety of special effects that can be used to enhance type and make it work for special purposes.

Type Runaround

avoid very wide columns; they're difficult for the eye to track without conscious effort on the part of the reader.

Avoiding Widows and Orphans

Widows and orphans are terms for leftover bits of type that appear in undesirable places. A widow consists of a word or less than half a line of text that appears at the bottom of a paragraph. Widows catch the eye, particularly if they are

Ultimate Survival Tip

Avoid Unusual Type Treatments

When studying a design's body copy, look for readability and carefully consider any unusual treatments, such as the use of reverse (small white type printed on a color background) or right justification. While the right designer can make both of these approaches work, keep in mind that a designer's intent is to create a stunning design. Sometimes the designer doesn't care if that means making the type hard to read. You should. Another design approach that sounds better than it works in practice is to use foil stamping. While stamping a short headline, logo, or tagline can be eye-catching, stamping an entire paragraph is ill-advised. It's difficult to read and expensive to produce.

followed by another paragraph, because they expose more white space than balanced paragraphs do. An orphan is the first line of a new paragraph that falls at the bottom of a column of text or the last line of a paragraph that spills onto the first line of the next column. In practice, these terms are often used interchangeably because no one can remember which is which. They also may also be used to describe the last word or sentence of a paragraph that spills onto an otherwise blank column or page.

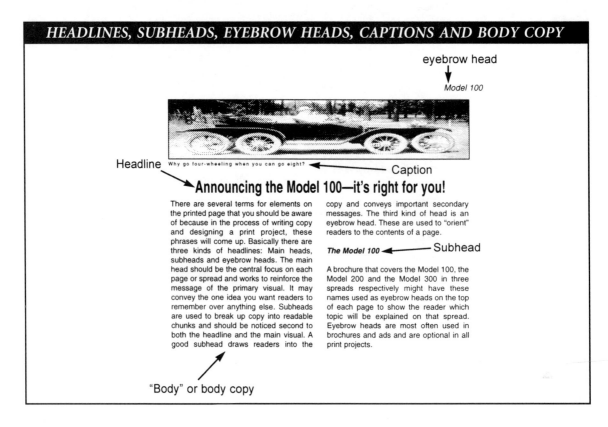

HEADLINES, SUBHEADS, EYEBROW HEADS, CAPTIONS AND BODY COPY

eyebrow head

↓

Model 100

Headline → Why go four-wheeling when you can go eight? ← Caption

→ Announcing the Model 100—it's right for you!

There are several terms for elements on the printed page that you should be aware of because in the process of writing copy and designing a print project, these phrases will come up. Basically there are three kinds of headlines: Main heads, subheads and eyebrow heads. The main head should be the central focus on each page or spread and works to reinforce the message of the primary visual. It may convey the one idea you want readers to remember over anything else. Subheads are used to break up copy into readable chunks and should be noticed second to both the headline and the main visual. A good subhead draws readers into the

copy and conveys important secondary messages. The third kind of head is an eyebrow head. These are used to "orient" readers to the contents of a page.

The Model 100 ← Subhead

A brochure that covers the Model 100, the Model 200 and the Model 300 in three spreads respectively might have these names used as eyebrow heads on the top of each page to show the reader which topic will be explained on that spread. Eyebrow heads are most often used in brochures and ads and are optional in all print projects.

"Body" or body copy

DESIGN 101

While entire books have been written on design, you can pick up some of the basic concepts just by reading this chapter. Design is highly subjective and tastes change by the minute, but the basics of design are easily illuminated.

When evaluating design, your most potent weapon is the first impression. A good first impression usually means that the design elements work well enough to warrant a second and more serious glance. A poor first impression probably means that the design suffers from basic problems. Your mission is to seek and destroy any design elements that alienate readers.

The four basic problems that can hinder any

design, whether print ad, trade show booth, architectural design, or brochure spread include:

1. **Too busy.** Too many elements compete with each other for the eye's attention.

2. **Unattractive.** An unattractive design stems from a lack of harmony between design elements. This may be a problem with color or poor integration of shapes. It may also be a quality problem, where the production is obviously cut-rate or inept.

3. **Uninteresting.** A boring design is usually the opposite of problems one and two. A boring design stems from a lack of elements or the use of quiet elements that work so well together that the eye can easily ignore them.

4. **Unbalanced.** In an unbalanced design, one insignificant element catches and holds the eye at the expense of other important elements.

Using a brochure layout as an example, some simple sketches of each problem are provided. Use your first impression to explore the problems of each. After each example is a pointer so that you can begin to make the design decisions for your communications.

Start by reviewing the sketch captioned, Too Busy. In this sketch, there are several different elements, each of which grab the eye at the same time. These elements are of similar visual weight, and the first impression focuses the eye between the blocks rather than on one of them or on the headline. The problem is also common when too many competing type styles are used on one page.

When you find that a design is too busy, throw out unimportant elements or merge them. Make the important items bigger or more prominent through the use of color. Make secondary elements secondary. Reduce the total number of typefaces used and consider eliminating all display faces. Too many bright colors can also make a layout busy. Consider reducing the total number of bright colors.

Now, consider the sketch captioned, Ugly. In this sketch, there are elements overlapping other elements and an obvious lack of visual continuity. The first impression rejects the layout because there is a total lack of harmony between the elements.

TOO BUSY

UNATTRACTIVE

When you are met with an ugly mess like this example, you may be working with a designer who would be better off in another line of work. If there's time, give the person a chance to fix it or get someone else on the project with an eye for aesthetics.

Next, there are two boring sketches to review. In the first sketch, there is only one

Ultimate Survival Tip

Design As Easy As 1-2-3!

A good design should do three things : (1) it should get your attention; (2) it should convey its chief message; and (3) it should convey any secondary messages in priority order. Design should not waste the observer's time by making him search for what's important or by making him sort out the vital from the trivial. It should also accomplish these steps in 1-2-3 order. A design that conveys a secondary message before the primary one has problems that should be corrected.

element with nothing to catch the eye. The first impression is one of disinterest. In the second sketch, all of the elements are balanced and fairly equal. The first impression is nonplussed. This second sketch might be acceptable for a page in a book or magazine but certainly not for an ad or promotional piece.

When are you dealing with an uninteresting design, simply adding elements will go a

UNINTERESTING

Announcing the Model 100—it's the one for you.

There are several terms for elements on the printed page that you should be aware of because in the process of writing copy and designing a print project, these phrases will come up. Basically there are three kinds of headlines: Main heads, subheads and eyebrow heads. The main head should be the central focus on each page or spread and works to reinforce the message of the primary visual. It may convey the one idea you want readers to remember over anything else. Subheads are used to break up copy into readable chunks and should be noticed second to both the headline and the main visual. A good subhead draws readers into the copy and conveys important secondary messages. The third kind of head is an eyebrow head. These are used to

long way in making your design more interesting. In the case of the second boring sketch, making some elements bigger than others will help, and you may want to move them around so the design isn't so painfully balanced.

Finally, review the example of an unbalanced layout. In this design, the important item may be the headline, but it is so dominant that the reader has to make a conscious effort to read the copy or interpret the graphics.

If a design is unbalanced, adjust the size and weight of the elements so that all of the important elements get attention. Anything that cannot be brought into visual balance according to its stature in the layout should be eliminated, if possible. Occasionally, this may be a case of trying to accomplish more than is possible in the available space. Set priorities and make adjustments to the offending items.

PRINTERS AND PRINTING: A BRIEF LESSON

There are a number of printing systems in use around the world, but the one used for almost all marketing communications projects is lithography. Printing techniques vary in the way they transfer ink to the page. Lithography uses water to resist grease-based inks; where water is present, no image is printed. Where there's no water, ink is laid down on the paper. This technique is capable of producing highly detailed documents and allows good control of the amount of ink applied. It also allows for long runs at high speeds before the press plates need renewal or replacement. In the Western world, lithography, with its inherent technical

UNBALANCED

Announcing
100—it's the one for you.

There are several terms for elements on the printed page that you should be aware of because in the process of writing copy and designing a print project, these phrases will come up. Basically there are three kinds of headlines: Main heads, subheads and eyebrow heads. The main head should be the central focus on each page or spread and works to reinforce the message of the primary visual. It may convey the one idea you want readers to remember over anything else.

advantages, is the most popular printing process.

Three Kinds of Print Shops

There are three kinds of lithographic print shops you may encounter:

1. **Quick Printers (also called Instaprinters).** These are small shops with a single one-color press and only two or three employees. If the job is simple and doesn't contain large blocks of solid color, quick printers are the best choice for the fast turnaround of simple documents (smaller than 11" × 17") with only one or two colors.

2. **Commercial Printers.** Most commercial printers have large shops and employ many people and a number of presses. The equipment in these kinds of shops varies considerably. The shop may have several two-color presses and a few larger presses for four-color work, or they may have only one press and a web for printing newsprint.

3. **Specialty Printers.** The most capable kind of print shop, specialty printers may own several four- or six-color presses. They are appropriate for handling jobs as complex as six-color brochures and elaborate annual

reports. The quality, however, varies from shop to shop, as does their specialty.

The Color Processes

There are several color processes employed in lithography. Unlike other kinds of printing technology, lithographic presses are only capable of printing a dot or not printing a dot. That means that they are incapable of directly printing a continuous tone image, such as the ones you see in a photograph. To get around this limitation, a number of color processing techniques are used. The techniques may be used together in one job or separately. The most common techniques include:

- **Halftones.** A halftone is simply a conversion of a black-and-white photo into a series of dots that can be printed by a lithographic press. The eye perceives these dots as shades of gray, ranging from black all the way to white. A solid dot is a black. No dot becomes white. Grays in between become partial dots. This system allows one color, typically black, to be used to produce a complete spectrum of grays.

- **Spot Color and the Pantone Matching System.** Spot color is simply the placement of solid colors (other than black) on the printed page. These colors may be used as type, decorative elements, or solid blocks of color. Spot color is usually specified through a recognized worldwide standard called the Pantone Matching System. This system provides designers and printers with a set of standard inks that can be mixed into a color chosen from the Pantone Color Formula Guide. Using this system, a designer in New York can specify a color that a printer in Los Angeles can match almost exactly.

- **Four-Color Process.** The most powerful innovation in printing so far this century was the invention and subsequent refinement of color printing. The four-color process, in which a complex color photo or illustration can be converted into a printed color image, begins with the assumption that three ink colors—cyan, magenta, and yellow—can be mixed in combinations to recreate any other color. While it doesn't quite provide every available color, this system is fully capable of creating convincing color images.

  To print a color image, the original image (usually a photograph or transparency) is color-separated. Simply, a machine is used to scan the photo for each of the standard colors and to break them apart. The separation creates a black-and-white halftone for each color, which is then used to make plates—one for each color.

  The colors are recombined when a four-color press prints the colors on top of each other. This recreates the look of the original image. But wait! Where's the fourth color? It's black, and it's used to compensate for the inability of the other three colors to create really dark colors and convincing shadows. A black halftone is also created with the other separations. So, the complete system includes cyan, magenta, yellow and black.

- **Screen Tint Color.** Cyan, magenta, yellow, and black can be used to reproduce a photo consisting of thousands of individual colors, and these four inks can also be used to create a single solid color. To create a screen tint color, a printer refers to a book to see what amount of each color must be added together to create the desired shade. Not all colors are available through this technique, but a solid color printed with the Pantone Matching System inks looks convincing and crisp.

The Print Production Process

Before a brochure or other marketing communications tool can be printed, there are a series of production steps that transform the designer's mechanical into a mask, a format that is then used to burn plates, which are used to print the piece. Here are the basic steps in the production and printing process that all print communications must go through.

Step 1. The printer estimates the job. He does this by looking at the steps required to get the job ready for press and by adding up the hours and materials charges. Next, he gets a quote on the paper he will use to print, sometimes getting a price from several distributors in order to find the lowest price and a delivery window that's suitable for the job. He then adds the time required for the press run to the estimate. A specialty printer running a complex job on a four-color press may charge $300 to $450 per hour for press time. That time includes the hours that the press will be tied up as well as the labor time for a pressperson and one or two helpers.

Step 2. The job is reviewed. When the bid is accepted and the art delivered, the printer reviews the job to make sure it's similar to the job he quoted and that there are no potential production problems.

Step 3. The job goes to the stripping room. The art is shot and converted into film. During this time, images are converted to halftones, and any required color separations are created. Printers may do this in-house or have the work sent out. For really high-quality color separations, most printers send out to houses that specialize in separation and color balance.

Step 4. The masks are created. The finished film of the type, separations, halftones and any screen tints are composited into a mask. This mask is approximately the same size as the press plates and usually consists of an opaque orange plastic sheet with the film stripped into cut-out windows.

Step 5. The masks are used to burn the plates. One mask is used for each side of the paper to be printed and for each color on a multicolor job. A machine called a plate burner is used for this process. To use it, the mask, with the film mounted into the windows, is placed on top of a photo-sensitive plate. Brilliant light then passes through the film windows and etches the image on the plate. Where the orange mask has not been cut away or where the film is black, no exposure takes place. The exposed plate is then developed in a special solution and is then ready for the press.

Step 6. The printer mounts the plates and adds the requisite inks to the press.

Step 7. The printer runs make-readies. Junk paper (maybe left over from another job) is run through the press, while the pressperson and his assistants adjust ink delivery and blanket pressure. These initial tests are called "make-readies."

Step 8. A press check is completed by the designer or client. After the client approves the run as accurate and as specified, the printer then runs the job.

Step 9. The job goes for final assembly or special treatments. This may mean going to a bindery for stapling or other assembly, either one in-house or at an outside shop. In the case of special processes, such as foil stamping or embossing, more vendors may be involved.

Step 10. The job is delivered or picked up.

Proofs

Depending on the nature of your job and the printer's equipment, you may see several kinds of proofs for your review and approval before your job gets printed.

- **Blueline Proofs.** These consist of a paper proof on either a bluish or a brownish paper. Bluelines allow you to look for missing elements in the design, improperly assembled jobs, and crooked elements and allow you to verify that the mechanical assembly of pages, die cuts, and folds are correct. Some shops do not stabilize these exceptionally fragile proofs. If unstabilized, the proof disappears instantly if brought into the sun or if photocopied.

- **Match Prints and Color Keys.** These proofs allow you to check for incorrect color use and colors that don't register properly. They are also useful for inspecting the overall appearance of a color job.

- **Chromalin Proofs.** These are used to check the quality of color separations, the color balance, and the size of the images.

- **Dummies.** Dummies are a kind of proof that the printer (or paper supplier) assembles using the actual paper. This sample is blank, but it allows you to get a better idea of how the selected paper will look and feel once it's assembled into its final form. Use a dummy to evaluate paper weights, opacity, complex folds, and/or die cuts. If your job is an expensive one, you may want to consider several papers and should have a dummy made from each before making a final decision.

The Ultimate Proof—The Press Check

Along with carefully checking the proofs described above, the ultimate proof of a print job is the press check. Press checks consist of looking at the job on the press after the make-ready phase is complete. There, you can check color and take one last look for mistakes.

If you plan to press check your job, be sure to let the printer know in advance. It's best to remind him when you check on the job's progress; it's quite common that printers will accidentally or deliberately forget to call you when the job is on press. If your job is in a shop that runs 24 hours, the press check may be held at any hour, so be ready to go on a moment's notice.

Once you arrive, you'll probably be put in storage somewhere until the pressperson has completed the make-readies. Large shops who cater to many people may have entire recreational areas available for the clients while they're waiting. One printer we have used in the past has a complete floor for waiting press checkers. Surrounded by small private rooms for resting and sleeping is a main hall complete with a kitchen, refreshments and, even a pool table.

Once on press, you will need to check for the following:

- **Hickies.** Small donut shaped marks caused by debris stuck on the rollers.
- **Registration.** If it's a color job, use a magnifying loop (borrow one from the pressperson) to make sure that all colors line up properly and that any four-color images have each color's dots aligned along the edges. If any of the images look slightly out of focus or soft, check the dot structure and alignment carefully.
- **Scratches.** Occasionally, a press plate will get scratched on its way from the stripping department to the press.
- **Color Balance.** You may want to raise or lower some colors in order to make them more lively or less intense. Sometimes in the case of a four-color image, one color, such as black, may print normally but will make the image appear too dark. With the pressperson's help, you can adjust the color. Make sure that the color is even across the sheet. Sometimes, a color may be normal in most areas but may be too light or too dark in one band. Check that the right paper is being used. Mix-ups or deliberate substitutions occur. If a Pantone Matching System Ink is being used, verify that the right color has been loaded into the press. Check the printed color against the Pantone chart.

After you make any adjustments and correct problems, you will be asked to initial and date the sheet that you approved. This means that you approve the job to run as is. Take a sheet from the job with you. If the shop speeds up the press after you leave (rare) and delivers a job with washed-out color, this sample is your proof that the delivered job was not run with the specifications you approved.

Color Is Subjective

Although a rose is always a rose, red is not always red. To give you some idea of how subjective color is, think of the color of Charlie Chaplin's hat when you watch him on TV. Black? Well, not really. What you perceive as solid black during the movie is really the dull green of the tube that you see when the TV is turned off. Color appears to change with the environment around it. For example, grass looks greener on cloudy days and just after sunset because the eye becomes more sensitive to green than to other colors in lower light levels.

Because color is so subjective and is based on lighting and its surrounding colors, study a color you select from the Pantone Matching System or the color proof under several kinds of light. If the color is to be used in an office environment, look at it under fluorescent lights. Take it out in the sun and review it. Then, look at it under the color-balanced lights at the print shop. You'll be surprised how different it will look in each of the three places.

Ultimate Survival Tip

Color Balanced Lights May Not Be
Most print shops will have a booth or room with a bank of color-balanced fluorescent lights for studying proofs. You can use these lights as a guide to color, but they may not be that accurate. Many printers spend the money to install the lights but then only replace the bulbs when they burn out. Some shops don't even keep the dust off the bulbs. In order for the lights to be color-balanced, the bulbs must be replaced regularly and kept clean.

Special Print Processes

There are several other "effects" that you may encounter in design and printing. These include:

- **Foil Stamping.** A shiny foil is applied by heat and a die to the surface of a page. This foil may be used to create a logo or to make a headline stand out. In the right design, foil can be elegant and tasteful, but foil stamping is overused in some pieces. It is an expensive process, and too much foil can be garish.

- **Blind Embossing.** Embossing is a process in which the paper is pushed up by a die. Embossing can be quite effective, but, like foil stamping, it is an expensive process. Some papers take embossing much better than others. Ask your printer for advice on which paper to choose.

- **Varnishes.** Varnishes are used to add subtle contrast to a design element. Varnishes may be either glossy or matte and may have a hint of color added to make them more noticeable. Varnish is applied by a regular press.

- **Die Cutting.** Some jobs may need to be cut into special shapes after the print run. Examples of jobs that have been die cut are ones with rounded corners and business card holders cut into literature holders. All kinds of shapes are possible, but the dies used to make elaborate cuts can be expensive.

- **Mar Coating.** Mar coating consists of applying a plastic layer to a printed piece. It is used to protect the printed surface of documents that suffer frequent handling.

Ultimate Survival Tip

Test Your Materials to See If They Photocopy!

When ordering letterhead or other materials that may be run through a copier, it's tempting to add a design element, such as embossing or foil stamping, to add a touch of class. Keep in mind that most embossed elements will get crushed during copying, and foil that is applied through heat will come off in the copier's heated rollers. In extreme cases, damage will result to the copier from the letterhead. Some kinds of raised print processes don't work either.

In addition to these potential problems, some color schemes do not copy well. Most copiers turn red into black and light blue into white. Some may drop out yellow. Silver foil will not copy well. If your materials will be frequently copied, test the colors before going into print.

PRINTING TERMINOLOGY

There are several printing terms that you'll frequently hear. Some of these terms will raise the price of your job, so you need to know what the designers and printers are talking about. Here are the most common terms you'll hear.

- **Solids.** Solids are solid areas of color. Depending on the paper and the size of the solid, they can be quite troublesome because pin holes may appear in the ink coverage, or the colors may come out looking uneven. They may also have to move the job to a more expensive press. Printers charge extra for printing pieces that make extensive use of solids because of the headaches involved.

- **Reverses.** Reverses are simply solids the with type reversed out of them, which allows the paper to show through. The type looks white or paper-colored on a colored background.

- **Bleeds.** Bleeds are necessary when ink is required all the way to the edge of the paper. Since no press can actually print all the way to the edge without causing a massive ink build-up on the rollers, bleeds are produced by printing on a larger-than-necessary sheet of paper and by then chopping off the edge to create the bleed. This may raise the price because larger sheets of paper are required, and trimming adds an extra charge.

- **Complex Registration.** Wherever one color abuts (touches) another, the registration becomes critical. Printers charge extra for this because it makes the job more complicated and may require a more expensive press. Never hand a quick printer a job that involves complex registration!

TYPES OF PAPER

There are a number of papers available for all kinds of jobs—everything from six-part NCR forms for bureaucracies to papers made of waterproof plastic. Most kinds of paper (also called stock as in "paper stock") fall into two categories—coated and uncoated. Coated stocks are made of fibers that have been combined with clay, adhesives, and additives to create a very smooth surface. Uncoated papers lack this smooth surface, but are processed to add color and texture. Most paper starts out as ground wood pulp or as pulp from recycled paper. The only exception is a new and expensive paper actually made from plastic, which requires special inks for printing.

From a printer's point of view, coated papers are much easier to print on because their surface is smoother and because less ink gets absorbed into the paper. Uncoated stocks, depending on how they are manufactured, can be highly absorbent, and printed colors become darker than they do on a coated sheet. Uncoated paper, on the other hand, offers a wide variety of colors and textures and is generally less expensive than the best coated papers (although there are some very expensive uncoated sheets available).

Paper is usually chosen by a designer in conjunction with the printer. Your designer may have already decided on a particular paper that takes color a certain way or has a special texture. Printers often have a say in the matter, too. Every printer has likes and dislikes when it comes to paper. Your printer may also know of a special deal where he can buy a sheet of identical quality and appearance at a price substantially less than the paper your designer specified, or the paper specified may only be available in an unsuitable size for your job and printing on it would mean trimming off and throwing away a large piece of each sheet.

Here are the kinds of paper you will encounter when printing marketing communications projects:

- **Newsprint.** The least expensive paper stock used for printing is newsprint. Most familiar in the form of the morning newspaper, newsprint is inexpensive and offers excellent opacity due to the lack of refinement of the wood pulp used to produce it. On the negative side, newsprint absorbs ink in a manner that prevents complex control of color, and it's quite susceptible to environmental elements. When wet, it quickly reverts to little more than pulp, and newspapers printed on standard newsprint turn yellow after just a few hours in the sun. That's why most libraries convert important newspapers to microfiche for preservation. Use newsprint only for very short-lived projects for which quantity and price are more important than quality.

- **Uncoated Options.** Uncoated papers are available in a variety of colors. They may also be run through pressurized rollers to add textures and patterns. Use uncoated stocks for letterhead (you can't type on coated stocks) and for projects in which colored paper and texture are important. If your project includes large areas of embossing, consider an uncoated stock because the fibers in this kind of paper are much more flexible than in coated stocks.

- **Coated Options.** Coated papers come in colors ranging from "bright-white" to creme. There are also different kinds of coated finishes, ranging from dull mattes to shiny glossies. Generally, matte-coated sheets absorb inks best, but they are also the most expensive. Avoid printing on glossy sheets, unless you are working with a specialty printer who can get the ink to lay down

evenly on the surface. Glossy and semigloss papers make for difficult reading but often make attractive packaging and covers. Most quality-coated stocks are rated by a number between one and three. A number three sheet is the cheapest and the least opaque, and absorbs ink inconsistently. A number one sheet is the most expensive because it has the most perfect surface and, therefore, takes ink and color the best. Use these papers for high-quality printing that involves process color and/or careful control of spot colors and for jobs where color registration is critical.

THE WEIGHTS OF PAPER

Paper is manufactured in different weights for different purposes. A paper's weight rating refers to the paper's actual weight for 500 sheets of a given size (different categories of paper use different sizes for measuring the weight). This weight is used as a method for specifying and ordering paper. Heavier papers are more expensive papers.

At the low end of the scale are "writing weights," such as 20-pound bond. This paper is most familiar as the limp sheets used in the office photocopier. As weight increases, so does the opacity and the stiffness of the paper. If you are printing on both sides of a sheet of paper, you want the paper to be quite opaque so readers can't see through the page to the printing on the other side. Stiffness is the degree of rigidity in the paper, and a given paper may have different thicknesses available, which affects rigidity.

Most printing-grade paper is available in both text and cover weights. Cover weight is a heavier, stiffer stock that is intended for use as the outside of a brochure or as business card stock. Lighter text-weight paper is used for the inside of a brochure or as letterhead. Cover weight costs more than text weight.

At this point, you have a basic knowledge and a basic vocabulary to get you started in the world of communications. There are more terms, jargon, and production proce-dures involved with video production and multimedia presentations, but they are beyond the scope of this book. Most libraries have excellent resources on these topics if you want to further delve into the jargon. For now, you have enough knowledge to keep yourself from being snowed by designers and other so-called advertising professionals.

CHAPTER

22

ONLINE ADVERTISING AND WEB SITE PROMOTION

This chapter explains the basics for getting started in Web-based and online marketing. We don't explain how to build a Web site (on the CD-ROM, there are plenty of links to sites that can help you), but, before you spend thousands of hours learning to program your Web site, be forewarned—the Web is not a "money ship" that just sails into your home office as soon as you set up your site. As in other marketing endeavors, it takes hard work to make the World Wide Web pay off. If you have a product that appeals to an easily targeted market and if you can attract those people to your Web site, there are several opportunities to make a profit by promoting your products or services on the Web and other online services.

These days, it seems to be common wisdom that, if you're in business, you need to have a Web site. In reality, for many businesses, a Web site will make little or no difference in the overall profitability of the business, and the time devoted to programming the Web site and keeping it up-to-date may pull time away from other more lucrative marketing efforts.

Think seriously about the needs of your market before you go onto the Web to make more money. It's hard to believe that Fred's

Service Station really needs a Web site to reap new profits. For some home-based businesses, however, the Internet and commercial online services (such as America Online, known as AOL to most people, and the Microsoft Network, known as MSN) offer viable marketing and distribution opportunities. Software companies, online magazines, and mail-order businesses can do quite well from the Web if the owners know how to promote their sites in the right places. The lure of the Web is its ease of entry—for less than $20 a month almost anyone with a computer and a modem can establish a small Web site (1 or 2 MB of storage) for no additional charge beyond the monthly fee for using the Internet or commercial online service. You can put up a lot of information in that free space, which is why people feel almost obligated to establish presence on the Web.

Merely having a site on the Web will do almost nothing to sell your products or services. To promote your Web site, there are three major things you must do:

1. You must register your Web site with the best search engines.
2. You should consider using the many advertising opportunities both free-of-charge and paid, on the Web.
3. You should search the Web regularly for competitive sites and related sites where you can attach a link to your site.

PRODUCING A WEB PAGE

If you decide a Web page is a good idea for your business, remember that good Web page design within the framework of a computer screen instead of paper, follows the same rules of type and visual design (or intentionally breaks them for artistic reasons) that you read about in the previous chapter. There are hundreds, maybe thousands, of Web design sites available on the Internet to get you started in using the basic tools for creating HTML codes (the basic Web programming language), developing page layouts, and publishing images on Web pages. Check out the Web design section, which is part of the Marketing category on the CD-ROM enclosed with this book, to find a starting place on the Web to help you create and publish your own Web site.

If you want to know what looks good on the Web, start some serious surfing to see what the best sites look like and to get ideas for how the sites work to lure you into their pages in search of more information.

PROMOTING YOUR WEB SITE

If you want people to find your Web site after you develop it, you first need to make your site information available through the major search engines (such as Yahoo , WebCrawler, Infoseek, and hundreds of others) that help people find the things they're looking for on the Internet. You can register your site one search engine at a time or you can use a search engine registration service, such as Submit It®, to register your site information on hundreds of sites at one time (although the more sites you register, the more it will cost.) Even so, the registration fees are quite affordable, and we recommend using a quality registration service to do the redundant work for you.

How To Use Submit It!® To Register Your Web Site

At this writing, Submit-It!® (www.submit-it.com) is one of the best Web site submission services. The service allows you to register your site on twenty basic search sites for free. Another option is to register up to two or more universal resource locators (URLs) at 400 sites for less than $100 per year (at this writing). Submit It!® services are used by more than 250,000 Webmasters, online marketers, and site owners, from Fortune 500 employees to individual hobbyists.

Submit It!® provides other, more costly services for Webmasters as well, such as consulting services, information monitoring services, and reports on access to the best sites (best, in this case, means most frequently visited). For site registration purposes, Submit-It!® supports more than 400 of the best, true Internet search engines and directories on the Web. However, the company has more than 1,200 search engines and reference directories in its database, and, every day, Submit-It!® gets 20 or more new requests from search engines and directories to be included in the Submit It!® service.

Why does Submit-It!® support only about 25% of the sites available on the Web? Because the company founders want to provide customers with the best, most relevant places to list their sites. The company visits and evaluates each directory and search engine to determine if the site will be around for a while, if it has an audience, and if it passes their technical evaluations. If a search site or registry passes the Submit-It!® scrutiny, the company categorizes the search site and adds it to the service listings. Someday, the company may have more than 1,200 sites in the service, and you can bet they'll be the best 1,200 on the Internet!

Submitting Your URL To A Search Engine

Whether you use Submit It!® or another registration service (there are links to a number of services and search engine registration sites on the CD-ROM), or even if you submit to services one at a time, here are some basic things to know about submitting your URL information to search engines and directories:

- Every day, new directories come into existence and others disappear. While companies like Submit It! try to keep up with all of the changes, the lists provided by the directories may be out-of-date simply because things change quickly on the Internet and World Wide Web.

- Some directories and search engines charge for listings, although most do not.

- Not all directories and search engines are relevant for all Web sites. For example, some are only for non-U.S. Web sites. Thus, if your site isn't relevant, the directory won't list your URL.

- Some directories and search engines periodically suspend submissions. Therefore, no number of submissions will get your URL into the service.

- When you submit the URL (Web address) for your Web site, you may find that it will take from one day to more than eight weeks for your site to appear in a search attempt on a particular site. This is because search engine sites are often critical of the information they list in their indexes. If your site isn't deemed relevant or professional by the site, it won't get listed. Sometimes, the wait for indexing your site is simply due to the volume of sites being submitted for review. Be patient and keep testing to see if your site comes up in a search.

For those search engine sites that use Excite, Web Crawler, or some other robot (also called crawlers and spiders) to categorize the information in a site, here are some tips on how to keep your site's information up-to-date in search engines.

Changing the Title and Content of Your Web Site

When you alter the title or content of your site, you don't need to contact each robot-automated search engine to point out the changes you've made. Excite and other such programs will perform automatic updates the next time the program does its update access (often taking the title from the title tag in your document's header, which is why it's a good idea to have the right title in your site's title). It may take a week or two for the spider to visit you, but it'll get there eventually.

Changing the Location of Your Web Site

When you change your URL, you'll need to submit a new add URL form to the search engine so that the robot can index your new site. If the old site remains at the old address, most spider programs will keep indexing your site unless you remove it or put a robots.txt file on your system. You can get information on using a robots.txt file in your site at info. webcrawler.com/mak/projects/robots/faq. html. These files point to your new site so that

automatic updating programs can find the information in your new location.

CHANGING THE SUMMARY OF YOUR WEB SITE

To change the site summary that the various spiders compile, you'll have to change your content. Spider programs typically build a summary of your site by taking sentences that contain the dominant ideas and concepts of your home page directly from the page. The designers of Web robots can't tell the spider to use only particular sentences in the summary.

Manually Updated Search Engines

Some search engine services complete their updating by hand (not through robots), therefore, you'll have to resubmit information about your site whenever you make major changes to the content. That's why using an automated submission service (like Submit-It!®) is a good idea. The service can help keep references to your site up-to-date.

ADVERTISING ON THE WORLD WIDE WEB

If you have some extra cash in your promotional budget, you may want to consider online advertising on the Web or one of the commercial online services. Advertising on a commercial Web site can range from a simple banner at the top of the site or a simple contact link (that the site charges to provide) for your Web site to a complete feature page of information on your product or services. Advertising on hot (meaning popular) online sites can be expensive. For example, it costs at least $2000 a year to advertise on the AOL NetFind search engine, and, if you want a big ad placed frequently, it will cost a good deal more.

If you want to find out about advertising on a major Web site, simply send an e-mail to the Webmaster and ask about advertising possibilities, which will vary by cost, number of contacts made on the site, and reach of the audience. (Read Chapter 15 on advertising if you don't understand these concepts. Advertising on the Web is much like advertising in other major media, such as newspapers or magazines. The larger the number of exposures, the more it will cost to have a company-specific advertisement on the Web page.)

If your own Web site ever generates enough exposure in your area of expertise, you can also sell advertising space on your site, just like other sites do. In fact, some Web entrepreneurs support themselves entirely through advertising fees generated by their site. The advertising fees enable the Web entrepreneurs to keep the site up-to-date and full of good information. Check out a high quality site for movie information at http://us.imdb.com, which supports its efforts entirely through advertising fees.

PROMOTING YOUR PRODUCTS THROUGH ONLINE SERVICES

Remember, there's more to the Net than the Web. The Internet also consists of newsgroups, chat services, and general information sites that contain shareware software and "free" reports (which can really be demos of your full-featured products and services). Best of all, online marketing beyond the Web represents some of the most effective and least expensive (often free) ways to market your products. You can use (often free) classified online advertising, direct e-mail promotions, and simple word-of-mouth ads on newsgroups and chat programs.

Using Newsgroups as Promotional Channels

Newsgroups, also known as Usenet groups, are bulletin board areas that draw people with similar interests to discuss their opinions. The Usenet newsgroups are topic-specific places (which work mostly in text-only mode as of this writing), where information is shared, ads are placed, and questions are answered. Some newsgroups allow outright advertising on the site for relevant products; some groups don't. However, if you become an information resource on a newsgroup and casually sign your name and add a reference to your Web site, you can do a lot to promote your wares without alienating the news readers.

To participate in newsgroups (there are thousands of them, so be selective before you get involved), you'll need a news reading program. Most Internet Service Providers (ISPs) include news service software in their package of support materials. If your ISP doesn't provide the software, consider buying something like Forte Free Agent, which allows you to access the groups, read messages, and post messages to the groups of interest to you.

Special Interest Promotions

SIGs (special interest groups) are similar to newsgroups, except they're available only to subscribers of commercial online services (such as America Online or Microsoft Network). These groups cater to chat discussions and often support bulletin boards and interest areas, which can be used for relevant advertising. If you have a special expertise, you can offer to become an expert who can provide special chat sessions or other support services (such as mentoring) for people who belong to the SIG. expertise.

E-Mail Promotions

We discussed how to use e-mail to promote your products in Chapter 19, which explains how to create direct mail promotions. Direct e-mail promotions should follow all the established rules of direct-mail marketing. The most important rule is to market to those people who are most likely to buy your product. Don't just send e-mail to everyone in the world, even though there are programs that enable you to do this with relative ease. The most important thing you'll need to assemble is a good mailing list and a well-written e-mail campaign in order to get good responses with e-mail. "Spamming" the readers with UCE (unsolicited commercial e-mail) will gain you little, unless you have an irresistible product. There are two sources of e-mail addresses you may want to look up: PostMaster Direct Response (www. PostmasterDirect.com) and Targ-it.com (www. targ-it.com). Both offer e-mail lists of people who have indicated that they actually like to receive commercial e-mail on topics of interest to them.

Online Classified Ads

There are thousands of commercial and private online classified areas where you can place an ad or product announcement for free. Some sites charge for these ads if the site is highly visible or in a premium location. Look in the marketplace areas of the commercial online services for their (mostly) free classified areas. Like most things, you get what you pay for, but the more you get mentioned, the better responses you can expect to receive from online classified ads. Keep your ads up-to-date if you want to get the best results. Old classified ads will not pay off over the long haul. Some sites keep their ads up for a long time, so be sure to make a list of all the sites where you place your ads and update them on a regular basis.

Links to Related Sites

You can use a search engine service such as Yahoo! (www.yahoo.com) or Infoseek (www. infoseek.com), to find sites related to your company's products or services. Expect to spend some time looking through the sites for their information links area (which are available on most high-quality sites). Then, write e-mails to the Webmasters of the relevant sites and ask to list your Web site on their lists. In return, offer to link their sites to your site. This free and cooperative advertising is a time-consuming (but often very rewarding) way of getting your site in front of interested Web surfers.

You can also place ads with the major online services, such as America Online, the Microsoft Network, Prodigy, and any others that survive or emerge in the future. Most online services offer SIGs, classified adds, on-screen ads, and other promotional opportunities—at a cost of course.

As with all promotions, the real key to making online promotions successful is targeted marketing. Find those people in the universe, whether online or on the ground, who want to buy your services, and you'll sell your wares. Although this sounds easy, the trick to online profits is consistent, high-quality promotions sent over and over again until you reach those people who really want your product. This trick is true for all of your promotions, so never give up after the first ad.

PART

5

LIFESTYLES OF THE RICH AND HOME-BASED

C H A P T E R

23

Time Management for Home-Based Workers

In this chapter, we look at the basics of time management for your business. Simple and practical suggestions for analyzing and improving your productivity are included, along with a brief section on managing and controlling your priority projects.

Time is money. Period. You can use it vacuuming the house, talking to telemarketers, or bringing in the bacon. The choice is yours. Whether you like it or not, every minute you spend tending to your business is paid back, and, usually, the payback is double what you put in. That's why you can't waste your time, even though everyone and everything around you attempts to soak up precious energy. Certainly you've heard that E= Money/Cash²!

MANAGING YOUR TIME

You may feel that nothing is getting done no matter how hard you work: "I worked 12 hours but didn't accomplish anything." In business, it happens every day when customers call and sales close, almost as if by accident. It's easy to focus a lot of time and energy on work that really has no germane purpose in bringing in money. If you think you're wasting your time, check out the time traps we talk about in Chapter 25.

No matter how hard you work, not all of your time will ever be used productively. You are, however, your own manager. All of us can manage our time more effectively and still stick to a realistic agenda. Procrastination is a common tactic, but effective time management eliminates the worst of it.

THE TIME LOG

A simple but useful technique for finding out where your time goes is to keep a daily log that details how you spend each waking hour in the day. After several days of recording your activities in this way, you will have a considerable amount of information about your current use of time. Write the log entries in detail and ask yourself these questions:

- Was the majority of my time spent on making money and the other priorities of the business?
- If I'm looking for leads to grow and/or build the business, did I succeed?
- What did I waste the most time doing? What can I eliminate or cut back?
- How can I better manage the telephone, kids, neighbors, and other distractions?
- Am I shortchanging customers because of time constraints?
- What am I doing right with my time?
- Is disorganization a problem? If so, get organized and try to stay that way. There are many good books on establishing filing systems and organization procedures. We've listed some of them on the CD-ROM.

Think Locally, Act Globally

Working for yourself requires both macromanagement and micromanagement of your time. Minute to minute you're focused (or should be) on what's immediately on your desk or workbench. In the long run, the big picture is keeping your company afloat and growing. This takes careful time management. For this reason, you need to mind your Ps and Qs while you watch how they translate into long-term survival habits. What seems immediate and vital this instant may waste money a year down the road. Sometimes, a careful review of your time usage points out problems where too much time is spent on tasks that aren't important.

Ultimate Survival Tip

Use a stopwatch.
Get an inexpensive stop watch or a digital watch and time your calls and tasks. Don't hang up on people after their three minutes are up. Instead, study the results of your log. Evaluate how much time you spent on the phone (per call) and how much of your time was consumed by tasks associated with each delivery and assembly, and even by closing up at night. Then, make changes to your work to effectively improve your productivity and prioritize your responsibilities.

SCHEDULING YOUR TIME

The manner of scheduling time is a matter of preference. Some people like physical organizers. Others laboriously use computers, even when it means booting up and waiting to get to a personal information manager to jot down an informal lunch for "noonish" next Tuesday.

For the home-based business person, you'll want to effectively organize your calendar dates and also have ready access to business cards and important addresses. For this task, a paper-based organizer is the most effective. Get one that handles 8½" × 11" forms, catalogs, and computer printouts, even though such a book is heavy to carry. Also get a three-hole punch so that you can add new information to the book. If you would rather computerize everything, use a scheduling and contact management program to track things on your PC. Then, print the material, punch it, and add it to your book.

The concept of the organizer dates from the simple appointment books and diaries that began appearing on desks in the nineteenth century. Today's paper-based organizers, like the popular DayRunner systems available from Harper House, have become comprehensive, personalized information systems in a binder. These loose-leaf organizers are available in several sizes and many styles, and a variety of fillers are available for organizing everything from your daily fitness routine to a list of favorite sushi bars.

Many companies make variations of these organizers. Besides the easy-to-find Harper House DayRunner systems, there are the classic DayTimer systems (sold through mail-order), the Day-at-a-Glance and Week-at-a-Glance organizers (available in almost every department, business, and stationery store), and the sophisticated Franklin system (available at special retail outlets and through mail-order). While manual organizers can fulfill the functions of an electronic organizer, they are larger and bulkier and contain no electronic "links" to other components of the home office. Even so, most businesspeople need a traditional paper-based organizer, because there are still times when it isn't feasible to use an electronic device.

We also recommend that you take a compact manual organizer with you to act as backup for your schedule when the electronic organizer is not feasible. Most organizer software programs allow you to print appropriately formatted schedule pages from your computer to put in popular paper-based organizer systems. This eliminates the need to duplicate schedule information and notes by hand.

Organizers

DayRunners from Harper House and similar organizers from other companies can track everything from a daily schedule to the names and locations of restaurants by city. DayRunners come in a variety of sizes and formats, which can be adapted to personal work habits.

If you don't want to buy an expensive manual organizer system, there are some samples of commonly used organizer pages that you can duplicate from the CD-ROM included with this book. Just punch the holes and put them in a binder, and you have a system personalized just for you and your business.

Contact Management Software

For some enterprises, a paper organizer is inadequate for tracking large numbers of accounts and billing phone calls. There are many contact and appointment packages on the market. Choose yours carefully, particularly the contact manager because it will be used to print mailing lists and to report on customer activity. The best bet is a program from a respected company. Many contact packages become obsolete and, no updates are provided to add features or to keep the product compatible with operating system upgrades.

Personal Digital Assistants

There are several personal digital assistants (PDA) that attempt to combine the easy-to-

ORGANIZE YOUR ORGANIZER

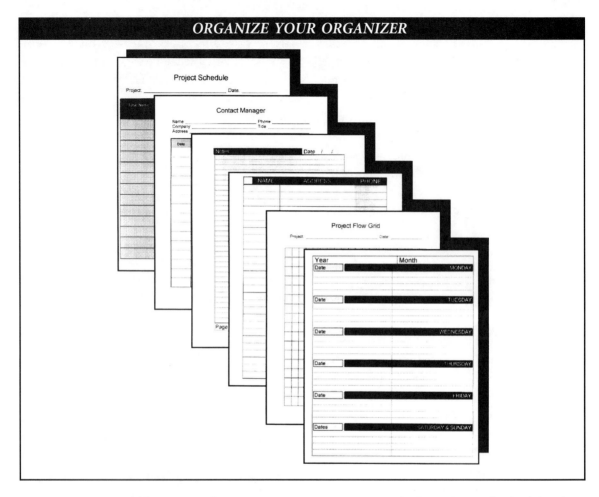

use DayRunner with the power of a computer. One of these might work for you, but before purchase you should test it in the store. These units don't always work as promised. For example, Apple Computer's first Newton featured automatic conversion of handwritten text into word processing text. Unfortunately, it turned most of the words into gibberish in the process.

Other Electronic Organizers
Less sophisticated than a PDA are handheld units, such as Sharp's Wizards. Capable of

managing a telephone list and schedule, these can be used in the field to track and manage resources. Then, at the office, they can be linked to with your computer to upload and download new information.

A Computer in Your Palm
Another option is the palmtop PC. Formerly limited to a propriety operation system or a downscaled version of Windows, a true handheld PC that runs a full version of Windows is now available from Toshiba. You can leave this computer running, ready to enter contact

NETWORK DIAGRAM

Complex projects are best controlled with a network diagram produced by project management software.

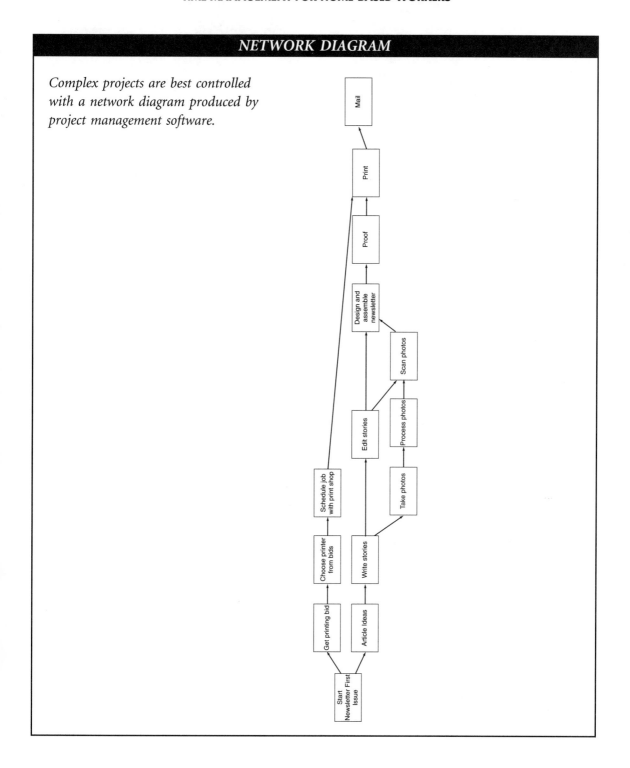

PROJECT SCHEDULING WORKSHEET

Name of Project: MyCo Newsletter

Today's date: 12/19/98

Task Name	Resource	Start Date	End Date	Actual Start Date	Actual End Date	Notes and Progress
Get printer quote for 4-page newsletter	Me	1/3	1/4	1/3	1/3	Cost for 500 copies in two colors, $289 at Joe's Printing
Write stories	Tom	1/15	1/31	1/15	2/3	7 stories completed
Photograph new product	Me	1/15	1/15	1/15	1/15	Film processed, image scanned into computer 1/20
Assemble newsletter on computer with PageMaker	Tom	2/1	2/20	2/5	2/14	"Rough" of newsletter complete. Added one more story to fill in blank space
Proof newsletter and make corrections	Kelly & Tom	2/20	2/22	2/20	2/22	Changes made and final proof complete
Print newsletter files to film at Joe's Printing	Me and Joe	2/25	2/26	2/25	2/26	Proofed one more time. No changes
Print	Joe	3/1	3/5	2/26	2/28	Looks good!
Stamp/address mail	Tom & me	3/6	3/8	2/28	3/2	Had Joe handle it for an additional $98
Mail	Me	3/8	3/8	3/2	3/2	Project done

data as you need to. The only limit to this arrangement is the PC's battery life.

PROJECT MANAGEMENT TOOLS

For managing large projects and complex schedules, such as starting or expanding your business or designing and delivering new products, there are formal tools and technologies available. They are called project management tools, and they are used to map out the project in terms of steps, time, and cost. Most project management is handled with computer software, although it can be done by hand. Invented in the 1950s for the purpose of managing huge projects like submarine design and construction, project management techniques can assist you with simple projects as well as large ones.

Simple projects can be listed by time on a worksheet. Just making a list of the steps or tasks will help you understand the process your project will require. Once listed, assigning a time and a resource person to each task clari-fies the amount of work required and gives you some idea of the cost.

There's a lot to know about project management. For novices, we suggest you read our book, *The Complete Idiot's Guide to Project Management* before purchasing a project management software package such as Microsoft Project®. You may decide that computerized project management tools are too complicated for your needs. We would guess that less than 20 percent of all project management software programs actually get used by the purchaser. It's that complicated to develop a full-blown project plan. That's why there are professionals who do nothing but manage projects full-time.

In this chapter, you received tips on improving your productivity and looking for hidden time sinks in your business day. We also touched on project management and have provided examples for you to use when you are managing simple projects. Remember that time is money, so spend it wisely!

CHAPTER

24

WORKING TOGETHER—MIXING FAMILY AND BUSINESS

Working together can be one of the most rewarding aspects of a good marriage or family relationship, but if you don't have the relationship together and the rules straight, it can be a disaster. In this chapter, we look at the issues of working together in the home office. In the home office, husbands, wives, and even the kids find that, by chance or by choice, they are working together for the first time. Eventually, the only dialog they have is about "the office," and work overcomes the relationship. This chapter provides hints for keeping your work and your personal life separate, so that you can be happy and productive as home-workers and as a family.

Certainly, one of the most difficult business arrangements is working with partners. Divided opinions lead to simmering resentments and hostility. "I'm working harder than him (or her)" fuels confrontation and the eventual disillusion of the partnership and the business as

well. In a traditional business partnership, each party goes home to live their lives with a respite from the disagreements of the office.

In a home-based business, however, partners sometimes don't have that luxury. Imagine that the pressure cooker builds up. When you go home to cool off and babble complaints about your partner's underhanded tactics, double dealing, and lack of commitment to the best interests of the business, who is waiting for you? Your wife or husband, who is also your disagreeable partner! Does it have to be this way? No, and in this chapter we talk about ways to save your marriage and your business at the same time.

GETTING STARTED ON THE RIGHT FOOT

A clear definition of the working relationship is as important as the comfort each partner feels in the underlying family bond. The best way to start a home-based enterprise with a spouse or other familiar person is to define all aspects of your mutual responsibilities up front. When adding a family member to an existing venture, the same procedures should be followed. That way, there are fewer chances of problems down the road. This section describes what "partners" need to agree on. Put the agreement in writing, because doing so helps to clarify responsibilities for all parties involved.

Establishing Working Hours

Who works when, who covers the phones (if relevant), and who handles the various chores of the business? Ultimately, a schedule is important to establish and maintain the hours each person contributes to each aspect of the business tasks. The most contentious part of working together is balancing the workload. An up-front agreement helps pave the way for a mutual support system in which each member of the team carries his or her weight and makes an equal and important contribution to the enterprise. Not all partners need a schedule, but for those new to working together, it's an important first step in learning to work cooperatively.

Establishing Responsibilities

In a home-based operation, each person's responsibilities must be tailored to his or her personal skills and experience. You—someone who doesn't like people much—might envision yourself as the salesperson. Your spouse, who isn't detail-oriented, may choose to do the books. You can imagine the potential pitfalls of this situation.

Avoid this problem with a frank appraisal of each person's skills and partition the responsibilities accordingly. Then, let people grow into other responsibilities, as conventional employers do. Avoid the trap of letting your partner lead the business; it may founder while he or she waits for you to become the leader.

Dividing Undesirable Chores

Every company has tasks that no one wants to do, such as reconciling the books or cleaning the office. If you ignore this work, the efficacy of the work day suffers. If you fail to assign them in an equitable fashion, your partner(s) will get angry. If you take them all on yourself, you won't get to the more important tasks. Instead, assign them as part of the schedule. In a small business, i.e., a husband and wife, everyone should take their turn, regardless of whether their unofficial title is "president" or "bookkeeper."

Dividing Household Responsibilities

If the household responsibilities were previously a burden, they will be doubly so in a home business. If they intrude on working hours or take one partner's time while the other completes "work vital to the business," household chores can become a festering source of resentment.

Ultimate Survival Tip

Changing Times
You may work together to establish a mutually agreeable business relationship that successfully expands the existing family arrangements. Remember that adaptability is the key to weathering the climates that are common in businesses and a standard part of fitting a new business into its market niche. Changes are de riguer and you'll see many of them. To avoid problems when "hell week" unexpectedly pops up, ground the evolution of the business in its original agreements instead of purely reacting to adverse situations. Modifications to the original covenants will result in smooth changes in responsibilities.

And the Kids
Children, even those who actively participate in the business, require special management and attention if you work at home. You may assume that your self-assured, 14-year-old science fair-winning daughter really knows as much as you do about keeping things on track. Chances are, no matter how astute she is, you still need to help organize her priorities and take her ideas under advisement before allowing her to move forward. Your kids may prove helpful in a number of tasks, but some children require a special incentive to turn a mountainous packing-and-shipping job into a molehill.

Short attention spans, a spate of unending questions, and beckoning interests intervene in the productive use of their time, and if there is no reward at the end of the work (say a movie, a treat, or a special privilege), they'll be less likely to enthusiastically help on the next big project.

For kids too young or too busy to participate productively in the enterprise, supervision is required to focus them on school and home tasks and to keep them out of your hair when you're busy. If you want cooperation when you work, you need to make sure the kids get some attention time in your schedule so they can talk about their own lives and play with you and have a bit of fun.

Here are basic guidelines to get you started on family happiness. (Note: You can customize these ideas to your kids, business, and lifestyle.)

- Cut the kids in on the business. Give older children a job with pay. If they perform, they get money and praise. Younger kids can participate, too, if only to do the most simple tasks and to benefit from your time and attention. Involving the young ones in the business gives you more time to spend with them, helps you out, and teaches them valuable skills in addition to patience and responsibility.

- Give the kids the opportunity to share your time during working hours. Include them in your plans. Take them on business errands and maybe stop at the ice cream shop for a treat. Traveling on business? Take a child with you so that you can mind him and provide a glimpse of the country, continent, world, etc.

- Show them the operations of your business. Your children will be intrigued by what you do and will want to become a part of it.

- You can isolate yourself physically and acoustically, but a window into your office allows the young ones to see your presence and enjoy watching you work.

- Have the kids call you from the home phone by dialing the office number. Make sure they know not to call too often, but offer this as an approach to reaching Mom/Dad at work should they feel lonesome or should an emergency arise.

- Awake with a sick child who is moving in and out of sleep without noticing you? Read up on important but dull matters, such as revisions to regulatory codes that effect your business. That way, you'll keep your child company while watching his health, and you might learn something useful.

- Try working with the kids in the room. For some offices (and home-based parents), the kids provide a marvelous addition to the work day. For companies that sell to other parents, the presence of your loved ones in the background reinforces your commitment to parenting in their eyes.

- Use breaks for constructive and child-engaging activities, such as baking a cake for dinner or that basic tune-up to the car you've been putting off. Your kids will learn from your activities, and you get to spend time with them while doing something that otherwise might break up the work day.

The Extended Family

According to the Census Bureau, from the 1950s through the early 1980s, more and more children grew up and moved away from home, never to return. Then, with the downsizing of the 1980s and 1990s, many moved home for free basement accommodations and Mom's home cooking. Many invited their aging parents into their homes to build a traditional extended family unit.

For the home entrepreneur, this may be either a blessing or a curse, depending on your personal relationships and the skills of the your relatives. Mom may turn out to be a wily accountant and bookkeeper. Dad may prove to be a super salesperson. Use your relatives' skills to remain close to the family; to provide an occupation (and a paycheck) to Mom, Dad, and Aunt Lucy; and to learn from their skills, which were honed in the years before you were born. This contribution can't be undervalued, unless their meddling in your enterprise becomes unbearable.

DEALING WITH PROBLEMS

When working with family members, all kinds of problems may interfere with operations. One spouse may feel that he or she is contributing a greater share of the workload. In many small businesses, the husband may leave for an afternoon at the bar or the golf course, assuming the his wife will stay on and handle the business, or the wife may leave to get her hair and nails done every Tuesday, abandoning the husband to answer the phone. No one says anything, but resentment soon builds. When one partner has a corporate job, he or she may make more money than does the other and assume an "I'm more important/better. I bring in more money than you do" role, which leads to disastrous consequences.

Be Honest

If you partner isn't pulling his or her weight, discuss it. It may be that your teammate is working harder than ever and that you have taken on too much and are getting worn out as a result. Discuss the problem amicably, preferably off-site and away from jangling phones and piles of files.

Rework the Agreement

Often, the agreement established before your operation began becomes outdated in the face of real-world business and the changing marketplace. Nothing (except the Ten Commandments) is set in stone. Make necessary changes to any formal agreement to repair problems in an otherwise working operation. Even the Constitution was amended, so you can certainly change your working rules!

Dealing with Clients

It's common in business for someone to shield a busier boss from phone calls. You can do this, too, by protecting your partner or vice versa, from interruptions, but never force someone into the position of keeping customers, vendors, or other annoying entities off your back. This is a major source of contention in any business.

Keeping At It

It's easy, when working together, to waste time. Since each spouse knows the other's hot buttons, it's easy to come up with something to do that will take both of you away from the office. Lunch out, a shopping trip, or a walk in the woods may come between you and work. If this proves to be an ongoing problem, set rigid working hours and force each other to stick to them.

Managing the Car

Many families depend on one car to get to and from work. When both spouses commute together, it often ends up that one has to wait for the other after a long meeting or working overtime before both can go home. Naturally, if this occurs frequently, the waiting partner will get tired of sitting around at work during what should be free time.

Working together with a spouse and/or kids requires time for adjustment. While you may recruit your family and your next-door neighbors to help out in a crunch, introduce family members to permanent responsibilities during slow times. That way, the need for adjustment can be recognized, and changes can be made that won't affect the business.

All-in-all, working with a family at home can be highly rewarding if you learn to communicate and work together.

25

Avoiding the Work-at-Home Traps

Humans are experts at wasting time, especially when they are faced with a difficult problem or an excess of hard work. Naturally, being your own boss contributes to this problem because there's no one to set deadlines and evaluate your performance as in a conventional business. In addition to basic procrastination, there are traps that must be avoided if a home-based enterprise is to succeed. Any one of them is capable of sinking a business, and more than one may be at work, sapping productivity and profitability. This chapter explains each trap, how to recognize when one is interfering with the "biz," and what to do should you get caught in one.

We suggest you flip through this chapter periodically, particularly if you're new to home-based operations or if your enterprise takes a nosedive for no apparent reason. Novices can get caught in any of the problems we present in this chapter and may not recognize them until conditions are bad enough to cause them to update the résumé and look for a day job.

Experienced home-based operators with plunging profits should reread this chapter. It's always possible that a trap is at work, invisible under the patina of otherwise smooth day-to-day operations, and based on our 15+ years of running home-based businesses, it's safe to say that *everyone* faces at least two or more of these problems sometime, regardless of experience.

WORK TRAPS

How you waste your time is largely a product of your personality, coupled with the work environment. You may trap yourself with your thoughts, or a family and its needs may intrude on working hours and productivity. That's not to say that you shouldn't have time off. Instead, scheduled work time must be used effectively to build and operate your enterprise. Time off can be scheduled separately to provide deserved breaks in the action. This chapter helps you to keep the latter from intruding on the former and to maintain an effective focus on the task at hand. A home-based business is, however, not for everyone. If you can't separate work from other activities, we advise caution before opening your shop. As one entrepreneur explained, his business didn't require an office, and when he ran it from home, TV reruns of "Leave to Beaver" were just too compelling miss. Could this be you?

"Rationalized Thinking" Traps

"It's one o'clock. I worked too hard yesterday. Should I work on the Forbin project or knock off early and head for the movies?" "After lunch, let's go shopping for that new computer again." "Honey, it's time for a glass of wine. I work better when I'm relaxed."

These are three examples of rationalized excuses. Generally, this is a process that starts when an unusually difficult, lengthy, or dull task is at hand. Be it cold-calling unenthusiastic prospects or pumping Mrs. Westley's septic tank when it's -12°F outside, there are thousands of reasons for not getting the job done. While you sit in your chair, your idle mind begins to explore justified excuses for procrastinating. Think long enough and you'll certainly come up with something.

What to Do About It

If you can't think of a way to get through a soul-testing, must-do piece of work, set a time period for the task and stick to it, instead of heading for the mall (or the bar). When daydreaming begins to provide reasons to knock off early ("I'll get to it next week"), snap out of it and stick to the schedule. For example, if your idea of home-office hell is wrapping, mailing, and invoicing 200 customer packages, try spreading the work out. If you have the time, try allotting the first three hours of each working day (instead of three consecutive 12-hour humdrum days) to complete the task. Of course, if you procrastinated until the absolute last minute, then you're in store for some long days. Ugh!

"Obligation" Traps

Corporate people often find that they spend more time in unproductive meetings than they do working. In the corporate world, employees can't skip a mandatory meeting, yet they're still accountable for their goals. This leads to the increasingly common 60-hour white-collar workweek in which workers put in unpaid after-hours time to make up for the interruptions.

At home, the same kind of trap wears different clothes. Family, neighbors, and day-to-day household responsibilities intrude on work time and productivity. Family members may not understand that you are actually at work even though you're home. If you pick up and drop off the kids at a day care, you could potentially waste an hour or more by sitting in rush-hour traffic, or the kitchen floor may need washing and waxing before the in-laws arrive for dinner. The list goes on.

What to Do About It

There's no easy workaround for obligations. Instead, you must prioritize each one, separating the "must-dos" from the "would-like-to-dos." Maybe completing the Web site and skipping a niece's birthday party is a better use of your time. Yes, you do have to pick up your kids, but maybe, with a quick sweep, the kitchen floor can go another day without a wash.

Responsibilities can also be distributed among other family members. Someone else in the household can surely wield a mop as well as you can. Possibly, your spouse can pick up the kids on the way home from a conventional job. Or, if his or her home-based workload is currently lighter than yours, pass them the task. Avoiding obligation traps is usually a matter of compromise. Short of a family funeral, you can always work out something.

A YARDSTICK FOR MEASURING

Another day is wasted amid a swarm of errands and leaves you too tired to remain focused on business after lunch. How can you keep tomorrow from becoming an encore of today? What measurement determines whether it's a trap, a must-do duty, or an enterprise-relevant activity? One simple criteria is to compare your home-based activity and actions to ones you would encounter in a conventional business. "Is this something I would do if I were working for a boss in a regular business?" If the answer is "no way," then you've identified a trap that requires disarmament.

For example, few employees would consider knocking off for a matinee movie after lunch or taking a trip to Houlihan's for a martini. Likewise, it's doubtful that a manager would tolerate an employee who heads home at 2:00 p.m. to clean the house for dinner

guests. When that voice in the back of your mind suggests a long lunch at a crosstown restaurant, consider whether or not a conventional boss would tolerate the resulting three-hour absence from your post. The midday "a-glass-of-wine-and-feet-up-on-the-desk scenario equally unlikely in any work environment, including home offices. Ask yourself: "Would I do this in a conventional job?" If they answer is anything but an unqualified "yes," then you're looking a time-wasting trap in the eye, and that's time, as a home-based entrepreneur, you can't afford to waste.

Ultimate Survival Tip

The Afternoon Blahs
If you've noticed the examples above are largely set in the afternoon, that's because after lunch (especially a large or wine-enhanced one) people naturally slow down. The afternoon nap is common because, due to afternoon hormone-level shifts, the body sends signals that create yawns. Nighttime workers are also familiar with this phenomena. Avoid it by taking a brisk walk or a cool shower, gulping a cup of coffee, or giving in and settling for a 15-minute nap, but promptly end a nap with a noisy alarm clock that will propel you back to work before REM sleep kicks in and smothers the day.

EIGHT WORK-AT-HOME BEAR TRAPS

Each "bear trap" is a little different and varies in nature by enterprise and the persona of the afflicted individual or group. (Yes, entire enterprises can be affected.) In those home-based businesses that are large enough to employ others, the owner or president may inadvertently force their own entrapment on employees.) When you read this section, it may appear that anything that isn't immediately business-related must be avoided during work hours. That's not our thinking. A ten-minute break from a task for a soda and a stretch of the legs is vital to well-being, but a three-person, all-day expedition for a new fax machine is trap behavior that turns a venture into the home-based Titanic. Keep your operation afloat with clear sailing, clear thinking, and hard work.

> *Note: When we refer to the "day" or "workday" in this section, it simply includes the time during which you are conducting business-related activities. It may be 9 to 5 or midnight to dawn, depending on your business. A few home entrepreneurs work a "day" that is broken up by other activities and easily pick where they left off. This mode of working won't lend itself to everyone.*

The "Noodling Trap"

Yes, it's a funny word, *noodling*. While it's not in Webster's, noodling is a very real trap. Put simply, noodling is the process of working hard but not accomplishing anything. A time-honored tradition in large bureaucracies, it keeps its users looking vital and busy. In a home-based business, noodling usually involves an inappropriate choice of work rather than an upkeep of appearances.

Days spent noodling are ones in which the "noodler" works (struggles) to accomplish a goal that is either beyond his or her current abilities, not of immediate benefit, or so time-consuming that it's not worth the effort. Another kind of noodling is equally common—the dedicated performance of tasks that don't need doing, including sorting 200 assorted rubber bands by size and recounting 500 pieces of inventory that were counted just two weeks ago. Essentially, you are a "noodler" when you work hard on anything that ultimately means nothing in terms of profit, personal gain, or personal satisfaction.

The Reverse Noodle

There's a related trap to the focused-but-largely-wasted day. We call it reverse-noodling. A reverse-noodle day is one in which nothing whatsoever is accomplished. Not even the rubber bands get sorted! It may consist of flipping through books in search of some piece of non-essential information instead of calling leads, sharpening 20 pencils by hand instead of learning a sticky new software package, or going through the aging accounts and subsequently failing to contact any of the offending parties. ("Oh, I'll just give them another week or two.")

What to Do About It

Reverse noodlers are in trouble unless they have someone else to take up the at-work slack for a while. For whatever reason, they have lost enthusiasm for their enterprise and, unless they regain it, the business will fail. While everyone has an off day now and then, accomplishing nothing for weeks on end (especially when business is tough) is a self-fulfilling prophecy. The reverse noodling rationalization is: "If it's already failing, why work anyway?"

Entrepreneurs in this boat should take a long, hard look at themselves. What seems to be the trouble? Do they dislike working in the comfort of their home? Are distractions keeping them too unfocused to work? Are they clinically depressed? Sometimes, it may take the opinion of a spouse, a close relative, or a friend to get an outsider's perspective on a problem you know exists but can't identify. If the enterprise is still sound and you can afford the time off, maybe a vacation is all you need to get a rest and to gain perspective. Do it!

Noodling Made Easy

Wasting time is easy. Like the old saying goes, "You can go to hell in your own way." It's much the same in a home-based business. Hard work that accomplishes nothing is an easy art to master—either through poor time management or basic bad priority management. You'll see variations of noodling in some of the other traps described in this chapter. Avoid noodling if it's a part of your basic working style by scheduling breaks and ensuring that the hands which should be dancing on a keyboard aren't occupied reshaping the paperclips.

The "I Thought I Could" Trap

The prospect of failure looms large. Can I do it? Can I make this business work and keep on working? It's a question faced by all people, from independent farmers to CEOs taking the reins of troubled corporations. This primeval fear is capable of hobbling the most aggressive home-based businessperson. The well-known quote, "The only thing we have to fear is fear itself," is true, but managing that fear is not always easy. Faced with the responsibilities of not only running a home-based business but also making enough money to support the business and the household while producing a profit is a very real challenge.

The "I Thought I Could" trap occurs when the anxiety-ridden bedroom-based proprietor throws in the towel. This trap affects new businesses when customers fail to immediately jam the phone lines and the seed capital (if any) runs out. Faced with such circumstances, it's easy to embrace the black shroud of failure. Naturally, once this point is reached, the operation will fail because there's no one manning the helm and doing the work. Compounding the paralysis of the "I Thought I Could Trap" is the additional anxiety of thinking, "What do I do now to earn a living?" Worrisome thoughts, indeed.

What to Do About It

This is a tough one. You should seek out, among your network of contacts, an experienced home-based entrepreneur who is willing to review your situation and help out. (It may take some looking. Successful home-based bosses are often too busy to manage their household affairs, let alone help you.) Talk to more than one person, if possible, to get a balanced perspective. It helps if your business and your adviser's business have similar operational characteristics. An adviser who provides high-priced consulting services may not be of much assistance to a struggling distribution operation. Still, listening to an adviser's advice and encouragement is better than watching daytime TV while your ship sinks.

Like the reverse-noodling trap, giving up may have its sources in other problems. Read the What to Do About It section there, too, if you're experiencing failure and find yourself wallowing in it.

The "Too Many Directions" Trap

You've certainly heard the phrase "core business." The core business consists of an enterprise's main product, its raison d'etre. The core product line usually provides the bulk of revenue and is closely tied to the company's marketplace identity. For example, when most people think of Borden, they think of milk and Elsie the Cow. Borden's core business is acquiring, processing, and distributing dairy products, but Borden makes many other products, such as adhesives. Obviously, glues and cartons of 1% milk go into different markets. (Yes, you can buy Borden's white glue in the supermarket isle next to the dairy case, but commercial adhesives are primarily distributed through channels to hardware stores and industrial users.) Borden has no difficulty with this arrangement because, as an old and experienced company, they move cautiously in new directions, confident that their core business will underwrite a new venture, which, if it fails, won't drain Elsie the Cow for keeps.

You, on the other hand, may not have that luxury. Your core business must remain your core business until it's 100% stable and runs like a clock. That may take several years. Only then can you decide to move into new markets and to expand your offerings. The "Too Many Directions" trap is just that—a home-based company, barely on its feet, decides to tackle too many new products and markets before it's time.

The demands of one product or service are more than enough to keep a home-based company busy. You must obtain sales leads, close sales, provide products in a timely manner, and manage your cashflow. Adding a second line that requires separate marketing can

become the proverbial straw that breaks the camel's back. With a second market, most of the functions of the first product line must be duplicated, as if you didn't already have too much to do. You may not have the time, expertise, personnel, and skills to run a different kind of business side-by-side with your core business. As a result, both businesses will, at best, suffer. At worst, you'll lose the entire enterprise because the workload is unmanageable, decision making is skewed from lack of time and rest, and unhappy customers turn their backs.

What to Do About It

You may come up with an idea for a product or service that's better than the one you started with. You may also find that your original core business is not financially feasible based on market reasons that are very real and not just a result of the "I Thought I Could Trap." (See the "Competition's Too Tough/There's No Business Out There Trap" later in this chapter.) Or, you may have a home-based business that's humming along nicely and want to risk throwing a wrench into it.

Your best weapon against unwisely venture adoption is the business plan described in Chapter 6. Pull it out of its drawer. (Hopefully, you look at and update it often enough that it doesn't require dusting.) Then, reread the plan and its goals, study the financial information, and look at your current schedule. Are you already working 11-hour days, 7 days a week and barely keeping your head above water? Will the new product require additional training, practice, setup, and new contacts in an entirely separate market? Can you afford what's required, both mentally and financially?

Discuss the entire decision with family members and/or partners. Since any action requires the consent and involvement of your business partners, take a careful look before you leap. Chances are that, unless you are underemployed in your current venture (unlikely, unless you aren't working hard enough) or, after careful analysis, you realize that your core business isn't viable, you should not add additional complexity. It's too risky. While it may be a possibility in the future, for now, building and maintaining the stability of your core business demands your unbroken concentration.

The "I Thought I'd Just Drop By to Say Hello" Trap

Working at home or hardly working? Worse, do you know the definition of a consultant: Someone who is unemployed but who has a watch and a briefcase. Since you don't have real job, others perceive you as not working. Friends, relatives, and, oddly, other home entrepreneurs have surprisingly little respect for your time, working hours, mission, or simple need to be left alone. Time is money and you can't allow others to squander it.

There are two sides to this problem. As mentioned, the first is that visitors don't consider your activities to be a job. After all, you don't get into a pin-striped suit or overalls at dawn and hit the freeway Monday through Friday, and you did answer the door, so what's a little chat going to hurt, even if it wastes 4 hours. The second perception is different but, for some personalities and schedules, it is equally problematic. Visitors assume that the

time they take from you can be made up, and you aren't working hard anyway. For those with a heavy workload and family and household obligations, this is major interference. Further, some people, once interrupted, find it very difficult to get back to work; a 10:00 a.m., "I Thought I'd Just Drop By" visit from Aunt Helda ruins the day.

The worst offenders are houseguests. Often consisting of family members and very close friends, houseguests are easily offended if you (in their eyes) ignore them in order to "putter around" in your home office. Why not take the day, the week, or the month off to go shopping and see the sights? Their interruptions and noise and the extra demands of caring for them make work impossible.

What to Do About It

How do you keep people away during work hours without hurting their feelings, especially those close to you? For the bored housewife or househusband next door, your company may be the highlight of the day. Neighbors may even let themselves in! ("Oh, you didn't answer the door, but your car was in the driveway and I thought maybe you'd injured yourself.") For relatives in many families, calling ahead isn't a requirement if they're "in the neighborhood."

Be polite but firm with visitors. Make them understand that your time is vital to your success. Do this by explaining, in business terms, why you can't be with them. "If I don't get Snell Corporation's proposal out today, I'll miss the bidding deadline." Only the most selfish person will ignore your need for peace and quiet when you're under the gun to produce. An imminent deadline isn't even necessary; naming the work at hand should be enough.

In addition, a sign goes on the front door (and also the back door, for overly neighborly neighbors) that states that you are not to be disturbed between the hours of X and Y. Please do not ring the doorbell for any reason. Delivery personnel please ring or knock twice. This discourages most visitors while still allowing UPS et al., to handle your goods. It helps that you politely mention this rule to all who may drop by so that they don't get steamed when they see the sign. Hopefully, the ring-twice rule for deliveries will convince offenders that you won't be pleased if they impersonate a FedEx driver.

Houseguests and Fish

Everyone has heard the Portuguese expression, "Houseguests are like fish. After three days, they both begin to stink." A houseguests interruptions are tougher than the drop-by visit to avoid. Houseguests will have made arrangements in advance, and you may really want to see them. The only approach is to inform them, in advance, that on X days and from X hour to X hour, you're "at work" and that they'll have to entertain themselves. We've put more than one visitor up in a hotel for a week, just to keep them from being underfoot, but not everyone can afford this. Relatives usually expect to stay with you, even in a 500-square-foot apartment.

Another solution is to move from a swanky Malibu, California, beach house to a ramshackle Churchhill, Manitoba, house (home, primarily, to 1,000+ pound polar bears). Few of your regulars will show up in Manitoba for

their annual free vacation suite. (Of course, if you can afford that beachfront house in Malibu, then you can probably don't need to run a home-based business!)

Ultimate Survival Tip

When Push Comes to Shove, Shove Them Out the Door

In 1994, two of our long-time friends, along with their son, decided to relocate to Phoenix, Arizona, where we lived at the time. After staying with us for a month and enjoying our pseudo-resort, complete with meals, a palm tree-surrounded pool, and their own guest suite, we realized that this was going to go on forever. They even left their 11-year-old boy with us for a week while they went home. (Our baby-sitting chore was announced to us. No one asked if we were willing to take on a child we hardly knew.) As you can imagine, this was one fruitless month, with no letup in sight. We discussed the situation with them, and, after they took no action to alleviate the situation, we finally kicked them out as nicely as possible. Sadly, it effectively terminated the friendship. Of course, with friends like that...

Avoid the Losers and the Dabblers At All Cost

Home-based entrepreneurs agree that as soon as you open a home-based business, you'll run into the losers and the dabblers. Almost every person we profiled told us so. Loosely described, the losers are a mix of people who like to sit around and complain rather than do any work. Their idea of running a company is waiting around for phone orders even though they never do any selling or promotion. Of course, when the customers don't materialize, it's time to blame the world, not themselves, for the failure.

Fortunately, this group is easy to recognize. At any given time, members of the loser's club make comments such as, "It's the miserable economy—there's no business out there, so why bother looking." As you become more successful, you may find that these people try to stick to you and your company like glue.

You'll meet some of these people in business clubs and organizations. They will try to get you to join their factions by involving you in their conversations and by luring you into their groups with offers of free rides to meetings and after-meeting cocktails to "talk business." The particularly persistent ones may even show up at your door and waste your afternoon by complaining about the world and telling you why your company isn't going to succeed. After they leave, you'll feel low enough to start updating your résumé to find a regular job.

A subset of this group is the dabblers. These are people who go through the motions of running home-based businesses by buying equipment, printing business cards and letterhead, and setting up a desk in the study, but they never get any clients or seem to do any real work. While they play at running an enterprise, they'll pester you for advice and waste your time over long lunches. Discussion topics will include long explanations of the companies they have started and agonizing explanations as to why clients have failed to place the big orders they were counting on. They may secretly hope that you will feel sorry for them and send them some of your customers, and by buying you an expensive lunch, they hope you will feel guilty and soon reciprocate the

warm gesture. Of course, when these people should be digging up sales leads and prospective work, they are actually off casing BizMart or other large office supply stores for the "right" answering machine to handle the customer calls that will never materialize.

One person we spoke to explained how a mixture of dabblers and losers almost made her go back to work at a regular job. Fortunately, a friend who was a successful home-based entrepreneur helped her realize where her time was going and how she was being emotionally manipulated into developing a negative outlook. She dropped the so-called friends and instead started a regular Monday lunch meeting with a handful of successful home-based businesswomen. With their positive feedback and proven advice, she built a company that makes a profit.

The thing to remember if you want to succeed in your own endeavor is to stay away from the dabblers and losers at all costs. If they start latching onto you, discourage them by becoming a perpetual optimist in their presence or by "accidentally" leaving them on hold when they call. Decline their invitations to lunches, parties, and dinners with the flimsiest excuses. Don't be home if they show up unannounced. Through these tactics, it will eventually sink in that you want nothing to do with the loser's club because you have no intention of becoming a member yourself.

The "Sales Call" Trap

Many home entrepreneurs handle all aspects of the business, including the sales cycle. Involving everything from cold calling to post-sales support, the sales cycle is an activity that varies in popularity among those who must perform it. For those who enjoy it (or learn to enjoy it), it can become a time trap like many other facets of home-based businesses. Surprising to introverted entrepreneurs who are uncomfortable when phoning an unfamiliar party, sales calls can be fun, especially when you are selling a product you have genuine enthusiasm for.

The trap snaps shut when selling becomes the primary activity you engage in each day. Unless you have a partner or employees who can take on the responsibilities of generating and delivering your products as well as managing other day-to-day activities, closing 10 or 10,000 deals won't build your business. It's surprisingly easy to spend your day on the phone chatting with friendly customers. While the best salesperson-to-customer relationship is one in which customers view you more as a friend than as a salesperson, these relationships can go to extremes: the long, business lunch, sales presentations conducted on golf courses, repeated follow-ups on dead leads (instead of finding new ones), and the list goes on.

What to Do About It
First, note the time spent with each customer contact in a log book. (You can use this same log to track business calls and consulting time.) Contact should be limited to less than ten minutes, with the exception of on-site sales calls, product presentations, and demos. Even then, long sales call may be little more than a way to avoid heading back to the office for real work.

If a problem is evident, then you need to learn how to effectively end the conversation. Carrying a beeper and having someone beep you at the appropriate moment is a great way to terminate long-winded and otherwise empty conversations. ("Looks like my next call is getting impatient. I'd better pack up.") Likewise, a business associate who "interrupts" you with something important during a phone conversation can lower the curtains on a talkative customer's chit-chat. If you don't have someone to page or otherwise interrupt you, set a timer for phone calls or program an organizer or digital watch to remind you of your "next meeting."

If you're spending so much time on sales because you fail to close them most of the time, you need to look at your sales skills (see Chapter 13), product marketing concerns and market viability, and the quality of your leads. There are also people who will totally waste your time. While it may seem odd, some "customers" will have you fly to their remote location (on your nickel), present your wares in a 2-hour talk, and then inform you that they were never interested in purchasing your product and that they just wanted information. Carefully evaluate your leads; quality leads are few and far between.

The "Immediate Family Needs" Trap
We have already mentioned that family and household responsibilities can dramatically infringe on your productivity, but they can be even more insidious. These responsibilities must be addressed, but their continued intrusion into your business day can keep you so unfocused that your work suffers. Nothing turns off a customer faster than hearing, "Mom, Mom," or a wailing baby in the background of your sales call. First, it nails you as a home-based business, and some people are—unfairly

and unwisely—uncomfortable with the notion of buying from a home-based business. Second, it's a distraction to both you and your customer. Third, you must deal with the problem so that you can concentrate your efforts on your company.

While household matters are legitimate responsibilities, less important ones are easy to rationalize. (See Rationalized Thinking earlier in the chapter.) It's easy to fill your workday by cleaning the house, minding the kids, or entertaining your spouse, but is washing dishes more attractive than making money?

What to Do About It

As was mentioned earlier, set a schedule that includes your business days and the hours during which you aren't to be disturbed. To make this work, you need firm control over those who are likely to interrupt you. Here are several tips:

- You can't leave younger kids to their own devices while you work. In addition to feeling abandoned, who knows what they'll get into. Instead, arrange for day care, just as you would if you worked outside the home. Your day care provider may be a traditional day care center, a spouse, or a willing relative or neighbor. For kids of all ages who remain at home, regularly scheduled breaks give you contact with them as well as a break in the office routine.

- Have a second phone line that only rings in the office. That way, personal calls won't disturb you and (hopefully) only clients will call your office number. You can even silence the office phone's ringer when you require absolute concentration. Likewise, when you're "out to lunch" in the kitchen,

you can ignore the office phone and let your answering machine, voice-mail, or answering service field the calls.

- Your office should have a door between you and the rest of the house to reduce noise intrusions. You can hang a "Do Not Disturb" sign on its doorknob. If no door is possible because your office is located in a portion of the family room, then a heavy curtain, a sound-damping, symbolic barrier that divides off your space, will suffice.

- Let the housework slide a little. Recent research shows that Americans aren't keeping their homes as immaculate as their parent's generation did. Why? Because, with the household's adults working full-time outside of the home, there's only enough time to keep up on the basics. If regular jobs force you to compromise on the chores, then there's no reason why your home-based business can't, too.

- Only you and other members of your enterprise can control distractions and shift household responsibilities to other shoulders. Don't let this common trap paralyze you and your productivity.

The "I'm Still Setting Up the Business" Trap

Many people dream of becoming their own boss and do just that—dream and dream on. Establishing a home-based business requires more than wishful thinking and a used desk in the spare room. There are apparatuses and supplies to acquire, procedures to be worked out, contacts to be established, and even licensing paperwork and planning commission approval in many communities. For a venture that involves manufacturing, tools and machinery may need to be selected, financed, and set up. Training may also be involved.

With all of the activities to do before startup, it's easy focus on the setup rather than get down to work. Instead of chasing down leads and closing sales, you find yourself spending several days selecting a computer or setting up detailed accounting procedures that you don't understand and probably don't need anyway.

Because you haven't officially opened for business, at least not in your mind, you waste days, which turn into weeks and even months, preparing to do business.

What to Do About It

At first, the basis of this trap is hard to see. For most people, it's a fear of failure. If you aren't ready to conduct business, then you aren't yet conducting business; therefore, the fact that cash is walking out the door instead of marching in is entirely justifiable. Once your business is open, measures of success or failure weigh heavily upon your shoulders.

Hopefully, you followed Chapter 6's advice and assembled a business plan that includes a schedule. It should also include a list of what must be purchased or accomplished before "opening day" and specify an exact date for opening. Stick with your plan and date, and you're in business!

Fail to get everything done by the starting date? Unless it's something vital, like getting a phone line installed in a telecommunications-challenged home, everything else can be postponed. Even equipment required for manufacturing can arrive late. What you needed today are closed sales to get

cash flowing. Otherwise, by delaying the operation's start date, your entire plan and business are at risk.

The "Competition's Too Tough/ There's No Business Out There" Trap

Related to the "I Thought I Could" trap, this one is an excuse for not working hard enough to acquire leads, close deals, and deliver a satisfactory product. (See the "I Thought I Could" trap if this applies to you.) Otherwise, it is caused by weak market analysis, unrealistic expectations, or inept sales and promotion. In most markets, direct competition exists. Your enterprise's widget or service must be tangibly superior in order to displace the competition, or you must reach a portion of the market that others are unaware of, unable to reach, or too big to care about. Every product—even those completely new in the market—competes for dollars. Many factors dictate consumer and business budgets alike. You must established priorities and make a safe choice for both. For example, a homemaker faced with the choice of meat and bread for her family or your snazzy and exciting new consumable will usually opt for the bread and meat.

What to Do About It

Before you assume that no one wants what you have to offer or that the competition really is killing you, more research is required. Is there really a problem with your working style or market analysis? Did you make people aware of your product? Failure to reach the right people at the right time can cause many products to bellyflop in the market. The usual solutions, explained in detail in this book, include:

- Cut price and/or improve value. While this may be impossible if your pricing was already set too low, it's an approach that works best when the competition is too big to consider you a competitor. In other words, they maintain their higher price while your company's market gains the interest of customers looking for a better value.

- Look for untapped or ignored markets. A company that made car wash equipment (no, not from home) saw itself rapidly losing domestic marketshares to slicker car wash equipment manufacturers. The company saved itself by recognizing its strong point—its use of parts commonly available worldwide. Today, the business has significantly grown by selling car wash equipment to third-world countries that couldn't wait six months for repair parts (as they had done when using other manufacturers).

- Change the product or what it's used for to gain market interest. No one wants a toaster that toasts only extra-thick bread, but if you changed that product's promotion and made it a sandwich toaster, you might boost sales overnight.

- Improve market visibility. Use the promotional mix described in Chapters 14 through 22 to make more buyers aware of your product. Look for alternate or superior distribution channels. Don't rely exclusively on Cousin Fred's distribution. He may be unable to effectively sell your product or may lack access to the right customers.

- There's always a way out of this trap. The tough part is coming to grips with it and staying operational long enough to see the results your changes will make. Don't let the

business die because your fear of failure paralyzes your ability to analyze the situation and take corrective action.

Variations On a Theme

It may appear that what you have to offer is not appropriate to the local market. So, what do you do? You consider moving elsewhere and starting over. Again, study the problem and analyze the potential of the new market. Add to that the costs of moving and the ensuing downtime. Is it a good idea? Probably not. A Web site might serve you better, and the whole thing can be run from your chair.

EIGHT MOUSETRAPS OF HOME-BASED BUSINESSES

You just read about the biggest traps that cause home-based enterprises to fail. But there are eight smaller traps that, while they won't break your operation's back like the ones above, take the fun, excitement, and profits out of being your own back-bedroom boss.

The "We're Out of Pencils" Trap

It's an important time in your company's growth, and you are the sole proprietor—president, middle manager, and employee. Come to think of it, you even empty the trash. A big proposal has come your way. Getting the work represents an economic high point in your business, but the proposal's preparation time is short, and you've got to look like a pro in front of a major corporation's senior management team. The laser printer is programmed to print a test page each time it's turned on. Thirty seconds after the printer powers up, the page appears. Out of the corner of your eye, you notice that the toner is nearly out and that the image is unreadable on one edge.

What do you do? Shake the cartridge gently to spread out the remaining toner and get to work or put off writing the proposal in favor of a trip to Staples for a new cartridge? If you choose the latter, you've slipped into the "We're Out of Pencils" Trap. You use any excuse to leave the house under the guise of "work," but for some reason, you never seem to get back to it. The next day, you are doubly pressured, have less time to complete the proposal, and have an attitude that degrades the quality of your work and your day.

What to Do About It

This is an easily avoided trap. Anytime you pick up the car keys, unlock the bike, or put on the walking shoes, take a step
back and consider what your actions mean in the context of business. Then, make a business decision. After a moment's thought, you (hopefully) realize that heading for Staples means other errands will come to mind. Soon, you will be running around town and the work day will be shot. This is a problem, particularly for one-person operations in which there is no partner to help "straighten out" your priorities when you announce your unnecessary plans.

The "TV" Trap

Everyone knows this one. On a break or before heading for the home office, you pause just to see what's on TV, or your open coin collection beckons from the kitchen table. Once you get caught in the web, hours pass and your workday with them.

What to Do About It

If you are easily distracted, have a written schedule and stick to it, even if it means setting an alarm clock to warn you when it's time to hit the computer again. This approach, with alarm bells and buzzers, got you through school, so it must be effective, and, for heavens sake, don't put a TV in the office so that you can "just watch the news." You'll never get anything done.

The "Office Remodel" Trap

Emphasized elsewhere in this book, a productive and comfortable work environment is essential to happy home office, but there's a trap lurking there, and it caught us once. What begins as repainting the office or putting in new carpet turns into a partial or complete home remodel. Once you repaint the office walls, the office carpet looks dingy. Once you replace the carpet, the office furniture looks worn. Once you replace the furniture, the rest of the house needs updating to make it match

During this period, little work gets done. Between moving furniture and the noise of hammers and saws—not to mention dust— you simply can't work. Plus, this is costing you far more than you originally expected. That puts your business at risk because you can't generate new sales when you can't work.

What to Do About It

Carefully plan all remodeling projects so that they can begin and end on your days off. (Shelve longer projects unless you work in a large shed in the backyard and have must-do repairs, such as a roof leak.) Once the project is completed, put aside additional remodeling for at least one year. If you plan to do it yourself, make sure the task won't leave you exhausted and leave the office dusty and disorganized so that work is impossible for a day or two.

The "Sickness" Trap

The easiest way to not do a day's work is to call in sick. When you called your old boss, you added a few coughs for effect, but when you are the boss, you answer to no one except yourself. Feeling blue? Got a mild cold? A stomachache? Better take the day off to get well so that you won't become more sick and need even more time off. Right? Next morning, the same minor symptoms mandate another day to recuperate. Meanwhile, nothing gets done and business slows to a crawl.

What to Do About It

If your condition is something that can be remedied with over-the-counter medication, buy some and take it. (Avoid sleep-inducing medicines, such as most OTC antihistamines, or take a smaller dose than the maximum.) Move to lighter work that doesn't require full mental or physical energy. Have a light breakfast and see how you feel. If nothing helps and your symptoms worsen, go see a doctor ASAP to get recovery under way. Otherwise, a couple of sick days may turn into a couple of weeks of down time.

The "Technology" Trap

Twenty years ago, a computer-minded friend used to joke about unnecessary technology. His favorite example was that someday someone would build a silly device like a microprocessor-controlled toaster. His argument was that too much technology was as bad as not enough and that customers would shun the microprocessor toaster. Guess what

appeared in stores in the late 1980s and gains popularity with each passing year?

Technology has an upside for the home-based business, and downward-spiraling prices have brought sophisticated computer hardware and software into the reach of nearly every operation. While technology can provide powerful assistance to your company, it can also waste your time, and you may not need as much as you can easily afford to buy. Here are examples:

- Purchasing powerful new software programs for market analysis, which you need only once a year (if that). The package requires a five-day manual thumbing to figure out how it works, but you made a mistake, which skewed the program's results. So you buy more inventory than your market will buy and are forced to stuff the overflow in a neighbor's garage where mice can get to it.

- Bulky and unusually complicated computers with constant problems that can't be identified. You find yourself spending more time formatting hard drives, reloading system and application software, and consulting with the dealer than you do accomplishing anything else.

- Lost files. "Oh no! Where has all the accounting data gone?"

These are just some of the problems encountered by would-be technology users. Likewise, an afternoon you spend struggling with a repeatedly jamming copier or programming a fax machine (with its cryptic menus and codes) is more time wasted. Some problems just don't go away and will ultimately drive you up the wall.

What to Do About It

The best tool for managing technology is to buy (or lease) only what you need. Test each product thoroughly before purchase and read reviews for background information. Recommendations from other home-based businesspeople are useful, but don't assume that they are familiar with all brands/kinds of the technology that interests you. Avoid products with steep learning curves unless they're central to your operation. Then, once acquired, test your purchase carefully to ensure it's reliable and does what's promised. Problems should immediately be corrected by the seller, or the merchandise should be returned.

Use the office computer only for business. Keep the kids and their game software off the machine. Use password protection, if you think it's appropriate. (Don't ever forget the password!) Protect the machine from harsh environmental conditions. For example, if you only heat or cool the office when you're in it, put the machine on a wheel-based stand and keep it in temperature-controlled areas when Jack Frost or the desert sun are at work. Back-up everything you do. Then, keep your fingers crossed, rub a lucky rabbit's foot, and hope for the best!

The "Hazardous Occupation" Trap

While it's unlikely that you will open an airbag assembly plant at home, home businesses have hazards, especially when manufacture or assembly work is involved. One successful lady who supported herself, her son, and her house by assembling fantastically complex candy baskets had to go out of business for several weeks. She badly burned her hand with glue from a defective hot-glue gun.

A variety of problems can occur. A computer with a defective power supply may (literally) shock you. Power tools may leap from your hands while in operation. A precious thumb may get hit when you miss the nail. Professional paints, dyes, and solvents may knock you out from their toxic fumes. You may get into a car accident while on your way to a sales call. Murphy's Law is in full effect in both the conventional and home-based business, and your neighbors won't appreciate it if you turn the neighborhood into an EPA SuperFund site.

What to Do About It

Do the obvious. Keep health insurance payments up to date. Read all instructions on new equipment and supplies. Follow the manufacturer's advice on handling dangerous products. Wear a breathing apparatus when conditions warrant one, instead of getting sick or french-frying your lungs. Operate power tools and machinery with care and never use them when you're tired, no matter how pressing the delivery date is. Read up on your industry to learn more about hazards and procedures for containing them.

The "Noise" Trap

This one is simple to avoid. All you need do is recognize it. In *Zen and the Art of Motorcycle Maintenance*, the author takes his frozen motorcycle engine to a shop for a rebuild. The shop rebuilds it three times, but the motor continues to malfunction. Finally, the narrator takes apart his motorcycle engine himself and finds that a tiny oil port is blocked and, with no lubricant, the engine overheated and froze after each rebuild. Thinking back, the author understands why the engine kept failing; the shop had a loud radio blasting all day. Its employees couldn't think straight and, therefore, lacked the focus needed to find the engine's underlying problem. Twenty more rebuilds won't have cured a problem that a toothpick, in the right place, easily remedied.

You may face the same situation. Living in a house full of noisy kids, dogs, and three TVs simultaneously blaring is an everyday occurrence. After you start a home-based business in such environs, you shouldn't fail to grasp why nothing seems to get done.

What to Do About It

Once you understand the problem, it's a matter of silencing noisy distractions—always easier said than done. Your choice of office space (see Chapter 10) must be central to peace and quiet. Otherwise, if options are limited, you'll just have to get a handle on noise control, possibly restricting the racket-makers to a portion of the house away from you office. Sometimes, soft background music or a background sound producers that generates the sound of softly breaking waves can be used to mask residual noise and to break the unaccustomed silence. Background sound producers come from Radio Shack or the Shaper Image. We use a 100-CD changer and select the "random" function. That way, the same song is rarely heard for several days. In addition, most cable TV systems offer 30 commercial-free music channels for $10 a month.

The "Overanalysis" Trap

Related tangentially to the "I'm Still Setting Up the Business" trap, the "Overanalysis" trap is one in which you plan commerce to death. While you should plan changes to your enterprise, too much time spent considering risks

and pondering prospects will find you missing the market window, if there ever was one. Overanalysis makes for rigid, can't-see-the-forest-for-the-trees execution. Of course, there are people who can't make a decision to save their lives. This is not a desirable characteristic of the home-based business set.

What to Do About It

Over analysis may fit a home-based accounting concern, but a fast-paced technology import enterprise will suffer when it takes six months to make a "buy" decision. With such plodding, the competition will already dominate the market, or a new technology may make the one under consideration obsolete.

Avoid the trap by setting a date when all research and pondering must be complete. Then, set a one-week window in which to make the decision. If it takes longer than that, then you lack adequate data, you have unresolvable doubts, you think the risk is too great, or you have trouble making decisions. If the last is true, have a partner make the decisions and stick to the aspects of the business that you feel comfortable with.

AVOIDING TRAPS

At the beginning of the chapter, we explained that most traps are recognizable to the experienced worker if he or she applies the values required for employment in any business, but like a serious illness, the onset of most traps is slow, and symptoms aren't obvious until the problem has progressed.

The best way to avoid traps is to carefully plan your business operations and to honestly appraise your improvement on

THE ULTIMATE HOME OFFICE SURVIVAL GUIDE

the bottom line. No one is always completely honest with themselves, but at least try. All of these traps can be avoided now that this chapter had made you aware of them. With observation and good fortune, you will recognize trouble before it creeps in the front door. Observing and acting on warnings before the trap snaps shut is the way to avoid the ensuing problems and the resulting negative impact on your enterprise.

C H A P T E R

26

EXPANDING OUTSIDE THE HOME

· ·

In this chapter, we'll look at the big decision: Should you remain home-based or get a larger office in the outside world? The decision to move away from your home-based office is not only a major step, but also a risky one. We explain the basics to help you make the decision to remain domestic or to pack your bags for the greener grass on the other side of the hill. We'll look at the decision process and what you can expect if you decide to move to outside quarters.

Yes, the foundation of this book is that working at home is more enjoyable, less expensive, and more productive than a "9-to-5" job in a conventional office, factory, or distribution center, but, as you'll see from the comments of others who have walked the path before you, the growth and expansion of a business can force you into leaving home—if that's a decision that meets your goals.

For rapidly expanding home-based businesses, staying at home may limit growth or constrain the kinds of products or services that can be sold. Not every home-based business should remain home-based, although there are plenty of good reasons not to move out. A space of your own means freedom and room to grow, but it also means freedom to make mistakes and not enough room for error.

381

MAKING THE DECISION TO LEAVE HOME SWEET HOME

For successful home entrepreneurs, moving out may be the only choice when expanding a company. If there's room (i.e., you don't rent or operate from an apartment), expansion at home is always a possibility. For some operations, going mainstream with a conventional store, office, or factory is the only way to go and grow. Otherwise, employee workspace, inventory, and manufacturing requirements absorb more and more of the house and lifestyle, leaving little room for living.

For these reasons, many entrepreneurs are forced to leave their home offices for larger quarters. Some people build new space attached to their homes, but other entrepreneurs must find new facilities outside their homes. In most cases, the transition to larger quarters can be a positive experience. By opening a store or moving into a factory or office, many business owners feel like they've finally made it. For others, moving out made their lives easier because the business was taking over too much of their lives and domiciles.

One former home entrepreneur finally gave up the home office because she realized that, to attract really large corporate clients, the company needed an office with a prestigious address. As she put it, "Big companies know that an address in the 7000 block is not exactly the Gulf+Western Building." For her, the move brought larger companies with deeper pockets, and the transition from home-based to office-based business was essential to growing the company from the million-dollar mark to the multimillion-dollar mark, where it is

today. For the majority of homemade entrepreneurs who leave their home offices behind, the move is not made out of choice. Instead, their business ventures grew at a fiery pace, which made transplanting the businesses to bigger quarters an inevitable consequence of success. A former home-based manufacturer of suntan products explained; "My entire living, dining, and family areas were just packed with boxes, a labeling machine, caps, and whatnot—you could hardly move around our house."

Another entrepreneur who experienced this kind of growth was genuinely pained at the prospect of leaving her comfortable New York loft. In her loft, her organization had blossomed from a one-woman enterprise to a million-dollar business in just a couple of years. Her success meant that she could no longer fit the eight people, the computers, the work tables, and enough telephones in her 10' × 10' office to meet the demand for her services. In fact, she and her staff were so comfortable in the home office, that they spent nine months looking for an office that felt like home.

What about the companies that choose to stay at home? Most people started their businesses at home for a simple reason—they couldn't afford an office, storefront, warehouse, or manufacturing plant. Most people contemplate moving out of the house at some point, but many decide to stay at home because they simply like working there. These people don't want to give up the flexibility of their home offices. For the businesses that require more room as time goes on, some entrepreneurs build additions to their houses or, in some cases, build new houses to accommodate the office requirements. Others control the growth of their businesses so that they can stay at home.

As one former Fortune 500 executive (who is now a multimillionaire) explained to us, "I already pay a mortgage payment and a phone bill and a heating bill. Why should I pay all of these bills twice and sit in an office all day? I bought my house because I like it, and my wife and I made it as comfortable as possible—we raised our kids here, too. So, I want to work here, play here, sleep here, maybe die here. I drove 26 miles each way to work for 14½ years before I was laid off. Nobody's going to make me rent an office and force me to commute again, even if the commute is around the corner. Besides, I get to go home for lunch when I walk down the hall." Attention office brokers and leasing agents: You can skip this guy when you're soliciting new business!

Home offices have distinct advantages for many businesses—including low overhead, no time wasted commuting, and, of course, all the comforts of home. For many of these reasons, people choose to work at home because these same luxuries go away once the nest is abandoned.

Likewise, choosing a conventional work environment has its advantages. If you can afford it, you can choose exactly the space you need in the location you desire, and having a traditional business increases the comfort level of those wary of home-centered operations.

The toughest part of going conventional is the transition period. You have all the complexity any company faces when it relocates. You also have to get used to the idea of commuting again—even if it's only a few blocks. Packing a brown bag or eating in a restaurant can feel downright alien after years of spending lunches in the kitchen. Relocating is a major business interruption, and the fine-tuning required to get the new office fully operational is always more work and more expense than you estimated.

WHO OUGHT TO RUN AWAY FROM HOME?

It used to be that a new business got started in the garage on a shoestring budget. When money became available, the business found more suitable digs and moved in. Beginning as a quiet rebellion in the last quarter of the century, people not only opened new companies at home because they had no other choice, many also stayed there because they liked it. The negative bias big companies held against home-based enterprises has all but vanished.

With that in mind, should you move? There are a triad of reasons for moving out of the house (or staying put). Is it the right decision or not? Ask yourself:

1. Is the business legitimately forcing me into a larger space or am I allowing something (such as excess unsold inventory in the hallway) to make me feel that way?

2. Am I considering a new address because, due to growth, moving is compelling or because I want to impress my associates and friends with my success?

3. Do I have sustainable cashflow to support the much higher overhead outside of my home? Will the new location financially benefit my business by covering the extra expenses plus improve revenue?

Ultimate Survival Tip

A Trap

Relocating a business from your house to a commercial location is a lengthy task that requires a lot of researching, calculating, looking, and thinking. This is the perfect sinkhole should you be looking for a reason to avoid real work, such as establishing new accounting procedures for the Xerxes Company. See Chapter 25 on work-at-home traps.

For the home entrepreneur who is considering a move because a new product or venture will require more space, consider renting temporary commercial space. A short-term lease allows you to see if you like running the company away from home and also offers an opportunity to test the new venture before signing a 5-year lease. In addition, should the exploratory venture collapse, you haven't really left home, so it's easy to retreat, if necessary.

If your major problem is inventory, consider renting stoage space in a secure ministorage location. Choose the space carefully. Look for adequate security, any evidence of rodent droppings, or watermarks on the walls, and fire protection. Another inventory option is to use a fullfiment house. These companies store your goods and ship them for you when orders come in. Because fulfillment operations vary widely, shop carefully before making a commitment.

Decisions, Decisions

The process of evaluating a business involves several steps. In the same way that you assembled a business plan for starting and operating your company, you should also document the results of each of the following steps and include your comments and any thoughts that result from your research. This will help you decide.

Step 1: Why Move?

When considering a potentially risky and always expensive move to a commercial space, you need to understand your motivations. That way, you can write down the reasons and study their grounding in reality. In two columns titled Reasons to Move Out and Reasons to Stay, respectively, write one sentence describing each reason to stay or go. For example, reason to go: Cost of a commercial shop is easily paid for if I don't send the jewelry line out for silver-plating. Reason to stay: Teenagers can't be left all day to themselves, and we can't afford to hire someone to mind them. You can try giving each reason a point value relative to its relevance and then add the totals for each category.

Step 2: The Cost

If Step 1 indicates that you should at least consider moving out, then it's time to look at the hard costs of the move and of keeping the new location afloat. You need to compile a list of all of the expenses you will incur and pencil in a number next to each one. Most spaces require a build-out and improvements to accommodate your needs. Depending on the lease and the market for commercial space, you may pay for all of it, you and the landlord may split the cost, or they may pay for all of it. In order to acquire reliable numbers, you need to choose three spaces that work for you. With the approximate costs of the remodeling and the additional wiring, lighting, and special requirements, you can get a hard number for your moving budget.

There are two estimates to prepare. The first estimate includes the one-time cost of readying the space, the furniture, the charges associated with the move, and any business profits lost during the interruption. The second budget is the monthly charge of occupying the space. In addition to the rent, certain taken-for-granted items, such as heat, insurance, and purified drinking water, add to the budget of an outside-the-home business. (See also You Can Go Home Again Sometimes later in the chapter should the outside venture hit the skids.)

The final tally of your expenses may floor you, so be prepared!

Ultimate Survival Tip

Add Ten Percent

No one ever remembers everything when budgeting for a new space. Add at least 10% to your total estimate to cover everything from under-the-chair carpet-protecting plastic panels to unexpected modifications and repairs not picked up by the landlord.

Step 3: Procedural Changes

What works at home may not work in a conventional business environment. You may not have noticed it, but at home, a set of routines and procedures for taking care of everything from managing inventory to getting the bills paid on time have worked themselves into place. To make a successful transition to an office, these procedures must be identified and then modified to suit the new environment.

Visitors may include anyone, from unannounced customers and the building inspector to unsolicited vendors selling "llama-hide" briefcases. Both the expected and the unsolicited visitors must be handled without turning the office on its ear. You should identify each procedure and note how you will handle it. Some tasks, such as using an accountant, instead of a spouse for processing bills and bookkeeping, add overhead you may not be able to support. It may also lengthen turnaround time for cashflow reports and complicate your thinking.

Is this what you want and can afford?

Step 4: Putting It All Together

This is a discovery period. Your investigations, thinking, and results are tabulated as notes, and the numbers are run. It's time to decide. To go or not to go? Only the numbers, coupled with your decision making abilities, will guide the way. Unless you have no choice and strong numbers support moving out, your best decision is probably to stay home. At least for now.

MAKING THE MOVE

It's a go—you're moving the home-based business to outside quarters. The numbers are there, and strong growth is on the horizon. All you need to do is move from one place to another without losing customers or seriously affecting your cash flow. Like anything else in business, planning is everything. You need to assemble a basic project plan (see chapter 6) to provide a timeline for the required steps and to ensure that nothing is overlooked.

Choosing the Right Time

Timing is everything. First, you must have a stabilized cash flow so that you can rely on receipts or accounts receivable to regularly generate the cash to underwrite a more expensive enterprise. You must also complete any work that would otherwise interfere with moving. Get it done early instead of postponing it. Second, your business must have a slow period during which you can relocate without a major disruption to your operations and customers. Third, if your new space requires improvements or equipment installation, you need to have everything done before you move. Since most remodeling projects run longer than scheduled, you should set the completion date for at least a week before you plan to occupy the space. That way, there's a little extra time to complete last-minute details and to correct any deficiencies you may find.

Moving Day

During the move, a specific window of time is required for the teardown, transport, and reassembly of furniture, computers, and personal effects. New furniture must arrive during this period as well. Plan on postponing your work during this period because you will have too much to handle with the move.

A Test Run

Your plan needs a scheduled open-for-business day. This is the morning when you arrive, ready to work. You will not move the furniture one more time, just to see how it looks. Often preceded by a grand opening party the night before, the first day is really a test run to ensure that everything is working and that you and your staff are ready to tackle new business

in the new space. Expect a few glitches—like the inability of the heater to produce an adequate 68° or a new computer that unexpectedly crashes. In short order, all will be well, and the business will come back up to speed.

YOU *CAN* GO HOME AGAIN— SOMETIMES

Once the thrill of expansion wears off, the realities of the day-to-day grind of running a company return. After the initial boost of excitement, a letdown period is to be expected, especially when costs exceed the budget and roses aren't coming up right away. During your planning, you should have expected that growth would occur, but it might take as long as six months for that growth to appear as hard dollars on the bottom line.

If, after half a year, you aren't seeing any worthwhile return and the problems with funding and working in the new space continue to exceed the benefits, you may think of moving home. Depending on the nature of your venture and the expansion steps you have already taken (increased headcount, leases, and infrastructure), a move home may require downsizing, although abandoning the longer-term leases common in commercial real estate (2 to 5 years, typically) is a business risk in itself. You will also have to explain to customers and vendors why you moved back. Saving face may be harder than saving money.

I'll Be Home by Christmas

Just as you made a plan for moving from home, you also need to plan how to go back.

This is a sometimes uncomfortable process of studying the required changes. The transition may require the disposal of assets that were purchased for the new space. When furniture and office equipment are to be sold, the return on their disposal is only pennies on the dollar. Unloading new employees is much more difficult. You will not win any popularity contests with those who must be let go, and you may also be on the hook for unemployment benefits and lawsuits.

The space you lease is another problem. If you can, amicably end the lease agreement with the landlord. The best plan is to find a substitute tenant who is suitable to the leasing party. Depending on the market for commercial space, this may be comparatively easy or next to impossible, especially if the space is highly customized to the needs of an uncommon tenant.

Keep this In Mind!

Part of your upfront "moving into outside quarters" evaluation should include a study of moving out of those new quarters. Condensing your operation back into the house will cost you. This added risk should figure heavily into the move-out decision. That's why a halfway step—a short-term lease, contract employees, and overall penny pinching—is a safer route than one that involves a permanent move to new quarters, which then proves less permanent than planned.

Your business is growing rapidly. It's a heady time to see all your hard work finally pay of as the market takes notice and growth comes your way at last. Should you stay home or move to commercial quarters? A commercial location may be right for you and your business, but don't let the adrenaline rush of success cloud your judgment. You may have to move out in order to keep pace with market growth, but if you don't absolutely need to, stay put. Consider taking over more space in the house. It's a safe decision that costs you nothing. Plus, you get all the comforts of home—free.

C H A P T E R

27

SUCCESS AT LAST AND FOR ALWAYS!

In this chapter we look at your smoothly humming home business and your satisfying personal lifestyle and offer suggestions on how to keep them both that way.

You've made it! You're a success! But don't let it go to your head. Instead, it's time to take stock in your accomplishments and follow the compass that is pointed to sustainable success.

When, exactly, do you become a success, and what are the measuring criteria? Tough questions. The limousine out front and fine cigars (if you can stand them) are not automatically guaranteed unless your business is a one-in-a-thousand success. Even though your business is up and running comfortably, you can't rest on your laurels and assume that it will run on its own.

LEVELING OUT

All companies require a combination of growth spurts and stabilization periods to achieve a degree of consistency in which the key partners don't worry about cashflow and income every waking moment. For most enterprises, stabilization is unlikely until the business is at least 5 successful years old. It takes time to build strong and consistent cashflow, and too many would-be entrepreneurs succumb to early success, only to watch as their business crumbles around them due to a lack of attention.

The hard work and personal sacrifice that go into building a successful home-based enterprise would appear to justify a period of relative leisure when the cash reserves begin to mount, but this is not the time to become complacent. In any new business, there are two risks that intervene in the successful transition from a start-up company to a stable one. They are:

- **Everything is new in a start-up.** New procedures, employee responsibilities, and customer relationships take time to be refined and reinforced. Change and evolution are inevitable in any start-up business, and these mean risks.

- **Luck.** It's entirely possible that the market forces that made your business an overnight success may shift the wind away from your sails. Many strong businesses have flopped in their second or third year when market changes caught the founders out buying Rolls Royces when they should have been minding their own businesses, so to speak.

For these reasons, until your home-based business is at least three (and preferably five) years old, you haven't reached a stable position in which you can occassionally let down your guard.

DEALING WITH SUCCESS

According to one Hollywood celebrity, success is like an addictive drug—you can never get enough of it—and, like a drug, success can cloud your judgment, involve you in bad decisions, and generally work against the forward momentum of your enterprise. You need a mechanism to keep you on track and away from the unwanted trappings that success sometimes brings. It's also important to keep a weathered eye on business to ensure that your participation is ongoing, adequate, and effective. Success can make you feel that everything is right with the world, even when it isn't.

YOUR NEW PALS

Is it that newfound positive attitude, thanks to your operation's growth, that's making you into a perpetual optimist? Are you instantaneously making risky decisions that would previously have taken a month of research and planning to make? These are indications of success gone wild. Strangely, the more risk that's involved and the more grandiose the result, the better you feel. Why not open an office in Katmandu? Why not sign on the dotted line for that sleek Mercedes sports car?

It could be the people around you who fuel your lack of judgment. Because of the recently hired bookkeeper who constantly tells you how much money you have to the newfound friends who hang on your every whim, no real feedback is getting through. Instead, a procession of yes-men are reinforcing your bad judgment and will ultimately run the business into the ground. These people hang onto you in hopes of money, jobs, referral business, and personal gain. Avoid them or learn to tune out their remarks. Otherwise, you'll start believing what they say. Want to test such a relationship? Tell everyone the business is headed for belt-tightening times and see who stays around to help.

Trusting Your Instincts

With a pack of yes-men surrounding you, you may become overly confident that your instincts are always right on the money, even when they're misdirected. The cure: Before making any decision that involves more than $100 or risks a business relationship, write it down. Then, put your notes away and reconsider the matter in the morning. You may be surprised by what you really see under the cold, cruel light of dawn.

Trust Other's Instincts

You may be running a company that, with continued careful management, is poised for success. Then, out of the blue, a friend, relative, or employee approaches you with an idea for a new line of business. Turning it over in your mind, the idea makes sense and seems to be a good fit for your company. Should you take it on?

Probably not until you've hit the 5-year mark, unless the idea requires little risk and even less of your time for implementation. Yes, you may miss an important opportunity, but if you've made it this far, such a risk could bring down the rest of the business if it fails or gobbles up more resources than you had estimated. If the idea is really hot, consider giving it to someone else in exchange for a percentage of the revenues.

SPENDTHRIFTING

As mentioned earlier, it's easy to feel that the "biz" is going so well that it's time for a new $10,000 computer workstation you don't need or to spend weeks shopping for the corporate Porsche. Watch out for this expectable phenomena even if it manifests itself in minor terms. If you spend more time shopping than you do working, you've got the spendthrifting bug.

Mind Your Pennies and Nickels

It doesn't take a company luxury car to blow the budget. Small expenditures mount up too.

Overhead is another source of nickel-and-dime depletion. Small expenses for services add up. You may find that, while careful management is keeping major expenses down, the $500 petty cash box is empty every Friday. Expense control dictates management of all expenses, from new toner cartridges for the laser printer to trips to the stationary store.

Keep tabs on all expenses and maintain control of the company's checkbook. If you don't sign a check or hand out cash, no one can spend your money without approval. Keep it that way until your company is large enough to justify an accounting department!

Dinner's On Me

Like the client lunches associated with too much time spent in sales mode, it's easy to blow the dough on expensive meals. You may find yourself in fancy restaurants—with almost anyone and for almost any reason, just to keep your ego afloat. While you wave hello to Barbra Striesand, work is foundering, as is your business' checking account balance. Yes, a fine meal in a fine restaurant is fun, but make sure you spend enough time on the business to keep the funds coming in for such entertainment.

Like There's No Tomorrow

Every enterprise sees monthly and annual fluctuations in cash flow and cash reserves. Expect this and budget accordingly. The best-run enterprise can see a busy year's receipts tide them through a lean year without the need for additional investment. Smug in the success of your venture, you may not hide enough nuts for the cold, cold winter.

FAMILY AND FRIENDS

Once you are rolling in dough—or at least pretend to be and make yourself look that way—you find people waiting for you at the door. Relatives will beseech you for bequests for poor, old Uncle Harry who's laid up with an unknown ailment. Friends you didn't know you had need money for their kid's must-do dental work, and your immediate family wants a bigger house to put up with both you and the business.

Again, it's easy to be flattered that others consider you a success, but you must handle such requests rationally, both from a business and friendship standpoint. Otherwise, once you make the first hand-out, recipients often come back for more and more. Those close to you may be the most difficult to handle. They may reinforce your success while demanding a piece of it. This is a hard path to follow.

REAL SUCCESS

Once you achieve a level of consistent success in your business, you are ready to reap the rewards—expansion, growth, and more revenue. Plus, you did it all by yourself. There's no boss except you, and you can celebrate the rewards of your hard work. The future is wide open. All it takes is you! Being a home-based success story is a great feeling, isn't it?

PART

6

How to Use the CD-ROM Included With the Ultimate Home Office Survival Guide

C H A P T E R

28

ABOUT THE CD-ROM

· ·

There are many times in your own home-based endeavor when you will need to ask yourself, "Should I do it myself or let someone help?" There is no pat answer. It depends on you, your willingness to look for advice, your comfort with networking with others, and the severity of your problems. Asking for help is not a sign of weakness—it is a sign of your determination to succeed.

We have assembled the most frequently used sources of help for home-based entrepreneurs and included them in the CD-ROM. You will find government agencies, private associations, book suggestions, information on computers and software, and many more sources of help for home-based entrepreneurs and teleworkers.

We've also included checklists (in Microsoft Word format) and spreadsheet templates (in Microsoft Excel format). Use these sources as much as you need. Copy them and modify them as you see fit. The files are here to help

you get started. If we have missed something that you need, you can write us and we will try to help you out if at all possible. Send e-mail to us at: *kimbaker@aol.com.*

HOW THE CD-ROM IS ORGANIZED

The CD-ROM contains four major sections:

1. The Netscape® folder, which contains a full copy of Netscape Navigator for both Windows and Macintosh

2. The HOMEBIZ folder, which contains files that can be viewed through Netscape or another browser (such as Microsoft Explorer)

3. The CHAPTERS folder, which contains folders numbered according to their relevant chapters in the book. These chapter folders contain Microsoft Word and Microsoft Excel documents that you can copy, print, and modify as desired.

4. A DEMO folder, which contains a demonstration of the PlanWrite software from Business Resource Software, Inc.

INSTALLING NETSCAPE—IT'S EASY!

If you don't have a Web browser, you won't be able to view the files in the HOMEBIZ folder. Netscape has been provided on the CD-ROM in case you don't have a browser. There are two versions for PCs (16-bit and 32-bit) and two for Macintosh computers (one for Power Macs and one for older Macs). Installing Netscape also provides you with a state-of-the-art browser for navigating the Internet.

Once you load Netscape and acquire Internet access, you can click on the hundreds of Internet Web addresses provided in the HOMEBIZ program. (If you don't have Internet access, read the section on Internet service providers for more information about gaining access to the Internet.)

Netscape Installation Instructions

For Pentium PC users:

1. Insert the CD-ROM into your CD drive.
2. Go to the Netscape folder on the CD-ROM. Click on the 32-bit folder if you use a recent model Pentium computer (Pentium II processor) or, for older (Pentium I) machines, click on the 16-bit folder.

3. Double-click the Setup.exe icon in the folder and follow the steps to install Netscape. Agree to the licensing terms by clicking Yes (I agree . . .) and then click Next in the dialog boxes.

4. Choose Typical Installation (recommended) unless you want to customize Netscape's setup by selecting Custom.

5. Choose a location for Netscape's installation. Use the folder the program automatically chooses if you aren't sure where to put it. (Netscape chooses a drive that contains enough room for installation.)

6. Click Install.

7. After installing the software, Netscape will ask you to create a new profile. Answer the questions. If you don't have an existing e-mail address, leave this field blank. (You can add it later.)

8. You've now installed Netscape and are ready to use the HOMEBIZ files.

9. To start the HOMEBIZ program, open the HOMEBIZ folder and double-click on the file named Default.htm. Netscape will open automatically. If you get a message that says "socket is unavailable," simply click on the Okay button. This message means that you aren't connected to the Internet. The program will work fine, but you won't be able to use the links to the Internet and the World Wide Web sites.

For Macintosh users:

1. Insert the CD-ROM into your CD drive.

2. For power PCs, click on the file named Navigator 4.031 PPC Export folder, or for older Macs, such as 68030 series Quadras, choose the Navigator 4.031 68K Export folder.

3. Open the Netscape Installer folder.

4. Double-click the Netscape Installer icon.

5. Agree to the licensing terms by clicking OK in the dialog boxes.

6. In the Install dialog, choose where you want to have Netscape installed and leave Easy Install selected unless you want to customize Netscape's installation.

7. Open Netscape from its folder and create a new profile. If you don't have an existing e-mail address, leave this field blank. (You can add it later.)

8. To start the HOMEBIZ program, simply open the HOMEBIZ folder and look for the file called Default.htm. Double-click on this file, and you're on your way.

9. If you're not connected to the Internet, click the Okay button in response to Netscape's message "socket is unavailable." This simply means that you aren't connected to the Internet. If you have an ISP, you won't see this message.

WHAT IS AN ISP AND WHERE DO I GET ONE?

To connect to the Internet, you need access through a commercial online service (such as America Online, Prodigy, or Microsoft Network) or a connection through an Internet Service Provider (ISP). Access is sometimes provided by companies and schools. You don't need an ISP or Internet access to use the HOMEBIZ program for *The Ultimate Home Office Survival Guide,* but you may want to access directly the many Web site addresses we've included. For this, you'll need an ISP. You can find an ISP in the telephone book under Internet Services, or you can ask your long-distance telephone company what it offers. The right ISP or online service should offer:

- Unlimited access without a contract for about $20 per month

- Local access telephone numbers without toll charges

- No busy signals at peak times

- Convenient billing methods, such as charging a credit card or monthly invoicing

- Free live technical support available as many hours as possible

- Shop around and ask other local home-based operations for recommendations or pick up a free copy of the America Online software in a computer magazine and try AOL for free for a month, then decide if you want to use another ISP.

HOW TO NAVIGATE AROUND THE HOMEBIZ FILES FROM YOUR BROWSER

Make sure you have a browser installed on your system before you try to use the HOMEBIZ program. Open the HOMEBIZ folder and find the file called Default.htm. Double-click on the Default.htm file to open it. This should start your browser (unless you already have it running) and display the home page for *The Ultimate Home Office Survival Guide* CD-ROM.

You can click on the buttons on the home page to learn more about using the HOMEBIZ files. Start by clicking on the *About the CD-ROM* button. This will take you to general information about navigating the HOMEBIZ files.

When you get to other pages on the CD-ROM, you'll notice buttons and purple underlined text. The underlined purple text indicates a link to another area on the CD-ROM or to a site on the World Wide Web. Some underlined links, including those that start with http:// and those that refer to Web sites or e-mail addresses, will not take you to the site or allow you to send e-mail unless you are connected to the Internet through your ISP or an online service company, such as America Online, Prodigy, or Microsoft Network. All other linked information is available directly from the CD-ROM.

If you are not connected to the Internet while using the files, you may get an error message explaining that a Web address (known as a URL) is not available (because you aren't hooked up to the Web). All other underlined links will take you to information that's stored on the CD-ROM.

The information and forms that are available through your browser can be printed, if desired, directly from the browser's print command (usually found under the File command on the task bar or by clicking on the printer symbol).

You can scroll through the information on a page by using your keyboard's arrow keys or by clicking on the browser's scroll bar. If you want to get back to a previous page, sim-ply click the back symbol (an arrow pointing to the left) in the browser. You can also get to information on the CD-ROM by clicking on buttons (found at the bottom of each major page) that will take you back to the main home page, the table of contents, the search routine, or the chapter index pages.

WARNING: Web sites move. Addresses change. Area codes for phone numbers change. The sites that are listed on the CD-ROM were current as of January 1998. If a link doesn't work, try a search engine (access is provided on the CD-ROM) to find the site's current address (if it still exists). Send us the new location of site or any information on new sites you find and we'll include them in the next edition of the CD-ROM. We will even give you attribution for your finds. Send us e-mail at kimbaker@aol.com.

HOW TO USE THE CHAPTER INDEX IN THE HOMEBIZ PROGRAM

We recommend that you start exploring the HOMEBIZ information on the CD-ROM through the *Chapter Index*, which provides links to those resources on the CD-ROM and on Web sites that are most relevant for each chapter. Click on the underlined words, and you'll go to that information on the CD-ROM, be transported to the World Wide Web site (if you're connected to the Internet), or be asked to send e-mail for information.

THE MICROSOFT WORD AND EXCEL FILES ON THE CD-ROM

There are some worksheets and spreadsheets in Microsoft Word and Microsoft Excel formats (as appropriate) on the CD-ROM. These files are available in the CHAPTERS folder. You cannot reach these files from the browser. You must have Word 95 or Excel 95 or a later version (Word 97 or Excel 97 for example) or a program that can read these files in order to use these files. Just put the CD-ROM in the drive and go to the CHAPTERS folder. Click on the relevant file to open it in Word or Excel.

You don't need Word or Excel to take full advantage of the information available through your browser on the CD-ROM, but, if you already have Word or Excel, you might want to manipulate or edit the available documents in Word or Excel form to suit the needs of your business. If you have another word processing program (such as WordPerfect) or another spreadsheet program (such as Quattro Pro or Lotus 1-2-3), most current versions of these products will be able to convert the files from Word and Excel to your programs.

THE PLANWRITE SOFTWARE DEMO

To view the PlanWrite demonstration provided by Business Resource Software, Inc., simply open the Demo folder on the CD-ROM and double-click on the Demo.exe file.

Note: If your computer does not run Windows 95 or Windows NT, you won't be able to view this demonstration.

COPYING INFORMATION TO YOUR HARD DRIVE

If you want to (and if you have enough room on your hard drive) you can copy the CD-ROM folders, including the HOMEBIZ folder that contains the browser files, to your hard drive and use them from there. As long as you copy the complete folders and don't make modifications to the locations of files within the folders, everything will work as it does from the CD-ROM.

Enjoy your time exploring and using the information on the CD-ROM. We hope the information and resources will make your home-based career or new business a great success.

About the Authors

The authors have successfully managed their own home-based careers since 1983. Former executives in major corporations, Sunny and Kim Baker now work at home exclusively as home-based writers, educators, and consultants using the methods and technology discussed in this book. Through trial, error, and perseverance, Sunny and Kim have learned how to make working at home both profitable and pleasurable, and in *The Ultimate Home Office Survival Guide*, they offer their experience to their readers. As a team, Sunny and Kim Baker have also authored books on marketing, publicity, project management, desktop publishing, and a restaurant review guide.

Sunny Baker founded Microsoft University and was general manager and director of marketing for Microsoft Corporation. At Microsoft, Sunny designed, tested, documented, promoted, and merchandised a full-range of PC and Macintosh applications. Sunny has held similar executive management and marketing positions at Intel, National Semiconductor, and Tymshare as well as a home-based entrepreneur who runs a marketing consulting firm from home.

Kim Baker is an artist and marketing communications professional. Currently running a successful high-technology advertising and marketing agency from home with his wife Sunny, Kim has also worked as a creative director for advertising agencies and has managed marketing communications departments for high-technology companies including Viasoft, Intel, Sydney Development, and Epic Data Systems. Kim has worked with desktop publishing since the early 1980s and with computers since 1972.

Index

S

Sacrifice, 38
Safety of equipment, 154–55
Sales, 40–41, 173–86. *See also*
    Marketing.
    big-ticket, 175
    break-even analysis, 44–45
    channels, 184–85
    closing, 175, 177, 181, 183–84
    commissions on, 174–75
    customer tracking, 185
    cycle, 176–77
    decision maker and, 181
    lead generation and analysis, 178
    methods, 41, 186
    methods to avoid, 186
    order taking, selling, and hard
        sell, 174
    persuasion and presentation,
        178–79
    prospects, 176
    qualification and objections,
        179–81
    reasons customers won't buy, 182
    success and, 14
Sales-call trap, 371–72
Sans serif type, 318
Satisfaction, 15
    customer, 184
Savings accounts, 116–17
Scanners, 156, 164
    in direct mail, 297
    in hybrid machine, 168–69
Scheduling, 6
    network diagram, 353
    project worksheet, 354
    publicity events, 267
    technology and, 153
    time, 350–55
SCORE, 62
Screen tint color, 331–32
Script type, 318
Search engines, 340, 344
    manually updated, 342
    submitting universal resource
        locator to, 341–42
Seasonal businesses, 46
Seating for guests, 137
Secured line of credit, 117
Securities and Exchange Commission
    Regulations, 80
Self-employment tax, 101–2
Sellers permit, state, 74
Selling. *See* Sales.
Selling propositions, in direct mail,
    288–89

Seminars, educational, publicity
    from, 263
Serif type, 318
Service businesses, 46
Service description, in business plan,
    64
Services, selling, 185
Setting up business, excessive time
    spent on, 373–74
Sharp's Wizard electronic organizers,
    152, 352
Shelf packaging, 191–92
Shelving space, 138
Shipping, breakage during, 193
Sickness trap, 377
Signs, for in-store visibility, 194–95
Size of work space, 130
Skills, 37–40
    management, lack of, 11
Small Business Administration, 62,
    118
Small business adviser, 40
Small Business Development
    Centers, 62
Snell, Mike, 18
Social Security tax, 102–3
Software
    for business plan, 63
    CD-ROM (included with book),
        395–99
    contact management, 351
Sole proprietorship, 77–78
Solids, in printing, 335–36
Space. *See* Work space.
Special-interest groups
    online promotion via, 343–44
    publicity from, 249
Specialty printers, 330–31
Speeches, publicity from, 264–65
Spendthrifting, 391
Sports groups, publicity from, 249
Spot color, 331
Stabilization, 390–91
Standard mileage rate, 100
Standard Rate and Data Service, 295
Start-up capital, 10, 117–18
Start-up costs, 43
State regulations, 74
States, multiple, doing business in,
    82–83
State taxes, 103
Stock, selling, 79–80, 81, 117–18
Storage space, 138–39, 384
Storefront, 22
Stores, product visibility in, 194–95
Strategic direction, 61
Structure of business, legal, 77–82

Subchapter S Corporation, 81
Subheads, 324, 326
Submit-It!, 340, 341
Success, xii, 389–92
    factors, 8–9
    roles needed for, 14–15
Support system, 24–25

T

T principle, 232
Tag lines, 188–89
Tape recorders, 155–56
Tapes, motivational, 24
Target market, 94, 202, 295
Tax accountants, 111
Taxes, 83–84, 101
    benefits of working at home, 7
    corporations and, 80, 101
    employment, 102–3
    estimated payments, 102
    excise, 103
    income, 101
    IRS (publications) and, 103–4
    self-employment, 101–2
    state and local, 74, 103
    success and, 14
Technology, 151–57
    business functions and, 152–54
    choosing, 159–70
    components of automated home
        office, 155–56
    evaluation, 154–55
    for integration and planning, 152
    success and, 15
    unnecessary, 377–78
Telecommuters, xiii
    use of book by, xv
Telecommuting, 27–35
    equipment for, 34
    starting own business vs., 29
    staying connected to office, 31–34
    steps to, 29–30
    tracking expenses, 34–35
    working with employer, 30–31
Teleconferencing, 34
Telemarketing, 176, 179
Telephone calls, to employer, 31
Telephones, cellular, 155
Television
    cable, 200–201, 225
    as distraction, 376
    interview and program proposals
        for, 241
    news releases for, 252
    publicity from, 247

Notes

LOOK TO PETERSON'S ONLINE AND PETERSON'S GUIDES WHEN SEARCHING FOR SUCCESS!

Starting a career is never easy. Peterson's Education & Career Center at petersons.com gives you the tools and the help you need to make any job a success!

At petersons.com you can:
• Search for career opportunities
• Get advice on building a portfolio
• Learn about education alternatives for busy professionals

Thinking about taking courses to improve your marketability and earning potential, but don't have the time?
Think about LifeLongLearning at petersons.com!

At **LifeLongLearning,** you'll find distance learning programs that deliver the education you want, when you want, and how you want, right to your doorstep!

Search by delivery format
• Correspondence courses
• Online courses
• Interactive TV
• Videoconferencing

Or by
• Geographical location
• Course level
• Cost

And the best part of all of Peterson's services? They're FREE!

Let Peterson's be your online guide to the future!

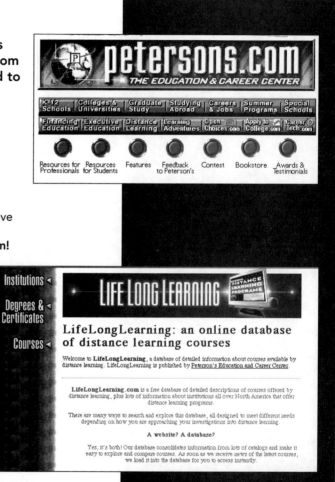

PETERSON'S
Princeton, New Jersey
www.petersons.com
1-800-338-3282

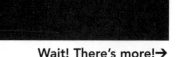

Wait! There's more!→